A HISTORY OF CANADIAN FICTION

A History of Canadian Fiction is the first one-volume history to chart its development from earliest times to the present day. Recounting the struggles and the glories of this burgeoning area of investigation, it explains Canada's literary growth alongside its remarkable history. Highlighting the people who have shaped and are shaping Canadian literary culture, the book examines such major figures as Mavis Gallant, Mordecai Richler, Alice Munro, Margaret Atwood, Michael Ondaatje, and Thomas King, concluding with young authors of today whose major successes reflect their indebtedness to their Canadian forbears.

DAVID STAINES is the former dean of the Faculty of Arts and now Professor of English at the University of Ottawa. He has authored and/or edited more than twenty books on medieval culture and literature and Canadian culture and literature. In 1998, he received the Lorne Pierce Medal from the Royal Society of Canada for outstanding contribution to Canadian criticism, and in 2011, he was awarded the Order of Canada and the Order of Ontario for his services to Canadian literature.

A HISTORY OF CANADIAN FICTION

DAVID STAINES

University of Ottawa

CAMBRIDGE
UNIVERSITY PRESS

CAMBRIDGE
UNIVERSITY PRESS

University Printing House, Cambridge CB2 8BS, United Kingdom

One Liberty Plaza, 20th Floor, New York, NY 10006, USA

477 Williamstown Road, Port Melbourne, VIC 3207, Australia

314-321, 3rd Floor, Plot 3, Splendor Forum, Jasola District Centre, New Delhi - 110025, India

103 Penang Road, #05-06/07, Visioncrest Commercial, Singapore 238467

Cambridge University Press is part of the University of Cambridge.

It furthers the University's mission by disseminating knowledge in the pursuit of
education, learning and research at the highest international levels of excellence.

www.cambridge.org
Information on this title: www.cambridge.org/9781108406468
DOI: 10.1017/9781108284554

First published 2021
First paperback edition 2022

A catalogue record for this publication is available from the British Library

Library of Congress Cataloging in Publication data
NAMES: Staines, David, 1946– author.
TITLE: A history of Canadian fiction / David Staines.
DESCRIPTION: Cambridge ; New York, NY : Cambridge University Press, 2021. |
Includes bibliographical references.
IDENTIFIERS: LCCN 2021024528 (print) | LCCN 2021024529 (ebook) | ISBN 9781108418089
(hardback) | ISBN 9781108406468 (paperback) | ISBN 9781108284554 (epub)
SUBJECTS: LCSH: Canadian fiction–History and criticism. | BISAC: LITERARY
CRITICISM / Canadian
CLASSIFICATION: LCC PR9192.2 .S73 2021 (print) | LCC PR9192.2 (ebook) |
DDC 813.009/971–dc21
LC record available at https://lccn.loc.gov/2021024528
LC ebook record available at https://lccn.loc.gov/2021024529

ISBN 978-1-108-41808-9 Hardback
ISBN 978-1-108-40646-8 Paperback

For Noreen

Contents

Acknowledgements

David Eso, Thomas Hodd, Helen Hoy, Wolfgang Klooss, Eva-Marie Kröller, and W.H. New commented on the manuscript. Neil Besner, Mary Rubio, Carl Spadoni, Natalia Vesselova, and Katherine Walton answered many queries. I am grateful to all of them for their time and their patience.

I am also grateful to Cambridge University Press, in particular to Sarah Stanton, who initiated the project, and to Emily Hockley, who saw it to completion.

A History of Canadian Fiction is a belated acknowledgement of a conversation with Jerry and Elizabeth Buckley on Dunster Street in Cambridge, Massachusetts in 1974; they suggested that I introduce Canadian literature courses at Harvard University. To them, I remain indebted.

Chronology

Date	Historical and Cultural	Literary
BC		
11500	Earliest records of human habitation on Haida Gwaii	
11000	Earliest records of the Bluefish Cave people in the Yukon	
9000	Earliest records of the Fluted Point people in Ontario	
7000	Earliest records of human habitation on the west coast of Canada	
AD		
1000	Viking settlement at L'Anse aux Meadows, Newfoundland	
1390	Mohawk, Oneida, Cayuga, Onondaga, and Seneca establish the Iroquois Confederacy	
1497	Jean Cabot sails from Bristol to Newfoundland	
1534	Jacques Cartier sails from St Malo to the Gulf of St Lawrence	
1576–8	Martin Frobisher sails from England on his three Arctic explorations	
1605	Samuel de Champlain founds Port-Royal, Acadia	
1608	Champlain founds Quebec City	
1610	Henry Hudson sails to Hudson Bay	
1625	Jesuits arrive in New France	
1632		*Jesuit Relations*, an annual, begins and continues until 1673
1670	Hudson's Bay Company begins operations	
1751	First printing press in Nova Scotia	
1752		First newspaper in Canada, *Halifax Gazette*
1759	Battle on the Plains of Abraham	
1763	Treaty of Paris cedes New France to Britain	
1764	First printing press in Quebec	

Date	Historical and Cultural	Literary
1769		Frances Brooke, *The History of Emily Montague*
1774	Quebec Act reinstating Roman Catholic religious freedom and French civil law	
1812–14	War of 1812	
1821		Thomas McCulloch, *The Letters of Mephibosheth Stepsure*
1824		Julia Beckwith Hart, *St. Ursula's Convent, or The Nun of Canada*
1829	The last of the Beothuks dies in Newfoundland	
1832		John Richardson, *Wacousta*
1836		Thomas Chandler Haliburton, *The Clockmaker*
		Catharine Parr Traill, *The Backwoods of Canada*
1839	Lord Durham's Report	
1847		George Copway, *The Life, History and Travels of Kah-ge-ga-gah-bowh*
1852		Susanna Moodie, *Roughing It in the Bush*
1864		Rosanna Leprohon, *Antoinette de Mirecourt*
1867	British North America Act, bringing into Confederation the provinces of New Brunswick, Nova Scotia, Ontario (formerly Upper Canada), and Quebec (Lower Canada)	
1870	Manitoba and North-West Territories join Confederation	
1871	British Columbia joins Confederation	
1873	Prince Edward Island joins Confederation	
1876	Indian Act	
1877		William Kirby, *The Golden Dog: A Legend of Quebec*
1888		James De Mille, *A Strange Manuscript Found in a Copper Cylinder*
1896		Gilbert Parker, *The Seats of the Mighty*
1898		Ralph Connor, *Black Rock*
		Ernest Thompson Seton, *Wild Animals I Have Known*

Date	Historical and Cultural	Literary
1900		Norman Duncan, *The Soul of the Street: Correlated Stories of the New York Syrian Quarter*
1903		Norman Duncan, *The Way of the Sea*
1904		Sara Jeannette Duncan, *The Imperialist*
1905	Saskatchewan and Alberta join Confederation	
1908		Nellie McClung, *Sowing Seeds in Danny*
		Lucy Maud Montgomery, *Anne of Green Gables*
1910		Stephen Leacock, *Literary Lapses*
1911		Pauline Johnson, *Legends of Vancouver*
1912		Stephen Leacock, *Sunshine Sketches of a Little Town*
1914–18	World War I	
1922		Frederick Philip Grove, *Over Prairie Trails*
1923		Mazo de la Roche, *Possession*
		Lucy Maud Montgomery, *Emily of New Moon*
		Laura Goodman Salverson, *The Viking Heart*
1925	United Church of Canada brings together Presbyterian, Methodist, and Congregational Churches	Frederick Philip Grove, *Settlers of the Marsh*
		Martha Ostenso, *Wild Geese*
1926		Robert J.C. Stead, *Grain*
1927		Mazo de la Roche, *Jalna*
1928		Morley Callaghan, *Strange Fugitive*
		Raymond Knister, ed., *Canadian Short Stories*
1929		Raymond Knister, *White Narcissus*
1932	Founding of the Canadian Radio Broadcasting Corporation	
1934		Morley Callaghan, *Such Is My Beloved*
1936	Founding of the Governor General's Literary Awards	Morley Callaghan, *Now That April's Here and Other Stories*
1939		Howard O'Hagan, *Tay John*
1939–45	World War II	
1941		Hugh MacLennan, *Barometer Rising*
		Sinclair Ross, *As for Me and My House*

Date	Historical and Cultural	Literary
1942	Internment of Japanese Canadians	
1945		Hugh MacLennan, *Two Solitudes*
1947		W.O. Mitchell, *Who Has Seen the Wind*
		Ethel Wilson, *Hetty Dorval*
1948		Henry Kreisel, *The Rich Man*
1949	Newfoundland joins Confederation	
1950	Founding of the Canadian Opera Company	
1951	Founding of the National Ballet of Canada	Robertson Davies, *Tempest-Tost*
	Report of the Royal Commission on National Development in the Arts, Letters and Science (Massey Report)	A.M. Klein, *The Second Scroll*
1952	Founding of the Canadian Broadcasting Corporation (Television)	Ernest Buckler, *The Mountain and the Valley*
		Norman Levine, *The Angled Road*
1953	Founding of the National Library of Canada and the Stratford Shakespearean Festival	
1954		Mordecai Richler, *The Acrobats*
		Ethel Wilson, *Swamp Angel*
1956	Founding of the *Tamarack Review*	Mavis Gallant, *The Other Paris*
		Adele Wiseman, *The Sacrifice*
1957	Lester B. Pearson wins the Nobel Peace Prize	
	Founding of the Canada Council for the Arts and the New Canadian Library	
1959	Founding of *Canadian Literature*	Mordecai Richler, *The Apprenticeship of Duddy Kravitz*
	Opening of the Saint Lawrence Seaway	Sheila Watson, *The Double Hook*
1960	Beginnings of the Quiet Revolution in Quebec	Margaret Laurence, *This Side Jordan*
1962	Completion of the Trans-Canada Highway	W.O. Mitchell, *Jake and the Kid*
	Founding of the Shaw Festival and the Neptune Theatre in Halifax	Rudy Wiebe, *Peace Shall Destroy Many*
1963	Founding of the Charlottetown Festival and the Vancouver Playhouse	Morley Callaghan, *That Summer in Paris*
		Leonard Cohen, *The Favourite Game*

(*cont.*)

Date	Historical and Cultural	Literary
1964		Austin Clarke, *The Survivors of the Crossing*
		Margaret Laurence, *The Stone Angel*
		Jane Rule, *Desert of the Heart*
1965	Founding of the Citadel Theatre in Edmonton	Carl Klinck, ed., *The Literary History of Canada*
	The Maple Leaf flag adopted	Robert Kroetsch, *But We Are Exiles*
1966	Medicare legislation passed (all provinces join by 1972)	Leonard Cohen, *Beautiful Losers*
		Harold Horwood, *Tomorrow Will Be Sunday*
1967	Canada's centennial Expo 67 in Montreal	George Bowering, *Mirror on the Floor*
		Timothy Findley, *The Last of the Crazy People*
	Report of the Royal Commission on Bilingualism and Biculturalism	Audrey Thomas, *Ten Green Bottles*
1968		Marian Engel, *No Clouds of Glory*
		Alice Munro, *Dance of the Happy Shades*
1969	Official Languages Act	Margaret Atwood, *The Edible Woman*
	New Brunswick is officially bilingual	
		Graeme Gibson, *Five Legs*
		Ray Smith, *Cape Breton Is the Thought-Control Centre of Canada*
1970	Report on the Royal Commission on the Status of Women	Robertson Davies, *Fifth Business*
		Richard B. Wright, *The Weekend Man*
1971	Official Multiculturalism Policy	Alice Munro, *Lives of Girls and Women*
		Mordecai Richler, *St. Urbain's Horseman*
1972		Margaret Atwood, *Survival*
1973	Founding of the Writers' Union of Canada	Maria Campbell, *Halfbreed*
		Rudy Wiebe, *The Temptations of Big Bear*
1974		Margaret Laurence, *The Diviners*
		David Adams Richards, *The Coming of Winter*
		Sinclair Ross, *Sawbones Memorial*
1975		Robert Kroetsch, *Badlands*
		Lee Maracle, *Bobbi Lee: Indian Rebel*
1976		Marian Engel, *Bear*
		Jack Hodgins, *Spit Delaney's Island*
		Alistair MacLeod, *The Lost Salt Gift of Blood*
		Michael Ondaatje, *Coming through Slaughter*
		Carol Shields, *Small Ceremonies*

(cont.)

Date	Historical and Cultural	Literary
1977	French is the official language in Quebec	Timothy Findley, *The Wars*
1979		Jack Hodgins, *The Resurrection of Joseph Bourne* Thomas Kusugaq, *Eight Inuit Myths/ Inuit Unipkaaqtuat Pingasuniarvinilit*
1980	Quebec votes against separation in referendum "O Canada" proclaimed official national anthem	George Bowering, *Burning Water*
1981		Timothy Findley, *Famous Last Words* Mavis Gallant, *Home Truths* Douglas Glover, *The Mad River* Joy Kogawa, *Obasan*
1982	Patriation of the Constitution Charter of Rights and Freedoms	Sandra Birdsell, *Night Travellers* Guy Vanderhaeghe, *Man Descending*
1983		Morley Callaghan, *A Time for Judas* Beatrice Culleton Mosionier, *In Search of April Raintree* Susan Swan, *The Biggest Modern Woman of the World*
1985		Jeannette Armstrong, *Slash* Margaret Atwood, *The Handmaid's Tale* Neil Bissoondath, *Digging Up the Mountains* Wayne Johnston, *The Story of Bobby O'Malley*
1986	John Polanyi wins the Nobel Prize for Chemistry	Jane Urquhart, *The Whirlpool*
1987		Rohinton Mistry, *Tales from Firozsha Baag* Michael Ondaatje, *In the Skin of a Lion* Carol Shields, *Swann*
1988	Canadian Multiculturalism Act Free Trade Agreement between Canada and the United States	Dionne Brand, *Sans Souci and Other Stories* Bonnie Burnard, *Women of Influence* Barbara Gowdy, *Through the Green Valley*
1989		Frances Itani, *Pack Ice* M.G. Vassanji, *The Gunny Sack*
1990	Meech Lake Accord fails	Thomas King, *Medicine River* SKY Lee, *Disappearing Moon Café* Nino Ricci, *Lives of the Saints*
1991		Helen Humphreys, *Ethel on Fire*

(cont.)

Date	Historical and Cultural	Literary
1992		Steven Heighton, *Flight Paths of the Emperor* Lawrence Hill, *Some Great Thing* Michael Ondaatje, *The English Patient*
1993		Caroline Adderson, *Bad Imaginings* David Bergen, *Sitting Opposite My Brother* Elizabeth Hay, *Captivity Tales* Alootook Ipellie, *Arctic Dreams and Nightmares* Thomas King, *Green Grass, Running Water* Yann Martel, *The Facts Behind the Helsinki Roccamatios and other stories* Carol Shields, *The Stone Diaries*
1994	Founding of the Giller Prize	André Alexis, *Despair and Other Stories of Ottawa* Gail Anderson-Dargatz, *The Miss Hereford Stories* Alice Munro, *Open Secrets* Shyam Selvadurai, *Funny Boy* M.G. Vassanji, *The Book of Secrets* Richard Wagamese, *Keeper 'n Me* Michael Winter, *Creaking in Their Skins*
1995	Quebec votes against separation again in referendum	Wayson Choy, *The Jade Peony* Rohinton Mistry, *A Fine Balance* Lisa Moore, *Degrees of Nakedness*
1996	Report of the Royal Commission on Aboriginal Peoples	Margaret Atwood, *Alias Grace* Dionne Brand, *In Another Place, Not Here* Ann-Marie MacDonald, *Fall on Your Knees* Anne Michaels, *Fugitive Pieces* Eden Robinson, *Trap Lines* Miriam Toews, *Summer of My Amazing Luck*
1997		Mordecai Richler, *Barney's Version*
1998		Dennis Bock, *Olympia* Lynn Coady, *Strange Heaven* Michael Crummey, *Hard Light* Tomson Highway, *Kiss of the Fur Queen* Wayne Johnston, *The Colony of Unrequited Dreams*

(cont.)

Date	Historical and Cultural	Literary
1999		Alistair MacLeod, *No Great Mischief*
2000	Founding of the Charles Taylor Prize for Literary Non-Fiction	Margaret Atwood, *The Blind Assassin* David Adams Richards, *Mercy among the Children*
2001		Darren Greer, *Tyler's Cape* Sheila Heti, *The Middle Stories* Yann Martel, *Life of Pi* Timothy Taylor, *Stanley Park* Madeleine Thien, *Simple Recipes* Jane Urquhart, *The Stone Carvers* Richard B. Wright, *Clara Callan*
2002	George Bowering is named Canada's first poet laureate	Robert Arthur Alexie, *Porcupines and China Dolls* Austin Clarke, *The Polished Hoe* Guy Vanderhaeghe, *The Last Crossing*
2003		Douglas Glover, *Elle* Frances Itani, *Deafening* M.G. Vassanji, *The In-Between World of Vikram Lall*
2004		David Bezmogis, *Natasha and Other Stories* Esi Edugyan, *The Second Life of Samuel Tyne* Anosh Irani, *The Cripple and His Talismans* Miriam Toews, *A Complicated Kindness*
2005	Same-sex marriage becomes legal throughout Canada	Dionne Brand, *What We All Long For* Audrey Thomas, *Tattycoram*
2006	Canada issues an official apology to Chinese Canadians for Headtax and Exclusion Act	Rawi Hage, *De Niro's Game* Heather O'Neill, *Lullabies for Little Criminals*
2007		David Chariandy, *Soucouyant* Elizabeth Hay, *Late Nights on Air* Lawrence Hill, *The Book of Negroes*
2008	Canada issues an official apology to former Indian Residential School students	
2009		Patrick DeWitt, *Ablutions*
2010		Emma Donoghue, *Room* Drew Hayden Taylor, *Motorcycles & Sweetgrass*
2011		Esi Edugyan, *Half-Blood Blues* Michael Ondaatje, *The Cat's Table* Steven Price, *Into That Darkness*

(cont.)

Date	Historical and Cultural	Literary
2012	Department of Foreign Affairs cancels "Understanding Canada" programme	Thomas King, *The Inconvenient Indian: A Curious Account of Native People in North America* Alice Munro, *Dear Life*
2013	Alice Munro wins the Nobel Prize for Literature	
2014		Michael Crummey, *Sweetland* Richard Wagamese, *Medicine Walk*
2015	Report of the Truth and Reconciliation Commission	
2016		Gail Anderon-Dargatz, *The Spawning Grounds* Emma Donoghue, *The Wonder* Anosh Irani, *The Parcel* Steven Price, *By Gaslight* Madeleine Thien, *Do Not Say We Have Nothing* Katherena Vermette, *The Break*
2018		Esi Edugyan, *Washington Black* Rawi Hage, *Beirut Hellfire Society*
2019		Margaret Atwood, *The Testaments*
2020	United States-Mexico-Canada Agreement of Free Trade The COVID-19 pandemic	Souvankham Thammavongsa, *How to Pronounce Knife*

The Chronology highlights important dates in Canada's history and culture; the literary dates usually include the first publications of important writers as well as their major publications.

Introduction

A History of Canadian Fiction identifies the major trends and problems that aided – and sometimes damaged – the steady growth of fiction in Canada. It also includes reflections on the British and American inspirations behind the blossoming of original and distinctive fiction writers within the Canadian borders. An overarching account of the development of fiction, this book records its growth from colonial times to the present, where Canadian-born and naturalized Canadian writers combine to create our country's fiction.

In February of 1982 I was lecturing on Canadian fiction in Sweden. Per Gedin, head of the publishing firm Wahlström & Widstrand, the foremost publisher of English-language titles in Swedish, and author of *Literature in the Marketplace* (1975), explained to me that his agents used to fan out to London and New York to learn what was happening every fall season. Now, however, he had stopped sending them. He was more interested in Australia, South Africa, and Canada. Australian Patrick White, he stated, had won the Nobel Prize for Literature in 1973; consequently, Australian literature was being discovered. South Africa had apartheid, and this precarious situation was commanding attention to itself and its writers. Canada, on the other hand, had no defining interest to the outside world – it had never won a war, it had no major problems to demand world attention, yet Canadian fiction was growing without the steady and sometimes overpowering gaze of the outside world. This last fact merited Per Gedin's attention.

As I put together this *History of Canadian Fiction*, the first detailed history, I have often thought of his wise reflections about the steady and unnoticed growth of Canadian fiction. Today we have major authors, Margaret Atwood and Rohinton Mistry, Alice Munro and Michael Ondaatje, and so many others, reaching out to national and international audiences. This book brings together the many individuals who have created this impressive history, using their texts, their words, and relevant criticism. Many writers comment on their fiction-writing background, and I have utilized their reflections as I write this story.

Much more than a century ago, a few fiction writers published highly regarded and incredibly popular books. Writers such as Ernest Thompson Seton and Marshall Saunders, Ralph Connor and Stephen Leacock, Nellie McClung and Mazo de la Roche had enormous sales. In his first three books, Connor, for example, registered sales of more than five million copies, though not in Canada alone.

Then came the early-to-middle years of the twentieth century when the outside world knew little about what was developing in Canadian fiction. The writings of Morley Callaghan, rooted firmly but not avowedly in his native Toronto, appealed to American audiences; the writings of Sinclair Ross and Hugh MacLennan, W.O. Mitchell and Ernest Buckler, whose first novels appeared from American publishers, were coming forward. And Ethel Wilson bordered the line between these writers and the new writers of the 1950s. Much of the writing was done inside Canada with the rest of the world paying little attention.

In the 1950s, Robertson Davies and Mavis Gallant, Mordecai Richler, Abraham Moses [A.M.] Klein, and Sheila Watson launched their literary careers with singular works which summoned praise inside and even outside the country. The 1960s saw first books by Atwood, Munro, and Ondaatje, the explosion of fiction that decade also producing the first fiction by Austin Clarke, Leonard Cohen, Marian Engel, Timothy Findley, Robert Kroetsch, Margaret Laurence, Jane Rule, Audrey Thomas, and Rudy Wiebe, and anticipating Richler's permanent return to Canada. The 1970s brought forward such new writers as Alistair MacLeod, Carol Shields, and Richard B. Wright. During this time the outside world began to heed what was happening in Canadian fiction. By 1982 it had developed steadily, as Gedin said, without the outside world's interfering gaze.

After World War II, writers from outside Canada began to arrive. Although there had been few immigrant writers coming to the country, such newcomers as Henry Kreisel, Clarke, and Rule became part of native-born Canadians as well as foreign-born Canadians, the two groups melding into fiction's multicultural world.

Since – and even before – 1982, Canadian fiction was slowly commanding attention from internal and then external sources. The Governor General's Awards were first presented in 1937, for example, the Writers' Trust Awards in 1973 and the Giller Prize in 1994. Fiction also began to reap international awards. Established in 1969, the Booker finalists often include Canadian writers, the award won four times by them. Established in 1994, the Dublin IMPAC Literary Award, later called the International Dublin Literary Award, has had even more Canadian finalists, the award being given twice to Canadian novels. And the Nobel Prize to Alice Munro is final testimony to the stature of contemporary Canadian fiction.

The history of Canadian fiction is not so old – not so old as that of European countries, not so old as that of American fiction. It begins in the nineteenth century, it blossomed in the mid-twentieth century, and it accepted its position on the world stage in the later twentieth century.

For the earliest writers, Canada was a colony, where *there* must be the centre for the colonial mind. For them, *here*, unknown and undefined, remained unexplored, a colonial and a critical preoccupation. Late nineteenth- and early twentieth-century attempts to probe the meaning of *here* were grounded in the colonial understanding of Canada's place as a settler colony in relation to its mother country. By the mid-twentieth century, there were constant denials of the existence of this colonial status. Then, as the twentieth century moved to its close, there was now a multicultural and multiracial world in Canada where Canadian-born writers were increasingly augmented by naturalized voices unafraid to write about their own chosen landscapes far from the supposedly safe world that is Canada.

CHAPTER I

The Beginnings

Where does Canadian fiction find its beginnings? Not so far back as about 11500 BC when Indigenous people, the first inhabitants of the land that would become Canada, moved across the Bering Plain to settle in the new land. Not so far back as about 1000 AD when the Vikings set up a small settlement at L'Anse aux Meadows in what would become Newfoundland. Not so far back as the late fifteenth century when Jean Cabot sailed to Newfoundland, or the sixteenth century when Jacques Cartier sailed to the Gulf of St. Lawrence in 1534, or even the early seventeenth century when Samuel de Champlain founded Port-Royal in Acadia in 1605 and Quebec City in 1608. Canada was a young country, beckoning settlers in the sixteenth and seventeenth centuries to plunder its plentiful natural resources for their own benefit. Fishing, forestry, and furs attracted many ravenous newcomers, the land itself seeming void of a cultural life. Canada was a country which, according to its possible Portuguese derivation, meant "nothing here."

The eighteenth century witnessed the political machinations of the French and the English to control the country. Identified as New France, the land became a battleground between the reigning French and the ascendant English. In 1759 the Battle of the Plains of Abraham outside Quebec City saw the English defeat the French. This engagement sealed the fate of New France and established English authority, the land becoming the new colony of British Canada. By the Treaty of Paris of 1763, when the colony's total settler population was about sixty thousand, France officially ceded it to England, gaining distinctive recognition and status within the colony; a policy of assimilation was rejected in favour of separate identities for the two peoples. The question of Indigenous cultural recognition was not raised.

Frances Brooke (1724–89), the wife of the Anglican chaplain to the British garrison in Quebec City, sailed from England in July 1763 to join her husband at Sillery outside Quebec City. Already an accomplished novelist and translator, she stayed for five years and wrote *The History of Emily Montague* (1769), her experiences in the new land providing material for a tale set against the backdrop of the colony. Enlivened by descriptions of the Canadian landscape and its inhabitants, this epistolary novel of sensibility centres on courtship and its many complications in the lives of three sets of lovers. By the end, the three couples are happily married and settled in England. Inaccurately termed the first "Canadian" novel, more accurately the first novel using, at times, a Canadian setting, *The History of Emily Montague* – by a temporary resident – is written and published for a British readership and employs the Canadian background to enhance its authenticity. Canada was still a country to be plundered.

The Beginning of Satire

The Atlantic provinces, specifically Nova Scotia, witnessed the beginning of satire. Born in Renfrewshire, Scotland, Thomas McCulloch (1776–1843), an ordained minister in the Secessionist Presbyterian Church, came to Nova Scotia in 1803 and accepted Pictou's call to establish a Presbyterian congregation there; he eventually set up Pictou Academy, a liberal, non-sectarian college which boasted standards of teaching and programs of study as demanding as those of Scottish universities.

Letters of Mephibosheth Stepsure, McCulloch's humorous letters published serially in the *Acadian Reporter* from 1821 to 1823 and as one volume in 1862, reflect his deep concern with the morals of Nova Scotian society. In creating his persona of Stepsure, supported by Dean Drone, who extols the virtues of domesticity, he makes him the ideal settler: pious, prudent, and thrifty, who overcomes poverty in his farming vocation, while his neighbours are often slovenly, spendthrift, and troublesome; Stepsure could well see what they failed to accomplish by not building up a strong basic economy, dreaming instead of becoming rich quickly. For Nova Scotians, their land, so rich in natural resources, allows good farmers to produce quality products. Family values and religious piety contribute to the well-being of individuals and communities.

Episodic in narrative form, the letters map society's virtues and vices; they are thinly disguised sermons which promulgate fidelity to society's traditional values. Establishing on Canadian soil the satirical sketch as a way of looking at his world, "McCulloch is the founder of genuine Canadian humour," commented Northrop Frye, "which is based on a vision of society and is not merely a series of wisecracks on a single theme.

The tone of his humour, quiet, observant, deeply conservative in a human sense, has been the prevailing tone of Canadian humour ever since."[1]

For Thomas Chandler Haliburton (1796–1865), born in Windsor, Nova Scotia, and graduating from King's College, Windsor, McCulloch's *Letters* were the direct antecedent and inspiration for his own episodic study of Nova Scotian manners. A distinguished lawyer and Supreme Court judge, who sought, among much else, to give a permanent grant to Pictou Academy, Haliburton wrote a series of sketches, *The Clockmaker; or, The Sayings and Doings of Samuel Slick, of Slickville*, first published in the *Nova Scotian* in 1835 and 1836 and revised and augmented as a single volume in 1837. He invented Sam Slick, a brash, loquacious, and itinerant Yankee clockmaker who meets the narrator, a reasonable Nova Scotian squire, and both ride together to Windsor. As they converse, Slick's American self-confidence contrasts with perceived Nova Scotian indolence. While he laments Nova Scotians' failure to realize their land's potential, offering unsolicited views in heavily accented Yankee English, he wants them to leave aside their lethargy to institute material reforms. At the same time he exposes and undercuts his supposedly perfect American society. The squire, meanwhile, lambasts the United States as a failed experiment that has "disappointed the sanguine hopes of its friends."[2]

The second series of sketches (1838) introduces Slick's recollection of his conversations with Rev. Hopewell, his ninety-five-year-old minister back home in Slickville, Connecticut. Hopewell has serious reservations about the direction American society has travelled since the Revolution, qualifying Slick's rosy view with his yearnings for a lost America. In the third series of sketches (1840), Hopewell presents his pre-revolutionary and pro-British view of America in contrast to Slick's passionate championing of the virtues of unimpeded progress. One has to weigh the alternative visions of these three men to appreciate Haliburton's own conservative view, which favoured a British system of government adapted to North American conditions.

Haliburton sought to raise the standard of living for Nova Scotians. Like McCulloch, he showed disdain for wayfarers who would not go about their traditional roles, refusing to applaud their agrarian world; he made a Yankee clock-peddler underscore the delinquencies and the strengths of the countryside. Like McCulloch, he believed that indolence was a feature

[1] "Introduction," *The Stepsure Letters* (Toronto: McClelland & Stewart, 1960), p. ix.
[2] All quotations from the texts, unless otherwise identified, are taken from their first editions.

of their citizens, though he wanted Nova Scotia to learn economically from the United States while ignoring its political ideology.

Haliburton's three volumes of sketches are another step towards a role for satire in the slowly accumulating literature of pre-Confederation Canada. Both McCulloch and Haliburton, deeply entrenched in Nova Scotia and writing for the progressive change of their rural economies, let satire be laced with irony to enhance their vision of an improved life.

The third satirist is James De Mille (1833–80). Born in Saint John, New Brunswick, and educated with a master's degree in 1854 from Brown University, he penned more than twenty-five popular novels. Filled with improbable coincidences and predictable people, his corpus included boys' adventure novels and light travel comedies. He was enamoured of Haliburton's writings, his *Dodge Club; or, Italy in 1859* (1869) revealing the comic exploits of American tourists in Italy and his own indebtedness to the figure of Sam Slick. *A Strange Manuscript Found in a Copper Cylinder* (1888), written as early as the mid-1860s and published posthumously, stands out from his many books as an exceptional piece of satire, influenced by Jonathan Swift's *Gulliver's Travels*.

Four friends and yachtsmen, sailing in 1850 "upon the ocean between the Canaries and the Madeira Islands," come upon a copper cylinder containing the curious handwritten report of Adam More, dated 1843, the first mate of an English sailing ship bound for home from Tasmania. Entering by a vortex near the South Pole a strange subterranean, semitropical land, More writes down his adventures among the foreign, cave-dwelling Kosekin people of Antarctica. A simple-minded spokesperson for Western civilization, he watches their extremism, their choice of poverty over money, their preferred darkness over light, their capacity to kill their natural instincts for an absurd ideal denying their humanity. He never realizes that their values are no less arbitrary than those of his home culture. De Mille maintains that people must choose the *via media* between More's simplicity and Kosekin extremism. *A Strange Manuscript Found in a Copper Cylinder* ends abruptly, the four men going off to dinner, the reading of the manuscript interrupted. Whether De Mille wished to end here or to add more is open to question, the novel being published eight years after he died. What remains is a satire on the ills of the Victorian world, where hypocrisy, materialism, and self-indulgence are everywhere.

At the turn of the next century, Stephen Leacock, who knew the writings of at least the first two of these Maritimers, develops satire and irony in his vision of contemporary life.

The Beginning of Romance

Romance, the literary form that, bypassing realism, chooses climes often remote from ordinary life, finds its earliest expression in *St. Ursula's Convent, or The Nun of Canada, Containing Scenes from Real Life* (1824), the first work of fiction by a native-born Canadian. Written at the age of seventeen by Julia Catherine [Beckwith] Hart (1796–1867), born in Fredericton, the daughter of a French Canadian father and an English Canadian mother, the novel, a historical, sentimental, and melodramatic romance, is set at the French defeat in Quebec City and the years immediately following the English victory. The complicated and tedious plot involves the central character who is taken prisoner at the siege and believed dead, and the plot follows his travels until he is back in Quebec where all ends surprisingly happily. Hart borrowed the style of the British romances, including their plot embellishments and their character stereo-types. The romance in Canada has begun.

At the same time, John Richardson (1796–1852), born in Queenston Heights, Ontario, began his military career at the age of fifteen by enlisting as a volunteer in the war with the United States; he would pursue this career intermittently for the next twenty-five years. As a militarist, military historian, and journalist, he penned several novels and Canadian histories. His major works, *Wacousta; or, The Prophecy* (1832) and *The Canadian Brothers; or, The Prophecy Fulfilled* (1840), combine historical realism with a penchant for elements from sentimental romances.

Wacousta acknowledges Richardson's two major influences, Sir Walter Scott, the father of the historical novel, and James Fennimore Cooper, the American author of frontier life, seeking to make his own country a setting for fiction by emulating what Scott had done for Scotland and Cooper for the United States. Following Cooper, he turned his setting to the North American frontier, the attacks carried out on the British forts at Detroit and Michilimackinac, furnishing the background for a fictional plot of love and revenge. Forsaking his European past, Wacousta, an outcast obsessed with vengeance, aligns himself with Indian savagery in order to take revenge against a man who once betrayed his trust. In the wilderness of this new landscape is the eternal struggle between good and evil, where the ostensible villain later gains sympathy while his worthy opponent has a chequered past. The conventions of Gothicism are present throughout this seemingly realistic novel, including, as its subtitle suggests, prophecies as well as mysterious coincidences, hidden identities, and fleeing maidens. Set two generations later than *Wacousta*, *The Canadian Brothers* employs the historical background of the War of 1812 for another study of revenge, this time with descendants of a character from *Wacousta*, and once again their fates lead them into another Gothic tragedy. In this war, Canada rejected the republican democracy of the United States, and once again were heard cries for Canadian freedom.

Richardson creates his historical and fictional plots and overlays them with all the trappings of the Gothic novel, making his fiction more romantic and sentimental than realistic. Yet he finds little in his own country to praise: "Should a more refined and cultivated taste ever be introduced into the matter-of-fact country in which I have derived my being, its people will decline to do me the honor of placing my name in the list of their 'Authors.'"[3] In 1849 he moved to New York City, where he continued to write. Dying penniless in 1852, he was buried in an unmarked grave.

Contemporary with Richardson's writings are the rebellions in Lower (Quebec) and Upper (Ontario) Canada that would lead to Lord Durham's *Report* (1839), a seminal document on the land's growth into nationhood and a further refusal to follow the American form of democracy. In advocating responsible government, which Haliburton opposed and Richardson supported, the *Report* shows preference for a government embodying the principles of the British parliamentary system and rejects American-style revolution. The British North America Act (1867) becomes the realization of the *Report*: set adrift from the mother country of England and fearful of possible annexation from an expanding United States, the four original provinces of New Brunswick and Nova Scotia, present-day Quebec and Ontario, come together in a Confederation to ensure their own continued existence.[4]

Encompassing in time the rebellions and the British North America Act is bilingual Montreal-born novelist and poet Rosanna Mullins, later Rosanna Leprohon (1829–79). Born to Irish Anglophone parents, she married a physician from an old French Canadian family in 1851 and bore thirteen children; she was at home in both cultures. In her early stories and novels, all set in British country homes and London mansions, she is a romantic, the plots filled with melodrama and sentimental yearnings and indebted primarily to Fanny Burney and Jane Austen. But when

---

[3] *Eight Years in Canada* (Montreal: H.H. Cunningham, 1847), p. 95.

[4] Manitoba joined the Confederation in 1870 along with the Northwest Territories, British Columbia in 1871, Prince Edward Island in 1873, Yukon Territory in 1898, Saskatchewan and Alberta in 1905, Newfoundland in 1949, and the territory of Nunavut, created from the eastern part of the Northwest Territories, in 1999.

she returned after four years from St Charles-sur-Richelieu to Montreal, she began the first of four novels that presented her own land. As she wrote in the preface to the second novel, *Antoinette De Mirecourt; or, Secret Marrying and Secret Sorrowing* (1864),

> Although the literary treasures of "the old world" are ever open to us, and our American neighbors should continue to inundate the country with reading-matter, intended to meet all wants and suit all tastes and sympathies, at prices which enable every one to partake of this never-failing and ever-varying feast; yet Canadians should not be discouraged from endeavoring to form and foster a literature of their own.

Like Richardson, she wants her fiction to focus on her own land. First published in serialized form in 1859–60 and set in the region of Montreal, *The Manor House of De Villerai* uses the backdrop of the British conquest of Quebec between 1756 and 1760 for the first historical novel, in English or in French, to portray the fall of New France from a French Canadian perspective. Blanche De Villerai, the beautiful and wealthy heiress of the Manor House, situated on the banks of the Richelieu, finally frees her childhood betrothed and erstwhile partner so that he can marry her servant, a farmer's daughter from Villerai, whom he loves. Forsaking the battlefield and the patrilineal manor house of Scott's historical writings, Leprohon makes her female manor house the scene for debates among upper-class women on the social value of love-based marriage, especially during the siege. At the end, as Quebec's dream dies, Blanche remains ever virtuous and alone.

Set in Montreal "in the year 176-, some short time after the royal standard of England had replaced the fleur-de-lys of France," *Antoinette De Mirecourt* studies the titular seventeen-year-old French Canadian Catholic heiress as she comes to Montreal and secretly enters a marriage with a Protestant British officer, Major Audley Sternfield, in an Anglican ceremony. A young neighbour, whom Antoinette's father had chosen for her husband, kills Sternfield in a duel, and a third man, himself a Catholic, asks for her hand in marriage, which represents the union of Anglophone and Francophone societies and the emergence of a new order in an "essentially Canadian" novel. An "interracial" marriage can be extremely happy, as Antoinette's promises to be. In advocating proper religious duty and filial devotion, the romance has two male protagonists and an innocent heroine who must learn to read clearly the ways of the world, yet it also is a call-to-arms for young women to avoid the handsome British officers, like Sternfield, on the streets of Montreal, for these same English had thwarted and eclipsed Quebec's destiny a century earlier.

Avoiding the historical distance of her first two novels, her third, *Armand Durand; or, A Promise Fulfilled* (1868), the most realistic of the four and deeply indebted to Charles Dickens's novels, focuses on the titular character, the son of a poor French aristocratic mother and a prosperous French Canadian farmer. When his mother dies and his father remarries, the latter has a second son, Paul. Both boys attend a Montreal college, where Armand pursues legal studies while Paul abandons college to rejoin his father in farming. Armand enters a mismatched marriage which leads him to drink. His wife conveniently dies in childbirth, and the woman he has long loved forces him to abandon alcohol. He marries her and fulfils his true ambition: he moves into politics with his new wife's support, she being a perfect mate for a rising young politician.

Her final novel, *Ada Dunmore; or, A Memorable Christmas Eve* (1869–70), set "not many miles from the beautiful Bay of Quinte," is a first-person narration of the much-maligned title character and her wayward brother. With an Ontario setting and an accumulation of troubles the perfect Ada has to endure, Leprohon altered her themes of Quebec affairs to pen a heavily moral tale, which ends with Ada and her husband reunited in peace and turning "our thoughts and aspirations to that life beyond the grave to which our paths on earth inevitably lead, whether they lie in shadow or sunshine, in joy or sorrow."

Leprohon wanted the first three of her novels to mirror the travails of English-French relationships in the past and the present. Her conclusion to *Antoinette De Mirecourt* emphasizes her deeply held belief that mutual respect leads to understanding, encouraging the bridging of differences. Her sympathies fall on the side of the French Canadians, the sentimental heroine being the victim who becomes strong, though the English male still has the controlling position.

Leprohon wrote for an English audience, though her works were quickly popularized in translation among French readers too, the first three novels being published in French within a year of their English publication. The fact that her fiction was more appreciated in Quebec than in English Canada reflects the accuracy of her portraits of Quebec people and their English compatriots.

For many of the published fiction writers of the late nineteenth century, the only avenue to some kind of success was romance, far from the real world of their own time.

Born in Kingston-upon-Hull in England and, from the age of fifteen, living in the United States for seven years, William Kirby (1817–1906) settled after 1839 in Niagara-on-the-Lake, Ontario, where he became editor of the *Niagara Mail.* A poet as well as a prose writer, he wrote *The Golden Dog: A Legend of Quebec* (1877), a novel and a perfect example of the classic historical romance, its story being of one woman's idealized but ill-fated love for a brave man in the Quebec of 1748. With characters of limited complexity, the book achieves its success with Kirby's research on the historical setting, which makes even the most bizarre elements have some degree of verisimilitude. He was responsible for establishing an English-Canadian tradition of historical fiction going back to Scott. Like Richardson and Leprohon, he returned to an earlier period of Canadian history to fashion his romance, though he does not share Leprohon's moral purpose.

Gilbert Parker (1860–1932), born in Camden East, Ontario, enjoyed national and international success for his romances. After travelling and working in Australia, he settled permanently in London, England, in 1890. There he began to write on the Canadian Northwest, where he had never been, and later on Quebec. Of his more than thirty novels, the immensely popular *Seats of the Mighty* (1896) centres on an admired Scotsman, who had been imprisoned in Quebec at the time of the English victory there in 1759. Romantic, sometimes melodramatic, he wrote in the spirit of his times, interweaving his fiction with the facts of some historical situations. He was the first Canadian writer to make a comfortable living through his fiction.

The female novelists were generally disinclined to imitate their male counterparts. Although some female writers did use sentimental romances for the same reasons that men used them, others had ulterior motives for employing the form.

Agnes Machar (1837–1927), born in Kingston, Ontario, where she was a lifelong resident, followed the religious and social principles she inherited from her Scottish Presbyterian parents, advocating Christian ideals. Her fiction advocated better working conditions for poor labourers, charity towards the less fortunate, improved education for women, and patriotism. *Katie Johnstone's Cross: A Canadian Tale* (1870), written for Sunday-school readers, recounts the unending trials and tribulations of its fourteen-year-old heroine, a model of Christian tolerance, who chastises women for not taking seriously their own lives. Improved educational opportunities for women is a constant theme in her books: the heroine regenerates one impoverished family by sewing for them and teaching their children to read. In her most serious attempt at social and moral realism, *Roland Graeme, Knight: A Novel of Our Time* (1892), a novel for adults, the title character founds the newspaper *The Brotherhood*, "the new champion of the oppressed and downtrodden workmen," based on "the idea of Christian fellow-feeling." The paper has "the temperate and moderate tone in which it set forth existing wrongs and grievances, and appealed to the justice and humanity of those with whom it lay to remedy them." This new understanding will also rectify the town's growing labour strife, a solution reflecting her earlier Sunday-school writing and heralding "the spirit of Christian socialism." The first Canadian to write about labour relations when the subject occupied writers in England and the United States, Machar believed that the remedy to society's evils rests in the active use of Christian principles, which also accounts for her use of romance, her books leading directly to the popular fiction of Ralph Connor and Nellie McClung.

May Agnes Fleming (1840–80), born in Saint John, New Brunswick, wrote romances which combined sentimental elements with such Gothic trappings as mystery, disguise, and shocking happenings. With their convoluted plots and melodramatic incidents, they became the standard for their weekly or monthly appearance in serialized publication. The influential presence of Charlotte Brontë and Charles Dickens is apparent as couples find their happiness only after obstacles are overcome. After Fleming moved to Brooklyn in 1875 to be near her publishers, her romances tended to be less melodramatic and more realistic. Although she set a few novels and scenes in Canada, her plots occurred mainly in England and along the eastern seaboard of the United States. Author of more than thirty-five novels, she was Canada's first international bestselling fiction writer, sticking to the sentimental romance that won her a large readership among North American women. Like her male writers, she employed romance to assure her continuing success.

Born in Montreal, Lily Dougall (1858–1923) sailed to Edinburgh as companion to her aunt. She studied at the University of St Andrews for her Lady Licentiate in Arts, English and moral philosophy being her first areas of study. In her fiction, she assembles people who achieve holiness through dealing with their everyday actions, as her major inspiration, George Eliot, also assembled her characters. Not afraid to stray from the sentimental romance, she challenged the accepted values of her readers. In her first novel, *Beggars All* (1891), a young wife faces a moral dilemma: her journalist husband moonlights as a thief to fund an operation for her crippled sister. Orthodox religion with its absence of true charity contrasts with the husband's robberies of the undeserving wealthy. Of her ten novels, four set in Canada, the most important, *What Necessity Knows* (1893), studies the social and intellectual diversity of Scottish immigrants in the Eastern Townships of Quebec, recalling *Middlemarch* and its equally broad canvas of characters from all levels of society. Again faith, which is generous, contrasts with rigid fealty to established strictures. Like Eliot, Dougall sees the growth of her characters as exercises in attaining some advanced degree of self-knowledge and even holiness.

Born in Leshmahagow, Scotland, Joanna E. Wood (1867–1927) emigrated with her family in 1869 to New York, then to Queenston Heights, Ontario in 1874, where they settled on a large farm. Her first novel, *The Untempered Wind* (1894), depicts the fictional Jamestown and its disgraceful treatment of a woman, "a mother, but not a wife," trying to survive with her young son in a narrow-minded town, the setting recalling Ontario's Niagara area where Wood grew up. Influenced by Dickens and Eliot, even more by Elizabeth Gaskell, Nathaniel Hawthorne, and Thomas Hardy, she paints a harrowing portrait of a strong-willed woman who survives the town's cruelty and ostracism, challenging the evangelical faith that has made her the victim of its constant abuse. Jamestown stands at the front of a series of hypocritical, puritanical small towns which will dot the Canadian literary landscape. Her later novels are sentimental romances, never attaining the shocking realism of her first novel.

Many of these writers adhered to the vogue of romance, which continued into the twentieth century.

The Beginning of Immigrant Writing

"We are all immigrants to this place even if we were born here: the country is too big for anyone to inhabit completely, and in the parts unknown to us we move in fear, exiles and invaders," writes Atwood (b. 1939) in her afterword to *The Journals of Susanna Moodie* (1970). Immigrants we may well be, but there are two kinds of immigrants then and now coming to Canada. The first are those who, like Frances Brooke, come for a time, then return to their homeland. The others are those who come and stay, frequently derisive initially of their new home.

The first group includes John Galt (1779–1839), who came from Scotland to Canada a few times in his later years. After writing novels about West Scotland life, he published *Bogle Corbet; or, The Emigrants* (1831), set in Scotland, England, Jamaica, and finally Upper Canada. A generally unsuccessful entrepreneur, Corbet leads settlers to Canada to establish a new village. Practising "reciprocal civility," he invites his people to uphold integrity and enforce policing measures to keep the town at peace in contrast to the American Eden; some of his followers, however, leave, seduced by the allure of prosperity in the United States.

In the second, more populous group are the many people who came to Canada and published their fiction, often in such journals as *The Literary Garland*, which ran from 1838 to 1851. Among many contributors were the Strickland sisters, Susanna Moodie (1803–85) and Catharine Parr Traill (1802–99), who emigrated separately to Canada in 1832. Moodie had already begun a literary career with children's stories, her Anglican upbringing demanding in her fiction a commitment to education and moral behaviour; these religious romances are filled with Gothic excesses and hearken back to the prevailing romance tradition in early Canada: "From the age of twelve years," she "roamed through the beautiful but delusive regions of Romance, entirely to satisfy my restless imagination."[5] Her later fiction followed similar goals. Traill, too, wrote pious, edifying tales for children which follow natural facts and outlooks, her stories suggesting her later use of varied landscapes and surrounding botanical life.

In addition to her fiction, Moodie also wrote three books about her life in Canada. *Roughing It in the Bush* (1852), a series of loosely linked and interrelated sketches, is her testimony to the struggles and travails of newcomers to Canada. As people enter uncivilized terrain, they confront images and realities of imprisonment, decay, and death, Moodie's attitude "nearly allied to that which the condemned criminal entertains for his cell – his only hope of escape being through the portals of the grave." In her closing sentence she hopes that "the secrets of the prison-house" have been revealed. Challenging the optimistic written accounts of immigration, her book presents sober reflections on immigration's painful toll on its participants. Because of its immense success, she then wrote *Life in the Clearings versus the Bush* (1853), another series of interdependent sketches, which recount life in Belleville and other Canadian towns, now praising the country and its inhabitants. Her "novel," *Flora Lyndsay, or Passages in an Eventful Life* (1854), a highly autobiographical work and the third book in her trilogy, captures her and her husband's preparations to leave England and their long trip to their new world, all seen in a Christian perspective. At this point Moodie surrendered her interest in Canada.

Unlike her sister, Traill, a natural historian, preferred to study and record the delightful flora and fauna that graced her life in Canada. *The Backwoods of Canada: Being Letters from the Wife of an Emigrant Officer* (1836), for example, records her acute observations of the natural world around her in the middle-class Christian lifestyle she and her sister

---

[5] *Susanna Moodie: Letters of a Lifetime*, eds. Carl Ballstadt, Elizabeth Hopkins, and Michael Peterman (University of Toronto Press, 1985), p. 38.

espoused, offering at the same time practical advice to female settlers in the new world. "I daily feel my attachment to [the country] strengthening," she wrote in its conclusion. "Our present rude dwellings will have given place to others of a more elegant style of architecture, and comfort and grace will rule the scene which is now a forest wild."

These immigrants to Canada are slowly seduced by the glories of their new homeland. Some, like Brooke and Galt, remained only a short time. For others, like the Strickland sisters, their new dwelling place, while initially awkward and cumbersome, came to be their desired home.

In his sequential sketches Galt looks forward to Leacock, and all three writers anticipate the world of another immigrant, Frederick Philip Grove, as well as the many writings of post–World War II immigrants.

The Beginning of Animal Stories

The publication of *On the Origin of Species by Means of Natural Selection, or The Preservation of Favoured Races in the Struggle for Life* (1859) by Charles Darwin (1809–82) ignited an international debate among scientists and educators about the distinctions between human beings and animals. Accepting the kinship of these two, Darwin broke down the traditional barriers between them. Considered to be the foundation of evolutionary biology, his work advocated far-reaching theories of natural selection, which showed that all species of life are not created but evolved over time from common ancestors. For writers, animal stories, uniquely Canadian in that the animals are presented as they are in life, not as figures in allegories or fables, examine the Darwinian world that recognizes the animal dimensions of human nature. In Canada, where the land boasted many more animals than human beings, the animal story found its natural home.

Alexander Milton Ross (1832–97), a surgeon, abolitionist, and naturalist from Belleville, Ontario, wrote three workmanlike accounts of animal life. Supplemented by pencil sketches of his subjects, the books begin the attention paid to the animal world. For Thomas McIlwraith (1824–1903), who was born in Newton-upon-Ayr, Scotland, and emigrated to Hamilton, Ontario, in 1853, ornithology was an abiding interest. He published *The Birds of Ontario* (1886), a remarkable achievement in nineteenth-century nature-writing and a concise guide to every bird species. Based on his belief in close observation of birds, the sketches, refusing to acknowledge them as individuals, evoke a lamentation for a time when hunters were not the enemies of birds, when there was still a connection between human beings and their "feathered friends."

The young Ernest Thompson Seton (1860–1946), born in South Shields, England, and emigrating to Canada in 1866, purchased Ross's volume on birds and discovered that it contained wrongly classified birds and missing species. From McIlwraith, the young Seton, a budding naturalist, learned certain "birding" areas near Hamilton and received access to his collection of stuffed birds. He later provided some line drawings for the second edition of *The Birds of Ontario* (1894).

In his autobiographical *Trail of an Artist-Naturalist* (1940), Seton terms his first story, "Kingbird," written in 1876, "the earliest known animal story of the realistic type," that is, a story "giving in fiction form the actual facts of an animal's life and modes of thought." As he wrote in the prefatory "Note to the Reader" of *Wild Animals I Have Known* (1898), his first book-length account of animals in the wild, "We and the beasts are kin. Man has nothing that the animals have not at least a vestige of, the animals have nothing that man does not in some degree share. Since, then, the animals are creatures with wants and feelings different in degree only from our own, they surely have their rights." Here is Darwin's perspective on the natural kinship of human beings and animals in realistic animal stories examining not the type but the specific, individual animal. Not fables, his animal stories are uniquely Canadian fictional tales.

Of the first two thousand copies of *Wild Animals I Have Known*, Seton had offered his New York publisher a contract to forgo royalties provided the publisher pay him double the standard 10 per cent royalty on all copies over two thousand. The book's release date was late October 1898; within three weeks the first two thousand copies were sold, and before Christmas the book had been reprinted three more times; it had its twentieth printing in its eighth year of publication, its fiftieth in its twenty-fifth year.

In his stories Seton makes the animal the hero, the human being but a small, if necessary, complement. The life, presented from the animal's perspective, gives the animal psychology, showing how it lives and thinks and feels. The hero's adventures are developed from life, yet the whole story must be called fiction because the hero is composed of several individuals.

"Lobo, The King of Currumpaw," the opening story of *Wild Animals I Have Known*, is a tragic tale of an amazing animal. Lobo, as Seton's "Note to the Reader" states, "lived his wild romantic life from 1889 to 1894 in the Currumpaw region, as the ranchmen know too well, and died, precisely as related, on January 31, 1894." Seton had been invited to a New Mexican cattle ranch by a man who wanted an expert on wildlife to kill the wolf pack that was devastating his range stock. With a sterling reputation for cunning and strength, Lobo, the pack's leader, scorned the poisoned baits. When Seton learned that a small, white she-wolf named Blanca was Lobo's constant companion, he managed to capture and kill Blanca, an inhumane action. Lobo followed his mate's trail to his own capture. When he howled in pain, no member of the pack responded. Seton brought him back to the ranch house and chained him to a stake. The next morning Lobo was dead of a broken heart, unable to endure the double loss of his beloved and his freedom.

Here is the essence of Seton's stories. A wild animal is caught in a vicious encounter, most often with a male human being. The "humane" behaviour generally appears to be that of the animal. In the ensuing conflict, the animal succumbs to the superior taunts and tortures of the assailant. The life of wild animals, as Seton often said, always has a tragic end. Canadian animal stories are about animals, animals in the wild, and readers empathize with them because they are inevitably portrayed as victims. By carefully observing animals in nature, thus following McIlwraith's practice, Seton concluded that what he saw could be explained only by the animal's rational activity. He went on to publish nearly thirty books of animal stories, many of them illustrated with his own drawings, and his collections were major bestsellers well into the mid-1920s.

Contemporaneous with Seton's stories are the animal tales of Charles G.D. Roberts (1860–1943), a distinguished poet who rarely employed the Darwinian universe, and a fiction writer who utilized the Darwinian perspective. Publishing more than a dozen collections of animal stories, he was a philosophical writer compared to Seton, who was the finer naturalist and the more didactic of the two. Born in Douglas, New Brunswick, he received his BA and MA from the University of New Brunswick, becoming later and, for ten years, a professor of modern languages at King's College in Windsor, Nova Scotia. Although he wrote nine novels and five novellas, he is known chiefly as a fiction writer who was an originator of the animal story.

His first story, "Strayed," published in 1889 and gathered in his first collection, *Earth's Enigmas* (1896), recounts the exhausting journey of "a young ox of splendid build, but of a wild and restless nature," who dashes away through the forest, oblivious to his former home and his beloved yoke-fellow. He meets up with other dangerous animals, the most barbaric being a cruel panther who ultimately attacks him to his death. "League upon league back in the depth of the ancient forest, a lonely ox was lowing in his stanchions, restless, refusing to eat, grieving for the absence of his yoke-fellow." Like many of Roberts's stories, this one makes the ox as "humane" as possible in terms of his behaviour and his way of life. Roberts was interested in describing battles between animals over food, territory, or just for the challenge of an attack, all this promulgating Darwin's theory that there is continual struggle for survival in the natural world. And like Seton, he disliked fables and allegories, preferring to create a direct and sympathetic relationship between his subject matter and his readers.

"Introductory: The Animal Story," his preface to *The Kindred of the Wild: A Book of Animal Life* (1902), observes: "Within their varying limitations, animals can and do reason. As far, at least, as the mental intelligence is concerned, the gulf dividing the lowest of the human species from the highest of the animals has in these latter days been reduced to a very narrow psychological fissure." He created more than 250 animal stories, psychological romances "constructed on a framework of natural science." His "Prefatory Note" to *The Haunters of the Silences: A Book of Animal Life* (1907) concludes: "The actions of animals are governed not only by instinct, but also, in varying degree, by processes essentially akin to those of human reason."

Seton and Roberts came to be friends. Roberts had already dedicated *The Watchers of the Trails: A Book of Animal Life* (1904) "To My Fellow of the Wild, Ernest Thompson Seton." In his autobiography, Seton, on the other hand, concluded that *Wild Animals I Have Known* "founded the modern school of animal stories, that is, giving in fiction form the actual facts of an animal's life and modes of thought." Yet in 1933, Roberts commented that he antedated Seton: "My stories are a *new departure* in animal stories, dealing with the *psychology* of the animals."[6] Seton and Roberts were, independently, originators of the Canadian realistic animal story.

Complementing the stories of Seton and Roberts are the writings of Marshall Saunders (1861–1947), a native Nova Scotian who published adult novels and animal stories. In her adult fiction, she often resorted to the formulas of romance. Her animal stories, however, capture the harsh treatment of animals. The first Canadian book to become a world bestseller with more than one million copies sold, and the first to be translated into eighteen languages, *Beautiful Joe* (1894), winner of the American Humane Education Society's Award for the novel that repeats the appeal of *Black Beauty*, tells in his own words the story of Joe, an abused dog, whose first owner brutally mistreats him, flinging against a wall all the puppies in the litter except for Joe. When he escapes to a woman's kindness, there is still cruelty everywhere, most human beings being

[6] *The Collected Letters of Charles G.D. Roberts*, ed. Laurel Boone (Fredericton: Goose Lane, 1989), p. 455.

merciless and evil. The story, told in an unsentimental way, was one of fourteen books Saunders wrote which constitute animal biographies.

The animal stories of Roberts, Saunders, and Seton herald increasing emphasis on animal rights, showing human compassion for many kinds of animals. At the same time, their stories lead to literary realism evident in later writings of Robert J.C. Stead, Martha Ostenso, and Grove. The animal story continues to have a place in Canadian fiction. Mazo de la Roche's *Portrait of a Dog* (1930) memorializes her Scotch terrier, for example, Grove uses ants as the centre of his last novel, *Consider Her Ways* (1947), Marian Engel's *Bear* (1976) makes a bear the focal point of one woman's interaction with nature, Barbara Gowdy's *The White Bone* (1998) explores the inner life of elephants, and Colin McAdam's *A Beautiful Truth* (2014) examines the consciousness of chimpanzees.

As the nineteenth century ended, romance was the accepted form of reading despite the presence of satire and the immense popularity of animal stories. Canadians generally read romances, not the genre that was the domain of Hawthorne, Herman Melville, or even Henry James, but the form that leads to happy endings far from the world of realism. They were generally intent on fiction as polite wish-fulfilment, enticing them to read in the never-never land of adventures, exploits, and love entanglements.

CHAPTER 2

From Romance towards Realism

Canada was a law-abiding, conservative, and Christian nation. Toronto-born and one of the more distinguished publishers in the United States, George H. Doran (1869–1956) reflected:

> religious publishing was of considerable importance, for everybody was religious. On Sunday mornings and evenings the streets of Toronto were crowded by thousands of our ultimate consumers, wending their respective ways cheerfully and devotedly to their several churches armed with Bibles, prayer-books, and hymn-books, to the ringing of church bells and the music of chimes. It was essential that every man and woman and child should be an adherent of some church or denominational body. A business man, especially a retail merchant, did not dare not to be a church member.

Canadian publishers were often attached to a particular denomination:

> So highly controversial an atmosphere demanded literature and propaganda, and there were numerous religious publishing houses: the Presbyterian Board of Publication, the Baptist Publication Society, the Methodist Book and Publishing House, the Primitive Methodist Book Room, the Evangelical Churchman Company, and a branch of the English Society for Promotion of Christian Knowledge – a purely Anglican or Episcopalian enterprise.[1]

This mixture of literature and propaganda found its primary exponent in Charles W. Gordon (1860–1937) of eastern Ontario, who was ordained a Presbyterian minister in Calgary in 1890. Better known by his penname of Ralph Connor, he was the top Canadian fiction writer of the first quarter of the twentieth century.

First serving as a missionary to the lumbermen and miners of the Northwest Territories, Connor came in 1894 to Winnipeg's Saint Stephen's Church, where he remained for the rest of his life. Although

---

[1] *Chronicles of Barrabas, 1884–1934* (New York: Harcourt Brace, 1935), pp. 6–7, 8.

he never forsook the ministry, he transferred part of its intention to his fiction. The author of twenty-two novels as well as many short stories, he pioneered a special branch of literature called pulpit fiction. However well-written and empathetic his novels are, they are essentially sermons which inculcate in his audiences moral lessons. He creates a highly readable, didactic fiction, which transfixed his readers and propelled him into the ranks of the bestselling English authors of his time.

As a young missionary, Connor decried a movement to terminate further expansion of the Western Home Missions. As a consequence, the editor of the Church-sponsored *Westminster Magazine* invited him to pen a short story based on his missionary life. Connor submitted "Christmas Eve in a Lumber Camp," and the editor suggested the story be divided into three sections, further emphasizing that future episodes might well constitute a novel, which would be called *Black Rock: A Tale of the Selkirks* (1898). The purpose was simple: "to awaken my church in Eastern Canada to the splendor of the mighty religious adventure being attempted by the missionary pioneers in the Canada beyond the Great Lakes by writing a brief sketch of the things that as clerk of the biggest presbytery in the world I had come to know by personal experience."[2] The content is, as he wrote in the preface, religious: "The men of the book are still there in the mines and lumber camps of the mountains, fighting out that eternal fight for manhood, strong, clean, God-conquered."

Religious in outlook and purpose, *Black Rock* recounts the moralistic story of a widow (her husband had been a confirmed alcoholic) and a young Presbyterian minister, who eventually marries her. The teller of the tale is Mr. Connor, "sometime medical student, now artist, hunter, and tramp at large" and a refugee from the "cosmopolitan and kindly city" of Toronto. While the railroad is coming westward, the minister wants to give this new land a faith, which will be instrumental in the shaping of the country: "If society crystallizes without her influence, the country is lost, and British Columbia will be another trap-door to the bottomless pit."

The *Westminster Magazine* printed *Black Rock* in an edition of one thousand copies; the first edition sold five thousand copies. Although it was too late to copyright the book in the United States, Doran, "one of the three greatest publishers in America and one of the best and closest friends I have made during my life,"[3] published an American edition whose success led to the appearance of many pirated editions.

---

[2] *Postscript to Adventure: The Autobiography of Ralph Connor* (New York: Farrar & Rinehart, 1938), p. 148.
[3] Ibid., p. 150.

His second novel, *The Sky Pilot: A Tale of the Foothills* (1899), follows the path of the "sky pilot" or missionary, who comes to a town in the foothills of Alberta to help its citizens in their earthly journey, to minister to the sick, and to die contentedly. Connor, still a figure in his own text, says of his hero that he was a great man, "tender as a woman and with the heart of a hero." "The measure of a man's power to help his brother," the preface states, "is the measure of the love in the heart of him and of the faith he has that at last the good will win." This second novel, which singles out alcohol as the ultimate evil and extols religion as the only proper path in this world, had "an immediate sale of nearly 250,000 copies, which later reached well over 1,000,000 copies."[4]

For Connor, the reason for the phenomenal success of his first two novels was clear: they "gave an authentic picture of life in the great and wonderful new country in Western Canada." Yet there was another important reason for their triumph: the two novels

> possess a definitely religious motif. Religion is here set forth in its true light as a synonym of all that is virile, straight, honorable and withal tender and gentle in true men and women. And it was this religious motif that startled that vast host of religious folk who up to this time had regarded novel-reading as a doubtful indulgence for Christian people.[5]

In these novels, indeed in all his fiction, Connor was promulgating his own vision of Canada. His fiction was to mirror his concept of his country, the pockets of urban wickedness in the east and the wild west, governed by law and order, that was beckoning new settlers. The cradle of his new Canadian race, the west is home to mythic Canadian heroes who represent the best of modern civilization. Long the silent son of the mother country, Canada belongs to a great world empire. Connor is describing a new Canada of his own and of the popular imagination, a Canada neither British nor American, but a country peopled by Canadians, the greatest race of all. He recounts his tales as romances, long narratives which follow the trials of a missionary, the modern exemplar of the medieval knight, who fashions his exploits among these western outposts.

In *The Man from Glengarry* (1901), Connor retreats from the west in order to present his own upbringing in eastern Ontario. Although ostensibly the story of Ranald Macdonald and his coming of age in obedience to God's will, the book captures the humble and true pilgrims on their road of life: "The mark that reached down to their hearts' core was that of their

---

[4] *Chronicles*, p. 202.   [5] *Postscript to Adventure*, p. 150.

faith, for in them dwelt the fear of God," and to make this point evident is part of the purpose of this book. In the end, Ranald leaves the corrupt world of the urban east for the wholesome innocence of the west. With this novel, Connor achieved total sales of five million copies of his three novels. Later, between 1917 and 1937, according to an in-house history of McClelland and Stewart, he was the most successful Canadian author, "whose popularity was such that McClelland and Stewart used to order the latest title by the railway carload."

The Man from Glengarry was followed almost immediately by *Glengarry School Days* (1902), vignettes about a young lad, the son of the Presbyterian minister and his wife, and his coming of age in Glengarry. These vividly remembered episodes from the past anticipate Leacock's sunshine world: the mood nostalgic, the morality sentimental, and the genre again romance, where integration is the ultimate consequence of all the conflicts in the story.

Connor continued his practice of writing romances of the past by retelling early events in Canadian and American history. For his sources, he used the Bible and its many stories, and he also drew upon John Bunyan's *Pilgrim's Progress*, the archetypal treatise charting the way to salvation through sin, repentance, and forgiveness. These works were the inspiration for his sermons and for his fiction. "The darling of the earnest, book-buying, church-going public, he saw novels primarily as a means of attracting attention to pressing social, religious, and political issues," comments Guy Vanderhaeghe (b. 1951).[6]

Connor's vision of a great Canada had a few stumbling blocks, however. His portraits of French Canadians, too easily indebted to William Henry Drummond's doggerel poetry, ranked the French as inferior to the English, and his limited understanding of the place of immigrants led to their assimilation into the glorious world Connor envisioned: "to make them good Christians and good Canadians, which is the same thing" (*The Foreigner: A Tale of Saskatchewan*, 1909). His call fell on deaf ears as French Canadians and immigrants strove to uphold their cultural distinctiveness, and though his later books still had, for example, American first printings of two hundred thousand, he became "resentful and somewhat embittered that he no longer held the heart and attention of his great and adoring public. . . .. He still writes as well as ever, or nearly so, but the world has moved."[7]

---

[6] "'Brand name' vs. 'No-Name'," *The Urban Prairie*, ed. Dan Ring (Saskatoon: Fifth House, 1993), p. 114.
[7] *Chronicles*, p. 206.

For Connor, the didactic was the centre of his fiction's great success. He sought to bring people to their true calling as members of God's church here on earth. He catered to his readers and their need for comfort and for accessible tales of the Christian heroic ideal.

One summer in the 1880s, Connor lodged near Cartwright, Manitoba, at the homestead of Richard and May Stead. Their son Robert (1880–1959) paid attention to Connor's stories, going on to become a successful journalist and publisher of two weekly newspapers. With little formal education, he achieved fame as a poet and then as a novelist. His first work of fiction, *The Bail Jumper* (1914), is a Connor-inspired romance set in Plainville, Manitoba, where the embodiment of evil in the figure of Gardiner, the keeper of the general store, is overcome by the natural goodness of the hero, Ray Burton. Gardiner desires Miss Vane, the town beauty, and so does Burton. Their collision leads to complexities which result in the unmasking of evil and the triumph of goodness. *The Bail Jumper* extends the influence on the prairie of Connor's vision of the west teeming with newcomers,

> men of all nationalities, Canadian, American, British Islanders, German, Russian, French, Austrian, Pole, Italian, Hungarian, Scandinavian, Chinamen – here they were gathered from the corners of the globe and waiting patiently through night and day, through heat and cold, through wind and rain, through any trial and any hazard for the God-sent privilege, born of a new country, of calling the land beneath their feet their own.

Stead's *The Homesteaders* (1916) is a further depiction of Plainville through John and Mary Harris who arrive from Ontario. Beginning in 1882 and skipping down twenty-five years, the book observes some cracks in the world of the perfect romance. In the end, however, John and Mary, woefully estranged, embrace each other, while the evil villain drives his horses over a precipice. Evil is one man's refusal to embrace his proper calling, preferring to be a slave to his own materialism. World War I constrained the perfect romance ending, for example, in his next novel, *The Cow Puncher* (1918), where the romance ending is interrupted by the war and the hero's death at Courcelette. *Neighbours* (1922) has two young brother-and-sister couples of the same age leave Ontario for the western foothills where they find their true happiness, and *The Smoking Flax* (1924) returns to Plainville for a romance which ends, again, in complete happiness.

Only in *Grain* (1926) does Stead question the romance tradition. The setting now more realistic than in his earlier novels, *Grain* charts the progress of Gander Stake from the 1890s through the end of World War I.

External forces are now acting upon the citizenry of Plainville. Stead depicts skillfully the documented changes in the farming life of the 1910s – he relishes uncovering the new worlds that greet the dwindling numbers of farmers. Yet Gander, at the end of his story, does not win his woman; he does not have the education or imagination to deal well with society around him. Ending with him leaving suddenly and going to the city, the novel refuses a romantic conclusion yet has no resolution. Stead himself knew only disappointment with *Grain's* lack of commercial success, and he returned to his usual tales, his next, *The Copper Disc* (1931), a thriller trying to mask an essentially romance world.

Stead could not venture far outside Connor's fictional world, though the times were suggesting other modes of writing. He made Connor his ideal and fashioned romances out of his materials, only briefly attempting to document something more than trite versions of prairie romances. Other writers, more attuned to the 1920s, would reshape their approach to prairie life.

The Expatriate Vision

At the turn of the twentieth century, Canada still lacked publishers who would gamble on Canadian titles. On 25 January 1888, Sara Jeannette Duncan (1861–1922) wrote of the comparative paucity of women writers in Canada: "New York is the place above all others for a woman with a facile pen; and the hundreds who live there very comfortably by its exercise testify that this is generally understood. The opportunities there for descriptive work are almost unlimited, and it is in descriptive work that women accomplish most."[8] Five years later, the poet Archibald Lampman advised his readers:

> No doubt a time will come when the more populous life and increasing interests of our own country will keep a larger proportion of its enterprising spirits within its own borders. For the present, however, it is quite natural that those who seek the widest field for their abilities should wander abroad. Let us find no fault with them on that account. They probably bring more honor to their country in the fields which they have chosen, than they would if they had remained at home. Here their energies might have withered away in petty and fruitless occupations, and their talent have evaporated in the thin sluggishness of a colonial atmosphere.[9]

[8] *Selected Journalism*, ed. Thomas E. Tausky (Ottawa: Tecumseh, 1978), p. 49.
[9] *Archibald Lampman: Selected Prose*, ed. Barrie Davies (Ottawa: Tecumseh, 1975), p. 72.

Although there were a number of Canadian writers who made their journeys from their homeland to elsewhere, there were, at this time, three Canadians who did "seek the widest field for their abilities": Arthur Stringer (1874–1950), Norman Duncan (1871–1916), and Sara Jeannette Duncan. These individuals from southern or southwestern Ontario represent the visions of the expatriate writer. Stringer never recaptured his native idiom; Norman Duncan was comfortable in an exile which did not separate him from his fictional homes; and Sara Jeannette Duncan, despite her wide wanderings, remained perfectly faithful in her fictional rendering of small-town Ontario.

Poet and novelist Stringer – he published fifteen volumes of poetry and more than forty novels – was an exceptionally versatile man, winning critical acclaim for his many works and gaining commercial success. Of these three expatriates, Stringer was the most successful and the most celebrated. In his first novel, *The Silver Poppy* (1903), which went through five printings, he embarked on a series of novels, completely Americanized, which depict life in the big city. Focusing on John Hartley, a young poet from England and educated at Oxford, who comes to New York to work for the United News Bureau, the novel follows his adventures – in reporting and in love – through to a tragic denouement. Hartley falls in love with a young novelist whose second novel he is rewriting. When they spend a week together in Quebec City, he proposes to her; she responds that she has given him sole authorship of her second novel. After he returns to New York, he finds out that the novel has appeared – with her name as sole author! Their romance ends.

After his success with *The Silver Poppy*, Stringer began to write New York crime novels. His New York experiences had given him a first-hand knowledge of criminal activity and street life, and through these books he gained his formidable reputation as an experienced chronicler of American lower-class life.

In 1915 Stringer sought to return to his native land as the setting for his novel *The Prairie Wife*, but too long a stay in New York prevented his easy accommodation to Canada. A young woman goes to live on the Canadian prairies with her new mail-order husband, a dour Scotch Canadian wheat farmer. Her reading has been in the works of Dickens, Eliot, and George Meredith, and her marriage is happy and fulfilling, issuing a little boy. An epistolary novel, the book follows the conventional romance of pioneering. There is, however, no sense of location, no feeling for the texture and atmosphere of prairie life.

In the second and third volumes of this trilogy, *The Prairie Mother* (1920) and *The Prairie Child* (1922), Stringer continues his epistolary technique as the young woman encounters the demands, the difficulties, and the dangers of this marriage of opposites. Their union deteriorates as they encounter financial hurdles and amatory triangles. In the final scene, however, she goes off into the perpetual sunset. Yet the books give no evidence of a Canadian sensibility. The sections set in New York are so vivid that the other sections pale in contrast. The trilogy becomes an American writer's odyssey on Canadian soil, though the Canadian soil is never realized.

Among his many later novels, all of them having Canadian references and even settings, *The Wolf Woman* (1928) stands out as a most interesting though flawed work. John Caver, "a man of the world and a twentieth-century father," owns the Trail-End Camp in northern Ontario, 700 miles north of his home in New York City: "He came from the mysterious Big City, beyond the Line, the city of millionaires who traveled half a thousand miles to shoot a deer or catch a string of fish, the city of stately homes and paved streets and motor-cars and music and books and the uncompre-hended splendor of life." In a boating accident in the North, John is thrown from his canoe, and the chore girl, Aurora Mary, whose father is Irish, her mother Aboriginal, saves his life. As recompense for her singular action, he agrees to bring her to New York, much to the noticeable exasperation of his own daughter. Aurora Mary is treated there with uncommon disrespect, amounting finally to complete hatred. In the end, she returns to the North, now accompanied by the daughter's original fiancée. "I love you," Alan Somer tells Mary. "I've loved you in some blind and groping way from the first day I saw you." The romance cadence recalls Connor's prairie fiction.

Stringer had a large and faithful following for his many novels, yet his novels are finally not about Canada nor are they written from a Canadian perspective. An expatriate who became an American citizen in 1937, he chose to become an American writer and thereby lost his Canadian vision. When he returned to a Canadian setting, he could not capture the land he had once known so well. In 1946, the University of Western Ontario awarded him an honorary degree in recognition of his literary contribu-tions to Canadian letters!

Norman Duncan, born in Brantford, Ontario, left the University of Toronto in 1895 without a degree and moved to the United States, where he remained for the rest of his life, though he never became an American citizen. A peripatetic traveller who roamed the neigbourhoods of New York City, Labrador and Newfoundland, the Middle East, Southeast Asia, and Australia, Duncan spent his first two years as a reporter with the

Auburn (New York) *Bulletin* and then worked for the *New York Evening Post*. As a result of roaming the districts of New York, he published his first book, *The Soul of the Street: Correlated Stories of the New York Syrian Quarter* (1900). Of special interest in these stories is his ability to capture the idiom of his characters, for his book brings to life the many Syrian immigrants who populate this quarter. In fact, the racial stereotyping of the Arabs as well as the stories' drunken and child-beating Irish are painted directly in their own dialects. Duncan found his natural vehicle in the earthy idiosyncrasies of his characters' speech, reproducing phonological structures in their dialogue. Here was a writer trying to capture the reality of his people.

From the Syrian Quarter of New York, Duncan travelled on assignment to the outports of Newfoundland and the coast of Labrador; he called this landscape – the coast between Cape St John and Cape Bauld, the area he knew best – "the real Newfoundland." Among the people he discovered their unique idiom, similar in its power to the idiom of the Syrian Quarter, and he made their language and their way of life the source of much of his subsequent writing. What is important again is the language of his characters, the particular idioms and dialects. He brings to vivid realization the people of Newfoundland and Labrador just as he had brought to life the immigrants of the Syrian Quarter.

In *The Way of the Sea* (1903), his collection of ten short stories about Newfoundland, Duncan captured the lives, the troubles, and the defeats of the outport people. Each story captures particular features of their contained lives so close to the natural world. As the final story, "The Fruits of Toil," concludes: "The life of a man is a shadow, swiftly passing, and the days of his strength are less; but the sea shall endure in the might of youth to the wreck of the world."

From his closely observed stories of these people, Duncan moved to his first novel, *Doctor Luke of the Labrador* (1904), and then to *Dr. Grenfell's Parish* (1905), his account of Wilfred Grenfell's work among the outport people. In the latter, his purpose is straightforward: to spread the knowledge of Grenfell's mission on the coasts of Newfoundland and Labrador and to describe the condition of the people he seeks to help. After this book, his fiction centres itself mainly in this world of endurance, defeat, and hope.

Duncan also wrote fictional tales for young readers, and here he utilized his knowledge of the Newfoundland terrain. As he writes in his preface to *Billy Topsail, M.D.; a Tale of Adventure with Doctor Luke of the Labrador* (1916), as the tale is told of the spring of the year, when the ice breaks up and the floes come drifting out of the north with great storms, Newfoundland presents herself in her worst mood. Yet the sun shines in Newfoundland, tender enough in summer weather – there are flowers on the hills and warm winds on her sea; and such as learn to know the land come quickly to love her for her beauty and for her friendliness.

Herein lies Duncan's unique position as a faithful chronicler of Newfoundland life, as the teacher who wants his readers to know and appreciate the detailed studies he offers them of the outport world, as the fiction writer who maps the unmapped and therefore exotic terrain of a people enduring hard but hopeful lives. To this task he brings his exceptional ability to capture these people in their own language, creating in his dialogue the locale's idiom. He had already achieved this in *The Soul of the Street*. He now chooses Newfoundland and makes it the setting for most of his remaining fiction.

As a short story writer and novelist, he left Canada to pursue his writing in the United States. He never abandoned his Canadian perspective, that of an outsider who sought out people to investigate, to map, to record. Essentially romantic by nature, he observed, he recollected, then he wrote. And his own personality is subsumed in the fictional worlds he creates. An unheralded but important writer, he remained the observer, vividly recounting for the first time the busy life of the Syrian Quarter and, more extensively, the complex life of the outports of Newfoundland.

Born and raised also in Brantford, Ontario, Sara Jeannette Duncan – no relation to Norman Duncan – always desired to be a writer. She embarked on her writing career first as a journalist – working for the Toronto *Globe*, where she was the first woman hired on a regular basis, the *Washington Post*, and the *Montreal Star*. In her many columns for these papers, she lamented the absence of a defined audience in Canada. Maintaining that Canadians are "suffering for a renaissance," she mocked the appearance of Canadian books:

> The publication of a Canadian work of poetry or fiction, or any of the lighter arts of literature, by a Canadian firm, among Canadians, is apt to be received with peculiar demonstrations. Their facial form is that of an elongation of the countenance, a pursing of the lips, a lifting of the eyebrows. This is usually accompanied by a little significant movement of the shoulders which we have borrowed from our French-Canadian relations-in-law expressly for use in this regard. We pick up the unfortunate volume from the bookseller's counter to which its too trustful author has confided it, and we turn its leaves in a manner we reserve for Canadian

publications – a manner that expresses curiosity rather than a desire to know, and yet one that is somehow indicative of a foregone conclusion.[10]

Duncan decried the plight of a writer in a decidedly colonial environment, for the colony did not believe in itself, and as a consequence the writers could not believe in themselves.

An avid feminist before the term became fashionable, a suffragist before the time of the suffragette movement, Duncan the journalist embarked on a trip around the world with another journalist, and the result of their travels was the publication of Duncan's first book, *A Social Departure: How Orthodocia and I Went Round the World by Ourselves* (1890), and the chance meeting in India with Everard Cotes, an entomologist at the Indian Museum in Calcutta, whom she married the same year her book was published. From then on, Duncan became a resident of India with frequent trips to England and to Canada.

Duncan wrote of the world she knew, whether these worlds were Canada, India, or England. A distinct realist in the manner of William Dean Howells, whom she came to know, and Henry James, whom she admired immensely, she has a tone of irony running through her works which has its inspiration in the writings, not of Dickens, who had such influence on Lucy Maud Montgomery and Leacock, but of Jane Austen. In her teenage years, she spent her time writing romances, and her ironic detachment came to pervade her short stories and her novels.

When Duncan came to write her only Canadian novel, *The Imperialist* (1904), she brought to her study of Elgin, a small Ontario town which is a thinly disguised Brantford, the same ironic detachment of Austen's novels. The inhabitants of Elgin represent the worlds of Canada, "this little outpost of Empire," the Murchison family being the Liberal forces, the Milburns being the forces that seem to prevail in contemporary society. Into their midst comes young Lorne Murchison, idealistic, vibrant, and doomed to defeat.

As a young man and a young lawyer, Lorne is dedicated to the championing of one extreme of political persuasion, the imperialist cause. He sees the advantages in reinforcing the bonds between Canada and her mother country, and he is afraid that if these bonds are not re-established, Canada will suffer annexation with the United States, which will mean the annihilation of Canada. He thus seeks further ties with England, preferring renewed imperialism to the possibility of absorption by the United States.

[10] *Selected Journalism*, pp. 109–10.

As a candidate for the Liberal party, he runs in the South Fox riding on an imperialist platform. Although he wins, his own party then unseats him. Lorne has failed to observe the vision that Duncan herself espouses: the Canadian world is founded on a sort of ambivalence, and the winning candidate must fashion a balanced vision between the two poles of renewed federalism with England and annexation with the United States.

The narrator of *The Imperialist* is a cosmopolitan woman with verbal dexterity, appreciative understanding of her milieu, and superior knowledge of the social forces at work in her community. She is most clearly allied with Lorne's older sister, who alone shares the narrator's capacity of standing outside the action and understanding its ironies. She thus becomes an Elizabeth Bennet, capable of recording the activities of her world while at the same time being outside of them, too. In a letter of 8 January 1905, Duncan explained the purpose behind her novel:

> It might be worth while to present the situation as it appears to the average Canadian of the average small town, inarticulate except at election times, but whose view in the end counts for more than that of those pictorial people whose speeches at Toronto banquets go so far as to over-colour the British imagination about Canadian sentiment. I thought it might be useful to bring this practical person forward and let him be seen. I hope I have not made him too prominent, but he is there. My book offers only a picture of life and opinion, and attempts no argument.[11]

This is precisely the nature of her creation, "no argument" through her carefully constructed veil of irony. Written thirteen years after Duncan had gone to India, the novel testifies to her abiding interest in and commitment to Canada and to her formidable evocation of her Canadian world. She wrote out of her knowledge of the place and its times, and yet she wrote from a distance from the place and its time.

In a letter of 4 May 1905, Duncan wrote to Archibald MacMechan of Dalhousie University:

> The spirit of place always seems to me strong in the land. I want to come back and work at it from closer range, and soon I think this will be possible .... My mother is a New Brunswicker – Shediac and all that country has the charm for me of nursery description. I am sure it is as different from Ontario as Massachusetts is from Illinois. We feel that we have been almost long enough in India and I hope to sail through the "Ditch" for the last time, westward bound, and be in Canada next summer.[12]

---

[11] *The Imperialist*, ed. Thomas E. Tausky (Ottawa: Tecumseh, 1988), p. 316.   [12] Ibid., p. 317.

Unfortunately, the prospect of her permanent return to Canada never materialized.

The first major novel in the history of Canadian fiction, *The Imperialist* stands as a fine achievement, evoking a particular time and place in Canada and its history.

Stringer and both Duncans were Canadians who left their country at a time when Canadian fiction was just beginning to find a voice and an audience at home. Expatriates all, they show, each in his or her own way, the glories and the dangers of embracing an expatriate vision. Stringer, stranded between two worlds and surrendering to the United States, was the true expatriate, never finding any valid connection to his own country. Norman Duncan, though a resident of the United States, found his literary home in the rugged terrain and personalities of the Newfoundland outports; the question of being an expatriate never dawned on him, content as he was in his fictional worlds. And Sara Jeannette Duncan, the most travelled of the three, never forsook her own land; she created a novel of social realism, which has endured more than any of the writings of the other two expatriates.

Stringer is buried in Boonton, New Jersey. Norman Duncan is buried in Brantford, Ontario. Sara Jeannette Duncan is buried in Ashtead, Surrey, England, in a lead-lined coffin to be sent home to Canada; it still rests there.

The First Feminist Wave

In the early twentieth century, the first feminist wave appeared in fiction. Sara Jeannette Duncan had already written the first Canadian novel, *The Imperialist*, though it was not published in Canada and came to be recognized only when it was reprinted in the New Canadian Library. At the same time, three writers, Nellie McClung, Lucy Maud Montgomery, and Mazo de la Roche, remained in Canada, two of them bringing changes to the Canadian nation, McClung through her views on women and women's rights, and Montgomery through her many novels, poems, and stories; meanwhile, de la Roche was capturing the largest international audience of the three. In 1908 McClung and Montgomery published their first novels, *Sowing Seeds in Danny* and *Anne of Green Gables*, the former dominating the bestseller lists of the time, the latter enduring through all time; de la Roche had to wait until *Jalna* was published in 1927 before she came to dominate the bestseller lists, especially outside Canada.

Born on Ontario's Bruce Peninsula, McClung moved at a young age with her family to rural Manitoba. As a young teacher on the prairies, she was depressed by farm women's unbearably hard lives and set out to relieve their burden. An active proponent of women's right to vote, she proclaimed her commitment through her writings, her public appearances, and her confrontations with government officials. With her deep religious commitment to Methodism, she rallied her supporters to promote not only women's working privileges but also complete abstinence from alcohol. An effective public speaker, she brought to her fiction many of her public concerns: women's right to vote, the evil effects of alcohol, and the stifling domination of men in business and in the bedroom.

In her youth McClung read all Dickens's works, concentrating on the later and more socially oriented ones, and she began to imagine what her role would be in her own country: "I wanted to write; to do for the people around me what Dickens had done for his people. I wanted to be a voice for the voiceless as he had been a defender of the weak, a flaming fire that would consume the dross that encrusts human souls, a spring of sweet water beating up through all this bitter world to refresh and nourish souls that were ready to faint."[13] The emphasis falls on Dickens as "a defender of the weak," who points out the failings of and to his society. McClung knew her Dickens well: her two autobiographies are filled with Dickensian references; she had her own set of Dickens, feeling "immeasurably rich in the possession of these long, paper-backed books, tea-colored and closely printed."[14] When she had her own family, she "got a set of Dickens when the children were small and read aloud to them in the evenings. *David Copperfield* was, I believe, the greatest favorite."[15]

All fiction writers, McClung believed, should envision a better world where they can frame their writings of the present world: "If you love your fellowman, and want to do them a service, with the gifts God has given you, hold fast to the faith, and the ethics of the Sermon on the Mount, which is the Common Denominator of all nations, and the only way of peace." Writers "must hear the church-bells ringing, above all the noise of the streets. We promise not to be quitters, deserters, or neutrals, cynics or mere observers."[16] The writer's art must serve the ways of the Lord.

In 1902 McClung wrote the first Pearl Watson story, set in Millford, Manitoba, afterwards the first chapter of *Sowing Seeds in Danny*, the first novel of the trilogy that focuses on twelve-year-old Pearl, the impoverished

---

[13] *Clearing in the West: My Own Story* (Toronto: Thomas Allen, 1935), pp. 281–2.
[14] Ibid., p. 281.
[15] *The Stream Runs Fast: My Own Story* (Toronto: Thomas Allen, 1945), pp. 91–2.
[16] From her papers at the University of Manitoba.

eldest of nine children, who displays wisdom in all her adventures. While her mother works in the home of a middle-class woman, Pearl cares for her brothers and sisters six days a week, glorying in her mature acceptance of work: "I pretend I'm the army of the Lord that comes to clear the way from dust and sin, let the King of Glory in." A sense of conversion begins to enter Pearl's world. The novel proceeds from episode to episode of Pearl's benevolent work; meanwhile, the Watson family is living happily but in abject poverty.

Pearl's second conversion focuses on Mrs. Motherwell. Moving into the Motherwell family to pay off a ten-dollar debt her family owes on their rail car that is their home, she instructs her second maternal figure in the ways of influencing her mean husband and helping her son Tom, who turns to alcohol as an outlet against the horrid life of his parents. And Pearl's third convert is not a woman, but a young English farmer-in-training who lies dying of appendicitis. While Tom is dispatched for the aged Dr. Barner but instead ends up in a bar, Pearl waits anxiously for the arrival of young Dr. Clay. When he arrives, he is traumatized by his supposed misdiagnosis of another patient; Pearl inspires him to operate, and the patient is saved. Dr. Clay and Dr. Barner, who has resented the younger physician, embrace now, the older physician aware so late of his own alcoholism. All ends happily. Throughout the novel Pearl embodies many of the major themes of McClung's philosophy: the need for women's suffrage, the evils of alcohol, for example. But she is never presented as a child, only as a mouthpiece embodying McClung's beliefs.

In McClung's second novel, *The Second Chance* (1910), the Watsons move from their shabby home to a finer location. Now fifteen, Pearl meets the Cavers. When Mr. Caver, a confirmed alcoholic, dies from drink, the owner of the town bar realizes his error and closes the bar permanently. The novel's focus, however, falls on Arthur Wemyss, the recovered patient from the first novel, who is awaiting his bride-to-be from England. When she arrives in Manitoba, she confesses that she has fallen in love with another man. Allowing her to unite with him back home, Arthur returns to England, now aware there that he loves a Canadian woman; he comes back, aware that this lady "makes me love this country." All ends happily.

In the trilogy's conclusion, *Purple Springs* (1921), Pearl, now eighteen, still loves Dr. Clay, a sick man being urged to spend no more winters in frigid Manitoba. All again ends happily. Embedding autobiography directly in this novel, McClung recounts the struggles for female enfranchisement in Manitoba. Focusing on the premier's opposition to women's suffrage, Pearl offers a veiled account of McClung's similar experiences.

The novel is an uneasy balance between autobiography and fiction, and in the newspaper account of one of Pearl's speeches, there is an acknowledgment of the paralleling of Pearl and McClung: "Pearl is an out and out believer in temperance and woman suffrage, and before she was through, she had every one with her – as one man put it, he'd like to see the woman vote, if for nothing else than to get Pearl Watson into parliament."

In the trilogy, McClung surrounds Pearl with a supporting cast of drunkards, farmers, and good people ostracized by suspicious neighbours. These people are Dickensian in character and nature. Yet Pearl herself does not have the commanding power of those around her, for she remains a mouthpiece, the stories themselves lessons on the rights of women and the evils of alcohol.

In her fourth and final novel, *Painted Fires* (1925), McClung depicts the trials of Helmi Milander, a thirteen-year-old Finnish immigrant who begins her new life in Winnipeg. Through a series of adventures and misadventures, Helmi grows into womanhood. Entrusted by the local doctor's wife to visit a Chinese "doctor" to obtain a little box, she is arrested in a raid. Unwilling to reveal who sent her, she travels to Eagle Mines, Alberta, where she obtains a job in a rooming house. Here she falls in love and marries Jack Doran, who then travels north with a trusted companion Helmi does not respect; meanwhile, she has their child. Jack goes off to war, returning home at last to find Helmi and their daughter Lili waiting for him. McClung praises the union of an immigrant and a Canadian, who espouse the goodliness and godliness of their western Canadian community. Successfully assimilated to this ideal, Helmi represents the best hope for English Canada's renewal as a vital and viable entity.

Throughout her career McClung wrote impressive short stories as well as four novels, all of them didactic studies to illustrate her themes. Her collection of essays, *In Times Like These* (1915), a strong feminist statement, outlines the themes of her fiction. Her fiction, on the other hand, is a less natural environment for the same themes.

In 1908 *Sowing Seeds in Danny* was the bestselling novel of the year, with sales exceeding one million. Now McClung's reputation rests on her political engagements, not her fiction. No literary figure since has expressed indebtedness to her fiction.

Long relegated to the position of a children's author, Lucy Maud Montgomery (1874–1942) is a major figure in the development of Canadian fiction. An inhabitant of Prince Edward Island who strayed far from it in her lifetime but never strayed from it in her fiction, she lost her mother to tuberculosis when she was only twenty-one months old; when she was six, her father departed permanently for the West, leaving her in her maternal grandparents' care. In effect, she was, like so many of Dickens's figures, an orphan from the age of six. In the course of her long career, she would publish more than five hundred poems, five hundred short stories, and twenty novels.

Looking back on her childhood, she remembers the few novels that were in her home: "I did not have access to many novels. Those were the days when novels were frowned on as reading for children. The only novels in the house were *Rob Roy*, *Pickwick Papers*, and Bulwer Lytton's *Zanoni*; and I pored over them until I knew whole chapters by heart."[17] By the time she was forty, she reflects on her favourite prose writers: "Nay, nay, there are too many of them – Scott, Dickens, Thackeray, Collins, Trollope and fifty others. I love them equally well, one for one mood, one for another."[18] Nearly twenty-five years later, she would continue to insist:

> I still love Scott and Dickens and Thackeray and Trollope and Kipling and Barrie – and the antics of today say they are 'outmoded.'!!![19]

The continuing presence of Scott and Dickens suggests the influence these two writers had on her creativity. From Scott, she created for Canada what Scott had created for Scotland: a fictional representation of the people and the places of her own country. From Dickens, she learned how to create and develop her exceptional young people and how to fashion sympathetic and intriguing characters. "The writer," she wrote, "must *create* his characters, or they will not be life-like."[20]

Her first novel, *Anne of Green Gables* (1908), originates in a newspaper clipping:

> In the spring of 1904 I was looking over this notebook in search of some idea for a short serial I wanted to write for a certain Sunday School paper. I found a faded entry, written many years before: "Elderly couple apply to orphan asylum for a boy. By mistake a girl is sent them." I thought this would do. I began to block out the chapters, devise, and select incidents and "brood up" my heroine. Anne – she was not so named of malice afore-thought, but flashed into my fancy already christened, even to the all important "e" – began to expand in such a fashion that she soon seemed very real to me and took possession of me to an unusual extent. She

[17] *The Alpine Path: The Story of My Career* (Don Mills, Ontario: Fitzhenry & Whiteside, 1917), p. 49.
[18] *The Journals of L.M. Montgomery*, eds. Mary Rubio and Elizabeth Waterston (Don Mills, Ontario: Oxford University Press, 1985–2004), 2, p. 146.
[19] *Journals*, 5, p. 193.   [20] *The Alpine Path*, p. 73.

appealed to me, and I thought it rather a shame to waste her on an ephemeral little serial. Then the thought came, "Write a book. You have the central idea. All you need do is to spread it out over enough chapters to amount to a book."[21]

Montgomery began her novel in the spring of 1905, not 1904 as she remembers here, and finished it in January of 1906. In the influential figure of Dickens she found many interesting children, including such orphans as Oliver Twist, David Copperfield, and Pip, to serve as models for her creation of Anne.

Into the rural farming community of Avonlea, Prince Edward Island, comes the eleven-year-old orphan from Nova Scotia. A self-willed and imaginative girl, Anne arrives to the surprise of Matthew and Marilla Cuthbert, an older brother and sister who were expecting a male orphan to aid Matthew on his farm. Winning over the affection, first of Matthew and later of Marilla, she finds acceptance and love in her new home. Both adults allow Anne to stay with them because their sense of duty tells them that they can do some good for the little waif. As she grows up – to the age of sixteen – she enriches the lives of her adoptive parents and the entire Avonlea community. When she is about to take flight and attend an "away" school, death claims Matthew. At the same time, Marilla, now on the verge of losing her eyesight, can stay at Green Gables only if someone stays with her. Anne decides to curtail her ambitions and repay Marilla her debt of gratitude.

From the intensely imaginative dreamer at the beginning who renames geographical locales in Avonlea which intrigue her, Anne becomes a more thoughtful and less selfish young woman. Her dreams must be rooted in reality, and she realizes that dreams on their own cannot be adequate. The novel is a series of steps in which Anne understands her true position in the life of the community and in her own world.

Like her dreams, romance, too, attracts the mind of the orphan. In a parody of Tennyson's "Lancelot and Elaine," the worlds of romance and of practical reality confront each other. Anne is Elaine, and drifting slowly down the river, her vessel springs a leak. This sorry episode leads Anne to conclude: "I don't want ever to hear the word romantic again." As she tells Marilla, "I think my prospects of becoming sensible are brighter now than ever." From the fanciful youngster, Anne becomes the pride of Avonlea.

Anne's growth takes place under the watchful and changing perspective of Marilla, who grows as Anne grows. Anne brings to Marilla that force of

[21] Ibid., pp. 71–2.

life, that realm of experience her own life has been lacking, at least from the time Marilla foolishly rejected John Blythe's affection. Marilla's final confession to Anne is the novel's conclusion: "It's never been easy for me to say things out of my heart, but at times like this it's easier. I love you as dear as if you were my own flesh and blood and you've been my joy and comfort ever since you came to Green Gables."

The supporting cast plays significant roles in Anne's growth, too. The three Dickensian women, Mrs. Rachel Lynde, the Avonlea busybody, Mrs. Barry, Avonlea's upper-crust arbiter of taste, and Aunt Josephine Barry, Charlottetown's answer to David Copperfield's Aunt Betsy Trotwood, change from scepticism and distrust of Anne to a quiet acceptance, even, in Aunt Josephine's case, to adoration of the young girl. And then there are the two other women, Mrs. Allen and Miss Muriel Stacy, who offer Anne exemplary portraits of womanhood that balance propriety, warmth, and common sense. Anne charms all these women and eventually wins over the entire community.

Although Montgomery sent the manuscript to five American publishers before it was accepted for publication, the fifth one, L.C. Page in Boston, accepted it "because a P.E.I. girl on their staff gave them no peace till they did."[22] The novel was an immediate bestseller. Published on 10 June 1908, the book was already into its second printing by the end of that month; the fourth printing occurred two months later.

In October of 1907, Montgomery began a sequel, exactly eight months before her first novel was published. Although she would write eight more novels and countless short stories which present Anne's teaching career, her marriage, and her many children, not one has the unity, the timeless story, or the enduring fascination of her first book. Only in *Rilla of Ingelside* (1921), a portrait of Anne's daughter named affectionately after Marilla, does she create a unified work where World War I impacts seriously and tragically on the lives of Prince Edward Islanders.

One of the reviews of *Anne of Green Gables*, Montgomery confided in her *Journals*, "said 'the book radiates happiness and optimism'. When I think of the conditions of worry and gloom and care under which it was written I wonder at this. Thank God, I can keep the shadows of my life out of my work. I would not wish to darken any other life – I want instead to be a messenger of optimism and sunshine."[23]

---

[22] *My Dear Mr. M: Letters to G.B. MacMillan from L.M. Montgomery*, eds. Francis W.P. Bolger and Elizabeth R. Epperley (Toronto: McGraw-Hill Ryerson, 1980), p. 141.

[23] *Journals*, 1, p. 339.

In turning to Emily Byrd Starr, a new heroine in her fiction, Montgomery wrote three novels, *Emily of New Moon* (1923), *Emily Climbs* (1925), and *Emily's Quest* (1927), to chronicle the life of an orphan from her eleventh year until her marriage. Although Emily, like Anne, is an attractive and articulate orphan with a strong imaginative streak, Emily herself is an artist. "People were never right in saying I was Anne," Montgomery remarked, "but, *in some respects*, they will be right if they write me down as Emily."[24] Later, she observed: "*New Moon* is in some respects but not all my own old home and 'Emily's' inner life was my own, though outwardly most of the events and incidents were fictitious."[25] Such observations are testimony to the fact that *Emily of New Moon* is the first Canadian bildungsroman, the novel of youth and initiation into a full life. This form also possesses to varying degrees some dimensions of autobiography; the bildungsroman, then, is subject to intrusions from areas of the author's personal experience beyond the limits of the fiction. Emily is a female artist battling the late nineteenth-century pressures that art is frivolous and a young woman should have as her primary goal to become a loving and obedient mother.

Dickens himself published his own bildungsroman, *David Copperfield*, where even the initials of the title character, DC, are Charles Dickens in reverse. It presents Dickens's autobiography as the product of an inherently strong memory going through his experiences from childhood to early maturity; Montgomery presents Emily from the age of eleven to thirteen, the formative years of a young girl, and her account is similar to Copperfield's account of his early years.

Beginning with her father's death and the Murray family taking charge of "the lonely, solitary little creature," *Emily of New Moon* chronicles the orphan's new home at New Moon under the tutelage of Aunt Elizabeth, a later version of Marilla, and Aunt Laura, a later version of Matthew, and her unceasing attempts to become a writer. From the start Emily is an author in need of a place where she can write, unimpeded by her new family's negativity towards writing. It is possible to read Emily's struggles as veiled approximations of the struggles Montgomery herself suffered on the way to her publishing career. Details about her early readings, found in her transcribed *Journals*, are included in *Emily of New Moon*, and events in her own life and her writing habits find themselves outlined in the novel.

---

[24] Mollie Gillen, *The Wheel of Things: A Biography of L.M. Montgomery* (Toronto: Fitzhenry & Whiteside, 1975), p. 134.
[25] *Journals*, 3, p. 147.

Maintaining that it is better to heal than to hurt in written composi-
tions, Mr. Carpenter, the teacher who best instructs Emily about writing,
becomes a spokesperson in *Emily Climbs* for Montgomery's views on the
creative process. "I read a story tonight. It ended unhappily," Emily
remarks as would Montgomery herself. "I was wretched until I had
invented a happy ending for it. I shall always end *my* stories happily.
I don't care whether it's 'true to life' or not. It's true to life as it *should be*
and that's a better truth than the other."

Herein lies the achievement of Montgomery, who took her plots,
executed them, then gave her stories happy endings, fearful of giving a
tragic ending to her main characters. Her writings are ultimately sentimental rather than realistic, always opting for the happy conclusion rather
than the dangerous, perhaps forbidden path that leads to forceful realism.
As Montgomery confided, "If you insist on seeing sky and river and pine
you are a 'sentimentalist' and the truth is not in you."[26] She was a natural
realist who always veered towards sentimental endings.

In her lifetime Montgomery brought the sentimental novel to a peak
which it would never reach again with any other Canadian writer. She
followed her rules in fiction and created lasting characters who, while
fashioned on Dickens's orphans, come into their own life on the pages
of her books. Yet she did not always have an easy path ahead of her.
William Arthur Deacon, the powerful literary journalist for *The Globe and
Mail* and her long-time personal enemy, decreed that Canadian fiction
could go no lower than *Anne of Green Gables*. And with the modernist
movement rising in Canada, she was demoted as modernists sought to
purify the scene of books which seemed sentimental, popular,
and feminine.

The books of Montgomery remained popular with general readers, and
in the 1960s writers, mainly female, started to acknowledge their indebtedness to her. Atwood and Margaret Laurence, Munro and Adele
Wiseman, for example, all of them speak of the importance she played
in their upbringing, their desire to be writers, and their
writings themselves.

For Mazo de la Roche (1870–1961), born Mazo Roche, the worlds of
Victorian fiction, especially the novels of Dickens, were her home. "The
only reading I remember seeing my grandfather indulge in was the novels
of Dickens. He read them over and over," she writes in her autobiography
Ringing the Changes (1957). Her childhood consisted mainly of Dickens:

[26] Ibid., 3, p. 387.

"By the time I was ten I read every book that came my way – *Oliver Twist* several times, *Old Curiosity Shop* once, for I hated Quilp, and even found the death of Little Nell too sentimental." Later she remembered: "My father had bought a bookcase and handsome sets of Dickens and Scott. Even while I admired the new furniture I could not keep my eyes from the books." When she was growing up, she "spent my happiest hours in one of the deep window seats living with the novels of Dickens and Scott – *David Copperfield*, *A Tale of Two Cities*, *Rob Roy*, *Quentin Durward*. My mother cared little for Scott but she delighted in Dickens, the Brontës, Jane Austen."

Born north of Toronto, de la Roche was an inveterate reader and writer from an early age. Her cousin Caroline Clement came to live with the Roche family when she was young, and the two girls became inseparable, forming a life partnership which would endure until their deaths. From their first encounters, there was "a delicious intimacy" between them, and later they adopted two children as part of their family. When de la Roche published her autobiography, she dedicated it: "For Caroline, From First to Last."

In 1902, de la Roche published her first short story and two more the following year. Her young adulthood was marred by frequent battles with illness and depression, and she did not attain her writerly position until the 1920s. The frenzied world of the Brontë sisters stands behind her first two adult novels. In *Possession* (1923), a man inherits an Ontario fruit farm from his dying uncle. Surveying his new property, he falls in love with one of his neighbours, a beautiful blonde. Unfortunately, he has a brief encounter with a young Indian, and when she bears a child, he reluctantly marries her. Echoes of Heathcliff and Catherine are everywhere. *The Thunder of New Wings* (1932), rejected by her publisher and printed a decade later, centres on a man whose mysterious birth, his almost evil nature, and his childhood beatings echo *Jane Eyre*.

De la Roche's achievement is *Jalna* (1927), winner of the Atlantic Monthly's $10,000 prize for the best new novel, and the first of sixteen novels which present the sometimes comic, sometimes tragic escapades of the Whiteoak family, the inhabitants of Jalna, "an old manorial farm house, set among its lawns and orchards" on the banks of Lake Ontario. Renny Whiteoak, the Master of Jalna, presides over his family, including the centenarian Adeline, his sister Meg, and his four stepbrothers. The plot is simple. Piers, one of Renny's stepbrothers, elopes with Pheasant, the illegitimate daughter of their neighbour Maurice Vaughan, who had once been engaged to Renny's sister. Another stepbrother, Eden, marries

Alayne, then has an affair with the married Pheasant. And Meg finally marries Maurice. All these details precede Adeline's one-hundredth birthday. The success of the novel depends not on its plot but on the explosion of people who populate its pages. Its many characters are painted by a few gestures, significant mannerisms, or other Dickensian touches.

Despite de la Roche's fascination with Dickens, the ultimate literary inspiration behind the saga – for *Jalna* and subsequent novels in the series that make up an extended family saga – is John Galsworthy. Although de la Roche admitted to reading only Galsworthy's *The Man of Property*, her characters exhibit many traits associated with Soames Forsyte and his family. Both family sagas treat the landed gentry sympathetically, while casting side glances at the below-stairs happenings of the lower-class servants. On the other hand, Forsyte's family is treated with a degree of irony missing from de la Roche's family groupings, and this absence makes her a romantic writer who cannot allow tragic endings.

For Timothy Findley (1931–2002), *Jalna* represented a British world of the past "more British than the British." It was "the aristocratic ideal of colonialism," with de la Roche allocating "roles based on British traditions that were already passé in the United Kingdom when she gave them their Canadian face."[27] But de la Roche's world appealed to the mentality of the 1920s and 1930s, presenting a dream world which existed in Canada only in the briefest way. For readers of the time, and especially with the Depression engulfing their consciousness, *Jalna* represented a retreat from reality into a fortified upper-class world of bygone and perhaps wholly fictitious eras.

For Robertson Davies (1931–95), "This family is an English family living in Canada, which is quite a different thing from a Canadian family," he wrote in 1940. On her death in 1961, however, he prepared a eulogy to contradict his earlier statement:

> There were many others who knew Canadians in whom there were all the Whiteoak strains – the colonial attachment to England mingled with a resentment of modern England, a democratic spirit at war with a desire for personal privilege, a pride in pioneer family blood with a consciousness that all the pioneer energy was being strained out of that blood. Oh, the Whiteoaks were Canadians, right enough! ... Mazo de la Roche was writing about a Canada which was perfectly real, and which persists today.[28]

---

[27] Quoted in Daniel L. Bratton, *Thirty-two Short Views of Mazo de la Roche* (Toronto: ECW Press, 1996), p. 160.

[28] *The Well-Tempered Critic: One Man's View of Theatre and Letters in Canada*, ed. Judith Skelton Grant (Toronto: McClelland and Stewart, 1981), pp. 141, 226.

The creation of the *Jalna* series is the single most protracted literary event in Canada until this time, and de la Roche judged her audience with care. A popular bestseller both in Canada and abroad, *Jalna* and its subsequent volumes came to dominate buying habits in Canada, the United States, and especially Europe. From the 1920s through the 1940s, de la Roche gave Europeans in particular their vision of Canada, even though her fictional creation was rooted in an earlier time and in another country.

Nellie McClung, Lucy Maud Montgomery, and Mazo de la Roche gave early Canadian fiction its first encounter with feminism. While McClung was instrumental in the development of women's rights, Montgomery and de la Roche gave their readers satisfying novels which underscored their themes, the former through her fixation with her time and place in Canada, the latter through her readings of the past in a fictitious landscape.

Stephen Leacock

"Personally," Stephen Leacock (1869–1944) declared in his preface to *Sunshine Sketches of a Little Town* (1912), "I would sooner have written 'Alice in Wonderland' than the whole Encyclopedia Britannica." Yet the representations by *Alice* and the *Encyclopedia*, seemingly years apart, are central to an understanding of the many worlds that commanded Leacock's attention.

Humorist and humanist, economist and educator, professor and pundit, Leacock, who graduated with a BA from the University of Toronto and a PhD from the University of Chicago, devoted his life to education, first through the classroom (at Upper Canada College in Toronto and later at McGill University in Montreal), then through his writings on history, economics, and political science, and finally, and most enduringly, through his many volumes of humour. "Humour is essentially a comforter," he wrote in his preface to *The Garden of Folly* (1934), "reconciling us to things as they are in contrast to things as they might be."

During Leacock's lifetime, his top-selling book was *Elements of Political Science* (1906), a textbook which was translated into nineteen languages. He later used it as the intellectual foundation for an influential series of articles on practical political economy which appeared in *Saturday Night*. An avid amateur historian, he contributed a volume on responsible government to the important Makers of Canada series in 1907 as well as three volumes in 1914 to the heavily promoted Chronicles of Canada series. And he wrote two popular biographies, *Mark Twain* (1932) and *Charles*

Dickens (1933), Victorian writers with whom he felt an imaginative and philosophical affinity.

Despite his success as a skilled essayist and historian, Leacock's humorous works secure for him a fatherly position in the development of Canadian fiction. In 1909 he gathered together nineteen of his early pieces, added twenty-one new sketches, and published them privately in 1910 under the title *Literary Lapses*. The volume's immediate popularity – and its successful publication the following year in England and the United States – established his reputation as a humorist, complementing his standing as a political economist. From 1910 until the time of his death, he published a book of humour almost every year.

Opening *Literary Lapses* is "My Financial Career," his narrative of an everyman overwhelmed by an august and sombre banking establishment. As a result, "Since then I bank no more. I keep my money in cash in my trousers pocket and my savings in silver dollars in a sock." The nameless hero is a typical Leacockian protagonist, a little man who finds himself bewildered by the alien world around him. The success of *Literary Lapses* led him to write *Nonsense Novels* (1911), which always remained one of his favourite books. In *Humour: Its Theory and Technique* (1935), he confessed that the book had "no small vogue in the last quarter of a century. The ten stories that make it up are not parodies of any particular stories or of any particular author. They reproduce types." But in reproducing original genres, he also recognized their inherent limitations. The parody is, he noted in *Humor and Humanity: An Introduction to the Study of Humor* (1938), "a protest against the over-sentimentality, or the over-reputation of the original." Leacock the parodist, never irreverent to his literary models, makes their extravagances a source of laughter: "The essential point is the use of parody as corrective to over-sentiment, of humour as a relief from pain, or humour as a consolation against the shortcomings of life itself."

In 1912 Edward Beck, managing editor of the *Montreal Star*, invited Leacock to contribute a series of comic pieces for the Saturday edition of the *Star*. "The only really large-scale commission that Leacock ever received for a fictional job to be done for a purely Canadian audience,"[29] *Sunshine Sketches of a Little Town* is a twelve-part account of the happenings in the fictional small town of Mariposa, introducing into Canadian fiction a number of characters and images that continue to resonate in the cultural imagination.

[29] B.K. Sandwell, "How the 'Sketches' Started," *Saturday Night* (23 August 1952): 7.

Leacock's definition of a sketch, which is a story "to make people glad, to take people out of themselves,"[30] reflects his close reading of the works of Dickens, in particular his first book, *Sketches by Boz: Illustrative of Every-day Life and Every-day People* (1836), his collection of separate pieces about people in the poor east end of London told by an omniscient third-person figure named Boz. Dickens's sketches are of a metropolitan area, whereas Leacock was writing his of a little town, as he states in his preface to *Sunshine Sketches of a Little Town*, in "a land of hope and sunshine where little towns spread their square streets and their trim maple trees beside placid lakes almost within echo of the primeval forest." His sketches are filled with sunshine, only hinting at the underbelly of this society, for example when Dean Drone has to be removed from his church because of dementia or when Judge Pepperleigh cherishes the memory of his dead son, never being told that his image of his son's nobility is a delusion.

After relating all the varied activities, excursions, and scandals of the small town, the narrator states in "L'Envoi. The Train to Mariposa" that his portrait of the town is not contemporary, that is, it is not of 1912, but of the Victorian period. "I suppose," he states, "very probably, you haven't seen one of these wood engines since you were a boy forty years ago." Then he adds: "Lake Wissanotti, where the town of Mariposa has lain waiting for you there for thirty years." The book's closing paragraph concludes: "How vivid and plain it all is. Just as it used to be thirty years ago."

Leacock's Mariposa existed as it is depicted thirty years ago. It is a community bound together by camaraderie, bound together by the essentially fraternal nature of its residents. Just as *Sketches by Boz* is a tableau of English life at a time when the country was in the process of inevitable transition into a modern consciousness, Mariposa, a relic of a world that is no longer, acts as a tableau of Canadian life that is no longer valid. The book is a loving recreation of life as it used to be lived in a small community, and the narrator, a survivor of this life, captures or rather recaptures a community that was and now will be *only* in the pages of a book, a detailed and close portrait that is affectionate, warm, and humorous. *Sunshine Sketches of a Little Town*, "easily the most cherished of his books, as much good honest fun to read today as when first published," is a triumph of the comic spirit. "Sunshine sketches is what we are promised," wrote Mordecai Richler, "and sunshine sketches is what we get, albeit

---

[30] "Letter to Frank Dodd, 18 February 1943," *The Letters of Stephen Leacock*, ed. David Staines (Don Mills, Ontario: Oxford University Press, 2006), p. 496.

delivered with assurance and enviable skill."[31] In his persona of Samuel
Marchbanks, Robertson Davies called the book "one of the finest, if not
the finest, book ever written about Canadian life."[32]

This remarkable collection introduces a familiar constellation in
Leacock's writing: a deftly managed combination of subtle ironies, genial
satire, and kindly humour deployed in support of his Tory-humanist
vision. Distinct from the more rigid Tory conservatism, his is a view of
the world that underscores the value of tradition, order, and a sense of
social responsibility. Mariposa is the kindly embodiment of many of its
social and cultural questions to which Leacock returns throughout his life:
the role of memory and imagination in the present and the future of the
individual and community; the complex and often divisive relationship in
modern politics between commerce and human emotion; and the essential
need for a sense of home, a word and a concept Leacock often used in the
abstract sense, which continues to haunt the Canadian imagination.

Leacock chose the title of his volume, *Arcadian Adventures with the Idle
Rich* (1914), a book he began shortly after the publication of *Sunshine
Sketches*, from Dickens's second book – and Leacock's own favourite – *The
Posthumous Papers of the Pickwick Club* (1836) – where the subtitle notes,
"Containing a Faithful Record of the Perambulations, Perils, Travels,
Adventures and Sporting Transactions of the Corresponding Members."
He turns from the seemingly minor foibles of the little town to
their metropolitan manifestation in an American city, a thinly
disguised Montreal.

"Avarice, nefarious rather than endearing hypocrisy, social pretensions
that infuriate more than they amuse, and lust, are strangers to Mariposa,"
Richler observed,[33] yet they are manifestly present in *Arcadian Adventures*.
Including some of the more bitingly satiric of his non-fiction writings, this
volume points directly to the moral and philosophical defects Leacock saw
as rending the social fabric of Plutoria, an imaginary city in which
predatory capitalism and plutocratic decadence become symbolic of the
American expansionist spirit which he pondered with both admiration and
fear. At times a heavy-handed counterpart to the little town of Mariposa,
these stories of Plutoria and its less-than-kindly citizens serve as a warning
of the dangers facing a community which turns away from the social ideals
set forth in *Sunshine Sketches*. With the reappearance of the aptly named

---

[31] *The Diary of Samuel Marchbanks* (Toronto: Clarke, Irwin, 1947), p. 64.
[32] "Introduction," *Sunshine Sketches of a Little Town* (London: Prion, 2000), pp. ix, xii.
[33] Ibid., p. xii.

Mausoleum Club and the noticeable slums visible from its rooftop, hyper-manipulative rich and victimized working poor, and hypocritical denominational rivalries, this city serves as a catalogue of what was to be opposed and corrected in the modern world. The Tory-humanist ideals Leacock often celebrated are subsumed in *Arcadian Adventures* by the rise of a destructive spirit of individualism and materialism, a spirit antithetical to the kindliness he considered the foundation upon which to build a shared humanity.

Besides his many other popular collections of humorous tales, Leacock was a popular anthologizer of humour, including his own, and one of the first Canadian writers to consider humour from a critical as well as a practical perspective. Although not always a consistent or precise critic, and clearly indebted to such antecedents as Meredith, William Makepeace Thackeray, and Henri Bergson, he published numerous books on his specialty, and though he knew the writings of McCulloch and Haliburton, he always found his comic home among the English and American humorists. Ironically, given his position within Canadian fiction, he was quick to assert that there was no such thing as Canadian humour; he also denied a Canadian literature which was distinct from British or American literatures.

Central to all of Leacock's writings, whether fiction or non-fiction, humorous or serious, is his concern for the condition of the contemporary world, which he saw as marked by a deep and increasingly troubling contrast between civilization's highest aspirations and the modesty or even disappointments of its grandest achievements. For him, comfort or consolations were rarely to be found in the world he saw before him. His stories are most often backward-looking, shaped by various strategies which allowed him to illuminate what he considered the beneficial aspects of vanished or vanishing sensibilities, those that shaped a much more open-handed social world.

This is not to suggest that Leacock was merely nostalgic or sentimental. He saw progress as inevitable, and in his non-fictional writings he showed himself to be an astute social critic whose sense of the fissures and energies shaping North American culture at a moment of rapid social change and dramatic economic developments is remarkably prescient. The past represented a stable, knowable point from which one might gauge the progress and stature of contemporary society. Although some of his later essays are tinged with a tone of bitter disappointment and a myopic detachment from what he considered less than tasteful sociocultural movements, he remained a writer confident and optimistic in temper.

A comic master of the short story or sketch, Leacock set the standard for many of the country's future writers in their recollections of their growth into maturity in little towns or ethnic pockets of cities. In *Sunshine Sketches*, his one strictly Canadian book, he presented a paradigm of the affectionate, humorous, and loving recreation of early life in a small, close-knit community.

The Immigrant Perspective

From his pastor's desk in Winnipeg, Ralph Connor confirmed to his many readers the changing nature of the Canadian population in his preface to *The Foreigner: A Tale of Saskatchewan*: "In Western Canada there is to be seen to-day that most fascinating of all human phenomena, the making of a nation. Out of breeds diverse in traditions, in ideals, in speech, and in manner of life, Saxon and Slav, Teuton, Celt and Gaul, one people is being made. The blood strains of great races will mingle in the blood of a race greater than the greatest of them all." Connor meant that the new immigrants would be assimilated to an essentially Anglo-Saxon standard. In the statistics of the time, there were 49,000 immigrants to the prairies in the year 1901, 146,000 in 1905, and 402,000 in 1913. In Manitoba, for example, there were at least four language groups at the turn of the twentieth century: English, French, German, and Icelandic, with the Icelanders maintaining their mother tongue in the home and in their own Icelandic press. By the 1920s, these immigrants were contributing to Canada's developing fiction.

Into this changing world arrived Frederick Philip Grove (1879–1948) in Winnipeg in 1912. Although his autobiographical *In Search of Myself* (1946) invented a new life in which he fabricated an Anglo-Swedish background and claimed to have been born into a wealthy cosmopolitan family, he was born Felix Paul Greve in 1879 in Radomno, Germany. He became a translator and writer who developed through contacts with the neo-Romantic circle around Stefan George. Following the common practice, he translated English and French works in order to prepare himself for his writing career. His first works were translations of and essays on Oscar Wilde, and he introduced German readers to Balzac, Flaubert, and Gide, Dickens and Hardy, and Meredith and H.G. Wells.

In his first German novel, *Fanny Essler* (1905), the title character, an attractive, middle-class woman brought up on romances and incapable of not dreaming, is too honest and frank to accept the harsh facts of life where marriage and money are concerned; she thus challenges the pervasive and repressive male attitude to women. In his second, *The Master Mason's House* (1906), the inequality of the two partners destroys the marriage. A tyrannical father and an overly obedient mother underline the need for the struggle against male tyranny, the novel a plea for the emancipation of women.

In his fiction Grove was following the naturalism of his time, that trend of using a close realism which suggests that environment and social conditions, like male tyranny, shape human beings trapped in their power. This naturalism is essentially pessimistic, for the characters of Grove's two German novels are victims trying to avoid inescapable dilemmas. Fanny, for example, is never treated with respect as a human being, and when she encounters a succession of princes, all interested only in exploiting her, the novel comes to an end, the solutions to her life in no way evident, all hope dashed.

Grove's literary works did not stave off his economic ruin, and faking his own suicide, he left Germany and emigrated with his wife to the United States. Then, without his wife, he arrived in Winnipeg, relatively penniless and looking for employment. Under his adopted name of Frederick Philip Grove, he took up teaching in rural schools and married a fellow teacher, thus beginning a new life of an invented homeland, background, and career.

In 1922 Grove launched his Canadian writing career with *Over Prairie Trails*, a set of nature sketches describing seven weekend trips by horse and buggy between Gladstone, where he was teaching, and Falmouth, where his wife was teaching. During their year of separation, he visited his wife and his two-year-old daughter thirty-six times, and seven of these journeys form the structure of his book. In light of the lead of John Burroughs, whom Grove admired immensely, his trips have the detailed and precise recounting of what he saw and encountered on his journeys: the trails themselves, the scattered wildlife, the few homes of the other settlers, and his relationship with his horses. The prairie landscape becomes a meaningful place as he focuses on the stunning beauty of his surroundings. Historian and naturalist, he is the scientific observer who must familiarize himself with a whole unfamiliar landscape, who must find his home in a world which seems impossible to inhabit as a home.

In his observation of the natural world, Grove aligns himself with the Romantic movement. His observation marks the first step in his approach to the natural world. The second step is his deliberation on the picture. And his third step, "emotion recollected in tranquility," illuminates the scene and the memory. "I was not content with recording a mere observation," he writes. "I had watched the thing a hundred times before. 'Observing' means to me as much finding words to express what I see as it means the seeing itself." In *Over Prairie Trails* he delineates the landscape that will be the setting for much of his fiction and that of future writers, including Sheila Watson and Rudy Wiebe.

Grove's first and arguably best English novel, *Settlers of the Marsh* (1925), focuses on Niels Lindstedt, who emigrated from Sweden and took up a homestead in the Big Grassy Marsh district of central Manitoba. He has a dream: to settle his land, to have a wife, and to build her a home. He falls in love with Ellen Amundsen, who has vowed not to marry because of her father's brutal cruelty to her mother. Into this sorry plight comes Clara Vogel, six years Niels's senior. Niels marries her, unaware that she is the town prostitute. For five years their marriage deteriorates, and when he arrives home to find her dallying with two men, he kills her. After serving six-and-a-half years of his ten-year sentence for manslaughter, he returns to his farm where Ellen is waiting for him. At the age of forty, Niels finds life beginning anew. Both he and Ellen are formed by their social conditioning, he by his naivete, she by her father's cruelty. His dream is given a second chance – he atones for his mistake, he pays for the tragedy he precipitated, and he achieves, for the first time, true happiness with Ellen.

Grove creates his first pioneer, a shrewd and upright calculator who sets out to amass wealth for his planned homestead. Young, strong, and determined, Niels is the perfect immigrant. His ideal, however, is thwarted, first by Ellen, his perfect mate, then by inner forces which prevent him, and Ellen too, from realizing themselves as feeling human beings. Both cannot express their human need for affection and love. What Grove set out to demonstrate in his German novels is now his expression of the social conditioning that breaks down human communication. In the end, after much suffering, Niels and Ellen are ready to reject their own paths and live off the vitality of the new land. The novel is a tragicomedy, a tragedy redeemed through Niels's imprisonment and eventual release, though it might well have ended as a tragedy with his imprisonment.

In its original version, *Settlers of the Marsh* was a "Three Book Series entitled Latter-Day Pioneers," and the three books consisted of "The Settlement"; "The White Range-Line House: A Story of Marsh and Bush"; and "Male and Female". Pressured into performing extensive cutting, Grove modified his original outline, producing a shorter version whose prose is frequently pedestrian: many passages have ellipsis marks, and the finished product lacks the style and sophistication of *Over Prairie*

Trails. His passion was for inclusiveness, yet his best writing was factual, selective, and precise.

At this time, Grove chanced upon the fiction of Thomas Hardy, destined to be the major influence on his subsequent writing. Hardy's tone appealed to his own pessimism, and he came to regard Hardy as the greatest teacher of the second half of the nineteenth century, his thought exacting a complete re-evaluation of accepted values. For Grove's pioneers, combating nature is the essential conflict in their lives, and Hardy's reasoned statements asserting that nature does not operate according to any standards rings true.

Under Hardy's influence, Grove wrote a trilogy of novels on the prairie experience: *Our Daily Bread* (1928), *The Yoke of Life* (1930), and *Fruits of the Earth* (1933). Each of these cumbersome books continues to explore prairie life, ending with the death of a central figure. The original title of *Fruits of the Earth* was *The Chronicles of Spalding District*, and though Grove did not approve of his publisher's demand for the new title, the original offers an important clue to these novels. All three are less novels than chronicles, accounts of the lives of the people according to their chronologies. The central figure, indeed the hero of each, is the prairie itself. For the immigrants who ventured into this desolate world, the prairie is a world they must relish and which must ultimately defeat them; no longer is a happy ending possible.

From his depiction of the trials of prairie pioneers, Grove moved on to a critique of industry and capitalism. In his semi-autobiographical *A Search for America* (1927), he attacked the wasteland of industrial North America. In *The Master of the Mill* (1944), his final and only industrial novel, the disintegration of the mill heralds the destruction of that ideal society that had been fostered in the country. Now city life means the disruption and end of the prosperous world of the countryside. Leaving behind the prairies, Grove enters the world of the modern novel. Rejecting his chronological studies, he embraces discontinuous time shifts and intermingles reminiscences, associations, and historical sketches. It is the meaning of events and not their orderliness that matters in this evocation of his horror of modern industry. Yet this final book is less a novel than a family chronicle, which charts three generations of men and women caught up in the battles, not with the soil, but with the increased mechanization of society.

In 1948 Grove died, almost as penniless as he was when he arrived in Winnipeg thirty-six years earlier. His German literary career was unknown in Canada, remaining so for many years. His Canadian literary career, starting with *Over Prairie Trails* and continuing for more than two decades, met with almost total indifference. He relied on Canadian publishers for his livelihood, and though he counted many publishers as his friends, he could not survive on his writings. He was and remained a Canadian, who suffered the plight of the destitute artist.

Born in Winnipeg, Laura Goodman Salverson (1890–1970) was an Icelander at heart, her parents having arrived in Canada two years before her birth. She grew up in a family where Icelandic was spoken, and she learned English only at the age of ten when she started school. An avid reader, she knew the Bible: "I knew the contents of the New Testament almost by heart";[34] the classics of British and French fiction: "Hardy, Eliot, and Victor Hugo, who always held first place in my affections"[35]; and, most importantly, the Icelandic sagas with their grim realistic details about families and their progeny. While the railroad job of her husband, a Montana native of Norwegian parentage, took them across the country, she always made time to write.

Unlike Grove, who studied people's confrontations with the prairie and, later, Ontario worlds, Salverson memorialized the Icelandic spirit in her Canada. Her first novel, *The Viking Heart* (1923), documents the plight of Icelanders who, driven from their homes by a volcanic eruption, come to Canada. In this new land, Borga Halsson marries Bjorn Lindal, and this chronicle focuses on their three children. All the people pride themselves on their Icelandic heritage, never losing their original identity in Canada; in fact, their nationality is their gift to the new land. Although the disjointed novel, charting four generations, is a chronicle filled with references to Viking gods and folk heroes, it is another romance, nationalistic in import, celebrating the steady and confident love of Icelanders which "revitalizes life and makes a nation indestructible."

A good friend of Nellie McClung, Salverson gave her the manuscript to *The Viking Heart*, and McClung suggested adding an opening section about Iceland and its volcanic eruption. "I had loved her for painting with sympathy, obscure, inconsequential folk, and more especially for the work she had done on behalf of women,"[36] wrote Salverson. Her own portraits of women, however, do not match Grove's depiction of downtrodden prairie wives.

In her second novel, *When Sparrows Fall* (1925), the heroine, "hot on the trail of romance," is reading *The Sky Pilot*. Connor's novel is

[34] *Confessions of an Immigrant's Daughter* (Toronto: Ryerson Press, 1939), p. 336.
[35] Ibid., p. 477.   [36] Ibid., p. 502.

mentioned only once, yet his romances stand behind this and her other novels. When she tells the tale of another group of settlers in Manitoba, this time Norwegian in origin, *The Dark Weaver* (1937) becomes a tedious romance with the hero's triumphant death in World War I. Perhaps her finest writing came in translations and adaptations of earlier tales, especially Icelandic sagas. In her novels she brought the saga tradition to the world of popular romance, *The Viking Heart*, despite its shortcomings, being the first novel of prairie life written by a Canadian.

When *Wild Geese* (1925) by Martha Ostenso (1900–63), her first novel, won the first prize of $13,500 in a first-novel competition sponsored by the American consortium of *The Pictorial Review*, Dodd, Mead and Company, and Famous Players-Lasky Corporation, Grove commented: "The book is deplorably, even unusually immature . . . . It is the old story: only trash wins a prize. That is why, for the last twenty years, I have steadfastly refused, for myself, and disadvised, in the case of other, younger people, submitting anything in competitions."[37] His reaction is less a commentary on the novel than a reflection of Grove's bitterness towards his reading public. *Wild Geese* was published in serial form in *The Pictorial Review,* in book form later by Dodd, Mead and Company, then filmed as a silent movie.

Born in Norway, Ostenso emigrated with her family to the United States when she was two years old, spending her early years in Minnesota and South Dakota, then in Manitoba. She attended high school in Brandon, and in 1918 entered the University of Manitoba, where she studied with Douglas Durkin, a married writing instructor and henceforth her romantic partner. He was invited to New York to give courses in the novel and novel-writing at Columbia University, and she travelled there to study the techniques of fiction under his tutelage.

The setting of *Wild Geese*, the remote lake district of northern Manitoba, is where Ostenso taught for one term in the rural school of Hayland, one hundred miles northwest of Winnipeg, before she started university. Hayland becomes Ostenso's fictional village of Oeland with its racial mix of Canadians, Hungarians, Icelanders, Norwegians, and native people. And in Lind Archer, the new schoolteacher who has arrived from Yellow Post, the railroad stop ten miles away, she found a projection of her own position: "My novel, 'Wild Geese,' lay there, waiting to be put in words. Here was the raw material out of which Little Towns were made.

---

[37] Letter to Austin M. Bothwell, 18 November 1925, *The Letters of Frederick Philip Grove* (University of Toronto Press, 1975), pp. 25–6. See also his letter to H.C. Miller, 14 November 1926, pp. 40–1.

Here was human nature stark, unattired in the convention of a smoother, softer life."[38]

A boarder at the Gare homestead, Archer is the external guide to the internal, stifling world of Caleb Gare and his downtrodden wife Amelia, their twins, the dull Martin and the whining Ellen, and their two younger children, the rebellious Judith and her kid brother Charlie. The patriarch who demands complete subservience from his wife and children, Gare is "a spiritual counterpart of the land, as harsh, as demanding, as tyrannical as the very soil from which he drew his existence." In fact, he is Jane Eyre's Rochester: "His tremendous shoulders and massive head, which loomed forward from the rest of his body like a rough projection of rock from the edge of a cliff, gave him a towering appearance." A figure out of Gothic romances, Gare is, unlike Rochester, maliciously cruel. Watching Judith, Archer notes the hidden enmity: "The high romance which had attended her setting out for this isolated spot in the north country was woefully deserting her. She had never before looked upon the naked image of hate. Here it was, in the eyes of a seventeen-year-old girl." Archer's former residence in the civilized world contrasts sharply with the spiteful world of the Gares.

Archer meets and falls in love with the apprentice architect Mark Jordan, who, unbeknownst to himself, is the illegitimate son of Amelia and her dead suitor, Del Jordan. Their romantic involvement is the antithesis of Gare's attempts to kill the love of Ellen for the half-Indian Malcolm or of Judith for the Norwegian Sven Sandbo. And all the while Gare suffers pangs of premarital jealousy over Mark Jordan.

At the novel's centre resides the bitter strife between father and daughter, between a raging tyrant and his rebellious offspring. Enslaved by his relentless commitment to his land, Gare disposes of any attempts to throttle his megalomaniac desire for solitary perfection. Trapped under his demands, Judith refuses to compromise. In the end, Gare is destroyed by a fire which threatens to consume all his flax crops; in trying to keep the flames away from his holdings, he is overtaken by the smoke and drowns in a bog before he has revealed Mark Jordan's parentage. Meanwhile, Judith escapes with her lover to the city where they will have the occasion to realize their dreams.

Archer and Jordan, too, set off for the city, aware that they are returning to their true home; she promises Amelia that they will return some time,

---

[38] Grant M. Overton, *The Women Who Make Our Novels* (New York: Dodd, Mead, 1928), pp. 247–8.

even though Amelia knows that they will never come back to this den of cruelty. The romance world gives way at the beginning to the pitiless world of the Gares; then the romance world returns at the end. Gare's narrow religiosity stands against the beauty, the physical strength, and the life-affirming sexuality of the indomitable Judith. He dies, Judith flees to a new life in the city, and romance returns after a detailed portrait of sterility masking as omnipotence. In the end, Archer and Jordan, Judith and Sven escape Gare's stultifying world; Amelia remains behind, unable to dream an alternative to her sorry existence.

Commenting on Judith, Archer tells Jordan: "Judith is a beautiful creature. She's like a – a wild horse, more than anything I know of." In her simile lies a reference to the major influence behind Ostenso's writing, the realism of such writers as D.H. Lawrence, whom she studied with Durkin. When Judith later meets Sven, "she hurled herself against him and he fell to the earth under her. Then something leaped in Sven. They were no longer unevenly matched, different in sex. They were two stark elements, striving for mastery over each other .... Her panting body heaved against his as they lay full length on the ground locked in furious embrace." Such frank realism now enters Canadian fiction.

In her subsequent novels Ostenso gravitated between American and Canadian settings, while moving closer to the conventions of romance. Her sales justified this move, for she was a mainstay of the American reading public. Her next two novels have American settings. Her fourth, *The Young May Moon* (1929), returns to the Canadian setting of *Wild Geese* to delineate again the repressive nature of Puritan religion: the heroine faces a life of loneliness and despair as a natural product of the human condition, exiled as she is from her mother-in-law and her faith. The sterility of her faith, which poisons her life, recalls the sterility that marks Caleb Gare's weekly sermons to his family. Set in British Columbia, *Prologue to Love* (1932) reveals a good woman who comes to realize her true feelings for her childhood friend, now her beloved. And as the dust jacket states about her next novel, *There's Always Another Year* (1933), Ostenso writes "a romantic novel – one that is appealing and dramatic. Against the stark, wild beauty of the Dakota prairies she has unfolded a story that is tense in emotion, strong in character, and infused with high spirit." Romance proved popular; this last novel went through five print-ings in its first three months of sales. Only in *The Mandrake Root* (1938) does Ostenso return to an unspecified Red River Valley to capture another strong-willed woman who ends up all alone with her child, her lover completely distraught and returning to the city.

Wild Geese is a trailblazing novel at the beginning of the movement in Canadian fiction towards an embrace of realism. But as her career continued, Ostenso was swept up by the popular world of American romances. The promise of her first novel was never realized later; she became a popular writer succumbing to the temptation of massive sales. With her understanding of the social and economic biases of small western towns, she could excel at grasping their stultifying natures. Although Caleb Gare reigned supreme in the worlds she was depicting, her passion for realism did not overcome her commitment to romance.

Through this early period in Canadian fiction, there was a struggle to move from romance into a fictional world which represented realistically the projection of the writer's perspective. But romance proved too potent an attraction, and many writers succumbed to its charms. Although such writers as Sara Jeannette Duncan evaded its temptations, these proved too hard to resist for some publishers and their audiences.

CHAPTER 3

Emerging into Realism

In 1928 Raymond Knister (1899–1932), a poet and short-story writer from southwestern Ontario, published *Canadian Short Stories*, seventeen short stories by such authors as Morley Callaghan, Norman Duncan, and Stephen Leacock. In an appendix he lists other writers such as Sara Jeannette Duncan, Nellie McClung, Lucy Maud Montgomery, and Martha Ostenso. He had read almost everything written in the Canadian short-story form to prepare his encyclopedic introduction, "The Canadian Short Story," the first public statement about the need for realism in Canadian fiction: "What is known as realism is only a means to an end, the end being a personal projection of the world. In passing beyond realism, even while they employ it, the significant writers of our time are achieving a portion of evolution. But most tale-spinners did not even achieve realism."

Knister understands the difficulties confronting the Canadian writer: "Conventions have held sway with the compulsion of a tradition of romantic externals ... much of our writing has seemed mechanical, and the literary flowering whereby it may be seen that the roots of a nation's life are sound has often had the aroma of wax and paper." Although Canadian magazines encourage "in the main, third-rate imitators of third-rate foreign models," a new movement is asserting itself: "Many thousands of Canadians are learning to see their own daily life, and to demand its presentment with a degree of realism." Into this new literary flowering, Knister contends, the short story is a major artistic form, and writers must follow the finest models, taking whatever they can from a broad selection of sources while remaining aware that the natural outlets for their work are across the border and across the ocean.

"A perfect flowering of art is embodied in one volume, *In the Village of Viger*, by Duncan Campbell Scott," he concludes. "It is a work which has had an unobtrusive influence; but it stands out after thirty years as the most satisfying individual contribution to the Canadian short story."

In 1896 Scott (1862–1947) published his ten interrelated stories about the citizens of Viger, Quebec. A reflection of his youth with his minister-father in several Quebec towns, they are tragicomic offerings which often suggest the encroaching urban blight. They also look ahead to fiction's embrace of realism.

In his own readings, Knister, who attended the University of Toronto for only a few months because of pleurisy and pneumonia, was international, bringing a cosmopolitan vision to the Canadian scene. He read British fiction of the nineteenth and early twentieth centuries as well as Balzac, de Maupassant, Flaubert, and Hugo in the original French and, in translation, the Russians, Gogol, Tolstoy, Turgenev, and especially Chekhov. The moderns also fascinated him: Galsworthy and Lawrence in England, James Joyce and John Millington Synge in Ireland, and Sherwood Anderson and Willa Cather in the United States.

Knister's first story, "The One Thing," published in the American magazine *The Midland* (January 1922) which H.L. Mencken called "the most important magazine America had produced,"[1] explores the increasingly isolated world of Billy Dulckington, who operates an unproductive farm in Knister's own area of southwestern Ontario. Instead of farming for the marketplace, he provides pasture and upkeep for prize horses, estranging himself from his relatives and neighbours. A stupid misunderstanding with his own brother leads only to their enmity. In this and subsequent stories, Knister depicts realistically the farm world of his childhood. Indeed, so entrenched were his stories in his Ontario world that no Canadian editors would publish them, and so *The Midland* and other magazines including *This Quarter* (Paris) became his home.

Jonathan Cape of London printed Knister's first novel, *White Narcissus* (1929), another account of the failure in communication between human beings; Macmillan published the book in Canada in May, and Harcourt and Brace in the United States in August. Richard Milne, now a successful novelist and the book's hero, returns to his small Ontario farm community to persuade his childhood sweetheart to marry him. She, however, is still trapped as a mediator between her parents, who have not spoken to each other for many years. Milne has a mission: to free her from the bondage of responsibility, but to no avail. Her father's rage leads him to destroy his wife's treasured white narcissi, and the spell between them suddenly snaps; all ends happily for the young couple. Like Grove's *Settlers of the Marsh*, *White Narcissus* suffers from a typical romance ending which undercuts the

[1] "This Land is Full of Voices," *Saturday Night* (1 December 1928): 6.

story's credibility and power. Although the character portrayal is at times wooden, Knister succeeds in his major aim: to make the landscape authentic to his readers. The moods of nature, the charms of the countryside, the workaday world of farm life, all these he captures in realistic detail. When he accidentally drowned on 30 August 1932, he left behind a mass of finished and unfinished novels, poems, and short stories.

To the budding literary scene in Canada, Knister gave an authentic Ontario landscape. He placed before his readers experiences and objects as directly and as fully as possible. He stayed in Canada, attempting to bring a new direction to its literature, moving from Victorian romanticism into the demanding rigours of modernism.

Like his friend Knister, Morley Callaghan (1903–90), a graduate of the University of Toronto, set out to be a professional writer, though of the urban setting of his native Toronto. He, too, sought to be a realist, "looking at the appearance of things, call it concrete reality, the stuff of experience, or simply 'what is out there'," and to do this he had to "strip the language, and make the style, the method, all the psychological ramifications, the ambience of the relationships, all the one thing, so the reader couldn't make separations. Cezanne's apples. The appleness of apples. Yet just apples."[2] In his long career, he published more than one hundred stories, fourteen novels, and six novellas. He also inaugurated *The New Yorker* practice of publishing short stories.

In his first published story, "A Girl with Ambition," which appeared in *This Quarter* (1926), Mary Ross, a lower-class, sixteen-year-old "neat clean girl with short, fair curls and blue eyes," is working in the shoe department of Eaton's, where she meets a middle-class high school student employed there for the summer holidays. He symbolizes for Mary what is respectable in life: "Thinking of how he liked her made her feel a little better than the girls she knew." While intrigued by him, Mary goes to a party with the grocer's son. In time she marries him, and then, in the story's final scene, a pregnant Mary is sitting beside her husband delivering groceries, sighted by her one-time beau.

This story has many features of Callaghan's fiction: the reporter's stance as he observes his characters; focusing on a few key scenes with the reader meant to fill in the rest; the use of irony as Callaghan weighs the drama of his story; and the stripped-down language with the words as transparent as glass. A girl with ambition becomes the pregnant wife of the grocer's son,

[2] *That Summer in Paris: Memories of Tangled Friendships with Hemingway, Fitzgerald and Some Others* (Toronto: Macmillan, 1963), pp. 115, 148.

and the reader ponders the respectability of her new position. "No one today – if one may venture to claim Toronto as part of the American scene – is more brilliantly finding the remarkable in the ordinary than Morley Callaghan," remarked Sinclair Lewis. "His persons and places are of the most commonplace; his technique is so simple that it is apparently not a technique at all."[3]

Callaghan knew many of the same writers Knister had read, though he did not read French authors in their original language. From Russian writers, he took the strategy of carefully delineating the setting while never naming an exact locale. From the British and Irish, especially Joyce and Lawrence, he continued their habit of dismantling the Victorian novel and substituting a heightened realism. From American writers, especially Sherwood Anderson whom Callaghan acknowledged as his "father," he inherited the technique of depicting realistically the dramas of the everyday world.

In his early novellas, *An Autumn Penitent* (1928), *In His Own Country* (1929), and *No Man's Meat* (1931), Callaghan expanded the themes and techniques of his short stories. Again he focuses on a few key scenes; there is irony as he depicts his people; and the language is direct and neat. In Eastmount near Toronto, *An Autumn Penitent's* Bill Harding lives with his wife Lottie and his sixteen-year-old niece, whom he has seduced and made pregnant. In the second novella, a man seeks to reconcile science and religion, finally going mad and living "in his own country." *No Man's Meat*, set in Echoe Lake in the Algoma district of northern Ontario, presents a lesbian couple: Jean Allen, the stylish woman returning from her travels, and Teresa Beddoes, the wife of the protagonist. Callaghan depicts realistically the lives of ordinary people. Not interested in upper-class men and women, he notes that his stories "touch times and moods and people I like to remember now. Looking back on them I can see that I have been concerned with the problems of many kinds of people but I have neglected those of the very, very rich."[4]

His first novels break dramatically from the romance world. Although, like Stringer, he turned to the underworld for his first novel, *Strange Fugitive* (1928), he set it in his own city. In the 1920s Prohibition era, Harry Trotter, a permanently restless and unimaginative man, loses his job as a lumberyard foreman. Trying to secure another good position which will satisfy his own self-importance, he abandons his wife and becomes a

[3] *New York Herald Tribune*, 24 April 1929, Books Section, p. 6.
[4] *Morley Callaghan's Stories* (Toronto: Macmillan, 1959), p. xi.

successful bootlegger. After a year in which he is involved with hijacking and murder, he is murdered by a rival gang. He does not realize his own limited possibilities, so eager is he to honour his insatiable lust for power as well as his continuing sensual needs. Although this first urban novel offers no full portrait of Harry, it does depict the pressures of his social environment which debilitate and ultimately destroy him. In *It's Never Over* (1930), Callaghan creates fully realized characters. With a psychology of characterization more complex than in *Strange Fugitive*, his people are aware of the situations in which they find themselves and cognizant of the workings of human nature.

Callaghan continues to treat life realistically. In *Such Is My Beloved* (1934), *They Shall Inherit the Earth* (1935), and *More Joy in Heaven* (1937), he depicts Toronto and its citizens, always looking at the failures of such major institutions as the Catholic Church and the justice system.

Such Is My Beloved makes a Catholic priest, Father Stephen Dowling, the centre of a study of the debilitating effects of social betrayal on a good human being. Jacques Maritain (1882–1973), the philosopher of theocentric humanism, gave Callaghan the plot of his novel and received, too, its dedication. Father Dowling's increasing interest in the welfare of two prostitutes meets with opposition from the surrounding society and from his church, first from his pastor and then from the bishop, at whose instigation the police arrest the prostitutes and force them to leave the city. "What a great pity Marx was not a Christian," Father Dowling observes. "There's no reason why a Christian should not thirst after social justice." *They Shall Inherit the Earth* focuses on Andrew Aikenhead as he confronts his stepson's mysterious drowning north of Toronto. While he endures growing ostracism from his society, his son Michael confesses to hearing but not heeding cries for help. The defeated father and the recalcitrant son leave together to confront the crime.

More Joy in Heaven returns to the downtrodden in convicted bank robber Kip Caley. After serving his prison sentence, this new prodigal son, paroled on Christmas Day through the efforts of Senator Maclean and the prison chaplain Father Butler, returns to his city eager to embark on a new life. But his sincere effort at reform is cast in doubt by all those in a position to help him. Anxious for sensational headlines, the reporters distrust his good intentions. The bishop "had to believe it possible in a man to change the pattern of his life, but he knew it hardly ever happened." Judge Ford, who passed the original sentence on Kip, regards him as incorrigible and refuses to believe his sincere desire to rehabilitate former prisoners. An idealistic Kip Caley wanted to be a reformed robber, seeking only the betterment of people. He set out to be a bridge between the outcasts of his society and the right-thinking people who seem to control that society. Unfortunately, social pressures exert such force on him that he fulfils Judge Ford's prediction, though never intending to do so.

Callaghan was setting his landscape firmly in the contemporary streets of Toronto, his home territory, breaking from his predecessors who preferred to write of far-off lands or romantic visions of their own land. Like a good reporter, he peopled his landscape with figures out of his own time. His favourite people were lower middle-class people battling against the evils of their society's ways. So often they would come up against law and order, but these social mechanisms were destructive of all natural justice. While many of his American contemporaries were embracing technological or Marxist solutions to their social dilemmas, Callaghan refused to write according to the dictates of the politically engaged, content to depict the problems and offer no solutions, merely showing the wayward nature of his spiritually inert world.

From the grimy streets of Toronto, he set his next two novels in downtown Montreal. In *The Loved and the Lost* (1951), the first English novel to depict Anglophone Montreal from Westmount down to the lower-class areas of dingy apartments and black nightclubs. He presents the safe inhabitants of Westmount, an enlightened liberal enclave of business men and their families, along with an academic from Toronto eager to leave his profession and a young woman who irritates the more conventional world of Westmount with her affection for blacks. In his presentation of post–World War II materialism, Callaghan does with Montreal what he had already done with Toronto: he paints a social portrait which encapsulates the bigotry and spiritual malaise affecting its people. *The Many Colored Coat* (1960) returns to his theme of the innocent man trapped, this time in legal manoeuvres which defeat him. A man of dangerous guiltlessness, he wonders too late if "innocence was like a two-edged sword without a handle, and if you gripped it and used it, it cut you so painfully you had to lash out blindly, seeking vengeance on someone for the bleeding." A lawyer tells him, "Innocence is a very fragile thing." Innocence is dangerous, leading him, like Father Dowling and Kip Caley, into recesses of his own self which he had never explored.

In his later years Callaghan went back to his past work, rereading, re-evaluating, and rewriting some of his earlier fiction, and publishing one new novel, *A Time for Judas* (1983). Nineteen centuries ago, Philo of Crete, the scribe to Pontius Pilate and another Callaghan outsider, held his unique manuscript of the story of the ultimate betrayal in human history, Judas's betrayal of Christ, told by Judas himself, "a man who had intelligence, perception, and curiosity about the mystery of life and who should have been a poet." He tells his story to Philo, who confronts the dilemma of betraying either Judas's trust or the truth. The story requires the personification of evil – betrayal – as the exact opposite of Christ's faithfulness, and Judas, always questioning, finds the answers to his questions in Christ and becomes his intimate disciple, whose faithfulness even embraces the betrayal Christ sees as absolutely necessary.

Philo suffers from the affliction depicted in many of Callaghan's writings: "What do you do with a great and fine old man who permits a thing to be done as the good right thing in the service of an institution which has been his whole life, when he knows that in acquiescing he'll be haunted and ashamed the rest of his life? Ashamed of doing the right thing." He finds in Christ's teachings that loyalty, such as practised by Judas, must be not to the external world of law and order but to one's own conscience. The same thinking propelled Callaghan's fiction.

From the beginning of his career when he was hailed as a master of the short story and often compared to Chekhov, Callaghan has occupied a major role in the history of Canadian fiction. The first Canadian writer to set his short stories and novels realistically in urban Canada, first Toronto and its dingy streets and alleys, and then Montreal with its equally squalid regions, he moved fiction from its romantic underpinnings to a revolutionary confrontation with the people of contemporary Canada, never forsaking the present – except in *A Time for Judas* – and its social problems. He maps out no particular outlook; he offers no simple answers; he is content to record the world as he sees it. Always at the centre of his fiction is the dignified stature of people trapped in situations which may question and ultimately deny their sense of self, but the dignified stature endures as society's mechanisms would seek to uproot and destroy it.

In his early years, Callaghan was writing for a distinctly North American audience; all his stories and novels were first published in Paris or New York. He wrote to the younger writers of Canada

> who were trying desperately to get started, and who, being Canadians, seemed to think they ought to get published in their own country. I was simply trying to tell them that if they were very good and had a distinctive talent and wrote honestly the chances were that they would not get published at all in this country unless they were first of all published some place else.[5]

---

[5] "The Plight of Canadian Fiction," *University of Toronto Quarterly* 7 (January 1938): 152.

Canada was still a country without a solid publishing base; writers had to sell their fiction abroad before they might obtain a distributor in Canada.

The experimental novelist Graeme Gibson (1934–2019) intended to write his thesis on Callaghan's fiction, and though Gibson's and Callaghan's novels might seem strange bedfellows, Gibson's indebtedness to the older writer emphasizes the fact that Callaghan was an example for younger writers in Canada. "Morley Callaghan prevailed," he commented.

> There were some individuals who had written remarkable individual books, but Callaghan had insisted on producing a body of work. In that sense he was a real writer. Even when his books didn't do well or were poorly received, he insisted on writing finished stories and novels. For me, he was the best example of a professional writer, he was the best example that it was possible to be a professional writer in Canada.[6]

Robertson Davies reiterated Callaghan's singular role: "An inspiration and a flag-bearer for all Canadian writers . . .. You have fought strongly and bravely for the establishment of an indigenous literature and so long as it lasts your name will be held in honour."[7]

Of equal importance with Callaghan in fiction's development, though not so prolific, is Saskatchewan's Sinclair Ross (1908–96), who dropped out of school after grade eleven to become a bank teller, a position marking the beginning of his forty-three-year career in banking. As a youth, he read Scott and Dickens, his mother's favorites. Like Callaghan, he also read Tolstoy and Dostoevsky, as well as Hardy and Joyce, Faulkner and Hemingway. Like Callaghan, too, he came to read many contemporary French writers, including Camus and Gide, often in the original French. The only Canadian book he read was Ostenso's *Wild Geese*, which chronicled prairie life in a manner similar to Ross's own fiction; he read none of Grove's works, having tried but quickly abandoning the challenge.

His first story, "No Other Way," was published in *Nash's Pall-Mall* in October 1934 after winning third prize from among eight thousand entries in the magazine's short-story competition. A struggling wife in a now loveless marriage of twenty years endures a hard-working farm existence which has robbed her of her beauty while her husband, a wheat and land speculator, boasts a still youthful-looking manner. She comes to realize that she has "no other way" but to continue working stoically. Endurance

---

[6] Conversation with the author, 2 February 1981.
[7] *For Your Eye Alone: Letters 1976-1995*, ed. Judith Skelton Grant (Toronto: McClelland & Stewart, 1999), p. 98.

is the only possible way to survive, and she is trapped by her circumstances. This story represents Ross's first attempt to depict prairie women who remain engulfed in failed marriages, struggling to live their lives against the lifeless prairie landscape. His women are, in Margaret Laurence's words,

> farmer's wives, most of them still fairly young, trying to resign themselves to lives of unrelieved drabness. They are without exception terrifyingly lonely, shut into themselves, shut out of their husbands' inner lives . . . . These women are intensely loyal, and as driven by work-compulsion as their men, but they still long, hopelessly, for communication and tenderness with their husbands – who desperately need the same thing but can never permit or accept it lest it reflect unmanfully upon themselves.[8]

In future stories, he will expand his depiction of the drought-ridden farms and the bleak landscapes that confront and often paralyze his characters.

In "A Field of Wheat," his next published story, after sixteen years of marriage, a couple watch the awesome power of a hailstorm ruin their crops and, by extension, their future hopes. Confronted with the vast power, beauty, and indomitability of nature, they must face again their own grim struggle to survive. In Ross's stories, human beings confront the external world of nature which often mirrors their own inner tensions and disappointments. They cannot reach out to each other, trapped as they are in their own inability to communicate. The stories capture realistically his people's struggles with nature, with the bleakness of the landscape, and with each other, the characters remaining isolated individuals trying to win out some kind of existence for themselves.

In his eighth published story, "Cornet at Night," Tom, a mature man, narrates an event which happened when he was eleven. Sent into town to hire a farm hand to assist with the harvest – the first time someone in a Ross story leaves for town – young Tommy realizes for the first time that there are men different from farm folk and music different from his teacher's metronome-based piano lessons. Against his own better judgment, he hires a stranger, a cornet player, who proves a failure at stoking hay and is relieved of his duties the next day. But his night-time cornet-playing brings a moment of transcendence to the lives of Tommy and his quarrelling parents. In fact, the sound of the cornet marks the first time Tommy becomes aware of the beauty and power of music, escaping as he does from everyday farm labour into the unfettered realm of the

---

[8] "Introduction," *The Lamp at Noon and Other Stories* (Toronto: McClelland & Stewart, 1968), p. 9.

imagination, symbolized by the cornet. In the farm's little parlour is a pansy-bordered motto on the wall: As for Me and My House We Will Serve the Lord. Here is the beginning of Ross's first novel.

As for Me and My House (1941) is the concentrated diary of Mrs. Bentley, the wife of a United Church minister, who pens occasional entries from April 8 until May 12 of the next year. The diary, a unique form of communication, is a private world where the diarist is speaking to no one but herself. It assumed a special importance for prairie wives, who frequently had no close friends or company to whom they might confide their feelings; keeping a diary is a way of preserving their sanity and securing times of privacy.

The Bentleys have moved to the town of Horizon, Saskatchewan, a bigoted Protestant town, to resume his ministry, this being the fourth time in the last twelve years that they have set up their home in a new town. Philip Bentley is an agnostic, trying to lead his congregation in rituals which have little or no meaning for him personally, and his wife, a seemingly patient woman, aids him in his calling. Ross restricts his novel to this small prairie town with the family taking only one brief vacation in Alberta. The novel conveys the atmosphere of the drought and depression of the 1930s, and in this way it is a continuation of Ross's short stories. But the Bentleys have an inner tension apart from their movements under the strictly controlling eyes of the town; they share a marital unease which affects all they do.

In the course of the diary's entries, Mrs. Bentley suggests that they adopt a twelve-year-old boy, and though this adoption gives Philip's life a new purpose, the boy is eventually taken away from them, and Philip lapses again into his bitter aloneness. What follows, then, is his brief affair with Judith West, a young choir member, and when Judith dies in childbirth, Mrs. Bentley suggests that they adopt this boy. At the end, she reveals to Philip that she knows the child is his. At the same time, the Bentleys are about to leave this latest town, and Philip will start a new life again with a bookstore in the city.

"Philip himself is an artist," writes Mrs. Bentley, "sensitive and impressionable, wary of life because he's expected too much of it." He is an artist, a painter and sketcher, but the portrait of Philip as artist is visible only through his paintings and sketches, which we know only through his wife's comments. His wife, too, is an artist, an organist and a pianist, who once "had ambitions too. The only thing that really mattered for me was the piano. It made me self-sufficient, a little hard. All I wanted was opportunity to work and develop myself." By insisting again and again that the only artist in her family is Philip, she tells the story of a failed artist, which is precisely what she is.

The central fascination of the novel lies in approaching the text. Mrs. Bentley is the narrator, yet the reader always has to measure how much truth there is in her statements, how much veracity there is in her reflections. And so, too, does the reader wonder about the accuracy of her depiction of her husband. How much the diary entries reveal depends upon how much truth is attributed to the narrator. "The reader has much to decide in this story," commented Robert Kroetsch (1927–2011). "The reader must read with a vigilance and with an imagination that dare, as does Mrs. Bentley, to wonder at the exact and to risk the feverish."[9]

As for Me and My House was published by Reynal and Hitchcock of New York in 1941, with McClelland and Stewart importing some copies for the Canadian market. Although the reviews were solid, sales were poor, only one reviewer, Robertson Davies, noting its importance:

> Mr Ross is keenly aware of the subtleties of the human mind but he knows when to let the reader draw his own inferences, and does not load his book with clinical detail. The book, though not precisely gay in tone, is deeply stimulating and is, as I have already said, a remarkable addition to our small stock of Canadian books of first-rate importance.[10]

It would not be until the novel's appearance in the New Canadian Library in 1957 that it came to be read widely and recognized as a singular work in the history of Canadian fiction.

Ross's next two novels were disappointments. Lacking a tight structure and believable characters, *The Well* (1958) is a conventional murder mystery, perhaps even a conventional thriller, which fails to exploit Ross's capacity for subtle characterization. Montreal is the setting for *Whir of Gold* (1970), a return to Sonny McAlpine, the thirteen-year-old prairie boy of Ross's short story, "The Outlaw," published in 1950. Now a clarinetist in Montreal, he agrees to join in a robbery, the pedestrian scenes in present-day Montreal alternating with vivid scenes of Sonny's prairie upbringing. His childhood was a time of imagination, the scenes recreated realistically. The Montreal scenes never depict the city, this foreign environment proving an alien world for Ross's imagination.

Ross's last novel, *Sawbones Memorial* (1974) is his return to the prairies to depict the town of Upward, Saskatchewan. On 20 April 1948, Doc

---

[9] "Afterword," *As for Me and My House* (Toronto: McClelland & Stewart, 1989), p. 221.
[10] "As For Me and My House: 1941," *The Well-Tempered Critic*, p. 143.

"Sawbones" Hunter is retiring after forty-five years as the town's physician. Again Ross limits his time and place here to an evening farewell party in the lounge of the new Hunter Memorial Hospital. Consisting solely of dialogue and monologue – in forty sections – of the thoughts and reminiscences of the townspeople, the novel, Ross's most innovative, represents the town's collective conscience as it tries to pay tribute to the retiring doctor.

Ross had read Claude Mauriac's novel, *Le Dîner en ville* (1959), which follows the conversations of six characters dining in a fashionable apartment overlooking Notre Dame Cathedral. He, too, wanted to create a novel which would capture the words of people gathered together for a few hours, eschewing any introduction to his characters and any narrative intervention. As he wrote, "No introduction, no descriptions, people just talk and think and the reader has to watch for clues and decide who is talking and thinking …. For some reason the manner or technique appealed to me and I thought I saw possibilities, although with some concessions to the readers so that the amount of figuring out required wouldn't discourage them."[11] People move about the lounge, chatting with one person or with one group, as clusters of people form, disperse, and reunite, filled with all the varying qualities of small-town prairie life, with its hypocrisy and cruelty but also with its generosity and good nature.

The structure of *Sawbones Memorial* is the celebratory party itself, the reader as partygoer moving naturally from character to character. Throughout the evening, as memories and perspectives come together to form a mosaic of the town and its past, four separate generations have their social positions and attitudes defined and analyzed. Then, at the climactic moment of the evening, refreshments are served, speeches are made, and Doc Hunter receives a watch to mark his retirement. The town is both the centre and the circumference of the book, its boundaries are the boundaries of the novel, and within its pages is a startling history of the doctor, four generations of his patients and his friends, and the generosity and the cruelty of the townspeople.

By "writing novels and stories that make us feel the wind and the dust and the sun of prairie landscapes with a new kind of sympathy," observed Kroetsch,

---

[11] *"Collecting Stamps Would Have Been More Fun: Canadian Publishing and the Correspondence of Sinclair Ross, 1933-1986*, ed. Jordan Stouck (Edmonton: University of Alberta Press, 2010), p. 220.

he gave us, along with bleakness and denial, a way to clear one's vision. He showed us a new world that was not a garden, as it was in the American dream, but rather one of such an elemental nature that we might create ourselves brand-spanking new, out of a flirtation with despair. He was a daring originator who suggested to many writers a way to proceed.[12]

For Knister, then, Callaghan and Ross embodied what he himself wanted: to see Canadian daily life presented realistically. Knister became the Moses of Canadian fiction, urging the writers of his country to assume the mantle of realism and avoid imitation "of third-rate foreign models." In the urban wasteland of Toronto and on the bleak landscape of the prairies, Callaghan and Ross met the challenge of writing realistic fiction with a careful delineation of their settings.

But the 1930s and 1940s still clung to their penchant for romance. A classical scholar by training and an early devotee of Hemingway, Hugh MacLennan (1907–90) spoke for young Canadians who had also felt afraid in a strange world: "Like hundreds of thousands of other young men, I was for a time a Hemingway addict, and the word is well chosen. There is something hypnotic about his strangely perfect prose."[13]

Rejecting his own country as a setting for his fiction, he wrote two international novels which are inferior imitations of *A Farewell to Arms* and *The Sun Also Rises*. Crucial in his literary development, these novels, *So All Their Praises* and *A Man Should Rejoice*, both originally unpublished, taught him that Canada, the world he knew, had to be the setting for his fiction. His task would be the exploration and delineation of his own uncharted country, and from experimentation with the international novel, he turned to the national novel where the nation, not its inhabitants, has the central role.

Published in 1941, the same year as *As for Me and My House*, and also using a carefully defined time frame, MacLennan's third novel, *Barometer Rising*, an account of the explosion in Halifax Harbour on 6 December 1917, has Halifax as its main character. In the two earlier novels, Halifax had a peripheral role; now it stands at the centre, the town that survives the explosion and reveals the promise of being a major city. The explosion propels Halifax into a new era just as the larger canvas of World War I awakens the entire country to its position within a world framework. The

---

[12] "Shaping an elusive landscape," *The Globe and Mail*, 2 March 1996, p. C15.
[13] "The Hemingway mystery unveiled," Ottawa *Citizen*, 25 January 1986, p. C3. See also his "Homage of Hemingway," *Thirty and Three* (Toronto: Macmillan, 1954), pp. 85–96.

novel becomes a study of a town and a country growing suddenly and painfully into maturity.

Barometer Rising brings together three segments of Canadian society. The younger people, represented by the returning soldier, Neil Macrae, and his future wife, Penelope Wain, are the new Canada, young urban pioneers anxious to see their country realize its limitless potential. Opposing the new Canada is the colonial mentality, represented most forcefully by Colonel Wain, Penelope's father, "the descendant of military colonists who had remained essentially a colonist himself, never really believing that anything above the second rate could exist in Canada." Between these attitudes stands the undecided Canadian, represented by Angus Murray, a friend of Colonel Wain; a man loyal to British tradition, he is, nevertheless, understanding though apprehensive of Neil's vision. The characters always remain secondary to the depiction of Canada, for they are only mouthpieces for particular attitudes to their country. In the course of eight days, Halifax becomes the victim of the explosion, the worst human-made disaster until Hiroshima and Nagasaki, and the characters suffer their fates: Colonel Wain is killed in the explosion, Neil and Penelope are united at last, and Angus Murray espouses Neil's praise of the future. The novel is a perfect romance, bringing the young couple together for a happy ending.

MacLennan saw himself as an essayist, even more, to use Edmund Wilson's phrase, as his country's "secretary of society":[14]

> The Canadian novelist would have to pay a great deal of attention to the background in which he set his stories. He must describe, and if necessary define, the social values which dominate the Canadian scene, and do so in such a way as to make them appear interesting and important to foreigners. Whether he liked it or not, he must for a time be something of a geographer, an historian and a sociologist, to weave a certain amount of geography, history and sociology into his novels.[15]

Choosing Halifax, a town he knew well, instead of the foreign panorama of his earlier works, he depicts Canada growing out of its colonial lethargy. The country, which at first he rejected as a setting for his fiction, was to become the realm of his fiction. Finally, and like Ross, he had an American publisher, Canada still being a country without a fully functioning publishing world.

---

[14] *O Canada: An American's Notes on Canadian Culture* (New York: Farrar, Straus and Giroux, 1965), p. 68.
[15] "Where is My Potted Palm?" *Thirty and Three*, p. 52.

Two Solitudes (1945) is a chronological and thematic continuation of *Barometer Rising*. The action, beginning in 1917 and ending in 1939 at the outbreak of World War II, focuses on the emergence of a new Canada in the figures of a young Frenchman, Paul Tallard, a writer and another version of Neil Macrae, and his English wife, Heather Methuen. *Two Solitudes* follows *Barometer Rising* in its patterning of characters to represent various dimensions of Canadian society. In the first half, set in a Quebec village, Father Beaubien embodies traditional, agrarian, authoritarian Catholic Quebec; opposing him is Athanase Tallard, Paul's father, a reasoned, passionate man who constantly thinks of the future, not the past, of his culture. When the setting shifts to Montreal, the priest's rigid authoritarianism is replaced by Sir Rupert Irons, who clings to British tradition as firmly as the priest clings to ancient dogma. Tallard becomes an opposing force as he strives to assist English financiers, only to see them desert him and negotiate directly with the local bishop. Despite his vision of a peaceful Canada with the French and English united through understanding, he belongs to the old world; he must be content to remain a prophet, a voice of intelligence ahead of his time.

The second half of the novel is devoted to Paul and Heather. After eight years of wandering and obtaining an Oxford degree, Paul learns the same lesson as a writer MacLennan himself had learned: his readers' ignorance of Canadian clashes and values presented him with a unique problem, and he would have to create his story for his readers. For Paul, the abandonment of the international novel in favour of the national novel is a necessary artistic decision, and a hybrid character of a French father and an English mother, he becomes anglicized, finding his artistic roots in British literature. His marriage to Heather represents the hope, albeit Anglophone, for the future of Canada.

Two Solitudes shares the naïve optimism of *Barometer Rising*. Though exploring the past, both novels are oriented to the future. In *Barometer Rising* the romance of Neil and Penny offers the only hope for a new Canada arising from the stupor of Halifax and the country's capitalism during World War I. *Two Solitudes* ends with Canada's active participation in World War II. Addressing the central problem of the nation, the dialectic between the French and the English, the novel offers a hopeful, happy, and simple resolution to the national tension.

In *Two Solitudes* MacLennan left behind Hemingway in favour of John Galsworthy, who had influenced the fiction of Mazo de la Roche and whom MacLennan had heard lecture in his own Oxford days. Galsworthy's mastery of time was a crucial component of his narrative, and so he fixed on *The Forsyte Saga* as his model for this Canadian version of the traditional chronicle. To tell his family saga, he chose the omniscient point of view as well as the chronological narrative he so admired in Galsworthy. He controlled the passage of time, just as Galsworthy had done, by alternating large scenes of world events with detailed scenes which reveal the effect of these gigantic events on his characters' personal lives. Yet the novel's form is that of a romance, though loosely structured in contrast to the neat patterns of *Barometer Rising*.

The Precipice (1948) completes the trilogy of MacLennan's national novels by studying Canada in contrast to its southern neighbour. Beginning in August 1938 and ending at the conclusion of World War II, it is a continuation of *Two Solitudes*. The Quebec village finds its English counterpart in Grenville, Ontario, where "the ferments and the revolutions of the past twenty years might never have existed so far as the town was concerned." Following the pattern of *Two Solitudes*, this town finds its contrast in New York City, an urban setting. The three Cameron sisters live in a cloistered world where Stephen Lassiter, an American businessman, comes to analyze the operational efficiency of his firm's Grenville plant. He represents the developed, money-oriented American society, finding Grenville's economic stagnation and indifference depressing. When Stephen marries the middle sister and they move to New York City, his own Puritan background asserts itself. He seeks monetary success as proof of his goodness, and his maniacal commitment to business destroys his marriage. Stephen and his wife become the embodiment of their Puritan heritages. He is energetic, anxious, and desperate for success; she is cautious, careful, and uncertain; both are guilt-ridden by their native tradition. The cautious Canadian, MacLennan suggests, is less destructive than the modern American, though each can complement and complete the other.

No longer content with the national novel, MacLennan sought a new form. His characters embody the theme, but they are assuming an increasingly important and independent existence. *The Precipice* is closer to the novel of character, and the almost-romance ending seems out of place. His three-novel confrontation with Canadian society has been the natural and necessary prelude to a delineation of individual lives in a Canadian landscape, and with his new-found development of characters he prepares to leave behind the national novel.

In the 1950s MacLennan turned to the character novel where people, not themes, dominate in a Canadian terrain. Set in 1913 in the fictional town of Broughton on Cape Breton, *Each Man's Son* (1951) is Dr. Daniel

Ainslie's journey to self-knowledge and self-understanding, though his search is personal with no national overtones. Driven by the Calvinistic doctrine of human damnation, he cuts himself off from his friends, his wife, and his own emotions. Eight-year-old Alan MacNeil becomes the childless Ainslie's charge and ultimately their surrogate son. And *The Watch That Ends the Night* (1959), a second novel of character set in contemporary Montreal, is one man's journey to self-knowledge, for he comes home from the Nazi death camps to have a startling effect on his former wife and the man whom she married after learning of her first husband's death.

MacLennan's final novels, *Return of the Sphinx* (1967) and *Voices in Time* (1980), return to his 1940s world where thematic concerns rule out the humanity of his characters. The former recounts the frustrated attempt of Alan Ainslie, Daniel's adopted son and now Canadian minister of cultural affairs, to bring understanding and harmony to the English-French dialectic. Although his presence suggests that the novel is a sequel to *Each Man's Son*, in theme and in form it is another national novel, a later and less optimistic version of *Two Solitudes*. Three decades after the tragic political career of Athanase Tallard, separatism, not coexistence, is the goal of many Québécois, and *Return of the Sphinx* is an uneasy reenactment of the 1940s' trilogy where characters embody ideas. The central figure is Canada, breaking apart into factions, and Alan Ainslie tries to be an older version of Neil Macrae and Paul Tallard. In the end, he resigns from public office, returns to Nova Scotia, the province of his birth, and travels from there across the continent. But the transcontinental panorama is no longer possible. Although the novel attempts to delineate complex characters, the theme of Canada in ruins returns MacLennan to the national novel, a form more appropriate in the 1940s when Canadian fiction needed such depictions of society.

Voices in Time, whose actions are recounted from the perspective of the fourth decade of the twenty-first century, is a seventy-year-old's retelling of the past, most specifically the times that led up to the Nazi control of Germany and much more. The novel resembles more a treatise than a narrative, a didactic author attempting to define the principal forces that shaped the twentieth-century world.

Accepting his country as the domain of his fiction, MacLennan animated Canadian society for his audience and mapped the terrain for future Canadian writers. He created a series of novels, most notably his novels of the 1940s, that sacrificed human characterization to depict a still uncharted social pattern. These earlier novels record the country's growth into maturity, and subsequent novels, though flawed, take place in a clearly defined terrain which was not mapped until Knister, Callaghan, Ross, and MacLennan appeared.

About Callaghan, MacLennan is relatively silent: "I never feel easy talking about Morley Callaghan, and I don't think he feels any easier talking about me. We both like each other, certainly I greatly respect him, but perhaps we are too alike to see each other with clarity, being also extremely different in our traditions and education."[16] Callaghan and his Catholic background differed from MacLennan's Calvinistic stock, and Callaghan, unlike MacLennan, pursued his writing on an international level, MacLennan pursuing the national route. MacLennan never ventured into the world of shorter fiction which was central to Callaghan's creative life. He often stated that the finest Canadian was a perfect mixture of the best of the American and the best of the British; he could not renounce his colonial terminology in describing his land and its people.

Amid this realist movement in fiction, *Tay John* (1939) by Howard O'Hagan (1902–82), born in Lethbridge and educated at McGill with a BA in economics and political science, stands out as an example of mythic realism. Originally published in England in 1939, the novel attracted attention only when it appeared in the New Canadian Library in 1974; since then it has become an important work in the development of Canadian fiction.

In the summer of 1880 in the area of Alberta's Yellowhead Pass, a man of mixed blood born from the grave of his mother, a Shuswap woman, who was violated by an Irish trapper, Tay John is a larger-than-life protagonist who soon becomes the hero of his people. "His yellow hair marked his different birth. His rifle was his own, and no man could touch it. His red coat was a sign of the white man's favour. His name was no more the name come from his people but the name he had earned when he was far from them." His adventures, told in the novel's opening section, "Legend," by an omniscient voice, give way to the second and final sections, "Hearsay" and "Evidence – without a finding," told by Jack Denham, which chronicle his later adventures. Denham's account, the distortion of a faulty memory, sees only fragments of Tay John's life, the tale retaining its sense of the legendary and the marvelous.

Confrontation with Tay John witnesses the making of a mythic hero: his strange birth, his loss of his first love, his chopping off his left hand, his

---

[16] *Dear Marian, Dear Hugh: The MacLennan-Engel Correspondence* (University of Ottawa Press, 1995), p. 42.

wrongly attributed charge of sexual molestation, his final love, and his death. A legend has its final effect on those who come into contact with him, and this effect is evident in all his encounters.

Based closely on his readings of Joseph Conrad, E.M. Forster, and others, O'Hagan shaped his novel as a mixture of history and legend, making it less a realistic than a mythic work, less a novel of the 1930s, when it was written, and more a precursor of the postmodern fiction of the 1970s. Thus he mirrors the concerns of Margaret Laurence, Rudy Wiebe, Robert Kroetsch, Michael Ondaatje, and others in their fiction.

Meanwhile, W.O. Mitchell (1914–98) was pursuing the less populated realm of comedy. A native of Weyburn, Saskatchewan, and a student at the University of Alberta, he would seem to be following Ross, but Ross's writings, especially his novel *As for Me and My House*, did not attract Mitchell's attention; he read only "Cornet at Night." Although he knew Leacock, his heroes were Hardy and Joseph Conrad, especially Conrad, who pointed out in the preface to *The Nigger of the 'Narcissus'*: "My task which I am trying to achieve is, by the power of the written word to make you hear, to make you feel – it is, before all, to make you *see*. That – and no more, and it is everything."

Who Has Seen the Wind (1947), Mitchell's first novel, is the tender story of Brian O'Connal, the four-year-old son of a small and nameless Saskatchewan town's druggist. Brian's imagination struggles, as the prefatory note says, "to understand what still defeats mature and learned men – the ultimate meaning of the cycle of life. To him are revealed in moments of fleeting vision the realities of birth, hunger, satiety, eternity, death. They are moments when an inquiring heart seeks finality, and the chain of darkness is broken." From the age of four through twelve, he encounters many experiences which make him at once a small-town boy living between the two World Wars and a tireless explorer after order amid the random chaos of this world. His home is the prairie, which forms the backdrop for Brian's adventures, and as he grows in age – the novel is divided into four sections, each of them covering a two-year phase taking him to new levels of awareness – he witnesses the fun and the foibles of small-town life. Although he experiences his own spiritual transcendence, he also endures the many hardships of his people: Mrs. Abercrombie and the school board who fire the town's good teacher; the Wong children and the suicide of their father; even Reverend Powelly and his zealous followers. Then there are his encounters with death in a variety of manifestations: his dog Jappy, a tortured gopher, his own father, and then his grandmother, too, which provide Brian's introduction to the hard facts of mortality. Yet through all these stands out his unflagging search for enlightenment and meaning. The story shifts between death and life, between the finite and the infinite, between the uniquely prairie and the universal until what remains is Brian's "maturity in spite of the formlessness of childish features, wisdom without years."

Mitchell had studied the writings of Swiss psychologist Jean Piaget, and Piaget's insights crystallized what Mitchell had already observed in children. He became a close observer of young people's development, and in *Who Has Seen the Wind*, he recreated the inner life of the child, especially the growth of a child's creative love of life. This domain, the world of the growing and perceptive child, was new to Canadian fiction, where children were seen and not usually heard. For Mitchell, the child is the centre of his fictional universe.

In addition to Piaget's formative influence was a second and more crucial force in Edmonton, the Medieval and Renaissance scholar F.M. Salter, who taught creative writing at the University of Alberta. He became Mitchell's friend and mentor, advising him on his writing, urging him to add more plot to his work, even suggesting and dictating the prefatory note. Salter first met Mitchell while the latter was trying to pen some stories, later gathered together as *Jake and the Kid* (1981), and his meticulous guidance was Mitchell's introduction to the craft of writing. Mitchell believed that the stories were popular as opposed to serious literature. "I don't mean that there is anything wrong with the Jake and the Kid stories; we have had fun out of them," Salter told him.[17] Later the Canadian Broadcasting Corporation broadcast more than 150 scripts for the series.

The power of Mitchell's first novel is a reflection of *Sunshine Sketches of a Little Town*. Leacock's "sunshine" portrait contains a few moments which undercut the comic tales of Mariposa and reveal the deeper thinking of the narrator himself. Mitchell's novel goes further, showing the comic glories of the small town yet revealing the sinister forces at work among the town's inhabitants, all these forces seen through the questioning vision of a young child.

Mitchell spent many years teaching, robbing him to some degree of the time to write fiction. When he turned again to the novel, he had trouble plotting an original story; too often his penchant for the quick comic tale denied him the novel's natural flow. Only in *How I Spent My Summer*

[17] Barbara and Ormond Mitchell, *W.O.: The Life of W.O. Mitchell: Beginnings to Who Has Seen the Wind* (Toronto: McClelland & Stewart, 1999), p. 258.

Holidays (1981) does he return and darken the world of *Who Has Seen the Wind*, as a man in his sixties remembers the summer when he was twelve and adult trespassers violated the children's secret cave.

As fiction editor for *Maclean's* magazine from 1948 to 1951, Mitchell helped many young authors in a manner reminiscent of the way Salter had helped him. On the acknowledgement page of a first novel, *The Mountain and the Valley* (1952), by Ernest Buckler (1908–84) appears Mitchell's name, for he had been instrumental in fostering Buckler's writing. Through their correspondence they became pen pals: "We feel we know you the best we know anyone – which is almost magic since we've never met you or talked with you."[18] A native of the Nova Scotia's Annapolis Valley and a graduate of Dalhousie University in Mathematics and Philosophy, Buckler was a sometime critic of contemporary literature, as *Esquire's* editor, Arnold Gingrich, recalled:

> Buckler began, when the magazine was very young, writing me a sort of critique of each issue as it appeared, and I began sticking his letters into the correspondence columns. People began writing in that they'd prefer to save their issues and read them only after Buckler's exegetical comments on them had appeared in subsequent numbers; some other people wrote that they'd rather read what Buckler said about the issues than read the magazines themselves. And some began saying they hoped I was paying Buckler a lot of money, because he was worth Hemingway, Fitzgerald, Dos Passos, Dreiser, and all the rest put together. I was paying Buckler nothing, of course, as we were only pen pals, but after enough of such chaffing from the cheap seats I began to feel guilty about this myself, and began urging Buckler to write.[19]

Buckler wrote short fiction out of his farming world. "You don't have to wander all over the bloody world and explore every niche and cranny in it to find out how people behave," he reflected.

> In a small community like this even, you have a representation of every kind of action, of every kind of psychological mode. The whole thing, the whole macrocosm, is here in microcosm. You don't have to know any more people than these to know what is going on in the human psyche. So this is why I haven't felt the exorbitant need to travel; I feel it's pretty well all here.[20]

---

[18] Barbara and Ormond Mitchell, *Mitchell: The Life of W.O. Mitchell: The Years of Fame, 1948–1998* (Toronto: McClelland & Stewart, 2005), p. 106.

[19] *Nothing But People: The Early Days of Esquire, a Personal History 1928-1958* (New York: Crown, 1971), pp. 252–3.

[20] Donald Cameron, *Conversations with Canadian Novelists* (Toronto: Macmillan, 1973), 1, 8.

The only major writer Buckler read in his early years was Hardy, whose hold on him continued throughout his life: "I know of no other place where one gets such intolerably moving pictures of the exquisite melancholy at the heart of things."[21] He then started to read major writers, including Hemingway and Faulkner, the former he admired for stripping the language to its bare bones, the latter for orchestrating the many and full levels of language. Along with these and other modernists was his professed love of E.M. Forster, whose immense shadow falls over *The Mountain and the Valley*. Among his papers and letters is no reference to any Canadian writer save for Callaghan.

With the publication of his first two stories, "One Quiet Afternoon" and "The First Born Son," in *Esquire* in 1940, Buckler began his writing career. The scene is usually a farming community where continual friction occurs between the rural way of life and the far-off urban scene. In "The First Born Son," for example, the tension between a father and son leads to their battle about the farming world and city life; there is no final resolution, only the careful delineation of two modes of living. In his stories Buckler is experimenting with his narrative point of view, the narrator being the person in the action or an omniscient and silent third person. And these stories were frequently reworked into a fuller presentation and transformation when they became part of his novels. In *The Mountain and the Valley*, his best novel, he gathered together all his themes and some earlier stories and created a unique work about the farming community of the Annapolis Valley and David Canaan, intelligent and precocious, a young artist who is obsessed with his urgent need to capture in words his feelings and his emotions. Published, at Mitchell's insistence, by Henry Holt of New York, the book propelled the *Esquire* writer to early success in the United States and Canada.

In the novel's prologue, thirty-year-old David is about to climb the mountain south of his farming home in the valley. The subsequent six sections chronicle his growth into adulthood, the first giving his childhood memories at the age of eleven, the second his sexual awakening and his intimation of the world outside the valley, the third his distress at his girlfriend's death, the fourth his unresolved conflict with his father, the fifth his unresolved conflict with his brother, and the sixth his unresolved conflict with his brother-in-law. These parts lead naturally to the epilogue, which takes place at the exact moment of the prologue: David is now

---

[21] "Letter to Ted Bentley, 9 September 1937," quoted in Claude Bissell, *Ernest Buckler* Remembered (University of Toronto Press, 1981), p. 36.

climbing the mountain to his death. All the moments come together to make this final ascendancy the total of all that preceded it, just as the rug his grandmother Ellen is making brings together all the discarded clothes of various members and generations of the Canaan family. The rug comes to be the artistic union of past and present and the human ability to triumph finally over time, the rug outlasting the Canaan family and enduring in – and outside of – time.

As its title suggests, the novel places in sharp relief the world of the valley, the loving rural community of David's home and family, and the world of the mountain, the embodiment of David's romantic dreams beyond the valley. Poised between these two poles, David confronts his choice: he can stay in the village of Entremont, embracing his rural realm, or he can follow his twin sister Anna and her husband Toby, free himself from Entremont's restrictions, and pursue his artistic intentions. He becomes increasingly aware of the limitations of the valley while remaining steadfastly loyal to them. His final decision is to climb to the top of the mountain regardless of the consequences.

The outside world encroaches steadily on the values of the Entremont community, just as Forster's *Howard's End* studies the gradual encroachment of modern society on the increasingly less remote life of Howard's End. Buckler himself described "the gradual dispersal of family oneness and (in parallel) in the village itself, as progress (?) laps closer and closer."[22] In his readings David comes upon "a novel by someone called Forster. It gave him such a lyric feeling to recognize the absolute truth of what the author said about whatever people he dealt with (though he himself had never known anyone like them, actually) that sometimes he'd have to look away from the page." Forster's vision of the creeping movement of modern life becomes David's – and Buckler's – Canadian parallel.

With a style which frequently resembles more a prose poem than prose, Buckler created a strong Canadian bildungsroman, the first since *Emily of New Moon*, of the early years and the growth of a young artist, whose final vision is being "the greatest writer in the whole world." The centre is the consciousness of its protagonist, and that protagonist is ultimately Buckler himself. Although he did eclipse himself when David dies, the valley remains a fixed and timeless place.

A few days after *The Mountain and the Valley* was accepted for publication, Buckler wrote to his agent about his next book:

---

[22] "Letter to Dudley H. Cloud, 24 March 1951," quoted in Alan Young, *Ernest Buckler* (Toronto: McClelland & Stewart, 1976), p. 32.

Maybe a non-fiction about the myriad, fast-disappearing, unduplicated anywhere facets of life in a Nova Scotia village as I knew it in my younger days, written in the light vein of the old 'Esquire' letters . . . . Or maybe a more sophisticated novel, with a background of Greenwich's Belle Haven district, where I spent a good deal of the time working in the 20s.[23]

He chose the latter, penning *The Cruelest Month* (1963), centring on seven people from sharply differentiated backgrounds who come together at Endlaw (an anagram for Walden) in rural Nova Scotia to obtain their bearings about who they are. As indicated by its original title of *The Cells of Love*, the novel watches both the strengthening and the restricting nature of love, though his people, wanting love as security, often fail in their quests; Buckler failed in his search for a method of getting inside these people. In *Ox Bells and Fireflies* (1968), he returned to a memoir which fuses fiction and fact in his endless search for a bygone paradisal world. A world of exquisite beauty, the memoir's setting has all the perfection of a real world. The urban destroys the rural Eden, and the book becomes a nostalgic memoir of a bygone world.

Buckler captured a rural Nova Scotia world which brings his fiction into the realm of universal art. "The universal is (even more than Blake saw it) seen in the particular; and if you are made small by the comparison, you are also made great (in the only way that greatness has a meaning) by feeling (even if unconsciously: what the hell does the how of it matter?) that you are pantheistically a part of the whole universe," he commented. "And if one must be a part of something, as human necessity rules one must be, what better than to be a part of a goddam immutable mountain or a goddam immutable valley or a goddam unsubornable sea?"[24]

Unlike Buckler himself, who knew little of Canadian fiction as he was starting his career, future writers would praise him. "I have been thinking of you lately, I don't know why," Munro wrote. "I guess because I've been writing a story called *Home*, which I was thinking you would understand. I don't know if it's similarity of background or vision, but I feel very close to you as a writer."[25] Canadian fiction was definitely "breaking away from this crocheting of little tea-cosies of genteel prose for the excruciatingly prim – and is turning out stuff of real flesh, blood, bone, *and* spirit," as Buckler said in 1953.[26]

[23] "Letter to Harold Ober, 21 January 1952," ibid., p. 37.
[24] "Author's Questionnaire for *Window on the World*" in the Ernest Buckler papers at the Fisher Rare Book Library, University of Toronto.
[25] *Ernest Buckler* Remembered, p. 139.
[26] Gregory M. Cook, *Ernest Buckler* (Toronto: McGraw-Hill Ryerson, 1972), p. 26.

In this movement towards realism stands Ethel Wilson (1888–1980). Born in Port Elizabeth, South Africa, she lost her mother when she was only eighteen months old; her father, a devout Methodist minister, returned home to England, where he died when his daughter was nine years old. Orphaned, she travelled to Vancouver to live with her maternal grandmother and her family. She knew an upbringing similar to Montgomery's, though there is no evidence that she had read Montgomery's writings.

Wilson matured in a world where she devoured books. Her literary mentors were the great writers of British literature: Shakespeare and John Donne; her idol Henry Fielding with his frequently autobiographical intrusions into his novels; Austen who "displays the people, poor fools, and they don't know that she knows them. It's all so harmless, and so awfully clever";[27] Anthony Trollope, "a story-teller of real people";[28] and Conrad, Forster, and Joyce, to name the most important. When she wanted to publish her short stories, she sent them to the left-leaning *New Statesman and Nation*, which printed them in 1937 and 1939. This weekly publication was her "first introduction to literary and artistic criticism and political polemics. I soon read in all directions, regardless of politics and schools. What would have happened in my own mental life in a geographical area that was then still a periphery, not a centre, if this very fortuitous influence had not arrived and at that time, I don't quite know."[29]

Wilson's "Englishness" did not blind her to the realities of contemporary Canada. She loved her British Columbia landscapes: "There are other places in the world that I know and love, but none that I know, and feel, and love in the same way. But I did not choose it. It chose. It is very strong."[30] Her stories appeared in the *Canadian Forum* in 1942 and *Chateleine* in 1945. After she began her correspondence with John Gray of Macmillan, she came to admire Canadian fiction, including *Such Is My Beloved* ("a novel whose setting is a city. This seems to me one of the very finest of Canadian novels") and *As for Me and My House* ("the remarkable achievement of a man speaking through a woman's voice. The monotony of the prairie heat, the prairie wind, the prairie cold, constricted life in the little town of false-fronted buildings, the boredom, the despair, the living

---

[27] *Ethel Wilson: Stories, Essays, and Letters*, ed. David Stouck (Vancouver: University of British Columbia Press, 1987), p. 188.
[28] Ibid., p. 150.   [29] Ibid., p. 101.   [30] Ibid., p. 104.

too close together in a small frame house – all this beats upon the reader. It has a terrible validity").[31]

In the process of writing her first novel, the weirdly Gothic and psychological near-thriller *Hetty Dorval* (1947), Wilson sought to capture the rural beauties of her own province, which "do not change, except for the exquisite and surreptitious signatures of the seasons, the surface and movement of waters, the glory of skies, the seasonal flighting of birds, the great isolated ponderosa pines each with its solitary tall shadow that moves with the sun, the pale virginal trembling aspens, the laughter of the loon on the lake."[32] She employed Lytton, a small town situated at the point where the Thompson River, "flowing rapidly westwards from Kamloops, pours itself into the Fraser, flowing widely and sullenly southwards." And up above, throughout the book, appears "the musical clamour of the wild geese," an allusion to the similar sounds and imagery of Ostenso's novel.

"No man is an Island" wrote John Donne in his famous meditation, and Wilson makes this passage her epigraph to the novel. Hetty Dorval is an enigmatic, sinister figure who acts threateningly and decisively on young Frankie Bernard, the novel's narrator, and Frankie's growth from a twelve-year-old schoolgirl to a young woman who finally spurns Hetty's continual and menacing advances into her life mirrors her evolving relationship with this older woman. In terms of plot, *Hetty Dorval* is simple. Frankie Bernard falls under the spell of Mrs. Dorval. Her parents do not like the mysterious outsider and warn their daughter of her ways. Wherever Frankie goes – to school in Vancouver, to England on a ship, in London – she keeps meeting Hetty, becoming less attracted to her and more repelled by her. She learns of her marriages and scandalous affairs with wealthy men, finally thrusting her from her life.

"No man is an Island," yet Hetty remains isolated and alone, isolated from her communities and alone in her thoughts, alone save for the equally disoriented Mrs. Broom, her housekeeper. Still she remains a force, an influential person whose power rests, not in developing her own self, but in helping to form the identity of those around her. At the end she is, as she was at the beginning, always on the move, though her moves may be halted by her final travels, with her latest companion Jules Stern, to Vienna on the eve of the Nazi invasion.

Wilson has a beautiful writing style, a clear form of narration, and an ability to capture scenes and their people with eloquent understatement. In her subtle form of irony she displays her understanding of the warfare

[31] Ibid., p. 93.   [32] "Preface," *Hetty Dorval* (Vancouver: The Alcuin Society, 1967), p. 8.

between a dominating woman and her one-time protégé. *Hetty Dorval* looks forward to Wilson's other literary creations, for this book, like her other fictional works, is less a novel than a novella. With a confined narrative focusing on a natural though unexpected conclusion, the novella became the major form in her writing career.

Wilson wrote several short stories, frequently using her family background for tales, autobiographical or fictional, about family members. In *The Innocent Traveller* (1949), she chronicles her family. Ostensibly not a work of fiction but a chronicle, the book is an account of "*this* kingdom, here, in this place, to a large degree. The Vancouver of that day is now obscured, but was in itself a foundation of the Vancouver which now is, and which we see, but which may some day also be obscured."[33] The early days of Vancouver are the background for the one-hundred-year life of an "innocent traveler." All the activities, events, and traumas of these loosely connected sketches do not deflate or harm the ever-recurrent heroine, who sails through her life – as daughter, sister, aunt, and great-aunt – always dependent upon others and always the perennially "youngest" of the group until she becomes "a memory, a gossamer."

In *The Equations of Love* (1952), Wilson took two novellas, "Monday and Tuesday" and "Lilly's Story," each about the same length as *Hetty Dorval*, and published them together. Focusing on the lives of working-class characters, she paints detailed portraits of her people and their dreary yet strangely uplifting lives. With an epigraph from Dickens's *Bleak House*, she sets out to explore the nature of truth, though "in a spirit of love," with the ironic detachment of an omniscient narrator.

Set in urban Vancouver, "Monday and Tuesday," Wilson's favourite of all her writings, follows two days in the lives of Mort and Myrtle Johnson, two lower-class working people whose boring workaday patterns betoken their bitter, almost defeatist attitudes. The story's climax consists of Victoria May Tritt's account of Mort Johnson's death, which took place, she avers, as he was trying to save his friend from drowning. No longer the figure of the drunken husband, Mort becomes a posthumous hero, and Myrtle must now live with the privileged duty of being a hero's widow. The lie Vicky tells is true "in a spirit of love," for it represents the opposite of self-pity, one of Wilson's deadly sins. In early drafts this story had too many authorial intrusions, Wilson's consistent indebtedness to her heroes, Fielding and Forster. Excising some of them, she revised the story, which was then accepted.

---

[33] *Ethel Wilson: Stories, Essays, and Letters*, pp. 87–8.

Wilson was the first writer to explore the Chinese presence in British Columbia. *Hetty Dorval* had a brief appearance by Wong, a grandfather who owned the Chinese café, "an old fat Chinaman whose father was one of the Chinese who mined for gold in the Fraser and in the Cariboo country in the early sixties." Originating in the figure of Yow, the Chinese cook from *The Innocent Traveller* and the first *extended* recognition in fiction of the Chinese presence, "Lilly's Story" follows its poor and forlorn heroine, a "pale slut" and a "homeless worthless bitch" from downtown Chinatown through a period of more than thirty years. When she gives birth to an illegitimate daughter, she invents a new identity for herself as Mrs. Walter Hughes and a new history, so that her daughter Eleanor will know an ordered and secure world. Lilly's lies transform her from a materialistic young woman into a devoted and selfless mother. Her roles as maid in Comox, hospital aide in the Fraser Valley, and chambermaid in a Toronto hotel lead to her sudden middle-class marriage as a "very very lovely woman" to a Winnipeg widower.

Both novellas feature an omniscient narrator unfolding shocking events in a compassionate way. At the end of "Monday and Tuesday," a lie has redeemed a degenerate and dead Mort in the eyes of his unsympathetic wife. At the end of "Lilly's Story," Lilly's horrid existence is redeemed by her constant and consistent attempts to win respectability for herself and her daughter. Lilly is that rare individual who realizes the innate possibilities of personal heroism. She is, as Donne's meditation concludes in the epigraph to *Hetty Dorval*, "involved in Mankinde."

Her longest novella, *Swamp Angel* (1954), recounts Maggie Lloyd's plight in contemporary Vancouver. She had been previously married; she had a child; both her husband and her child have died. Now married for the second time to Edward Vardoe, she experiences the misery and the suffocation of a marital nightmare; her marriage is slavery consisting of the nightly humiliations she endures with Vardoe. Unexpectedly to her husband's horror, she flees her male-dominated marriage to go into the interior, to the lakes around Kamloops, where she becomes a cook and restorative force in a failing lumber camp. Taking her life into her own hands, she designs her own future in the open country she now inhabits, finding her own secure place. Like Frankie Bernard and Lilly, Maggie Lloyd reaches a new understanding of herself and her position in the world. She refuses to burden herself with thoughts of the past, preferring to dwell in the inescapable present, the only stability in a world of ceaseless change.

Wilson's fictional universe involves a faithful depiction of her beloved Vancouver and the interior of British Columbia. Her people consist of the working class and those from the more privileged social classes, and their presentation is a realistic celebration of their unique determination to become more than what they originally were. Her main characters are women who take themselves out of their familiar settings in order to discover their true selves. They soon learn that this world is not benign, but chaotic, shaped by chance. Yet each woman must establish by herself the connection with the larger human community of which she is a part. A complex dilemma, life is, quoting Edwin Muir in the epigraph to her collection of short fiction, *Mrs. Golightly and Other Stories* (1961), "a difficult country, and our home."

A staunch moralist, Wilson subscribes to the Christian teaching that all people must strive to ennoble themselves, even if there are obstacles in their path. "I am indeed a Christian," she once said, "and very grateful but not a good enough one, and not entirely conventionally a Christian – in formal belief and observance."[34] She portrays "a wide variety of characters with perception, compassion, humor and a sense of the mystery at the core of life. I think of her as a deeply religious writer, although not in any orthodox way, perhaps, and not in any didactic way," wrote Margaret Laurence.[35] Wilson's women achieve their final self-understanding, not in the traditional male sense of power, but in a spiritual notion of selfhood which influences the lives of others. Their achievement rests in their self-realization in the Christian meaning of life.

The ultimate accolade for Wilson's fiction comes again from Munro. "I *was enormously* excited by her work because the style was such an enormous pleasure in itself," she reflects. "It was important to me that a Canadian writer was using so elegant a style. You know I don't mean style in the superficial sense, but that a point of view so complex and ironic was possible in Canadian literature."[36]

While Wilson embraced her Canadian world, Norman Levine (1923–2005) had an ambivalent attitude to Canada. Born in Ottawa, the son of Polish Jewish immigrants, he received his BA and MA in English from McGill University, then moved to Cornwall, where he lived for much of his life. Starting out as a poet, he went on to publish two novels, *The Angled Road* (1952) and *From a Seaside Town* (1970), and eight collections

---

[34] "Series of Combination of Events and Where is John Goodwin?" *Tamarack Review* 33 (Autumn 1964): 6.
[35] "A friend's tribute to Ethel Wilson," *Toronto Star*, 24 January 1981, p. F8.
[36] J.R. (Tim) Struthers, "The Real Material: An Interview with Alice Munro," *Probable Fictions: Alice Munro's Narrative Acts*, ed. Louis K. MacKendrick (Toronto: ECW Press, 1983), p. 18.

of short stories. "The publisher in Toronto had read it," he wrote regarding his first novel, "and said I would have to get it published in New York or London; then he would look after the Canadian market."[37] The country still lacked a publishing tradition.

The Angled Road is less a novel that a series of reflective episodes, almost short stories, which follow a man from his early impoverished life in a Canadian city, a thinly disguised Ottawa, to his enlistment and travels to England as a flyer in World War II, then his return to Canada with his decision to attend university. What is impressive are the myriad impressions of people on his young artistic sensibility as well as his affairs with two English women. Yet Levine would admit in 1970: "I already knew the book wasn't any good. And here I was a writer. Writing things that weren't anywhere as good as I wanted them to be."[38] There are no detailed settings in Canada or in England; there is only one controlling perspective, the protagonist, who narrates his story; and the plot is so closely tied to events in Levine's own life, though there are no references to his Judaism.

His other novel is a first-person account of a fictitious writer, Joseph Grand, and his attempt to write in an English seaside town. A Canadian Jew, he has spent his life submerging his past; now he is nowhere. The book is a series of separate short stories unified by his observations. As he ends his book, he admits: "Life seems to be a series of unconnected brief encounters." One of these encounters, the seventh chapter, "A Trip to London," became a separate but unchanged story, "I'll Bring You Back Something Nice." The novel's momentum diminishes when such intrusions can be read independently from their original context.

It was in the short story form where Levine excelled. Often taking an episode from his life and painting it with little attempt to draw out its moral, he does not follow Callaghan or Wilson in their close studies of the world outside of themselves; rather he looks forward to the short fiction of Margaret Laurence and Munro. "I would try to make lists. A list of all the stores and businesses going up and down the main street and who owned them, a list of family names, names on the tombstones in the cemetery and any inscriptions underneath," Munro's narrator, for example, says in *Lives of Girls and Women* (1971). "Names of the streets and the pattern they lay in." In "A Writer's Story" from Levine's *Thin Ice* (1979), the narrator comments:

[37] "Why I am an Expatriate," *Canadian Literature* 5 (Summer 1960): 49.
[38] "Norman Levine: An Interview with John D. Cox," *Canadian Literature* 45 (Summer 1970): 63.

How was I to earn a living if I couldn't write my next book? I started to make lists. Of the people I grew up with in Ottawa. Of the popular songs I knew when I was at school. Of the streets, the streetcar lines, the market, the library, the parks.

In his short stories, Levine often depicts a sensitive narrator who watches his world with detached bemusement, often preferring an explored but usually lost past. These male figures are isolated, cut off from life around them and making their stories reflect their loneliness. The reader is more conscious of their reflexive minds than of the delineated world outside. The title story of *The Ability to Forget* (2003) ends, "Later a For Sale sign appeared by his house. Then the Sold sign. People disappear. And that's that." People come and people go, scarcely leaving any trace of themselves.

Levine knows the people who come to inhabit his short fiction. "I've always been attracted to all kinds of people that society frowns upon. I've been attracted to the ordinary, the everyday. These are people who get pushed around, who are not significant, and in my own kind of cockeyed way I think I try to show that these lives people lead should have some kind of dignity."[39] This preference for the ordinary is not far removed from Callaghan's lower middle-class people finding their way in this world. While Levine's uncluttered, terse style owes a debt to Hemingway, his major influence was Chekhov, who "wrote out of the experiences of his own life. That he did not impose 'plot' onto his material. But by giving all sorts of insights into his characters (by telling us enough about them) he made you get to know them intimately. So all that was needed was some small incident for us to be touched, as we would be with people we know well in life."[40] Chekhov was his ideal, and he made his stories akin to Chekhov's own tales.

Unlike Wilson who knew so much about Canadian literature, Levine did not evince any true knowledge of his country's burgeoning fiction. He stayed in Cornwall for much of his life, creating realistic fiction which plumbed the depths of his intimate realm, often retaining his role as the lonely outsider.

Realism entered the world of Canadian fiction, in Knister's and Callaghan's novels and short stories, in Ross's prairies, to some degree in

[39] David McDonald, "Simplicity and Sophistication: A Conversation with Norman Levine," *Queen's Quarterly* 83 (Summer 1976): 219.
[40] "A Racy Chekhov," *Atlantic Advocate*, 66, 5 (January 1966): 71.

MacLennan's fiction, in Buckler's East Coast fiction, in Wilson's elegant novellas, and in Levine's short stories. These writers successfully infused their work with realistic techniques and attitudes, few of them now maintaining the Canadian penchant for romance. Laurence reflected,

> For me and for most of my generation, in Canada anyway, that kind of social realism which took in an analysis of the whole social pattern was not necessary because it had been done by people like Hugh MacLennan, like Ernest Buckler, like Sinclair Ross, and various other people – Morley Callaghan – so that when I began to write I realized quite quickly that what really grabbed me the most, what I really would like to do the most in a novel, was to, as far as possible, present the living individual on the printed page, in all his paradox and all his craziness.[41]

---

[41] *Conversations with Canadian Novelists*, 1, 103.

CHAPTER 4

The Foundational Fifties

With realism slowly supplanting romance as a major mode in fiction, Canadian writing emerged from its romance origins. After the end of World War II, writers were espousing their commitment to the development of fiction along lines which marked the modernistic foundations of their voices.

The Massey Report of 1951 urged the country to broaden support for arts and artists. The Canadian Opera Company traces its origin back to 1950 and the National Ballet of Canada to 1951.The Stratford Shakespearean Festival opened in 1953. The Canada Council for the Arts was established in 1957 to foster the arts. In 1957, Malcolm Ross launched the New Canadian Library to publish out-of-print classics of Canadian literature; in 1959, the quarterly journal *Canadian Literature* began its life at the University of British Columbia. The arts were becoming celebrated across the land. And fiction introduced four major writers, Robertson Davies, Mavis Gallant, Mordecai Richler, and Sheila Watson, as well as a major poet, A.M. Klein, who ventured into the expanding worlds of Canadian fiction; one of them looked back to romances, two of them confronted the reality of the present, and two of them explored new areas leading to innovative forms of fiction.

From his earliest years Robertson Davies, born in Thamesville, Ontario, was interested in the stage. He remembered his first public appearance in an opera when he was only three years old. At Queen's University he was active in the Drama Guild and went on to Balliol College, Oxford, where he obtained his B.Litt. for a thesis he published the following year, *Shakespeare's Boy Actors* (1939).

For Davies, Canada was a land of writers. He began his literary career as a journalist. He filled review pages extolling the writings of world literatures – he particularly loved the novels of Dickens, Arnold Bennett, and the Edwardians – and he appreciated his Canadian world, expressing his reasoned thoughts on de la Roche, MacLennan, and, most of all, Leacock. "There was nothing of the dry humorist or the pawky joker about him. He was plenteous and bountiful in his evocation of laughter," he remarked. "He was in the greatest tradition, not of wit, not of irony or sarcasm, but of true, deep humour, the full and joyous recognition of the Comic Spirit at work in life."[1]

As a humorist, Leacock had, according to Davies, a vision of tragedy while preferring the realm of comedy. He extended people's range of vision by speaking the truth. Yet he was a lonely man, who,

> living among us, fought the solitary fight of the literary artist in a special state of loneliness, for in spite of the vast audience which admired and waited for his work, he was lonely. He lived at a time – a time which is still not completely past – when Canada was ready to acknowledge that a poet or a novelist might be an artist, worthy of the somewhat suspicious and controlled regard which our country accords to artists, but when a humorist was obviously a clown.[2]

Davies identified with his understanding of Leacock's supposed personality.

When he turned to the writing of fiction in the late 1940s, he chose to emulate Leacock in his choice of plot and character. He fashioned his early novels as "the full and joyous recognition of the Comic Spirit at work in life," seeing himself as surpassing Leacock's comic genius, for Leacock restricted himself to the short story: "If Leacock had developed into a genuine heavyweight novelist the course of Canadian literature during the past thirty years would have been very different."[3] There is, however, a strong tradition in Canada which sees the short story not as a novel manqué but as a separate form of art.

Tempest-Tost (1951), Davies's first novel, was "a light and amusing story with a Canadian setting . . . light and amusing stories are rather uncommon at present."[4] Set in the fictional town of Salterton, a thinly disguised Kingston, Ontario, where its author was residing, it follows the many efforts of an amateur theatre group to mount an outdoor production of *The Tempest*. Salterton is "a detailed portrait of an Ontario community which is not only extremely funny, but also ferocious and mordant . . . a self-important, gullible, only moderately honest collection of provincial

---

[1] "Introduction," *Literary Lapses* (Toronto: McClelland & Stewart, 1957), pp. x–xi.
[2] *Our Living Tradition: Seven Canadians*, ed. Claude T. Bissell (University of Toronto Press, 1957), p. 148.
[3] Ibid., p. 142, p. 136.
[4] *Discoveries: Early Letters 1938–1975*, ed. Judith Skelton Grant (Toronto: McClelland & Stewart, 2002), pp. 64–5.

folk." There is, as in Leacock, "love in the portrait, certainly, and indulgence for the folly of humankind."[5]

Leaven of Malice (1954) explores further the foibles and follies of Salterton. It is "a lot better than *Tempest-Tost*. It is about newspaper life in a small Canadian city, and it uses the setting and many of the people from *T-T*. Now *T-T* was criticised for having a thin plot; *LM* has enough plot for a Trollope novel."[6] Another comedy of manners of a small city, it opens with a false notice of an engagement, maliciously published in the Salterton *Evening Bellman*, and through the course of the novel the young pair, wrongfully maligned, realize they care for and love each other. The novel closes, appropriately, with their true wedding announcement. The two comic novels explore the dark underbelly of provincial society, the negative dimensions being the sinister side of provincial society which was left comparatively unexamined in Leacock's sunshine world.

Although Davies was, to this point, an avid follower of Freud, he found Freud's impatience with religion disturbing, and so turned to the Christian writings of Carl Jung, who had come to disagree with a few fundamental principles of Freud, namely his obsession with sex as a primary element in human behaviour as well as his belief that the human unconscious stored repressed emotions. For Jung, and for Davies, the psyche can be understood not only through Freud's dream theories but also through religion and mythology. Human beings have an individual unconscious as well as an inherited collective unconscious which is filled with spiritual archetypes common to all peoples. Jung would now play a major role in Davies's fiction.

The third Salterton novel, *A Mixture of Frailties* (1958), begins with the death of a tyrannical mother, who established a trust fund for the education abroad of a young Salterton woman until such time as her son's wife gives birth to a son. The local recipient of the legacy receives extensive musical training in England from the best singing coach in London, who teaches her to sing with "the most compelling and revealing of sounds"; an international conductor who shows her that dedicated study can lead to self-knowledge; and a formidable composer, who instructs her to extend her range of emotions. Unfortunately, the composer, the embodiment of destructive egotism, commits suicide. The conductor, though much older than her, seeks her hand in marriage. Meanwhile, the son and his wife have a son of their own, thereby regaining his mother's estate.

---

[5] *Our Living Tradition*, p. 147.   [6] *Discoveries*, pp. 100–101.

Davies uses the Jungian collective unconscious to explore the depths of his characters. As the winner explores her musical world, she follows a Jungian path, leading her to a deep knowledge of music and of herself. Davies provides a clear understanding of the townspeople, which distinguishes this novel from its predecessors. The Salterton trilogy reworks Leacock's Mariposa, the third novel exploring more fully the tragedies that lie beneath the town's surface.[7]

When Davies spoke at Glendon College of York University in 1968, his subject, "The Conscience of the Writer," used Jung's writings as its basis. "In the early part of life – roughly for the first half of it – man's chief aims are personal and social," he announced. Then the personal life becomes more complex as the more mature person realizes he is "the object of a supraordinate subject. And he seeks wisdom rather than power . . . . If he has the courage and wisdom to advance courageously into the new realm of values and emotions he will age physically, of course, but his intellectual and spiritual growth will continue, and will give satisfaction to himself and to all those associated with him."[8] Although the address predated *Fifth Business* (1970), Davies's major and finest fictional creation, it outlined the journey of the novel's narrator, Dunstan Ramsay.

Davies returned to Robert Browning's *The Ring and the Book*, a poem he had read first when he was sixteen: "There we have a story told to us by a variety of people, each from his own point of view, each stressing what he thinks important, and each bringing his own understanding of life and his own store of wisdom and egotism to the problem."[9] His books would now be first-person narrations, revealing more about their narrators than they themselves realize.

In a letter to his employer, the headmaster of Colborne College, Ramsay, a seventy-one-year-old teacher, sets out in *Fifth Business* to prove that though he has been teaching there for forty-five years, his life has been adventurous. The novel is

> autobiographical, but not as young men would do it; it will be rather as Dickens wrote *David Copperfield* – a fictional reworking of some things experienced and much re-arranged – a spiritual autobiography in fact, and

---

[7] In 1961 Davies became Master of the new Massey College in the University of Toronto and resided there for twenty years. During this time he sought to make Massey more Oxfordian than the Oxford colleges, looking back to a world which no longer existed, retreating into a dignified if antiquated college system. He was a colonialist, looking to England for the true values of the academic life.

[8] *One Half of Robertson Davies: Provocative Pronouncements on a Wide Range of Topics* (Toronto: Macmillan, 1977), pp. 127–8.

[9] "A Contrast in Novelists," *Saturday Night*, 6 August 1955, p. 21.

not a sweating account of the first time I backed a girl in a corner. I choose
the word 'spiritual' with intent, for during the past ten years the things of
the spirit have become increasingly important to me ... through Carl
Gustav Jung's ever-thickening veils of thought and fantasy I discern something that gives great richness to my life.[10]

Ramsay's life has been a series of epochal moments involving his two
childhood friends, Percy Boyd Staunton and Paul Dempster. When he was
only ten in Deptford (a thinly veiled Thamesville, Ontario, Davies's
birthplace), Staunton throws a snowball at him with a stone in it; when
he ducks, the snowball hits a pregnant Mary Dempster. As a consequence,
she delivers prematurely her son Paul, then proceeds to go mad: she
wanders the town in disarray and with uncertain judgment. Meanwhile
Ramsay befriends Paul, introducing him to the world of magic, and
considers Paul's mother a modern-day saint. After fighting in World
War I, he becomes a teacher and an expert on saints, discovering in his
research truths about himself. In his European travels, he meets the
renowned Magnus Eisengrim, the stage name of his old friend Paul.
When Eisengrim's troupe arrives in Toronto, he discloses to his two
friends that the snowball held a hidden stone. The next day Staunton's
car is dragged from Lake Ontario, his corpse at the wheel and the stone in
his mouth. Like a good Jungian, Ramsay learns that myth, alongside his
study of saints and their miracles, offers a firm foundation for human
identity; the mythic underlies each person's life.

Although Davies was not intending a sequel to *Fifth Business*, he used
many of its characters to explore further Jungian ideas. *The Manticore*
(1972) focuses on Staunton, not through his own testimony but through
the reflective thoughts of his forty-year-old son David, an alcoholic criminal lawyer, who travels to Zurich to undergo analysis at the Jung Institute.
In these sessions David learns that his father, a superficial man, was a poor
parent, who exploited David's fragile ego and encouraged his alcoholism
and his instability. By coincidence – if there are coincidences in Jung's
world! – David travels to St. Gall where he chances upon Ramsay, his
teacher, and Paul Dempster, who explains that his father was not murdered, but committed suicide. Penetrating beyond the personal to the
collective unconscious, he learns he can delve into the primordial connections of the collective unconscious while attending to his personal obliga-
tions in Canada; the inward journey must be taken.

---

[10] *Discoveries*, pp. 211–2.

Although Davies did not intend to write a second trilogy, the success of *The Manticore* convinced him to write one more novel, thus completing the unanticipated trilogy. Now he focuses on his other friend, Paul Dempster, *World of Wonders* (1975) being his autobiography, opening with his involvement with a circus in Deptford and his sexual abuse by Willard the Magician. He becomes the world's leading illusionist and magician. Despite his cruel upbringing, he learns from his past, the collective unconscious being a primary legacy. The world of wonders is the realm beyond mere appearances, the spiritual reality that is the underlying pattern always beckoning to knowing human beings.

With the completion of the so-called Deptford Trilogy, Davies now toyed with the idea of a planned trilogy. His focus is the university with its medieval origins, its unfettered love of enquiry, and its central position in the history of Western civilization. He made his setting, Coulter College, his frame of reference now smaller than it was in his last three novels. *The Rebel Angels* (1981) has two narrators, a twenty-three-year-old graduate student who is studying with a paleo-psychologist researching how medieval people viewed their world, and a middle-aged Anglican priest engaged in writing short biographies of the university's faculty. There is a central problem with these two narrators, for they speak alike, not even trying to voice the cadences of the young woman. The people fall into two categories, the self-absorbed egotists and the more serious egoists, who acknowledge and recognize religion as a mode of feeling and of thought. Religion is an essential component of a great university, offering a moral perspective impossible if people allowed their baser instincts to dominate their thinking. *The Rebel Angels* is a university novel, burdened with factual information and frequently burying its plot under a wealth of detail.

What's Bred in the Bone (1985), the sequel or, more appropriately, the prequel to *The Rebel Angels* and a finalist for the Booker Prize, is a biography of Francis Cornish, a young artist, who attends Colborne College, studies with Ramsay, and, after graduating, continues his schooling at Oxford. Trapped into a bad marriage and subsequently leaving his wife, he swears never to marry again. Thus ends his Jungian apprenticeship and his search for his anima figure as a completion of himself. By his life and his forged art, he proves that art is masterful deception which reveals hidden truths.

In *The Lyre of Orpheus* (1988), the third in this trilogy, Davies brings his knowledge of Victorian theatricals to an opera production. A young doctoral student receives her doctorate, the biography of Cornish is published, and all ends happily. The comic ending emphasizes Davies's primary concern in his fiction, the denouement that is never tragic but essentially comic. His plots reveal the unhappy side of life, including murders and suicides; nevertheless, they have romantic endings with realism kept at a discreet but telling distance.

In his final two novels, *Murther and Walking Spirits* (1991) and *The Cunning Man* (1994), Davies set out to explore the city of Toronto in a projected Toronto trilogy. Essentially a ghost story narrated by a ghost, the former includes one family's history, a history akin to Davies's own: "It is based in the history of my family, and although it is a good deal fictionalized, the basic facts are true, and the whole thing is, in my opinion, truer to the reality of what happened than a strictly historical book would be."[11] The labyrinthine narrative undercutting the innate power of its story, *The Cunning Man* represents an older writer's withdrawal from the ideas of the Deptford trilogy. "I seem to be one of those authors who writes the same book over and over again," he said. "The reason it has cost me so much anxiety is simply old age: I cannot do the job now as readily as I did twenty-five years ago, and there is no great mystery in that."[12]

With a formidable knowledge of literature, Davies set out initially to emulate the comical world of Leacock, painting his Salterton world in the bright colours of Mariposa. As he succeeded in his fictional constructs, he brought to Leacock's vision an understanding of the psychological insights of his mentor, Carl Jung, which added new depth to his fictional world. That world, however, remained the romance, even though Davies had embellished it with a dose of realism. "My books are not novels in the sense of being artistic constructs formed on something which reaches back to a French origin, or Henry James, or something," he admitted. "They're romances. I just write romances, and when you write romances you have to be Scheherezade [sic] and bear in mind that if you do not hold the Caliph's attention he will cut your head off in the morning."[13]

Davies's fiction did not admit emulators or progeny. His world was his own. Although a bestselling author, he was a solitary writer, fashioning his well-told stories for his reading public, few of whom knew the restricted Canadian worlds he was depicting or the bygone worlds of England he was evoking.

In early 1951, John Sutherland (1919–56), the editor of the little magazine *Northern Review*, invited Mavis Gallant (1922–2014), who had published

---

[11] *For Your Eye Alone*, p. 242.   [12] Ibid., p. 295.
[13] "Interview: Robertson Davies in conversation with Michael Hulse," *Journal of Commonwealth Literature* 22, 1 (1987): 134.

a story in his journal, to have lunch with another Montrealer, twenty-year-old Mordecai Richler (1931–2001), who was intending to leave Canada to travel in Europe. She was a devotee of Montreal, unique in her eyes for its "two solitudes" of the English and the French, a city "unique, unclassifiable. All those small worlds of race and language and religion and class, all shut away from one another. A series of airtight compartments. But a handsome city, the most attractive imaginable."[14] Unlike Gallant, Richler found the city stifling: "I wasn't going somewhere as much as I was getting to hell out of Montreal which I found suffocating and excruciatingly boring and provincial."[15] Both young writers wanted to be on the world's stages.

Like Callaghan and Davies, Gallant had an early career in journalism, though, unlike them, she never pursued a university education. After briefly working in the cutting room of the National Film Board of Canada in Ottawa, she took a position as a reporter for the *Montreal Standard*. "Newspaper work was my apprenticeship," she wrote,[16] which meant piecing together the details of her stories and giving her the background and the preparation for her career as a writer of fiction. She remained with the *Standard* for six years. In her many articles and profiles, she reveals an encyclopedic range of interests from Freud and psychoanalysis to contemporary happenings in Montreal, across Canada, and around the world. Her articles display a solid reading in both English and French writing in Canada as well as a thorough familiarity with the Quebec and the Canadian cultural scenes, her features including profiles of such important figures as Paul Hiebert and Roger Lemelin, MacLennan and Gabrielle Roy. She also wrote features on war brides, immigrants, and displaced people in alien cultures, the people who would populate her later stories.

Her articles also portray the sad life awaiting writers in Canada. As early as 1946, she queried the stagnant life of Canadians. "Caution and neutrality, our most distinctive traits, have kept us from producing anything new and original in every field but radio," she reported, adding that "Canadians get violent over Americanization, yet nine times out of ten won't buy, read, or listen to a home-grown product," and concluding, "We have driven so many creative people to more congenial surroundings."[17] Three years later, she was even more explicit: "In voice and

---

[14] "An Interview with Mavis Gallant," *Canadian Fiction Magazine* 28 (1978): 25.
[15] *Eleven Canadian Novelists* (Toronto: House of Anansi Press, 1973), p. 281.
[16] *The Selected Stories of Mavis Gallant* (Toronto: McClelland & Stewart, 1996), p. xiii.
[17] "Why Are We Canadians So Dull?" The *Standard*, 30 March 1946, pp. 2–3.

opinions most of the speakers vary from the academic groan to the petulant whine. Over everything they say, in the case of the book critics, lies the terrible pall of Canadian literary pedantry, that feeling that the speaker has read all the back issues of Partisan Revue and is just as smart as anyone else."[18] Her response was to leave Canada for a congenial home abroad.

Although steadfastly Canadian – "a Canadian is someone who has a logical reason to think he is one. My logical reason is that I have never been anything else, nor has it occurred to me that I might be"[19] – she left Montreal to become an international author, someone who wrote about people everywhere unfettered by geographical restrictions. She travelled through Europe, settling permanently in Paris, where she continued to write in English.

"I owe it to children's books – picture books, storybooks, then English and American classics – that I absorbed once and for all the rhythm of English prose, the order of words in an English sentence and how they are spelled," she reflected.[20] Although she would spell out her major influences, Guy de Maupassant, Chekhov, Hemingway, and Katherine Mansfield, she was familiar, too, with Canadian literature, including Leacock's comic tales, Callaghan's short stories, and the many contemporary writers featured in her *Standard* profiles. By early 1951, now ensconced in Paris, she turned her full attention to fiction writing.

Gallant made the short story her chosen, indeed her favourite, form. In more than fifty years of short fiction, she perfected the genre, using it to cast light on contemporary reality. As her principal focus, she always chooses alien, often alienated, people, either refugees, expatriates, or exiles from their homeland, and studies them in their reactions to the people and the places where they are resident; ultimately, they come to know or not to know themselves. Over the entire situation, Gallant's irony operates, her sense of the interior life that may or may not ensnare her characters.

In the title story of her first collection, *The Other Paris* (1956), Carol, a middle-class twenty-two-year-old American woman, has come to Paris in the postwar 1950s; shortly after she arrives, she finds herself engaged to her boss, corporation-minded Howard Mitchell: "The fact that Carol was not in love with Howard Mitchell did not dismay her in the least." The bitter irony of this observation focuses on Carol herself, a romantic figure who

---

[18] "On the Air," The *Standard,* 26 March 1949, p. 7.
[19] *Home Truths* (Toronto: Macmillan, 1981), p. xiii.
[20] *The Selected Stories of Mavis Gallant,* p. xvi.

cannot understand the Paris world around her. She came to experience the gay life she had encountered in the pages of books: "Where was the Paris she had read about? Where were the elegant and expensive-looking women?" But all she meets are "only shabby girls bundled into raincoats, hurrying along in the rain, or men who needed a haircut."

In contrast to the loveless engagement of Carol and Howard stand Odile, Howard's secretary, and her young lover Felix, "Austrian, [Howard] thought, or Czech," himself an indication of the massive displacements of the postwar years. Although Odile is ashamed of Felix in front of her family, she takes Carol to his dingy lodgings, and the unsuitability of Carol's own engagement becomes painfully clear. When Carol leaves, Felix walks her to the local metro station and holds her hand; "standing under the noisy trains on the dark, dusty boulevard, she felt that she had at last opened the right door, turned down the right street, glimpsed the vision toward which she had struggled on winter evenings." But this interior life she closes abruptly and resentfully: "What she and Howard had was better. No one could point to them, or criticize them, or humiliate them by offering to help."

In the end, Carol settles for her own engagement, believing that Howard would fulfill her desires. She will forget the dismal world of Paris; she will not recall Odile and Felix; she will remember instead the Paris of films, "and there would be, at last, a coherent picture, accurate but untrue." Carol's "memory" avoids the reality of postwar Paris; in fact, her flight to an untrue portrait is her eradication of the world she inhabited so fully but for such a brief time.

"The Other Paris" captures with precise details the world of postwar Paris with its poorly dressed people, spartan restaurants, and the incessant drizzle that engulfs all the people. This is the tangible background to the realist fiction which is the story itself, the horrid tale of Carol, who must avoid any attempt to break down her formidable enclosure. Gallant's irony functions well at the story's conclusion. Carol will make her memory conform to what she wants to remember, an easier solution than confronting the reality of what she has seen.

In the early 1960s, Gallant began her travels in Germany, a country which had horrified her since her days at the *Standard* when she had written about it; under the Third Reich life had reached such irrationality that reasoned explanations might distort the nature of the tragedy. Gallant's own repugnance for the war crimes meant that it was, until this time, impossible for her to venture into Germany. Her German short stories started appearing in 1963, many of them collected in *The Pegnitz Junction* (1973). Dealing not with the war years but with the postwar years and the Germans' response to their own history, the tales often feature people who have lived through the war, the past still haunting their precarious present.

In "The Old Friends," for example, Helena, a well-known West German television actress and a survivor of the Nazi persecutions, meets an unnamed fifty-three-year-old police commissioner for tea at "a garden restaurant on a height of land above Frankfurt." Accompanied by her young son from an unknown relationship ("The rumor is that the father was an American, but not a common drunken one, an Occupation leftover – no, it was someone highly placed, worthy of her."), she enchants her doting companion. In their conversations she allows him to pay her loving attention, then wounds him with repeated references to the death camps, her murdered family, and her own Jewish origins. As she recounts her personal history, the act of remembering filled with terror, her revelations cannot adequately encompass the absolute evil that is Nazism. She was the child who was rescued by chance from transport to the death camps.

These "old friends" are not "old friends," but only acquaintances; they are old friends only in the most ironic sense. Their conversation, always amiable, is constantly interrupted by her casual references to her family, her background, and her Jewish grandmother, who was killed in Silesia during the war. What began as a superficial acquaintanceship becomes an encounter between historical victim and willing victimizer, who now wants to exonerate himself from the known past. In his thoughtless rewriting of the past, he references a mental folder, so like the Gestapo files that arbitrarily assigned human beings to the death camps.

Helena's own rewriting of her history is equally suspect. She refuses to draw a clear picture of it, telling "a story that has long ago ceased to be personal." Although the death camps maintained that rape was forbidden, they reduce Helena to a number, obliterating her personal identity. In her reminiscences she seeks not to rewrite the past but to obliterate her full memories. In spite of her past, she, too, wants to live.

In "The Old Friends," as in so many Gallant stories, the narrator, frequently a third-person figure, stands outside the text with a detached voice, recounting the story and keeping appropriate distance from the tale. People can manipulate their history; they can falsify their own memories. Readers remark on the seeming multiplicity of voices and perspectives in Gallant's fictional universe. What they are sensing is Gallant's positioning of herself outside the story, creating a unique world in which the characters stumble through a series of awkward movements. The follies of our age she casts before us in their many variations, inviting us to see the complexities of her characters and the apparent rootlessness of modern life.

Although her characters are usually exiles from their homeland and often exiles from themselves, the French and German inhabitants are complemented by the many Canadians who also populate her fiction. Her editor-titled collection, *Home Truths: Selected Canadian Stories* (1981), brings together many stories of the preceding twenty years, including the six stories of Linnet Muir, a semi-autobiographical portrait of the young Gallant in Montreal. She often wrote her earlier stories about expatriates who had lost so many of their physical and mental possessions; as these figures begin to explore European landscapes, cut off as they are from their roots, they are similarly removed from their history and culture. In Linnet, who "is obviously close to me. She isn't *myself*, but a kind of summary of some of the things I once was,"[21] she portrays the return journey from exile to identity. Linnet comes home to rediscover her home, recreating the past from a route through history; she looks back in order to see her own past and to gain her selfhood in the contemporary world.

Gallant continued to write short stories. Her last collection, *Across the Bridge* (1993), unites tales of Montreal with stories of Paris. In the title story, an evocation of Paris in the 1950s, Sylvie Castelli rejects her father's proposed marriage of convenience; she longs for her true beloved, whom she has met only once. The arranged marriage is cancelled, her proposed marriage then rejected, and Sylvie must rekindle her father's proposed situation. At the end, Gallant's penchant for irony allows the naïve heroine a modicum of happiness.

Like Callaghan and Wilson, who sought American and British journals for their fiction, Gallant published in *The New Yorker*, evidence for the limitations of Canada's literary scene. *The New Yorker* proved ideal for Gallant, offering her fine editors for her stories and the necessary audience for this cosmopolitan author.

Gallant also published two novels: *Green Water, Green Sky* (1959) and *A Fairly Good Time* (1970). The former results from her uniting of three connected short stories, "Green Water, Green Sky," "August," and "Travellers Must Be Content," now with a brief concluding section; the latter began as the short story, "The Accident."

An examination of young Florence Fairlie's descent into madness, *Green Water, Green Sky* presents a kaleidoscope of images of a young woman smothered by her divorced mother, who understands personal identity only marked by social status and money. An American teenager now based in Paris, Flor is the subject of her mother's claustrophobic attachment and

---

[21] "An Interview with Mavis Gallant," p. 28.

her deluded aspirations for her daughter's future. The unnatural bond between mother and daughter is the first step on the road to Flor's mental breakdown, and her mother's constant manoeuvres finally cut off Flor's links to her past and destroy her fragile sanity. Flor continues to persist in the other characters' memories, even when she is lodged at "a sort of rest place," a mental institution outside of Paris, where she is a memoryless inhabitant. Her decline into madness cannot be stopped.

In *A Fairly Good Time*, Shirley Pettigny, a Canadian married to a Parisienne, is in the midst of a dissolving marriage. Her husband Philippe with his middle-class family background represents the triumph of reason and order; he lives confident in the stability of his own life, walking out on his wife because of the chaos of her mind. "Comfortable in chaos," Shirley represents the supposedly weaker version of the feminine role. Set in and around Paris from June 1963 until April 1964, the novel chronicles in a non-traditional, structural frame a Canadian expatriate's slow emergence into a reasonable, almost formidable human being. Shirley is a feminist protagonist, a victim of the male privileges of French society, for Gallant comically condemns women's subservient positions in nearly all aspects of life. All the females are subject to the oppression of males with their completely sanctioned power bases, exerting tyrannical control. Against all these people, women as well as men, Shirley slowly comes to realize her own personal identity, her divorce itself having freed her so that she can finally be herself.

Both novels examine women's adventures on the road to madness or to a much needed personal identity. Florence descends to madness, Shirley rises to self-understanding, conducive now to having "a fairly good time." When the woman is removed from her past, displaced from and deprived of any markers of her past, her origins, and herself, she will fall, as Florence does, or she will rise up to some degree of autonomy. Whereas *Green Water, Green Sky* is tragic, *A Fairly Good Time* is ultimately comic in the determined persistence of Shirley, leading her to an optimistic ending to her story.

In all her fiction, Gallant shows a preference for the short story; the novel eluded her talent. Her stories offer a mirror on contemporary reality in Europe and in North America. Her authorial neutrality testifies to her consistent attempts to highlight portraits of dislocated people, often cut off from their past or alien in their present, portraits that invite readers to unmask or see more clearly her characters, who often hide under layers of accumulated personal histories they may or may not know. She is, as Davies noted,

a great mistress of the art of implication. Her writing is beautifully economical, and by a hint here and a simple statement of fact there she
contrives to give us finely realized portraits of her characters, so that by
the end of one of her short stories we know the people better than those we
meet in many a full-length novel. We have learned enough about their past,
and have had enough hints about their future, to make their present firmly
apparent.[22]

She was, as Richler observed, "our most compelling short story writer since
Callaghan."[23]

Gallant's vision of the complexities of lives caught in the quagmires of
contemporary life placed her stories, along with those of Callaghan and
Wilson, on the permanent shelves of short fiction writers. Future generations, including such varied writers as Rohinton Mistry (b. 1952) and Lisa
Moore (b. 1964), would read her for the strength and the intricacies of her
fictional worlds.

Brought up in the orthodox Jewish faith, which he soon set aside,
Mordecai Richler had some background in his own country's fiction. He
knew well the writings of Leacock, who, he averred, was the only literary
ghost staring down on the young writers of Canada. He respected the
fiction of Callaghan, especially the short stories ("surely our most talented
writer ... his short stories are superb and add up to the best work ever to
have come out of Canada"),[24] and sought early in his career to begin a
correspondence with him; Callaghan politely turned him down; to him
Richler dedicated his anthology, *Canadian Writing Today* (1970). He also
knew the fiction of MacLennan and Wilson and of Lemelin and Roy. He
was most influenced, however, by American writers, including
Hemingway and Fitzgerald, Dos Passos and Faulkner, and Norman
Mailer and William Styron. Then in Europe he continued to devour the
writings of André Malraux and Jean-Paul Sartre. Unlike Gallant, who
claims the short story as her own, he prefers the less confined and
confining world of the novel, where he "set down a sort of honest record
of things of our time and our place."[25]

Richler's first published novel, *The Acrobats* (1954) – his earlier unpublished novel, *The Rotten People*, has disappeared – explores Franco's
postwar years of the early 1950s. The young protagonist is a Canadian

[22] "Afterword," Mavis Gallant, *Across the Bridge* (Toronto: McClelland & Stewart, 1997), p. 208.
[23] "Maple Leaf Culture Time," *Shovelling Trouble* (Toronto: McClelland & Stewart, 1972), p. 147.
[24] "O Canada," *Hunting Tigers Under Glass* (Toronto: McClelland & Stewart, 1968), p. 18.
[25] *Eleven Canadian Novelists*, p. 271.

expatriate painter, André Bennett, living in a rat-infested hotel in Valencia, having escaped his tedious life in Canada as the son of a wealthy father and his socialite wife and leaving behind the botched abortion and subsequent death of his Jewish girlfriend. He admires the International Brigades who assigned to themselves the defence of Spain; they epitomize the world of honour and truth, virtues he (and Richler) found lacking in their own times. But he comes to see that these once-idealistic men have "proven either duds or counterfeits – standing up in the thirties to cheer the revolution hoarsely, and in the fifties sitting down again to write a shy, tinny, blushing yes to capitalistic democracy." Although *The Acrobats* raises weighty issues, it never probes them in depth. The novel is Richler's apprentice work fashioned according to the writers he has been reading, including Malraux, Sartre, and Hemingway. His world is a post-Hemingway Spain where all romanticism has disappeared, where all rapture has gone.

Son of a Smaller Hero (1955) marks Richler's first treatment of Montreal's Jewish world. Presented in immense detail, it is neither complimentary nor denunciatory. Often wrongly condemned for being anti-Semitic, Richler paints his people as they are, never fearing to show the positive as well as the negative aspects of his characters. Noah Adler, the twenty-year-old titular hero, is the eldest grandson of Melech Adler, who rules his extended family with seeming justice based on punishment, firm in his belief in a vengeful God. He has moved into a downtown apartment, intent on finding his own way in the modern world. A born dreamer, always willing to see beyond the immediate, he seeks to know and cherish freedom in his own life. Although he feels isolated in his new home, he must define himself apart from the ghetto he has known. As a young boy of eleven, he had witnessed unethical dealings on his grandfather's part. This incident remains a vivid memory. Later, when his own father dies trying to rescue a secret padlocked box belonging to his father, he cannot believe the common understanding that his father was attempting to save the Torah inside the box, for he knew that his father believed that money was hidden there. What he seeks is knowledge of himself which is independent of all other people, finding his own livelihood apart from everyone else. He flees at the end, literally and figuratively, to Europe.

Unlike the serious tale of *The Acrobats*, *Son of a Smaller Hero* has fine comic moments, most notably the funeral of Noah's father with its cinematic montage of all the characters. "I've been enormously influenced by film, and it's a large part of our culture experience, so that we've absorbed certain film techniques into our novel writing," Richler reflected.

"We were accustomed to the quick dissolves and time-changes, we were all brought up on film and so part of the story-telling technique in film has become part of our novel-writing technique."[26] Movies will become a more pronounced presence in his later novels.

Son of a Smaller Hero is Richler's bildungsroman, a compassionate portrait of the artist as a young man, determined to break away from his ghetto upbringing and yet still uncertain of where the road will lead, certain only that the road must be taken. Noah begins to create his own self as the novel ends, his ethical independence now a part of his being.

A Choice of Enemies (1957) is *The Acrobats* in a London, England setting with the hero, Norman Price, a Canadian university professor who abandoned his teaching position in the United States for his socialist convictions. Like André Bennett and Noah Adler, Price learns that as a free individual he is not to embrace a community of people but to define himself as his own person. Through him, Richler argues that man is responsible for what he makes of himself.

The Apprenticeship of Duddy Kravitz (1959) returned to the Jewish Montreal of the 1940s for a comic tale of the rags-to-riches saga of the gifted young entrepreneur Duddy Kravitz. Much more humorous than the introspective story of Noah Adler's coming-to-maturity, it begins in the ghetto where Duddy is struggling as a sixteen-year-old for understanding and recognition from his unsympathetic family. To win their esteem and to gain his own financial independence, he tries to buy all the land around Lac St. Pierre, a beautiful region of the Laurentians, with the intention of establishing a holiday resort. He exploits other people; he lies and cheats; he uses his devoted French-Canadian lover Yvette and his epileptic friend Virgil. Yet he also reveals, as did Noah, sympathetic concern for members of his family, including his brother, who is saved by Duddy after he performs an illegal abortion, and his grandfather, who had cautioned him, "A man without land is nobody." Richler was ambivalent about his comic creation, revering him and despising him: "The moral idea behind Duddy," he said, "was to get inside, and show how sympathetic in many ways, the go-getter, the guy nobody has time for ... really is."[27] But Duddy is trapped by the business jungle surrounding him: his cruel and selfish deeds must be weighed against that environment, and he is a product of this world, learning from the mercenary examples thrust before him. Although "the scheming little bastard" who is Duddy is in evidence,

[26] Ibid., p. 272.
[27] Charles Foran, *Mordecai: The Life & Times* (Toronto: Knopf, 2010), pp. 245–6.

the "fine, intelligent boy" is also there in his land schemes, driven in part by his treatment of his brother and his comforting of Aunt Ida when her husband is dying of cancer.

Confessing that with this novel he had found his own style, "and then it all became easier in a way because it was all my own,"[28] Richler was acknowledging himself as a writer of comic fiction. Although he sometimes depicts the Jewish community as intolerant and ignorant, his satire extends to many groups, for he is keen to expose the hypocrisies that emerge when groups are unwilling to communicate. The world of manhood is a world of compromise, corruption, and ignorance. This rite, shared by many men and exemplified by the many corrupt figures Duddy encounters, fails to anticipate the type of men these boys become. Duddy Kravitz is both repellant in all his vices and charming in his few selfless moments. Richler presents him as an intricate and compelling figure, daring his readers to judge him.

This comic novel with its satiric moments leads to pure satire in *The Incomparable Atuk* (1963), a pungent account of a resourceful Baffin Island poet, who is brought to Toronto by a fur company and becomes the centre of attention for the city's cultural and social circles. Richler is not being anti-Canadian; he is being anti-everyone who seeks personal rewards at the expense of society; his society contains no one who sets up proper standards. Although focusing on Canada, he is satirizing all countries that are pretentiously pursuing false goals, that highlight the trivial, failing to notice the light of reason and justice. The cultural and social circles of swinging-sixties London are the setting for Richler's still more savage work, *Cocksure* (1968), "a satire dealing with caricatures and extremes and not with people."[29] The novel watches an "easily or glibly dismissed, middle-class, decent, bill-paying, honourable man" facing an immoral world.[30] Believing "in the possibilities within each of us for goodness," the hero strives to be himself, living by traditional values, in the face of continual harassment and persecution.

Richler's satires have the audacity and daring of Swift's, written as they are out of savage indignation and disgust at the ways of the contemporary world. "The book is a satire of those obscenities of thought, conduct and prejudice which a permissive society is so rapidly making available," remarked Anthony Burgess. "The moral force of the satire would have been much diminished if he hadn't deliberately rubbed away at the sore of

---

[28] *Eleven Canadian Novelists*, p. 279.   [29] Ibid., p. 287.
[30] *Conversations with Canadian Novelists*, 2, 117.

his own disgust."[31] The final word on the satires, however, belongs to the satirist himself. Asked about the novelist's role, Richler reflected: "I'm an unfrocked priest . . . . It's a moral office, and if I can leave one book behind, then that's the most I can hope for. If it can be said that I was an honest witness to my times, I would consider I've done my work well."[32] He chose satire as his weapon to deplore society's wanton disregard of traditional values.

In his last four novels, Richler returns to Jewish Montreal, creating massive canvases, eschewing a chronological time sequence, and incorporating as his central character an artistic man all too familiar with modern life.

St. Urbain's Horseman (1971), a finalist for the Booker Prize, depicts the complicated life of Jake Hersh from Duddy Kravitz's world, a thirty-seven-year-old successful but beleaguered London film director who left his native Montreal fourteen years earlier. Though a film director for the Canadian Broadcasting Corporation in Toronto, he found himself culturally suffocated in Canada and left for England. A decent man trapped in the machinations and evils of the world around him, he is standing trial for indecent assault, marijuana possession, rape, and sodomy. As he reviews his life, he looks back to his cousin Joey, known as the Horseman, whom he has known since they were kids on St. Urbain's Street. His memories point to an adventurous cousin, far from the straight man Jake is, who has been searching for Dr. Joseph Mengele, the Nazi war criminal and his personal antagonist, in the Paraguayan jungles. Jake always admired, indeed idolized Joey, and his life seems to be proof that evil will ultimately be punished. Meanwhile, in his trial, Jake and his Cockney acquaintance, his accountant's assistant Harry Stein, are convicted, though they are both innocent. For his part, Jake is fined five hundred pounds; Stein is sent off to prison. Now Jake can begin to pick up the pieces of his shattered life.

In a technique which now becomes standard in Richler's novels, the time sequence is carefully and deliberately non-linear. Although the current action covers only a few days, from Jake's appearance at the Old Bailey to a little while after the third and final day of the trial, flashbacks fill in Jake's Montreal childhood and later his time in Toronto, his first meeting with his wife-to-be, and many other earlier experiences. His present is conditioned by his past, which always haunts him.

Underneath the novel's many comic moments lies Richler's significant treatment of the Holocaust, which reveals his passionate commitment to

---

[31] *Mordecai: The Life & Times*, pp. 350–1. [32] *Eleven Canadian Novelists*, pp. 298–9.

and thorough knowledge of the subject. Drawn from a variety of sources, his account of Dr. Mengele, the officer in charge of the selection of victims, and his subsequent escape to South America, is true to fact, as is his account, for example, of the unsuccessful attempt of Hungarian Jews to buy Jewish lives in exchange for money and war materials. Richler focuses on the truth of his material, quoting from reliable printed accounts of the subject, wanting to be an honest witness to his times.

Written after his permanent return to Canada in 1972 and after the victory of the Parti Québécois in 1976, *Joshua Then and Now* (1980), adhering to a complex non-linear time sequence, focuses on the life, "then and now," of its forty-seven-year-old protagonist, Joshua Shapiro, another St. Urbain's Street boy. In the spring of 1978, Joshua, a distinguished journalist, television personality, and Westmount resident, is recovering from a critical car accident while his wife, Pauline, is suffering a nervous breakdown, caused by her brother's suicide; she had refused to give false testimony that might have acquitted him of embezzlement. Joshua, meanwhile, is being hounded by newspaper accounts of his supposed homosexuality, which began with letters he and another writer composed for the purpose of selling them to unsuspecting university libraries eager to acquire literary manuscripts. This story comprises the "now" of the book. The "then" is all the episodes of the past that intersect with Joshua's present life, including his relationship with his parents; his London life, where he woos Pauline, a Canadian senator's daughter; and his passionate experiences as a twenty-one-year-old in Ibiza. Intensely moral and responsible, though he shows some malicious streaks to his otherwise good character, he sifts through his past, attempting to understand both the past and the consequent meaning of the present.

Like *St. Urbain's Horseman*, *Joshua Then and Now* recounts an informed writer's look back at the events that created him. But unlike Jake Hersh, Joshua is intensely conscious of the passing of the years, of his own mortality in the face of time's constantly vengeful regard. His understanding of the past's influence on the present reminds him constantly of his growing awareness of man's mortality and of his own.

To recount the family saga of five generations of Gurskys, the noted Montreal bootleggers and errant rascals, Richler creates Moses Berger in *Solomon Gursky Was Here* (1989), another Booker finalist, a drunken writer and ex-academic, the son of "L.B. Berger, the noted Montreal poet and short-story writer" and a Gursky speech writer, to write the biography of Solomon Gursky, later reincarnated as Sir Hyman Kaplansky. Through this fifty-two-year-old, he distances himself from his protagonist, establishing him as the pitiable son of a father noted not for his writing but for self-serving artistic weakness and need. Following again a non-linear time sequence (now through the generations), the novel explores the Gursky stock, beginning in 1851 around Magog with the local people falling under the spell of the riddling "Brother Ephraim," swindler and founder of the Church of the Millenarians, and continuing to 1983, again near Magog, with Moses Berger seemingly adrift in vacuous meanderings, still contemplating the subject of his incomplete biography and still trying to sort out fact from fiction. Underneath the outrageous comedy and dirty dealings which characterize the Gursky family appears a deeply moral Richler, who targets the rich for their stupidity, their tyranny, and, above all, their greed on the corporate as well as the personal level.

In his tenth and final novel *Barney's Version* (1997), Richler writes for the first time in the first person, Barney Panofsky penning his autobiography, "the true story of my wasted life (violating a solemn pledge, scribbling a first book at my advanced age." Sixty-seven-years old, Barney was one of the friends of young Duddy Kravitz, and his Montreal world is the centre of his sometimes incoherent meanderings. Suffering from Alzheimer's, he is trying desperately to shore up these fragments against his own ruin. A film and television producer and writer, Barney has had three wives, thus dividing his reminiscences into three not-wholly-distinct parts: Clara 1950–52, who "had no time for other women and is enjoying an afterlife as a feminist icon"; the Second Mrs. Panofsky 1958–60, "an exemplar of that much-maligned phenomenon, the Jewish-American Princess"; and Miriam, 1960–, his one true beloved. As he tries to summon his memories, he cannot adhere to these divisions; memories overlap one another, and he is powerless to give full expression to his own thoughts. The comedy of the opening chapters gives way to the increasing tragedy of the closing chapters when Barney can no longer express his ideas coherently. His eldest son annotates his father's lopsided book, appending an afterword which chronicles Barney's descent into oblivion, though his many correcting footnotes reveal the traps baited just for his son.

Again eschewing a chronological order for a non-linear time sequence, which mirrors Barney's drifting mental capacities, Richler creates a comic and tragic masterpiece. Although the moments of comedy are hysterical, the overall tone is one of melancholy and sadness. "Oh God, it's too late for Barney," the novel ends. "He's beyond understanding now. Damn damn damn." Loveable and laughable, Barney Panofsky, Richler's supreme creation, is reduced to silence.

In his ten novels, written over a period of more than forty-five years, Richler mapped out his terrain as a comic novelist who could see both the comedy and the tragedy of human life. His six major books, *Son of a Smaller Hero*, *The Apprenticeship of Duddy Kravitz*, *St. Urbain's Horseman*, *Joshua Then and Now*, *Solomon Gursky Was Here*, and *Barney's Version*, paint the Jewish world of Montreal. Looking closely at the dimensions of his territory, he depicts it so lovingly and so exactly that it becomes a microcosm of a world both Jewish and non-Jewish. "I'm staking out a claim on Montreal Jew-ville in the tradition of H. de Balzac and Big Bill Faulkner,"[33] he stated early in his career. But his vision extends far beyond his creation of Canada's version of Faulkner's Yoknapatawpha County. From the beginning of his career he was engaged "with values, and with honour. I would say I'm a moralist, really. You may not find whatever code of honour I'm groping for as a way to live, acceptable, but that's really my obsession. And like most serious novelists I have one or two ideas and many many variations to play on them."[34] He sought to discover what would happen to an individual caught up in the frenzy of the modern world. An honest witness, he showed our times, rarely the past, keeping his vision fixed relentlessly on the present.

Richler "did not want to be known as a Canadian writer or a Jewish writer, but as *a writer*, to be measured against all other writers."[35] He was "the one serious writer we had who was sharp, funny, and unafraid," says Munro, "and that was rather startling for Canadian writing of the period."[36] "For my generation," Atwood reflects, "he was a trailblazer who went on to create and occupy a unique place in our national life and literature."[37]

While Gallant and Richler were fleeing the apparent provincialism of Canada for the international worlds of Europe, A.M. Klein (1909–72) was content to remain in Canada. Born in the Ukraine, which his family left when he was a year old, he received his BA in Classics and Political Science from McGill University and took his law degree from the Université de Montréal, then practiced law in Montreal until his retirement in 1956.

[33] *Mordecai: The Life & Times*, p. 245.   [34] *Conversations with Canadian Novelists*, 2, 124.
[35] Ted Kotcheff, "Afterword," *The Acrobats* (Toronto: McClelland & Stewart, 2002), p. 213.
[36] Conversation with the author, 10 July 2013.
[37] "Mordecai Richler: 1931–2001: Diogenes of Montreal," *Curious Pursuits: Occasional Writing 1970–2005* (London: Virago, 2005), p. 244.

One of Canada's more distinguished poets, he examined his personal relationship to his Jewish heritage in his early work. Then, distressed by the rise of Nazism, he moved into political and social satire. His final volume of poetry, *The Rocking Chair and Other Poems* (1948), explores and responds to a broad spectrum of Canadian traditions. In *Solomon Gursky Was Here*, Richler made him a possible basis for L.B. Berger, who "was sustained by larger ambitions and had already seen his poetry published in English-language little magazines in Montreal and Toronto, as well as once in *Poetry Chicago*." Then businessman Bernard Gursky offered him an annual retainer of ten thousand dollars to serve as his speech writer and cultural advisor. Berger accepted, Gursky giving public addresses using the poet's unacknowledged eloquence. Klein's one novel, *The Second Scroll* (1951), is a unique literary work, though it is not quite a novel, for it also includes a number of poems and fragments of verse drama.

In keeping with Klein's studies into the history of Jewish traditions, his novel delineates the Jewish scene, both historical and contemporary: the historical is the time between 1917, when Russian pogroms filled Jewish settlements with dread, and 1949, a year after Israel was formed. The story reflects the sufferings of Jews, their forced exodus from Europe, and their return to Israel, the Promised Land. Klein sees in contemporary events the remarkable achievements of the Jewish people, testimony to their destiny, which can be explained only in religious terminology. The loss of faith in God and its recovery – with a closing return to Israel, newly formed as an independent nation – constitute the novel's theme, and the eternal problem of the existence of evil has an important bearing on human beings' relationship to God and on God's relationship to human beings.

As the novel opens, Melech Davidson, a devout and dutiful scholar, confronts the atrocities in Russia in 1917. Unable to reconcile his belief in a loving God with the unspeakable depravities he witnesses, he pursues political battles, ending up as the sole Holocaust survivor of the appalling Jewish massacre at Kamenets. This experience leads him to identify completely with the martyred Jews and to express their lives in and through his own.

A Jewish Canadian journalist, his nephew is travelling to Israel to discover for his publishers the poetry of the reborn people; he has never met or even seen his uncle. He rhapsodizes,

> My life was, and is, bound to the country of my father's choice, to Canada; but this intelligence, issuing, as it did, from that quarter of the globe which had ever been to me the holiest of the map's bleeding stigmata, the Palestine whose geography was as intimately known as the lines of the palm of my

hand, filled me with pride, with exaltation, with an afflatus odorous of the royal breath of Solomon. . . . I was like one that dreamed. I, surely, had not been of the captivity; but when the Lord turned again the captivity of Zion, I was like one that dreamed.

He pursues Davidson's travels, following in his footsteps and finding in Casablanca his photograph, "a double, a multiple exposure." Then, in Israel, he comes to understand his uncle's role as the exiled Jew in a quest for truth. Before he has glimpsed his uncle, the latter is fatally shot by an Arab gang. At his grave, the nephew understands his uncle's spiritual embodiment of his race.

The Second Scroll focuses on the persecution of European Jewry and Klein's identification with the people and the land of Israel. As a Canadian Jew cut off from the Holocaust as well as from the founding of the state of Israel, Klein writes an impassioned account of one man's search for his God amid the painful realities of contemporary Europe. An ambitious experiment with form, the novel breaks up a strictly linear chronology and employs several narrative perspectives to focus on the plight of people trying to assert their own humanity.

A confirmed resident of Canada like Klein himself, Sheila Watson (1909–98), a native of New Westminster, British Columbia, sought to know how to be international within Canada:

> I began the writing of *The Double Hook* as an answer to a challenge . . . that you could not write about particular places in Canada: that what you'd end up with was a regional novel of some kind. It was at the time, I suppose, when people were thinking that if you wrote a novel it had to be, in some mysterious way, international. It had to be about what I would call something *else*. And so I thought, I don't see why: how do you . . . how are you international if you're not international? If you're very provincial, very local, and very much a part of your own milieu.[38]

Therefore, she set out to write fiction which denied any difference in the life lived in the local community and the life lived at the centre.

A devoted reader of the modernists, Joyce and Eliot, Faulkner and Wyndham Lewis – Watson received her BA and MA from the University of British Columbia and wrote her doctoral dissertation later at the University of Toronto on Lewis under the supervision of Marshall McLuhan – she decided to write about the only world she knew well, the

---

[38] "What I'm Going To Do," *Open Letter*, third series, 1 (Winter 1974–1975): 182.

world of Dog Creek in the Cariboo country of interior British Columbia. Going there as a teacher in 1934, she had no intention of writing about it; she went there to teach: "I didn't choose, it chose me." Slowly she realized "that if I had something I wanted to say, it was going to be said in these images."[39] For two years Dog Creek became her home.

Writing about British Columbia, Watson knew too well the dilemma of the colonial artist. British Columbia was emblematic of the country's colonialism; even its name celebrates a colonial mentality. The province, remote from whatever may seem to be the centre of Canada, redoubled Canada's own remoteness from the imperial centre. The British Columbia where Watson was born and educated was conscious of its status as province and colony, firm in its belief that whatever is significant takes place elsewhere. In her writing, she rejected regionalism, the seeming emancipatory force in the development of Canadian fiction as confining and limiting.

Her first novel, *Deep Hollow Creek* (1992), written in 1937–38 but not published for more than fifty years, focuses on a young woman's time in a small settlement in the British Columbia interior, where she takes up her first teaching post in a one-room schoolhouse. She is an intruder in the Indigenous community, and as she slowly becomes part of this isolated world, she finds herself immersed in the stories she is told. Living in her cabin, she ponders the variegated life around her while reading literary classics. The people, both Indigenous and White, have forsaken Christian rituals and Indigenous traditions, relying on Coyote, the presiding literal and mythical animal who represents the authority perceived by the Indigenous who live alongside nature. The schoolteacher becomes the narrative consciousness on whom events are noted and through whom the reader knows them. The novel "contained what I began to see as the menace to Canadian writing – the external observer, someone who has come into the community from the outside, schoolteachers, doctors," Watson commented. "I think it failed because of the narrator, so I decided to take narrators out of my writing altogether. That threw me into the dramatic dialogue form of *Double Hook*. I wanted the immediacy of the experience."[40]

Recognizing the distortion of an intrusive narrator, Watson eliminates in *The Double Hook* (1959) all references to any narrator who might control the action, something she did not achieve in *Deep Hollow Creek*.

---

[39] Ibid., pp. 182–3.
[40] George Melnyk, "A talk with Sheila Watson," *Quill & Quire* (September 1975): 14–5.

The reader then becomes the assembler of sequences, by association participating in the events of the novel; trusting her reader, she never allows any intrusion, setting up an immediacy between the printed text and the reader, who sees the action and responds to it directly. In 1938, as Watson noted, T.S. Eliot had praised Wyndham Lewis for "his impersonality, the impersonality of the artist who can out of the particularity of experience express a general truth or create a myth."[41] Watson followed this modernist pattern, creating out of a particularity of experience a general truth about life, death, and what happens in between.

Set again in the remote interior of British Columbia, *The Double Hook* is a typical western, but a western that reflects communities where westerns are supposed to take place. The first page lists the main characters:

> In the folds of the hills
>
> under Coyote's eye
>
> lived
> the old lady, mother of William
>   of James and of Greta
>
> lived James and Greta
> lived William and Ara his wife
> lived the Widow Wagner
> the Widow's girl Lenchen
> the Widow's boy
> lived Felix Prosper and Angel
> lived Theophil
> and Kip

This opening sounds like the prologue of an ancient tale, yet the layout of the page reads like the list of characters in the printed text of a dramatic play. Watson is attempting to fuse or collapse narrative and drama, bringing to narrative the kind of terseness and economy of a play and telling the story in five parts, all the time keeping the characters before us with no narrative intruder. The novel then continues:

> until one morning in July
>
> Greta was at the stove. Turning hotcakes. Reaching for the coffee beans. Grinding away James's voice.
> James was at the top of the stairs. His hand half-raised. His voice in the rafters.

---

[41] "Canada and Wyndham Lewis the Artist," *Open Letter*, 94.

James walking away. The old lady falling. There under the jaw of the roof. In the vault of the bed loft. Into the shadow of death. Pushed by James's will. By James's hand. By James's words: This is my day. You'll not fish today.

James Potter's murder of his mother sets the plot in action, beginning with murder and ending with birth, both these acts having James as their central agent. Yet the agent cannot control the consequences of his actions, and James must return in the end to the place of his crime; he must descend through the darkness to the now purified ground of what he had desecrated. The novel's ending leaves life happier than it was at the beginning, but the ending is not happy. For Watson life and death are inextricably linked.

In a language new to Canadian fiction, *The Double Hook* explores the guilt and fears of a family and a community. James, who finally flees this community, returns to that community, aware, like Watson herself, that one cannot escape one's own world. Taking one family's plight in one local community and recounting it uncompromisingly and unapologetically, observing fidelity to every detail to show how this particular world parallels the patterns of all worlds, Watson makes her rural British Columbia tale a haunting evocation of literary and human patterns traditionally associated with the world's centres and other places. By skilful use of language, by mythic references, by subtle rewriting of western material, she creates a fathomless study of life, death, and rebirth in a remote area of British Columbia. The novel becomes the ultimate anti-regional novel, rejecting the colonial implications of regionalism and embracing a self-sufficiency in place, a *here* defined without reference to *there*.

With remarkable intensity, *The Double Hook* relates the characters to their setting. As Watson commented, "What I was concerned with was figures in a ground, from which they could not be separated. I didn't think of them as people in a place, in a stage set, in a place which had to be described for itself, as it existed outside the interaction of the people with the objects, with the things, with the other existences with which they came in contact. So that the people are entwined in, they're interacting with the landscape, and the landscape is interacting with them."[42] In a draft for a preface he was writing for the novel, McLuhan echoed her sentiment:

> Instead of huge visual gestures or the social abstractions of the novel about the minister, the farmer, the teacher, the Indian, the Mennonite, or the French Canadian, the whole Canadian fabric is included in each moment of

---

[42] "What I'm Going to Do," *Open Letter*, 183.

experience in this novel. This achievement is possible only to a poet who can control a novel as a unified poem, including the totality in every part.[43]

The Double Hook stands as Watson's major contribution to Canadian fiction, bringing the everyday world of the local into the permanent place of world fiction. Earle Birney, who had originally evaluated the manuscript for McClelland and Stewart, called it "monotonous, self-conscious, artificial, and lacking in real fictional interest."[44] He argued that the book not be published, then became its proponent in the early 1960s when, as head of the Creative Writing Program he had established at the University of British Columbia, he always assigned Watson's novel as the only text his students were required to read; *The Double Hook* demanded that he change his mode of reading to accommodate what had once seemed monotonous. For Kroetsch, the novel enabled him "to *see* a new country."[45] For George Bowering, the novel "has since its publication been an icon for other writers who do not fit easily into the realist tradition."[46] And yet the novel is strikingly realistic while ushering in the modernist world in a timeless rural landscape.

When *The Double Hook* appeared in Swedish in 1963, poet and polemicist Artur Lundkvist, a member of the Nobel Prize Committee from 1969 to 1986, observed in his introduction, "It is contemporary life in isolation, geographical and cultural, which yields an impression of archaic timelessness. The whole picture has a sculptural effect. It consists of life figures in deep relief which are put forward for reflection. The abruptness does not exclude a sense of fullness, a repressed astringent richness. The text suggests far more than it spells out directly."[47] *The Double Hook* stepped away from the regional and realist tradition that dominated Canadian fiction, opening the door for more adventurous and experimental fiction.

Watson also published six short stories which frequently have characters named from Greek classical myths, though they live in apparently contemporary British Columbia. In "Antigone," for example, published the

---

[43] F.T. Flahiff, *Always Someone to Kill the Doves: A Life of Sheila Watson* (Edmonton: NeWest, 2005), p. 238.

[44] Ibid., p. 200.

[45] "Hugh MacLennan: An Appreciation," *Hugh MacLennan: 1982*, ed. Elspeth Cameron (Toronto: Canadian Studies Program University College, 1982), p. 115.

[46] "Sheila Watson," *Encyclopedia of Literature in Canada*, ed. W.H. New (University of Toronto Press, 2002), p. 1199.

[47] "Introduction," *Dubbelkroken*, trans. Berit Skogsberg, introduction trans. Eric Hanson (Stockholm: Tidens Förlag, 1963), p. 7.

same year as *The Double Hook*, the narrator has grown up in a mental hospital which makes the irrational appear rational. The mythic allusions, not inviting allegorical interpretations, are points of departure for a sustained treatment of the contemporary alongside but not parallel to the classical references.

Robertson Davies looked back to an Anglophone world which may – or may not – have been what he was transcribing. Mavis Gallant fashioned her short stories of contemporary life in Paris and Canada. Mordecai Richler laboured heroically to bring the novel into direct confrontation with the contemporary world. A.M. Klein wrote his one novel about the past and present history of the Jewish people. And Sheila Watson fashioned her international novels out of the Canadian ground she knew so well. The five writers heralded the solidification and the permanence of a strong and variegated Canadian fictional world, mapping their own routes to future glories.

CHAPTER 5

The Second Feminist Wave

By the 1960s, the first feminist wave, Nellie McClung, Lucy Maud Montgomery, and Mazo de la Roche, had receded, their fates now resting on the banks of time. De la Roche, who died in 1961, witnessed the dwindling sales of all her novels, most of them consigned now to oblivion. McClung, who died in 1951, is regarded only as one of the "Famous Five," the women who, in 1927, challenged the meaning of the word "Persons," which excluded women from Senate appointments; though they lost their challenge, the verdict was overturned by the British Judicial Committee of the Privy Council; none of her books, however, is in print. Only Montgomery, who died in 1942, survived as a major force, all her books still in print and many female writers espousing her inspiration and influence. In the 1950s, women again assumed a major role, Mavis Gallant and Sheila Watson heralding the unique place women held in the development of Canadian fiction.

Adele Wiseman (1928–92), the Winnipeg-born child of immigrant parents, looked back on the earlier feminist writers: "For several decades Canadian women have been able to function this way as free artists. The success of the earlier generation has made it clear to younger women that they could choose to function this way; it has legitimized their aspirations." Brought up on the biblical legends and tales of the Jewish exodus from eastern Europe, knowing many children's works, including Montgomery, and graduating from the University of Winnipeg in English and psychology, she regarded herself as holding a unique position in the development of Canadian fiction: "Not that I am by any means the first or the most noteworthy woman writer in Canada, but because as a writer I stand historically at a kind of watershed, as possibly the first of the Canadian women prose writers, in English, to emerge after the Second World War."[1]

---

[1] "Word Power: Women and Prose in Canada Today," *Memoirs of a Book-Molesting Childhood and Other Essays* (Toronto: Oxford University Press, 1987), pp. 53, 45.

In addition, she continued to bring Jewish culture into the landscape of the Canadian novel, augmenting what Henry Kreisel (1922–91), Klein, and Richler had started to do.

Her first novel, *The Sacrifice* (1956), was not a feminist novel, but a deeply moving, patriarchal portrait of a man removed from his eastern European roots and struggling to earn his living in an unnamed central Canadian city. The biblical portraits of Abraham and Isaac serve as the basis for a detailed account of modern Jewish life, the myth giving meaning and historical continuity to the tragic fate of Jews in the twentieth century. Abraham, his wife Sarah, and their one remaining son Isaac – his two older brothers were murdered by Christians in a pogrom on Easter Sunday – flee the Ukraine and settle in the New World. As immigrants, they encounter all the hardships associated with adapting to the ways of their new home. Because of his sons' murder, Abraham hates God. He expects so much from his only surviving son that, when Isaac dies rescuing the Torah from a burning synagogue, this moment is a necessary sacrifice to Abraham's God. His daughter-in-law Ruth becomes the widow, taking the initiative to support herself and her only son. After Abraham himself is widowed, he becomes entrapped by Laiah, an openly sensual woman who misunderstands him; he murders her in sacrifice. From the madhouse where he is imprisoned, he sends his visiting grandson Moses down into the city with his own message of love.

The Sacrifice adheres to the consciousness of Abraham, relegating his wife Sarah to a position of debilitating passivity; her untimely death expresses the novel's emphasis on female humility or humiliation. Laiah, the embodiment of female seduction, on the other hand, is marginalized by her position as a prostitute and by her single state. Cast aside even by the women, she endures emotional and material hardship in a society unable to permit even the expression or the understanding of female desire. She is ultimately a hypocrite, seeking acceptance by the very society whose patriarchal limitations she publicly rejects. Her murder silences her indiscreet, seductive guiles. Narrated by an omniscient observer, the novel is operatic in its orchestration of the great Old Testament themes of persecution, punishment, and ultimately redemption. Abraham's journey from exile to imprisonment is the timeless tale of the wandering Jew in the modern world.

Wiseman's other novel, *Crackpot* (1974), strikes a different chord. Centring on Hoda, the rotund matriarch whose physical amplitude leads to her economic success as a prostitute, the novel captures her earliest years through her unexpected pregnancy to her final meeting with her own son, who remains unaware of who his mother is. Told from the point of view of Hoda herself, the book is a celebration of her life in the comic mode as opposed to the tragic dimensions of Abraham's pitiable life.

Just before World War I in their north Winnipeg hovel live the blind Danile, his hunchbacked wife Rahel, and their young daughter Hoda, their story becoming a legend for the young Hoda with her parents playing heroic roles. When Rahel dies, Hoda, grossly overweight, is the subject of her classmates' humour and sarcasm. Bewildered by the treatment she receives, she longs for affection and love; what she discovers is fumbling sex with the local boys. Naïve and still trusting, she becomes a prostitute, winning money to help cover her and her father's living expenses. When she becomes pregnant, the birth must be concealed from her father, and she leaves her newborn son at the Jewish orphanage. Her own life continues until the climactic scene with her son, who comes to her as the neighbourhood whore: "As a mother she is forced, given the circumstances, to make love, to give her son love; it is a way of making it up to her son for having abandoned him. It is as if she is delivering him a second time, when ironically she is initiating him into his sexual life."[2] In a comic resolution, a man who has survived the horrors of World War II proposes to Hoda, thereby affirming the integrative nature of comedy. Her marital union brings her back into the fundamental tenets of the Jewish faith, having relinquished her profession as a prostitute and assuming the role of "a good wife."

Both novels suggest Wiseman's interest in people outside normative society. In the examples of Abraham and Hoda, she describes "people on the edge of society, people who are deformed either physically or psychologically. It is partly an extended metaphor of the Jews. I believe we should all try to open ourselves up to a wider acceptance of humanity."[3] In *Crackpot*, she subverts the orthodox tradition of Judaism, calling attention to her own understanding of women's positions in the Jewish faith.

The feminist movement had not come into being when Wiseman started writing, yet she and many of her followers were writing about feminist issues when these issues had not yet been considered openly: "Canadian women writers have tended to write not with the hope of achieving equality, but in the assumption of at least equality, and that both in relation to the number of women writing and to the quality of

[2] "The Charm of an Unorthodox Feminism: An Interview with Adele Wiseman," *We Who Can Fly*, ed. Elizabeth Greene (Dunvegan, Ontario: Cormorant Books, 1997), p. 137.
[3] Ibid., p. 129.

much of their writing, this has proved to be an accurate assumption."[4] The American feminist movement occupied itself first with theorizing its own right to exist in the 1960s, while Canadian writers had already begun to put into imaginative form what American writers were beginning to contemplate. This marks the second wave of feminism.

Among the writers fostered by Wiseman was her close friend and confidante, Margaret Laurence (1926–87). The two met in the summer of 1947 after they graduated from the University of Winnipeg and before Laurence's marriage. The married couple moved into an apartment opposite the Wiseman home in north Winnipeg, and Laurence and Wiseman became correspondents, mutual mentors, and lifelong friends.

In 1949 the Laurences left Canada for England; the following year they went to Africa for seven years, where Jack Laurence was appointed director of a dam-building project in the British Protectorate of Somaliland, now Somalia, and two years later, he continued his engineering work in the Gold Coast, now Ghana. Fascinated by Somaliland's extensive oral literature, Margaret Laurence began translating poetry and folk tales, her work leading to a volume of translations, *A Tree for Poverty: Somali Poetry and Prose* (1954), "the stories of a highly imaginative race without a written language." Somali literature heightened her natural interest in the past and in the social and familial roots that clutch and often cripple. Many contemporary African writers, she observes in "A Place to Stand On," the opening essay in *Heart of a Stranger* (1976),

> re-create their people's past in novels and plays in order to recover a sense of themselves, an identity and a feeling of value from which they were separated by two or three generations of colonialism and missionizing. They have found it necessary, in other words, to come to terms with their ancestors and their gods in order to be able to accept the past and be at peace with the dead, without being stifled or threatened by that past.

In another decade she would begin the arduous task of chronicling her Canadian past.

Laurence set her first two books of fiction in the Gold Coast, her novel, *This Side Jordan* (1960), and her collection of short stories, *The Tomorrow-Tamer* (1963). All her African fiction centres on independence, both personal and political, and rarely has an outsider captured with such pathos the struggles and casualties of an alien world coming into self-realization. The fiction shows characters caught between the biases of their traditions

---

[4] "Word Power," *Memoirs*, p. 45.

and the demands of their liberation. Frequent are the clashes between imperialists viewing with scepticism and bitter resentment the Africanization of their industries and Africans detesting their arrogant and condescending employers.

The stories in *The Tomorrow-Tamer*, written and published individually from 1954 to 1963, have first-person and third-person narrators; each narrator is an outsider, exiled from some aspect of his natural world. The outsider may be an alien to Africa or an African caught up in the new technology and rendered alien to his tribal values. The point of view is that of an ironist, watching the joys and sorrows, the hopes and disappointments of an emerging people.

The chapters of *This Side Jordan* alternately concern the African protagonist, Nathaniel Amegbe, who, though educated by Christian missionaries and freed in his own mind from his tribal past, remains attached to the ways of his people, and the English protagonist, Johnnie Kestoe, the son of poor Irish Catholics, who has rejected his religious upbringing and come to the Gold Coast as an accountant in a textile firm, even though he despises the country and its inhabitants. As their paralleling stories become increasingly interdependent, the novel becomes a chronicle of war between native traditions and the values of the imperialists. Although the symmetry of the plot may seem too neat, the novel has an abundance of carefully delineated and realistic characters on a rich canvas that captures the complexity of social change.

Laurence's final African writing, her critical study, *Long Drums and Cannons: Nigerian Dramatists and Novelists 1952–1966* (1968), had a major lesson for her: "Most Nigerian writers have in some way or other made an attempt to restore the value of the past, without idealising it and without being shackled by it." For Laurence and her fictional characters, life's journey is an exploration of the past to understand its connection to the present. Acknowledgement of the past and acceptance of its relationship to the present offer personal peace and contentment. Such understanding is both the purpose and the end of the mental meanderings of her characters as they free themselves from the stultifying aspects of the past and accept its proper significance. According to "A Place to Stand On," Laurence "began to see how much of my own writing had followed the same pattern – the attempt to assimilate the past, partly in order to be freed from it, partly in order to try to understand myself and perhaps others of my generation, through seeing where we had come from."

After her books of African fiction and non-fiction, written mainly in Vancouver where she lived for five years, Laurence had a strong desire to write about people from her own background. Her expressed hatred of colonialism and her love of independence, both political and personal, now translate themselves into her evocative portraits of five women from Manawaka, Manitoba.

Laurence regarded herself as belonging to the second generation of Canadian writers. The first generation, including Callaghan and Ross, MacLennan and Buckler, had rejected British and American models to write of the world through their own eyes. In Laurence's African fiction, she was focusing on people as they dealt with their pasts and the changes to their society. In her Canadian fiction, the focus became women confronting their pasts and their conflicting presents. American feminism had to confront and understand a male literary establishment, and so leading American feminists were theorizing at this time about their own ambitions. Even though the feminist movement had not yet been formed, Laurence came to embody many of its hopes and disappointments in her fictional portraits. Along with Wiseman, she "took the creative leap into the issues of our age which others still had not defined clearly as issues, and which they have since begun to use our fiction to help them understand,"[5] such issues as nuclear disarmament, a feminist platform with global implications. When she turned to Canada, she focused first not on her own generation but on that of her grandparents, reproducing the voice of that generation. To Vanderhaeghe, she was "an essential literary guide, a woman whose writing helped to open my eyes to what might be done with material that lay right under my nose."[6]

The Stone Angel (1964) is Hagar Shipley's personal account of the last days of her life. With memory rampant, the ninety-year-old narrator unconsciously weaves episodes from her past into her painful present. The novel's structure is the order of her mind, the entire book being composed of flashbacks occurring in a progressive chronological pattern and alternating with scenes in the immediate present. At the beginning, Hagar is blind, like the statue of the stone angel in the Manawaka cemetery. All her life has been a display of pride as she struggled to hide her emotions and live in self-sufficient isolation. During a lifetime of wrangling, she never learned how to express or accept love; she tried to hide her inner failure, that she had never known the ability to rejoice. In the end, however, her pride gives way to need. In Hagar,

---

[5] "The Writer and Canadian Literature," *Memoirs*, p. 88.
[6] "A Writer's Life," The 2014 Margaret Laurence Lecture, 30 May 2014.

part of her goal is simply survival – to survive until the moment she dies, with some kind of dignity and some kind of human value. But at the same time, the great theme at the end is the theme of freedom. She has always tried to put the hooks on people, to influence people, to manipulate them, her husband and her sons, and she has never allowed them to go free, so she has never been free herself: this is what she comes to understand in the very last days of her life.[7]

Hagar is blind and foolish, her pride both her fortress and her failing. In retelling her life, she confronts her past, her many deeds and misdeeds, and her miserable present state. As she examines her life, she provides feminist scholars with a spellbinding portrait of a woman trapped in the temper of her time.

Whereas *The Stone Angel* is set in the generation of Laurence's grandparents, her second Manawaka novel, *A Jest of God* (1966), is set in her own generation. The narrator and protagonist, Rachel Cameron, a thirty-four-year-old spinster schoolteacher returning home from university in Winnipeg, endures the long, hot summer of Manawaka. While resigned to the Presbyterian sterility of the town and the oppressive presence of her hypochondriac mother, she harbours a rebellious craving for love. Although her summer affair with Nick Kazlik, a schoolmate from early years who now teaches in Winnipeg, comes to an abrupt end, it has a positive effect. "What she wanted from him, and what was impossible for him to give, because it is not possible for any human being – she really wanted him to save her, to enter her life and say: Come with me and all will be well. One individual cannot save another in that sense," Laurence reflected.

> We are not God, but what Nick did for Rachel was to enable her to reach out, hold and touch another human being, which was what the sexual experience meant for her. It was the reaching out to another person and making herself vulnerable, as Rachel was able to do ultimately, with Nick, which led her to be able – to some limited extent – to liberate herself.[8]

The protagonist of the third Manawaka novel, *The Fire-Dwellers* (1969), is Rachel's thirty-nine-year-old sister, Stacey Cameron MacAindra, who buys a railroad ticket out of Manawaka as soon as she has saved enough money. Now through a series of flashbacks, memories, fantasies, through a mingling of first-person and third-person narrative, she examines her tangled life in Vancouver. Instead of the anticipated enlargement of her

---

[7] *Conversations with Canadian Novelists*, 1, 98.   [8] *Eleven Canadian Novelists*, p. 204.

personal horizon, she finds enslavement to her four children, her dull husband, and encroaching age. By the end of her mental journey, she sees the complexity of life and the problems other people face. Again Laurence created a woman who, like Hagar and Rachel, embodies the imprisoning pride that separates her from the external world of others. Like Rachel, Stacey has a brief love affair where she, too, learns to move outside herself into the life of her lover.

While writing the three Manawaka novels, Laurence also worked on seven short stories, fictionalized autobiography, which were published separately in the 1960s. Adding one further story, she collected them under the title *A Bird in the House* (1970). The protagonist, Vanessa MacLeod, is another young inhabitant of Manawaka, and the stories follow ten years in her life which coincide in part with World War II. Although Vanessa is the narrator and the protagonist, the centre of the book is her autocratic grandfather, and his centrality underlines the importance of the stories as cathartic autobiography. Her grandfather was a hard man who had a hard life, and near the end of the final story, she writes: "I had feared and fought the old man, yet he proclaimed himself in my veins."

In this collection Laurence enunciates the development of her own emotional and intellectual life as she describes her evolution into an artist. In this fictionalized version of her life, she explores Vanessa's movement from a romanticist, who, like Montgomery's Anne, lives in a romance world, to a realist writer who seeks truth through her art. As the stories progress, each one offers a further step in her understanding, and little by little Vanessa manages to sublimate the bitterness her young self felt towards the shackles her family put around her, and she becomes completely free at the end of the last story, where she returns to Manawaka after being away for twenty years. When she comes to her grandfather's house, she is hurt by its dilapidated condition. Laurence has laid to rest her upbringing and her grandfather, and professes her own commitment to the life of a writer who is committed to truth.

Her final Manawaka novel, *The Diviners* (1974), is a unique portrait of the town since Morag Gunn, the forty-seven-year-old narrator and protagonist, is not a woman of Manawaka, but an outsider, a girl who came to Manawaka and later tried to escape from it, only to realize that escape can be only physical. When Laurence suggested that this novel might be her last or at least her last about Manawaka, she underlined its epic significance, for the novel is the culmination and completion of her investigation of the town. It is appropriate that her investigation comes to an end with her employment of Morag, a novelist, for here is Manawaka from the perspective of a writer. Morag's personal search for understanding the pattern of her life complements a much larger ambition: *The Diviners* is an exploration of the role of the artist in Canada, the importance of time and place to the artist, and, more importantly, the centrality of the past to the artist's understanding of her own position in the flux of time.

Completed when Laurence herself was forty-seven, *The Diviners* is her bildungsroman, the novel that records the growth, education, and maturing of the individual, frequently with autobiographical overtones. While her early upbringing corresponds to the family life of Vanessa MacLeod, the autobiographical dimension of *The Diviners* is the embodiment in Morag of Laurence's ideas about art and life. For Laurence, Manawaka's creator, and Morag Gunn, Manawaka's historian in the fictional world, art is the distillation of the private and the fictional, and the mysterious process of literary creation provides the theme and the form of the novel. At the end Morag has summoned up all her past and discovers her own place in Canada: "This place is some kind of garden, nonetheless, even though it may be only a wildflower garden." Like her creator, Morag transforms her garden into art. At the conclusion of her mental journey she "returned to the house, to write the remaining private and fictional worlds, and to set down her title." With its final setting in eastern Ontario, *The Diviners* is Laurence's farewell to Manawaka. The epic dimensions of Morag's reliving of her life and, through stories and ballads, her ancestral past give the novel a quality of finality and summation that makes it a natural conclusion to its creator's imaginative involvement with the prairie town.

From her careful study of the colonial cultures of Africa, Laurence brought to her Canadian fiction a wise sympathy for the plight of the individual in a young nation, an understanding of the need for myths that give shape to human lives, and a dedication to the depiction of contemporary Canadian women in the pages of fiction.

When Laurence started writing her Manawaka quintet, the feminist movement had not yet found a confident social voice. Only in some liberal circles was the phrase "women's liberation" coming into play. In 1949 Simone de Beauvoir published her study of *The Second Sex*, translated into English in 1953, which provides a detailed examination of women's oppression and became a fundamental text of contemporary feminism. More important for North American feminists is Betty Friedan's *The Feminine Mystique* (1963), now considered the major impetus for the women's movement. Calling the contemporary situation with women "the problem that has no name," Friedan depicted the roles women assume in industrial societies, especially the full-time homemaker role she considered paralyzing. Women, she averred, were as capable as men of any kind of work or career. Three years later, she founded and became the first president of the National Organization of Women, which strongly advocated for the legal equality of women and men.

Unlike the United States, Canada tended to view equality between men and women as a given proposition, yet this equality needed to be explored and examined by the Royal Commission on the Status of Women, created in 1967 to "inquire into and report upon the status of women in Canada, and to recommend what steps might be taken by the federal government to ensure for women equal opportunities with men in all aspects of Canadian society." In 1970 the commission's report came out with 137 recommendations to guarantee equality.

Laurence's Canadian writings focus relentlessly on women coping with their problematic lives in trying circumstances; the women of Manawaka became a standard-bearer for the feminist movement that was asserting itself in contemporary society. "People sometimes ask me whether I'm consciously writing feminist novels. No, I am not," exclaimed Laurence in 1979. "Even though I myself feel I am a feminist, I won't write in any didactic or polemical way about it. My protagonists are women and I simply try to portray their dilemmas as truthfully as I can. I'm not doing it for any other reason than because I am interested in a character as a human individual."[9]

From Wiseman's writings and her personal involvement in fostering women writers and from Laurence's achievements as a major fiction writer, other female authors also developed their positions as proponents of the second feminist wave. Among them are Audrey Thomas (b. 1935), a native of Binghamton, New York, who became a graduate student at the University of British Columbia and adopted Canada as her homeland, and Marian Engel (1933–85), whose early death "was felt in the literary community like a sudden withdrawal of current, a dimming of lights. This consciousness of the loss of a distinct vitality is still with us," eulogized Wiseman at the time. "She has left those of us who knew her and respected her work with a continuing regret for a life too early, a unique voice too soon interrupted."[10]

[9] "Margaret Laurence," *Strong Voices: Conversations with Fifty Canadian Authors*, ed. Alan Twigg (Madeira Park, British Columbia: Harbour, 1988), p. 162.
[10] "Marian Engel 1933–1985," *Canadian Literature* 108 (1986): 199.

A graduate of Smith College, where she studied the classics of English literature, all by men, Thomas soon discovered the revelatory fictional and non-fictional writings of Virginia Woolf. When she accompanied her husband to Vancouver, she did graduate study in English literature, completing her master's thesis on Henry James and almost completing her doctoral dissertation on *Beowulf*; the department rejected her thesis. From 1964 to 1966 she travelled with her husband and two daughters to Ghana, where her husband taught art at the University of Science and Technology in Kumasi. (They separated in 1972.)

Caught between the male tradition of English literature, outlined by her Smith College professors, and the growing number of female writers, most notably Doris Lessing, Thomas dramatizes the unhealthy split in her female characters, the half that clings to the male-centred lifestyle and the half that seeks independence and freedom to be themselves. Much of her fiction, especially her early fiction, is rooted in her own life, her unhappy childhood, her African travels, and her later life in British Columbia, almost all her stories and novels female-centred. "You can't add 'feminism' to a story the way you can add vanilla to a cake, sticking your finger in and tasting, 'needs a bit more vanilla' (or lemon or almond essence)," she observes in the introduction to her collection, *Goodbye Harold, Good Luck* (1984). "I consider myself a feminist but I do not, consciously, think about feminism when I am making a story."

In her first published story, "If One Green Bottle ...," which would become the opening story of her first collection, *Ten Green Bottles* (1967), Thomas transforms her painful memory of her own miscarriage in Ghana into a harrowing account of a woman's mental suffering as she undergoes an equally painful miscarriage. Her distraught memories keep flooding her consciousness as she struggles to keep sane in this traumatic time. The many ellipses that interrupt the narrative flow in almost every line emphasize the pain she is suffering as well as the memories that continually break into her consciousness. "Salon des Refuses," the closing story of *Ten Green Bottles*, which reflects her early employment in a New York State asylum, is an equally terrifying rendition of the frail border between sanity and madness in a setting which promulgates the closing suicide. She writes out of her own youthful work and her African travails, transmuting them into painful and poignant stories. Always writing her fiction with women as narrators or women as the centre, she analyzes and assesses the position of women, using some details of her own life as part of her fictional transmutation as she looks at the struggles of women in contemporary society. Already in this initial volume is her rebellious intent to knock down the traditional modes of writing and to experiment in new ways, whether it be through constant ellipses or through the frightening third-person analysis of the asylum.

Thomas's short stories often lead to their treatment as novels. *Mrs. Blood* began life as a short story, as did *Latakia* and *Intertidal Life*. *Mrs. Blood* (1970), her first novel, has a split-person narrator, Mrs. Blood, the focus of her memory, and Mrs. Thing, existing uneasily in the present, who reflects upon her marriage, her extramarital affair, and her current miscarriage and earlier abortion, told in controlled hysteria from a hospital bed in Ghana. The traditional novel with its straightforward narration struggles to contain this split perspective, and the first-person narrator lapses at the end into fragmentary utterances. *Songs My Mother Taught Me* (1973) documents Isobel Cleary's coming of age in upstate New York; her father is ineffectual, her mother prone to sudden outbursts of anger; her response is to flee this chaos, which recalls the world of Dickens's *Great Expectations* with the ever-faithful Joe Gargery replaced by Isobel's loving grandfather. Through memory she unravels this former existence, realizing that "Life was cruel, people hurt and betrayed one another, grew old and died alone."

Dedicated to (among others) Margaret Laurence, *Blown Figures* (1974), the third novel of what is usually regarded now as a trilogy and a direct sequel to *Mrs. Blood*, follows its heroine on her return journey to Ghana to exorcise the child she miscarried in *Mrs. Blood*. Totally experimental in terms of pages and blank pages which isolate the textual fragments, *Blown Figures* is the most experimental novel written thus far in Canadian fiction.

Moving more and more into the dilemma of women in their relationships with their parents, their lovers, and their children, Thomas explores in these novels and in her later works the roles women take on, often bewilderingly, only to cast them aside and try to figure out alternative modes of existence. "What really interests me is the relationship between men and women and how we lie to one another," she comments. "I think one of the hardest things for women right now, because we've gotten so strong (and we really are strong) is that we're very intolerant of the weakness of men."[11] As she examines the relationships her characters are capable of developing, she further develops her understanding of the role of the female writer, which she had cursorily examined in some of her shorter fiction.

Taking the form of Rachel's letter to her departed lover Michael, *Latakia* (1979) continues the depiction of split women, reaching

[11] "An Interview with Audrey Thomas," *Room of One's Own* 10, 3 (1986): 58.

emotionally for independence yet needing sexual attachment. Being a successful novelist and relishing this interruption to her novel-writing, Rachel explores the many ways a woman can effectively write about herself and her passionate feelings, and by composing "the longest love letter in the world," she brings Michael's presence back into her life, eliminating for the moment his loss as he has returned permanently to his wife. Many female stories are fictions of weakness and dependence; Rachel discovers that there are layers of self-delusion which hide the strength inside her. "You made me bloom again, Michael, and you taught me just how strong a woman I really am," she writes. "I do not *need* to be 'looked after' or 'defined', even if I might want it." Yet there is a dichotomy between her needs as a woman and her needs as a novelist: the central fact in her life is her work, her novel-writing, yet when her affair with Michael no longer hinders her creativity, she feels forlorn and lost. She is a Thomas heroine, struggling with her needs and finding no adequate resolution to her predicament.

Like *Latakia, Intertidal Life* (1984) focuses on the relocation of writer Alice Hoyle and her three daughters to a Gulf Island in British Columbia and the subsequent dissolution of her marriage to Peter, who is left to continue teaching at a local university during the week and to commute to his family on weekends. The end of the marriage forces Alice to confront the meaning of commitment and love as she tries to piece her life together, to search through her past, like Laurence's Morag Gunn, in order to understand the cluttered jumble of the present. As the narrative weaves back and forth in time, Alice is on a voyage of discovery. "What's happening to men and women today is just as exciting and terrifying as the discovery that the earth was round, not flat, or even that the earth was not the center of the universe but just part of the solar system. But we all need new maps, new instruments to try and fix our new positions." But Alice has not found the map. Not always steering clear of cloying self-pity, she nevertheless emerges as a complex and caring woman, struggling and straining and surviving. With its liberated heroine questioning the foundations of her belief, daring not to shift blame to the opposite sex, confronting the agony of writing amid the more pressing demands of a painful reality, *Intertidal Life* does not provide answers, only disturbing questions.

In her three recent novels, Thomas eschewed her studies of contemporary women in their domestic situations for three women in near history who have their own set of problems dealing with their societies. In *Isobel Gunn* (1999), a male narrator tells the story of an Orkney girl who masquerades as a man to join the Hudson's Bay Company, making of her life a work of fiction; *Tattycoram* (2005) is the first-person narration of the life of Harriet Beadle, later Coram, a minor character of Dickens's *Little Dorrit*; and *Local Customs* (2014) is poet Letitia Elizabeth Landon's post-death account (along with three other narrators) of her marriage, her journey to the Gold Coast (Ghana), and her death two months later. Isobel Gunn and Letitia Elizabeth Landon were historical persons; Tattycoram is Dickens's creation. In each of the novels, Thomas captures their female worlds with scholarly accuracy.

Tattycoram, Thomas's finest novel, recounts the title character's upbringing at the London Foundling Hospital, including her adoption into a rural foster family for five years. Her return to the hospital leads to her ten-year dreary life there, followed by her domestic employment in the Dickens's burgeoning home. She then leaves the household to become a teacher, only to be lured back again to aid his plans to rehabilitate fallen women. Questioning his right to use her speech and mannerisms in *Little Dorrit* – "there is no excuse for bad behavior of this kind, this careless cruelty, this disregard for the feelings of others," her husband admonishes her – she wonders about this theft by a fiction writer, all the time being embedded in new fictive life by a contemporary writer.

Beginning with stories of her own life, transmuted into fictional works, Thomas went on to probe the debilitating world of women trapped by their past beliefs about themselves and poised to take on their impending independence. There are no easy answers, only the disturbing questions about the place of women in their own worlds. In her recent books she expands her study of contemporary women to look back on women, real or fictive, from near history who find their ways in their own worlds.

Born in Toronto and raised in a variety of southwestern Ontario locations, Marian Engel wrote her master's thesis, "A Study of the English-Canadian Novel since 1939," at McGill University under the supervision of Hugh MacLennan, who remained a lifelong mentor and friend. Maintaining that her thesis was "the best piece of critical writing I have ever seen in the field of Canadian writing,"[12] MacLennan developed in her a supreme importance for prose style as well as a sense of history for her country. Although she knew all the writings of the major women authors of the British tradition, she found her technique in Laurence's books, whose pictures of women are "difficult, sometimes half-disturbed;

[12] Christl Verduyn, *Lifelines: Marian Engel's Writings* (Montreal: McGill-Queen's University Press, 1995), p. 51.

always dealing with men to whom the word 'man' also means something they have not experienced, but been told."[13] Her thesis gave her the occasion for "surveying the territory to find a place for myself" among the women writers of her own country.[14]

Convinced that "in a society which is completely sexually divided, where the woman's role and the man's role is worked out very clearly according to a pattern that was laid down a thousand years ago, a woman's experience is very different from a man's,"[15] Engel set out to explore the lives of ordinary women. Her first novel, *No Clouds of Glory* (1968), renamed in subsequent printings with its original title of *Sarah Bastard's Notebook*, is a book as notebook, the interior monologue of a fragmented, non-centric woman trying to find a place for herself in a rapidly changing world. Thirty-year-old Dr. Sarah Porlock, a teacher at a Toronto university, has just ended two sexual relationships, one with her brother-in-law and one with a married friend, suggesting that she is eagerly moving beyond the bounds of propriety; she has also just suffered her father's death. At the same time, a *Toronto Star* interview hails Sarah as representative of a new generation of model young Canadians. Despite protests to the contrary, she resigns her job, which means social status and security, renames herself Sarah Bastard, sells all her books and possessions, and takes the train to Montreal, where, rather than teaching literature, she is going to be a writer. "Kill yourself, or decide," she hears herself say. In the end, she avers, "Jump, or you'll die, Sarah." Montreal represents her new beginning. The socially acceptable Dr. Sarah Porlock is reconfigured as Sarah Bastard, woman author: "I want to produce, I want to get into a world where creation – creation of anything – is a fact, where ideas are important, where people are tough on you and where if you turn out something good nobody, but nobody, will say it's 'cute'." No longer buoyed by her usual sarcasm, she can confront her problems by deciding to create her own story. She has become an ever-changing, decentred, and fluid subject-in-process, free from the constraints of the patriarchal order.

The Honeyman Festival (1970) examines a woman's life from the perspective of a mother. Her husband away on another trip, Minn Burge, seven-and-a-half months pregnant with her fourth child and nearing forty in age, epitomizes women's realities of motherhood rather than men's fictions about it. Although she is from the small, stultifying town of Godwin in southwestern Ontario, she lives now in Toronto, where she

---

[13] "It's the grit. Laurence is unforgettable because she is us," *The Globe and Mail*, 19 April 1975, p. 37.
[14] *Lifelines*, p. 51.   [15] *Eleven Canadian Novelists*, p. 97.

forges out her relationship with her mother, a perfect homemaker and disciplinarian, while focused on her own role as mother, ultimately not subscribing to her mother's vision of the world. In her stream of consciousness, she is an articulate woman who reveals her critical intelligence and solid understanding of the world around her. For Munro, these two novels look at the women of her time, drawing realistic portraits:

> here was a woman writing about the lives of women at their most muddled, about a woman who can't quite believe in the world of careers, academic strivings, faith in work, and another who is just managing to keep afloat in the woozy world of maternity, with its shocks and confusions and fearful love and secret brutality. You have to remember how shunned, despised, misused, this material was at that time.[16]

In *Monodromos* (1973), Audrey Moore spends several months on a Greek island, writing letters to Max, a married English poet living in London, befriending the island's only woman artist, and taking up a new lover. For Max, a man of the mind who lives in his world of books, she agrees to search out the icon of a dog-headed saint, and when Max dies, she goes to a distant monastery where she sees the disappointing statue. At first guided by men's instructions, she gradually sees the island world with her own eyes. This new land with its long history challenges her small-town southwestern Ontario upbringing. She slowly realizes her sense of self is changing. Too long living under men's guidance, she leaves the world of the mind and moves into the world of feeling and instinct, becoming at last both physically and psychically involved with her own spatial context.

Monodromos has another context significant for Canadian writers. In choosing a setting far from home, Engel wanted to "tell a lot about being a foreigner, trying to get into places, failing, whether it is moral to try at all. And about how the tissues of old societies come through the weave and give it texture."[17] As Laurence wrote to her,

> Your amazing sense of Exile. I guess I felt rather strongly about that, because for many years I lived in Africa, and I loved it, I really *did*. But I was in exile, all the same ... the knowledge of being an outsider, describing a land and a people with help from guidebooks, accurately, with a real sense of the details, the smells and touch and sights, but always from the stance of Another.[18]

---

[16] "An Appreciation," *Room of One's Own* 9, 2 (June 1984): 33.   [17] *Lifelines*, p. 115.
[18] *Marian Engel: Life in Letters*, ed. Christl Verduyn and Kathleen Garay (University of Toronto Press, 2004), pp. 136–7.

Yet Engel never again wrote fiction with a foreign setting.

Bear (1976) achieved the critical and popular success long denied to her. A bibliographer at the Toronto Historical Institute, who lives "like a mole, buried deep in her office, digging among maps and manuscripts," Lou agrees to catalogue the library of the Cary Estate on an island in the bush north of Toronto; like Audrey Moore, she relies on books as her guide through life, and she catalogues books as her way of recording the fragments of other people's lives. A colonial and patriarchal white octagon, the home also has a bear she befriends, then falls in love with it. To the bear, she bares her soul, revealing her innermost thoughts and desires, giving no heed to the intellectual and rational aspects of life. The bear comes into the house, finding its way into the library, where it spends evenings asleep by the fire. Lou feels loved and peaceful in the animal's presence. One evening she initiates sex with the bear, and its claw penetrates her back: "For one strange, sharp moment she could feel in her pores and the taste of her own mouth that she knew what the world was for." She heads back to Toronto at summer's end, though the island has transformed her from a lonely spinster to a woman capable of rejecting the rational in her own work and embracing the instinctual around and within her.

What happens to Lou after she returns to society? The answer is *The Glassy Sea* (1978), where Rita Heber, another woman from another southwestern Ontario hard-working and church-going family, joins the Eglantine Sisters of the Church of England in London, Ontario. She spends a decade working alongside the eight members of the Eglantine House, reading, thinking, and working. In light of the advanced age of many members of her small community, she is advised to leave and make her way in the world. She falls into a lifeless and withering marriage, embracing finally a divorce from her demeaning husband and fleeing to the east coast, where Philip, Bishop of Huron, proposes that she return and reopen Eglantine House, which she vows to make into a woman's hostel.

Written as a long letter to the Bishop of Huron, the novel hearkens back to that female form, the epistolary novel, as Engel explores the options society offers women for their social fulfilment. Although "the ideal for womanhood was not Mary but Martha," a hard worker who served her men, Rita wants more than a life of service. She demands personal fulfilment, involving both Mary, the intuitive, and Martha, the worker. The contemplative and the active need and demand integration. Eglantine House will be a place where women come, not to serve, but to belong. To Aritha van Herk, *The Glassy Sea* was a beacon of light: "If only everyone would dare to speak for us women like that – life would be so much simpler and easier and more straightforward."[19]

The setting of Engel's final novel, *Lunatic Villas* (1981), a series of renovated townhouses on Rathbone Place in Toronto, focuses on a "single, self-employed free-lance writer" and mother of seven children. Committed to the depiction of women's experiences in her newspaper articles, she is the novel's spokesperson for not an idealized portrait of motherhood, but motherhood as it is in her own world. Her household is not overseen by a father or by any other man; it does not work on principles of hierarchy; it operates on principles of mutual, though not always, smooth cooperation between her children and herself, often with the aid of some women friends and neighbours. The dream of cosy domesticity is now seen as a male dream out of touch with reality. Men and women, therefore, need not conform to traditional male/female roles; they may revise parental roles, alter family structures, and develop new, emancipatory roles for women. Engel now entered a new realm, more comic than her preceding five novels, more mature too, looking at "a large hearted and slightly fuddle-headed collector of stray children who lives on a street in Toronto," in Wiseman's words, "where palpable, if zany, people conduct their lives with a sense of magic and possibility always hovering and sometimes even descending to illuminate their days with small, bearable miracles."[20]

Not unlike Wiseman and Laurence, Engel sought to change her society in its approach to, and understanding of, women's lives. Using the novella, her chosen form until her final novel, she studies ordinary heroines in their search for the routes to female fulfilment. Torn between social dictates and their own personal desires, women often flee society to investigate alternative lifestyles. In the end, her women can fuse the biblical figures of Mary and Martha, the intuitive and the intellectual, ushering in a new time when women's roles, and men's roles too, will be radically transformed, redefined, and inexorably altered.

To an interviewer's question, "Were you an early feminist?" Alice Munro (b. 1931) replies, "I never knew about the word feminism, but of course I was." To the same interviewer's question, "Was it important that the story was told from a woman's perspective?" she responds, "I never thought of it as being important, but I never thought of myself as being anything but a woman . . .. When I was a young girl, I had no feeling of inferiority at all in being a woman."[21]

---

[19] Ibid., p. 194.   [20] "Marian Engel 1933–1985," 199–200.
[21] From the official interview on receiving the Nobel Prize in November 2013.

Raised near Wingham, Ontario, a rural community not far from Lake Huron, Munro attended the University of Western Ontario, from which she had received a scholarship which lasted only two years; for men, it was for four years, since they were expected to enter the sciences. In later years, she accepted her only honorary degree from the university, for she thought she deserved a degree denied to her. In the course of her distinguished career, she has published fourteen collections of short stories.

Munro grew up a young, incorrigible teller of tales. Her childhood was a time of fantasies, though her fantasies would become more formal, more detached, less personal daydreams. She read Montgomery when she was nine years old. Although she devoured *Anne of Green Gables*, she was more pleased and more troubled by *Emily of New Moon*, Montgomery's bildungsroman:

> In this book, as in all the books I've loved, there's so much going on behind, or beyond, the proper story. There's life spreading out behind the story – the book's life – and we see it out of the corner of the eye. The milk pails in the dairy-house. Aunt Elizabeth pouring the tallow for the candles. The slightly repulsive splendour of the parlour at Wyther Grange. The corners of the kitchen at New Moon. What mattered to me finally in this book, what was to matter most to me in books from then on, was knowing more about that life than I'd been told, and more than I can tell.[22]

In her teen years, Munro read writers from the American South, including Eudora Welty, Flannery O'Connor, Katherine Ann Porter, Carson McCullers, and Reynolds Price. These writers reverberated with her because she recognized their treatment of a similar regional terrain:

> I felt there a country being depicted that was like my own. I can think of several writers now who are working out of Southwestern Ontario. It is rich in possibilities in this way. I mean the part of the country I come from is absolutely Gothic. You can't get it all down . . . .. It's a very rooted kind of place. I think the kind of writing I do is almost anachronistic, because it's so rooted in one place, and most people, even of my age, do not have a place like this any more, and it's something that may not have meaning very much longer. I mean this kind of writing.[23]

She later commented,

> The writers of the American South were the first writers who really moved me because they showed me that you could write about small towns, rural people, and that kind of life I knew very well. But the thing about the

---

[22] "Afterword," *Emily of New Moon* (Toronto: McClelland & Stewart, 1989), pp. 360–1.
[23] *Eleven Canadian Novelists*, pp. 248–9.

Southern writers that interested me, without my being really aware of it, was that all the Southern writers whom I really love were women. I didn't really like Faulkner that much. I loved Eudora Welty, Flannery O'Connor, Katherine Ann Porter, Carson McCullers. There was a feeling that women could write about the freakish, the marginal .... I came to feel that was our territory, whereas the mainstream big novel about real life was men's territory. I don't know how I got that feeling of being on the margins, it wasn't that I was *pushed* there. Maybe it was because I grew up on a margin.[24]

The fiction writer she admired most was not O'Connor, a writer of ideas with a strong Catholic point of view, but Welty: "The writer I adored was Eudora Welty. I still do. I would never try to copy her – she's too good and too much herself."[25]

For Munro, writing is the crucial act of recording reality:

I'm very, very excited by what you might call the surface of life, and it must be that this seems meaningful in a way I can't analyze or describe .... Well for me it's just things about people, the way they look, the way they sound, the way things smell, the way everything is that you go through everyday. It seems to me very important to do something with this .... It seems to me very important to be able to get at the exact tone or texture of how things are.[26]

Her fiction attempts to see the reality that exists on the surface of life, to see that multicoloured surface clearly, to record it clearly and accurately, to probe the surface so completely that one gets somewhere near the essence of what is being described. This is the first step in Munro's artistic universe: she has to paint the everyday reality of her characters before she can notice the unfathomable depths of her creations.

When Munro depicts her world, she delves deeply into the surface exteriors; she paints the streaks of the tulip so closely, so naturally, that we accept the truth of her vision. Marshall McLuhan used to tell his students that the closer an artist penetrates in the descriptions of their subjects, the closer the artist penetrates to the universal, that is the more closely an artist goes to their particular subject, the more universal the subject becomes. This is the second step of Munro's art – she moves so penetratingly to the exact description of her subject, however localized it is, that her stories become universal in their meaning. Small towns in

---

[24] "The Art of Fiction," *The Paris Review* 36, 131 (Summer 1994): 255–6.
[25] Deborah Treisman, "On 'Dear Life': An Interview with Alice Munro," *The New Yorker* (20 November 2012).
[26] *Eleven Canadian Novelists*, p. 241.

southwestern Ontario finally become the universal settings of major stories that happen here, there, or elsewhere. This pattern occurs in her first collection of stories, *Dance of the Happy Shades* (1968), and continues through her last, *Dear Life* (2012).

Whether Munro's stories are in the first or third person, each one usually has a retrospective narrative technique which allows the older person, often the narrator, who was the younger person, to comment on what was back there, to comment on what happened, to wonder now about the past. Munro states,

> The adult narrator has the ability to detect and talk about the confusion. I don't feel the confusion is ever resolved . . .. And the whole act of writing is more an attempt at recognition than of understanding, because I don't understand many things. I feel a kind of satisfaction in just approaching something that is mysterious and important. Then writing is the act of approach and recognition.[27]

Her narrative technique allows her to approach the past through the present situation, to try to understand the past from the present, to use the writing on the past to offer an "approach and recognition." She plays off then and now, the past and the present, her stories moving back and forth from the past to the present and back again, reproducing the mind's capacity to recover the past, to reassess the impact of the past, to discover the torturous relationship of the past to the present, and perhaps to understand to some degree the present scene, event, or incident.

At the core of this technique is Munro's realization that "all life becomes even *more* mysterious and difficult." All we have is art itself to help us approach the past, to gain some understanding of where we stood in the past and where we stand now, and to bring us to some kind of increased awareness. "I believe that we don't solve these things – in fact our explanations take us further away," she concludes.[28]

In *Dance of the Happy Shades* Munro examines the immediate world around her in southwestern Ontario. "Postcard," for example, is a brief vignette of a young woman who lives a pedestrian existence save for the attentions of Clare MacQuarrie, a man older than her by twelve years. She cavorts with Clare; she drives around town in a small car he gave her; she looks forward to the day when they will marry. Every year he goes to Florida with his sister and her husband, sending back to her a postcard of

---

[27] Jill Gardiner, "The Early Short Stories of Alice Munro," MA thesis, University of New Brunswick, 1973, 178.
[28] Ibid.

his travels. One day the news is posted in the local paper that Clare married a woman in Florida and would be returning with his new wife. Infuriated, angry, deeply hurt, the narrator is beside herself. Her mother, a wise, older woman who always loved Clare herself, merely comments: "I am an old woman but I know. If a man loses respect for a girl he don't marry her .... You destroyed your own chances." Munro tells the story retrospectively – all the details are there, the cavorting, the happy encounters, the dreadful news from Florida. There she leaves the story, not drawing a moral, just painting the picture of the town and the anguished woman. There is no final understanding on the part of the main character, only the recognition of what has taken place.

Lives of Girls and Women (1971), Munro's second collection, focuses not on the external world around her but on the internal world of her heroine, Del Jordan, a surrogate for the writer who is Munro, for the copyright page of the first edition notes that the book "is autobiographical in form but not in fact." The book studies the artist, the female artist, growing up in this world, coming to grips with her sense of herself, rejecting the stereotypes the world places on her, and finally accepting her own vocation, as the older Del notes at the end, to the artistic profession.

Del is a girl who delights in seeing, recording, and ordering, the three paths of the artist who sees, records, and orders. She is an inveterate observer, standing outside the order of things even when she partakes in it. Being a perceiver, she must be an outsider: "I loved the order, the wholeness, the intricate arrangement of town life, that only an outsider could see." The book itself is an embodiment of what she and Munro believe art to be: it is a tour of the past, an affectionate and compelling attempt to summon up stories, episodes, incidents, and people in order to understand their significance now or at least to understand their importance in the present. The present is the cluttered fabric of the present, and by turning to the past, Del manages to piece together the world that created her, to make some sense of her own background, and to see the formative influences upon the person she is now.

By the last story, Del and Munro have come to know their own artistic creed: how to transform reality into art, which is the realm of the true artist. "People's lives, in Jubilee as elsewhere, were dull, simple, amazing and unfathomable – deep caves paved with kitchen linoleum." Del turns away from her attitude of derivative invention, of taking something and transforming it, into the recording of facts, listing all she can of the details of her own world, to make it everlasting as she moves through it and away into maturity. She has discovered that fiction fades in confrontation with reality when it is not true to the facts; authenticity is the key to her own version of the truth. She now knows that her art will record the profound drama of the ordinary and the trivial when confronted with honesty. Munro reflects,

> I don't feel that a novel is any step up from a short story. . . . When I began to write *Lives*, you see, I began to write it as a much more, a much looser novel, with all these things going on at the same time, and it wasn't working. Then I began pulling the material and making it into what are almost self-contained segments. I mean the sections could almost stand as short stories. They're all a little bit loose, but this seemed to be the only way I could work, and I think maybe this is the way I'll have to write books. I write sort of on – like a single string, a tension string – okay? That's the segment or the story. I don't write as perhaps, as some people say a true novelist does, manipulating a lot of strings.[29]

Freed from her own story, Munro puts into practice the lessons Del Jordan picked up during her journey through her personal past. By the time of her eighth collection, *Open Secrets* (1994), her stories have become longer, still more complex, a mini-novel in the short story form. In "The Albanian Virgin," for example, it is the 1920s, and a woman known only as Lottar has been kidnapped in the mountains of Albania by the tribe that killed her guide. Her captors fire their guns, ply her with brandy, and nurse her back to health in the town of Maltsia e madhe. A Franciscan priest visits her during her illness and explains that the tribesmen are not robbers; they were defending their family honour since the guide had murdered a member of their tribe. Then the story changes to the 1960s and the words of the unnamed narrator, a bookstore owner in Victoria, who is in St. Joseph's Hospital visiting her friend Charlotte, hospitalized with an unidentified illness. Charlotte explains that the story of Lottar, which she is telling, is her self-creation, which she hopes will be made into a film. As the story moves back and forth between Charlotte's account of Lottar's troubles and the narrator's account of her own history, including her uneventful marriage, her subsequent affair with her boarder in London, Ontario, and her steadfast hope that he may join her in Victoria, time is melded into a continuum; no strand of the story is separate, no story is self-contained. By the end, it becomes evident that Charlotte is Lottar, trying to piece together her own life.

---

[29] *Eleven Canadian Novelists*, p. 258. Munro's later collection, *Who Do You Think You Are?* (1978), was a finalist for the Booker Prize, which subsequently excluded short stories from consideration for the prize.

"Child's Play" (*Too Much Happiness*, 2009) centres on Marlene reliving again and again an event from her childhood. Now an older woman, an anthropologist who never married, she remembers a scene from her young days when she and her friend Charlene had a riotous time at their summer camp. Years later, Marlene had seen a picture in a Toronto newspaper of Charlene's wedding to a man named Christopher; she did not write to her. "Perhaps fifteen years later," Marlene, now a published author and a retired professor, receives a letter from Charlene congratulating her on the publication of one of her books; again she does not answer. She then receives a second letter, this time from Christopher, announcing that Charlene has cancer: "She had only a short time left to live." Charlene requested Marlene to come to see her in the hospital, but when she arrives, Charlene is hopelessly asleep. The nurse attending her gives Marlene a letter which Charlene wanted her to have, begging her to go to Guelph to see a parish priest, Father Hofstrader. When she arrives at the cathedral, she learns that the priest is on vacation.

Then follows the story's ending, a dramatic account in the present tense of the incident at their summer camp where Marlene and Charlene drowned the awkward camper Verna. Suddenly the story makes sense, from the opening questions of the past time through Charlene's letter to Marlene to visit this one priest. The ending, as so often in Munro, takes place after the story ends, after Father Hofstrader returns, after Marlene meets him, details left to the reader's imagination. Munro is masterful, suspenseful, and merciless. By retrospect, the narrator relives her life, starting with this one tragic incident, which is described last, and going through her entire life, wondering still – even after the story ends – what will happen because of this one terrifying incident. Munro's philosophical bent is so much in evidence here – art allows her to approach the subject, look back on it in the past tense, then gain some insight, if this is possible. "I feel a kind of satisfaction in just approaching something that is mysterious and important," notes Munro.

Munro's stories examine the lives of people who are confronting the myriad triumphs and confusions that plague their seemingly normal existences. As her fiction develops over her more than fifty years of storytelling, her stories become steadily bleaker, the bittersweet joy of *Lives of Girls and Women* giving way to the relentless search for some kind of contrition and forgiveness in "Child's Play." Art is, Munro states, "the act of approach and recognition." And this is what she does in her fiction. She looks at life, at the human situation, in all its complexity, and she looks at it directly and yet compassionately. She does not mince her words;

she applies herself to a careful depiction of the scene so that it is readily visible through her eyes. More often than not, her narrators are looking back in order to understand the meaning of the scene. The precise meaning is not available; we can recognize only its seeming importance. Munro is a modern writer, wondering about the ambiguities of the past, wondering, too, about the past's meaning on and in the present.

In 2006, Margaret Atwood opened her collection of Munro's fiction: "Alice Munro is among the major writers of English fiction of our time. She's been accorded armfuls of super-superlatives by critics in both North America and the United Kingdom, she's won many awards, and she has a devoted international readership. Among writers themselves, her name is spoken in hushed tones . . .. She's the kind of writer about whom it is often said – no matter how well-known she becomes – that she ought to be better known."[30]

On 13 October 2013, Munro was awarded the Nobel Prize for Literature, heralded as "the master of the contemporary short story."

For Carol Shields (1935–2003), "Alice Munro has shown us what the written word can do. She has been more than a model."[31] For Barbara Gowdy (b. 1950), Munro "is just so good. She is magically good in that when you try to pursue her technique, it vanishes. She strings her words together with invisible thread."[32] And for Souvankham Thammavongsa (b. 1978), Munro is her literary idol: "How bare and plain her language is, and also how brutal. When you grow up reading the best short story writer in the world, you notice and absorb what she does."[33]

Although Atwood (b. 1939) denies being a feminist, preferring the label "protofeminist," she belongs to the second feminist wave. Born in Ottawa and educated at the University of Toronto with a BA in English and Harvard University with an MA and a nearly completed doctorate, she finished all her doctoral requirements except for her thesis, "The English Metaphysical Romance." An accomplished literary critic, novelist, poet, and short story writer, she is the most intellectually gifted of all the writers of this feminist wave, penning a series of novels and short stories of the past, the present, and the future. While her knowledge of Canadian literature is encyclopedic, there is a special place reserved for Montgomery: "Readers of my generation, and of several generations

[30] "Introduction," *Alice Munro's Best: Selected Stories* (Toronto: McClelland & Stewart, 2006), p. vii.
[31] 2002 interview with Shields: bookbrowse.com/author_interviews/full,index.cfm?author_number=764.
[32] "Writing to reflect the darkness of life," *The Globe and Mail*, 22 May 2019, p. A15.
[33] Correspondence with the author, 26 May 2020.

before and since, do not think of *Anne* as 'written'. It has simply always been there."[34]

Although *The Edible Woman* (1969), Atwood's first published novel, coincided with the rise of feminism in North America, she sees her novel as protofeminist rather than feminist:

> There was no women's movement in sight when I was composing the book in 1965, and I'm not gifted with clairvoyance, though like many at the time I'd read Betty Friedan and Simone de Beauvoir behind locked doors. It's noteworthy that my heroine's choices remain much the same at the end of the book as they are at the beginning: a career going nowhere, or marriage as an exit from it. But these were the options for a young woman, even a young educated woman, in Canada in the early sixties. It would be a mistake to assume that everything has changed .... The goals of the feminist movement have not been achieved, and those who claim we're living in a post-feminist era are either sadly mistaken or tired of thinking about the whole subject.[35]

Atwood's novels testify, however, to her strongly feminist outlook on literature and on life.

The Edible Woman was revolutionary at its time of publication. Chronicling assumed gender roles and the ways in which women are expected to display their femininity, it focused on a heroine who could not accept the roles she was required to play. Working for a marketing research firm in Toronto in 1963, Atwood learned the background to *The Edible Woman*, a social novel about the possibilities and impossibilities for personal female identity in a consumer society. Marian McAlpin is about to assume the fixed social identity as the wife of Peter until her body rebels against this trap. Rejecting food, her body identifies with the victims of consumer society. An alternative, her potential liaison with a jaded graduate student pursuing an academic reputation rather than the more idealistic pursuit of knowledge for its own sake, ends in failure, too. Marian then bakes a cake in the shape of a woman and eats it herself. Her choices remain the same at the end of the book as they are at the beginning. The only difference is that she now accepts her own complicity in her victimization.

Rooted in Atwood's reading of 1950s and 1960s American novels, *The Edible Woman* focuses on a woman, described by another character as abnormally normal, who is trapped by her patriarchal society and by

---

[34] "Afterword," *Anne of Green Gables* (Toronto: McClelland & Stewart, 1992), p. 322.
[35] "Preface," *The Edible Woman* (London: Virago, 1980), p. 8.

herself in an untenable position. Her two alternatives in terms of the men in her life offer her no sense of herself; she is alone in her isolated and isolating position, the prototype for the common experience of white, middle-class women throughout North America.

Written as a ghost story, *Surfacing* (1972) is the mythic journey into nature and into the self as Atwood's nameless heroine struggles to find herself. With her lover and her two companions, she travels to the island cabin in northern Quebec where she had spent her early summers. Haunted by her missing father and dead mother and by a marriage that never took place and the child she aborted, she dives into the lake and surfaces a new woman. *Surfacing* offers a more optimistic view of its protagonist than does *The Edible Woman*. While the latter is lighthearted, it is also pessimistic; the couple is not united, and the wrong couple gets married. At the end of *Surfacing*, the woman returns to the surface, having shaken off past encumbrances and willing now to begin anew. Although the terrain of *Surfacing* is bleak, the portrait of the nameless protagonist is sensitive and sympathetic.

Although a feminist novel, *Surfacing* is simultaneously a study of victimization. The heroine "wishes to be not human, because being human inevitably involves being guilty, and if you define yourself as innocent, you can't accept that." As Atwood confesses,

> What I'm really into in that book is the great Canadian victim complex. If you define yourself as innocent then nothing is ever your fault – it is always somebody else doing it to you, and until you stop defining yourself as a victim that will always be true. It will always be somebody else's fault, and you will always be the object of that rather than somebody who has any choice or takes responsibility for their life. And that is not only the Canadian stance towards the world, but the usual female one. Look what a mess I am and it's all their fault. And Canadians do that too. Look at poor innocent us, we are morally better than they. We do not burn people in Vietnam, and those bastards are coming in and taking away our country. Well the real truth of the matter is that Canadians are selling it.[36]

The theme of victimization also stands behind Atwood's volume of literary criticism, *Survival* (1972), which sees "as clearly as possible those patterns of theme, image and attitude which hold our literature together."

Lady Oracle (1976) is a masterful comedy, as Atwood fashions her bildungsroman of a young Toronto girl who blossomed to 245 pounds by the age of nineteen. Red-haired and excessively overweight, her heroine

---

[36] *Eleven Canadian Novelists*, pp. 22–3.

is a romance writer who imagines alternative lives: the obese Joan Delacourt, the thin Joan Foster, and Louisa K. Delacourt, a successful author of costume Gothics. *Life Before Man* (1979) eschews the first-person narrator for the use of the third person and three centres of consciousness, as it explores two years in their lives; setting aside the comic tone of *Lady Oracle*, it studies the games the trio play in love and marriage, sex and power politics. With Toronto's Royal Ontario Museum as the background for a series of impersonal imprisonments, Lesje, the novel's centre, sets aside her birth control pills, finally accepting responsibility for her own life.

Bodily Harm (1981) marks a further development in her fiction. In removing her heroine from Canada and choosing a Caribbean setting, the first time Atwood has moved her fictional world outside Canada, she delivers a scathing commentary on her own country and its smug prefer-ence for the security of non-involvement. More than any of her contem-porary Canadian writers, she devotes much of her creative energy to her country's aspirations and fears. Her passionate commitment to Canada is audible in the admission of Dr. Minnow, the victim of an assassin's bullet. "'The love of your own country is a terrible curse, my friend,' he says. 'Especially a country like this one. It is much easier to live in someone else's country.'" *Bodily Harm* is an impassioned and pained plea to every-one who stands back passively, Marian McAlpin for example, preferring the role of voyeur to that of participant in the drama of life. The vacuum that is her heroine's life is ultimately her own creation, the consequence of her fear of commitment and her unwillingness to assume personal respon-sibility for her actions and her world. In the novel's closing pages, the heroine flies back to Canada, yet this ending is only her fantasized conclusion: we leave her still facing death in a Caribbean prison.

"Fiction," Atwood avers, "is one of the few forms left through which we may examine our society not in its particular but in its typical aspects; through which we can see ourselves and the ways in which we behave towards each other, through which we can see others and judge our-selves."[37] Fiction allows us to see others, to move outside the paralyzing entrapment of self, and to focus our gaze outside ourselves. Writing, the act of making contact with something outside the self, is the means to avoid the solipsistic and deadening retreat into the isolated self. "If writing novels – and reading them – have any redeeming social value," writes

---

[37] "An End to Audience?" *Dalhousie Review* 60, 3 (Autumn 1980): 424.

Atwood, "it's probably that they force you to imagine what it's like to be somebody else."[38]

With five novels set in the present, Atwood moves to future time in *The Handmaid's Tale* (1985), a Booker finalist, a first-person dystopian fiction set in the near future in Cambridge, Massachusetts. Offred records her memories of growing up in the old society, being formed for the new society, and belonging to one of the male Commanders. Society as we know it has returned to a constructed re-creation of Puritan New England; the government of the past has been toppled; women are slaves to men's desires in a loveless theocratic world. The novel's brilliance rests in the creation of a future that is a too logical extension of many dimensions of the present.

Perhaps only a Canadian, a neighbour as well as an outsider to the United States, could create such an unsettling vision of the American future. In implied contrast to Gilead is its northern neighbour, once again the final stop of a new underground railroad, this time one that smuggles handmaids to the freedom of Canada. Readers may wish to shy away from Atwood's warning about the present, which leads to Gilead, preferring to regard the book only as fiction. But the heroine realizes that people, unable to bear very much reality, escape into the hope that reality is only fiction. "I would like to believe this is a story I'm telling," she laments. "I need to believe it. I must believe it. Those who can believe that such stories are only stories have a better chance." With her readings in American Puritan literature and her eyes focused relentlessly on the present, Atwood offers a too convincing analysis of the future directions of the American destiny.

Atwood's next four novels have exclusively Canadian settings. *Cat's Eye* (1988), a Booker finalist, and *The Robber Bride* (1993) focus again on Toronto, the former, a first-person narrative, revealing a painter who returns from Vancouver for a retrospective of her work and for a confrontation with the many submerged layers of her past, the latter looking at one evil woman, who shapes and reshapes the lives and the safety of the two women who heed and hate her. Atwood then returns to the Canadian past, the mid-nineteenth century, in *Alias Grace* (1996), a Booker finalist, for Grace Marks's first-person account of her life, including her trial for murder; the novel even includes a brief appearance by Susanna Moodie, the nineteenth-century immigrant who had already cast her lot for many

---

[38] "Writing the Male Character," *Second Words: Selected Critical Prose* (Toronto: House of Anansi, 1982), p. 430.

years in Atwood's creative imagination. *The Blind Assassin* (2000), which won the Booker Prize, goes back to the early decades of the twentieth century for Iris Chase Griffen's mainly first-person journey through the detrimental effects of class and gender division in Toronto as she manipulates the truth and assigns the writing of her own novel to her now dead sister; both are fractured women, the pain they endure suggesting their collusion in their own victimization.

Atwood ventured again into the future, into a world beyond *The Handmaid's Tale*, into a post-apocalyptic future in her MaddAddam trilogy, "a speculative fiction," as Atwood herself says, "not a science fiction proper."[39] *Oryx and Crake* (2003), a Booker finalist, depicts a terrifying future where the one human survivor would seem to be Jimmy, who renames himself Snowman after the Abominable Snowman. Alone save for the Crakers, a genetically modified people developed to replace human beings, he recounts his previous life in little pieces: his unsatisfying relationship with his parents, his lifelong friendship with Crake, "the numbers man," and his many sexual entanglements, including his connection with the beautiful Oryx. Snowman emerges as a morally responsible man who tells his tale to gain some understanding of what has happened.

Taking place during the same years as *Oryx and Crake*, *The Year of the Flood* (2009) begins in the present, year Twenty-five, the time of the Waterless Flood. Now the focus is on two female characters, Toby (or Tobiatha) who speaks in the third person and Ren (or Brenda) who speaks in the first person, members of the cult of the pacifist God's Gardeners, who accept refugees from the outlying lands known as the Exfernal world and offer another mode of living. One of these Adams, Zeb, openly flouts the rules of the Gardeners and forms a breakaway group of bioterrorists known as MaddAddam.

MaddAddam (2013), the final volume of the trilogy, is the continuation of both *Oryx and Crake* and *The Year of the Flood*. For the innocent Crakers, Toby creates mythological stories, simple but glorified, of her old world of Crake, Zeb, and the Gardeners and of the world that will be. Listening to her all the while is the young Craker Blackbeard. Her lover Zeb had a chequered past, including a torturous life with his half-brother Adam One, who used the online codename MaddAddam to gather together a group of supremely intelligent gene hackers to infiltrate

---

[39] "Writing *Oryx and Crake*," *Curious Pursuits*, p. 322.

biotechnological corporations. It is a horrific future, built on Atwood's perceptions of her own world. "Although *MaddAddam* is a work of fiction," she writes in the acknowledgements, "it does not include any technologies or biobeings that do not already exist, are not under construction, or are not possible in theory."

The Heart Goes Last (2016) continues the journey into the future, though not the post-apocalyptic world of her trilogy, but a future already represented in *The Handmaid's Tale*. Again set in the United States, specifically the eastern part that became the Republic of Gilead, it takes place in an undesignated time when violence, a breakdown of law and order, and mass unemployment are everywhere, Atwood's aim being to portray the grim details of this futuristic world under the perverted ideals of its Scientology-like leader.

Thirty-four years after the publication of *The Handmaid's Tale*, Atwood wrote its sequel, *The Testaments* (2019), set fifteen years later and utilizing three overlapping narrators. Still a totalitarian theocracy with rigid control of women and their reproductive capacities, Gilead shows signs of internal decay, and there are now competing political systems elsewhere in the former United States. With increasing corruption at home, there are some hopeful signs that the future may return to a time when constitutional rights were not suspended, Canada meanwhile offering a plausible alternative. The novel won Atwood her second Booker Prize. Atwood's impressive fiction straddles all boundaries; she writes of the past, the present, and the future; she has her settings in Canada, the United States, the Caribbean, Europe, and nameless places in the near and distant future. Her fictive world invites readers to transport themselves into her compelling and realistic universe where modes of living are steadily open to questioning. She is, above all, an observer, and she wants her readers to observe, too.

Atwood denies herself a strictly feminist role, and she does not align herself openly with the feminist movement, though she is a writer adopted by feminist critics. When she began writing, the movement was scarcely visible. Now she pronounces its benefits to literature: "The expansion of the territory available to writers, both in character and in language; a sharp-eyed examination of the way power works in gender relations, and the exposure of much of this as socially constructed; a vigorous exploration of many hitherto-concealed areas of experience." She sees herself, as do the other authors in this chapter, as a fiction writer, not as a person advocating political causes or movements, which "are usually problematical for novelists, unless the novelist has a secret desire to be in billboard advertising."⁴⁰ Perhaps she is similar to Audrey Thomas: "I consider myself a feminist but I do not, consciously, think about feminism when I am making a story."

For the authors of this chapter, the feminist movement was happening while they were writing their fiction. Twentieth-century feminism began first in France and then in the United States, and the most influential modern feminist writing in Canada emerged first in Quebec with writers like Nicole Brossard penning elaborate treatises on women and their plight. In English fiction, the authors of the second feminist wave celebrate their feminist positions through and in their fiction. They write about women, their struggles and harassments, their triumphs and tragedies; they do not pen important treatises about women; they pen novels and short stories which depict the modern world and women's roles in it.

In the period between Wiseman's male-centred *The Sacrifice* to her later female-centred *Crackpot* rests the emergence of fiction writers who lead the way to a challenging future of feminist fiction, all the while not giving place to the celebration of a movement but sticking closely to the demands of a fictional world and the challenges of "making a story."

Laurence pioneered the writing of women's lives, her five Manawaka books setting the stage for depictions of women and their place in society. Thomas and Engel followed her lead with their presentations of women adrift in the contemporary world. Munro celebrated men and women, of the past and of the present, in her short stories. And Atwood broadened her treatment of men and women by setting her books in the past, the present, and the future.

Towards the end of her life, Laurence penned her autobiography, *Dance on the Earth* (1987), a feminist document unlike her earlier fiction, standing, in its opening pages, as a vengeful treatise: "I think it is outrageous that men are recognized as sexual beings whereas women are often left with either a burden of guilt over an abortion, or a burden of guilt over an adoption, or a burden not only of guilt but of eighteen or more years' work trying to raise a child alone with damn little help from anyone." The distance between Laurence's fiction and her autobiography is also the distance between early feminist theorizing and the solid feminist stance of the eighties.

For these six writers, fiction offers a way of viewing their world from their own female perspectives. "They have become among the most loved

---

⁴⁰ "Spotty-Handed Villainesses: Problems of Female Bad Behaviour in the Creation of Literature," *Curious Pursuits*, p. 179.

and appreciated writers not only in Canada but in the English-speaking world, honored by awards, honorary degrees, Orders of Canada," Jane Rule (1931–2007) observed. "They are household names, inspirations to generations of women coming after them that, yes, it is possible to do it all."[41]

---

[41] "Our Mothers" (September 2005), *Loving the Difficult* (Sidney, British Columbia: Hedgerow, 2008), p. 19.

CHAPTER 6

The Flourishing of the Wests

The Canadian fictional landscape holds many wests. From the Alberta strongholds of Ralph Connor's pulpit fiction through Frederick Philip Grove's Manitoba, Howard O'Hagan's mythic Yellowhead Pass, Sinclair Ross's Saskatchewan depression, and W.O. Mitchell's joyful Saskatchewan down to Ethel Wilson's British Columbia city and country life and Sheila Watson's interior British Columbia, there are more and different wests than can be imagined. Building upon these and other writers and forging their own identities, western writers have continued to create their own unique voices. Pre-eminent among them is Robert Kroetsch (1917–2011), a professor in both Canada and the United States, an essayist, novelist, and poet who contributed to a reimagining of the west and influenced many other writers.

Born near Heisler, Alberta, Kroetsch exemplifies the principles of the disciplined and engaged writer. First attracted to literature through a travelling library, he stumbled upon Conrad's *The Nigger of the 'Narcissus'* and James's *The Turn of the Screw* ("two books that puzzled me, fascinated me, held my imagination: because they weren't like anything I'd read, ever, before").[1] Then there was his exposure to W.O. Mitchell's short fiction ("He was the first Canadian writer to influence me. He gave me the realization that you could write about the Prairies. All the literature I had read was about people somewhere else. Then suddenly I read his *Jake and the Kid* stories and *Who Has Seen the Wind?*").[2] He then encountered another model, *As for Me and My House*:

> Where I had responded with delight to Mitchell, I remember responding
> with shock to Ross's portrait of a marriage, a prairie town, a prairie
> house .... Ross and his characters in his town of Horizon became a

---

[1] "Taking the Risk," *Open Letter*, fifth series, no. 4 (Spring 1983): 65.
[2] *For Openers: Conversations with 24 Canadian Writers* (Madeira Park, British Columbia: Harbour, 1981), p. 114.

generating principle, the enabling moment that releases me into a memory of the politics and the poverty, of the card parties and the funerals and the wedding dances and the sports days and the auction sales, the silence and the stories of the Thirties. Ross, by some alchemy, allowed me to recognize the binary patterns that the human mind uses to construct its days and its labyrinth.[3]

Finally, his reading of *The Double Hook* taught him "to *see* a new country."

The pivotal moment in his early career occurred at McGill University where he was studying in 1954–55. He enrolled in Hugh MacLennan's course on the development of English prose. MacLennan

dared to name the names of my world, and that truly was daring at the time. He had dared to root his story in the geography of our country. In that naming and in that concern with geography – the total implications for a particular people of a particular landscape – he was the role-model I had been seeking. He was – he is – the novelist as geographer: a man who reads rivers, who reads water . . . the cartographer of our dreams, be they social or political or religious or personal.

He inspired the young writer to fashion his stories out of his own land:

It was he who showed us, there in that classroom, in his writing, in his voice, in his presence, in the limited story of his life that we had in the absence of a biography, how to proceed . . . . It was he who, in the intricate mystery of his writing and his life, showed us how to live with and how to live those most oldfashioned of afflictions: love of place, love of country, love of language, love of friends, love of that indeed opposite sex.[4]

After graduating in English and philosophy from the University of Alberta, Kroetsch went North, the last of the Canadian frontiers, to work first as a labourer on the Fort Smith Portage and then for two seasons as a boat purser on the Mackenzie River. He then graduated with an MA from Middlebury College and a PhD from the University of Iowa, all the time reading Canadian and world literatures. Following MacLennan's example, he began to write a novel about the Mackenzie River: *But We Are Exiles* (1965) builds on Kroetsch's Mackenzie experiences in Peter Guy's third-person narrative. Having cast aside his eastern upbringing and now a pilot on the Mackenzie, Guy attempts to recover the body of the ship's exuberant and egotistical owner. The ending is deliberately open, suggesting incompleteness, indeterminacy, and the possibility of continuation. With

---

[3] "On Being an Alberta Writer," *Open Letter*, fifth series, no. 4: 74.
[4] "Hugh MacLennan: An Appreciation," pp. 136, 139.

MacLennan as the inspiration, *But We Are Exiles* is a traditional novel which dares to suggest the ambitious probing of Kroetsch's later fiction and its uneasy relationship with social realism.

"As a child," Kroetsch recalled, "I had that really strong feeling that I was living in a place that had no story to explain it and so I suppose one of the things I wanted to do was tell *that* story of nothing to tell."[5] Early in his career, he wrote: "In a sense, we haven't got an identity until somebody tells our story. The fiction makes us real."[6] His fiction makes his own world real. Following Heidegger's theories, he resolved that the major writers must, and do, uninvent the world, clearing their terrain: "Canadians still have to elect for this relatively unknown voice that is theirs, and make literature out of that."[7] Seeing Canada as a country where things are being formed though not already shaped, he enjoys the freedom to experiment, to challenge, and to defy the tenets of social realism: "one of the skills of the deconstructionist is to play with the possibilities of the text ... one is always moving back and forth between positions."[8] Incompleteness is the norm; resolution becomes impossible.

Moreover, Kroetsch is a student and product of the oral tradition: "I'm interested in what we call the oral tradition in literature, and I think that Western Canada is one of the few places left where men genuinely sit down and tell each other stories." This tradition expresses "the way people communicate legend to each other; often it leads to the tall tale tradition: the story has vitality; why not stretch it a little, make it a little better."[9] The unnaming, then, "allows the naming. The local pride speaks. The oral tradition speaks its tentative nature, its freedom from the authorized text."[10] He concludes: "I find a *source* in that oral tradition, rather than an answer of any sort."[11] After *But We Are Exiles*, the tall tale and its oral tradition become fundamental to his evolving fiction.

The Words of My Roaring (1966), *The Studhorse Man* (1969), and *Gone Indian* (1973) are set primarily in the pseudo-fictional region of Coulee Hill/Notikeewin, Alberta, which approximates the region where Kroetsch was from – Battle River Country in the Alberta Parklands. The first book

---

[5] *Labyrinths of Voice: Conversations with Robert Kroetsch*, eds. Shirley Neuman and Robert Wilson (Edmonton: NeWest Press, 1982), pp. 186–7.
[6] Robert Kroetsch, James Bacque, Pierre Gravel, *Creation*, ed. Robert Kroetsch (Toronto: New Press, 1970), p. 63.
[7] *Conversations with Canadian Novelists*, 1, 86.   [8] *Labyrinths of Voice*, pp. 63, 73.
[9] "Writing from Prairie Roots," *Alberta School Library Review*, 8, 1 (Fall 1971): 16, 10.
[10] "Disunity as Unity," *The Lovely Treachery of Words: Essays Selected and New* (Toronto: Oxford University Press, 1989), p. 32.
[11] *Labyrinths of Voice*, p. 164.

takes place in the drought of 1935; the second during World War II; and the third in contemporary times. Each book has the figure of the married undertaker and candidate for public office, Johnnie Judas Backstrom, the larger-than-life protagonist of the first book and a fleeting presence in the two subsequent novels. "There was a bit of romance about the North; a bit of mythology, adventure on the last frontier, and so I went up North," he recalled. "I did write a novel about life on the Mackenzie River, but part of what I discovered was my connection with Alberta, the stories that I had to tell about my home."[12]

But We Are Exiles' third-person narration gives way to the exuberant first-person narration of *The Words of My Roaring.* In the provincial election, Johnnie Backstrom promises to bring rain for the drought-stricken farmers. His older opponent, "minion of the Eastern high-muckie-mucks and front for the Fifty Big Shots," stoically accepts the economic facts of the depression, making an artificial world from his transplanted historical roots. In the end, it rains, and Backstrom wins the election, an outcome confirmed in a later novel.

Kroetsch is playing with the myth of the stultified East and the blossoming West: the East has a codified political myth unconnected to the unformed Western consciousness. Backstrom is creating a new order and mythologizing his world, speaking prophetically for the West's own sense of myth. Towards the beginning, he says: "We are so often mistaken; we confuse beginnings, endings." Halfway through his story, he laments: "You know – beginnings and endings. The old confusion." Then the final paragraph of his tale observes: "Beginnings and endings. I had to make amends." His "amends" is the ribald tale he has been telling.

The Studhorse Man has two protagonists: Hazard Lepage, the studhorse man, who is searching for the perfect mare for his prized blue stallion Poseidon, the last of the Lepage breed, and Demeter Proudfoot, a mad scholar who is writing Hazard's biography some twenty years later from a waterless bathtub in a mental hospital. Like Backstrom, Lepage, a larger-than-life character with his vitality, his exuberance, and his rampant masculinity, contrasts with Proudfoot, a sexually repressed man who interferes more and more in his seemingly objective biography. The treatise is a dialogue between a dispossessed elder on a fixed quest and a frightened young man asserting his role as biographer of a factual as well as fantastical scholarly work. The biography is the final triumph over time

---

[12] Robert Kroetsch and John Lent, *Abundance: The Mackie House Conversations about the Writing Life* (Vernon, British Columbia: Kalamalka Press, 2007), p. 68.

itself in Proudfoot's ability to assemble and shape a life out of the notecards, conversations, and other resources at his disposal, to give some kind of form to human experience, which Kroetsch consistently describes as formless: "The biographer in *The Studhorse Man* slowly usurping the subject of his biography is unwillingly deconstructing the notion of a hero. He starts to see himself as the hero as he sits in the bathtub writing the book."[13] Lepage cannot locate the perfect mare, and Poseidon is used for the new technology of Pregnant Mare's Urine and the subsequent production of birth control pills. Despite the realistic descriptions of Alberta's cities and towns, its rivers and roads, *The Studhorse Man* is Kroetsch's continuing creation of a mythologized comic land out of his Alberta world.

Gone Indian, the triptych's conclusion, continues Kroetsch's fascination with dual protagonists: J. Mark Madham, an adherent of the written word and, like his creator, a professor of English at the State University of New York at Binghamton, and his disgruntled doctoral student, Jeremy Sadness, an adherent of the oral tradition, who has flown to Edmonton for a job interview at the University of Alberta. Sadness sends Madham tape-recorded accounts of his travails, which Madham edits and finally destroys as he assumes authority over Sadness's story. In the process of editing, he engages in a process of self-reflection which prompts him to confront the guilt he has repressed following his own move from the West to the East. He, therefore, continues the tradition of the first-person controlling the narration of *But We Are Exiles* and Demeter Proudfoot's attempted authority over Lepage's life. He lives in the East, a sterile, fenced-in world, where he feels secure; Sadness flees to an open-ended realm of possibility, having successfully avoided closure and now finding a more authentic sense of self on the northern prairies, which resist human definition. The prairies become the last frontier, and, as Kroetsch quotes in his epigraph from Frederick Jackson Turner, "For a moment, at the frontier, the bonds of custom are broken and unrestraint is triumphant."

All three novels entail the mythologizing of Albertan life and livelihood. Each one is an open-ended comic travelogue, the movement from closure to openness the opposite of the traditional quest motif, the search for freedom the overriding concern of the novel's questing journey. Each novel questions where society is going. In his celebration of the frontier's unrestraint, Kroetsch introduces Indigenous people as full individuals, not having them as token gestures but portraying them as honest people. When Sadness, for example, finds surrogate parents, they are a man and

---

[13] *Labyrinths of Voice*, p. 179.

his Blackfoot wife. Alberta has many peoples, and they are all figured forth in Kroetsch's paean of praise for his mythologized landscape. "It's a lesson you have to learn over and over again," he observed, "trust the local, trust your place and its versions of stories."[14]

Modelled in part on *Surfacing* and recounting that novel's search in a western setting, and paying homage to *Heart of Darkness, Badlands* (1975) follows a 1916 paleontological expedition from a female perspective. Kroetsch's former wife "was reading all this literature way before it became a powerful movement," he recalled. "She was about ten years ahead of the whole thing, so I was exposed to a lot of feminism (coming out of Woolf of course – obvious sources to begin with). I heard about it and read some of it and I think in a novel like *Badlands* I am responding to that."[15] There were also his rereadings of *As For Me and My House*, a woman's diary. He thus made his expedition, following his earlier patterns, a narration though now by a woman who makes up her story out of her father's field notes. Kroetsch "had to write the story as a woman, to get it down," writes George Bowering (b. 1935), "because none of the men in the story would get it done. When she throws her father's 'end of words' into the lake she walks away, and she says that she 'did not once look back, not once, ever.' But of course the whole book, written after that walk, is made of looking back. The author had to be a woman to do that."[16]

In *Badlands*, William Dawe led the expedition down the Red Deer River to uncover dinosaur fossils to rival the famous paleontologists of earlier generations. He left behind notes which his daughter Anna, a repressed virgin from Ontario, uses in 1972 to follow his journey, giving some form to the formlessness of his jottings. She seeks to penetrate her father's protective exterior and to define her own identity. As she tries to understand her father, she is accompanied by Anna Yellowbird, an "Old Indian Woman" and a totally natural person, who had followed Dawe's team in 1916. Curiously, Dawe had named his own Anna after the older Anna. Throughout the novel are dreams of fame, tall tales, and raging sexuality, though everything is now seen through a feminist perspective which debunks male behaviour. In fact, the female voice often satirizes male rituals, using irony to remind the reader of the narrator's perspective. The quests of Dawe and his daughter Anna highlight the many-layered texture of Kroetsch's novels, the allusive, indeed mythopoeic dimensions of his literary works. In his fiction as in his poetry, he is giving voice to the

[14] *Abundance*, p. 23.   [15] *Labyrinths of Voice*, p. 34.
[16] *Errata* (Red Deer, Alberta: Red Deer College Press, 1988), p. 46.

West and its many dimensions, whether on the archetypal raft on the Red Deer River or the boat on the Mackenzie.

In his subsequent novels, Kroetsch expands his playful exploration of the boundary between fiction and truth, between the manipulation of his reader's mind and the more usual strain of social realism. In its third-person narrative voice speaking for the entire community of Big Indian, Alberta, located somewhere along the Saskatchewan border, *What the Crow Said* (1978) recounts a series of fabulous events in a matter-of-fact way, illustrating that the oral narrative is still the background of Kroetsch's literary work. *Alibi* (1983) has an American-educated Albertan working as an agent for a millionaire oil producer, whom he has never met; trying to find his employer a perfect spa illustrates the futility of all attempts to make collections of objects, systems, and even language. *The Puppeteer* (1992) continues the oil producer's penchant for collections in new and exotic settings, where Kroetsch as compiler can range widely in his employment of language and its wide possibilities. *The Man from the Creeks* (1998), a fantastic recreation of the Klondike gold rush, uses the final lines of Robert Service's poem, "The Shooting of Dan McGrew," "While the man from the creeks lay clutched to the/breast of the lady that's known as Lou," as the touchstone for the reminiscences of Lou's now 114-year-old son Peek, who still resides in Dawson City.

Using social realism as the springboard for his fantastic explorations of the myth of the west, Kroetsch illuminated Canadian fiction with a knowledge of Canadian as well as world literatures, introducing postmodern literary theories into his closely planned novels. He gave fictive expression to the western landscapes in a buoyant and raucous style.

For Rudy Wiebe (b. 1934), writing fiction is a craft and an august calling. "Throughout history the most original religious thinkers have also been great storytellers," he wrote early in his career, and the writers he selected for his anthology "are standing in the greatest of all human traditions – when we read their stories we not only experience pleasure, we also experience the desire to be better."[17] Raised Mennonite, he writes from the perspective of a committed Christian: "I've always felt pretty strongly about my Christian vocation. I'm a Christian so I write from that viewpoint, there's no point in being apologetic. I write as a Christian just as Camus writes as an existentialist." His sources are many, including the panoply of books he read in university, especially the stories of Joyce and

[17] *Double Vision: An Anthology of Twentieth-Century Stories in English*, selected by Rudy Wiebe (Toronto: Macmillan, 1976), p. xii.

Faulkner, the writings of Frederick Philip Grove, "a writer who wrote mythically and imagistically about the world I knew," and Sheila Watson, "I read Sheila Watson's *The Double Hook* practically the month it came out. I would suppose that my striving after language in *Peace Shall Destroy Many* – and I think it must be seen in some sense as striving – is trying to do what Sheila Watson does seemingly effortlessly."[18]

Born in Fairholme, Saskatchewan, Wiebe spoke only German until he started school. After his family moved to Coaldale, Alberta, in 1947, he continued his schooling, attending the University of Alberta as an English major. As a graduate student, he took a creative-writing course from F.M. Salter, who convinced him, "Write about the stuff that you know, that you've lived yourself. That's the way to be a genuine writer."[19] He encouraged him to ponder his northern Saskatchewan, *Peace Shall Destroy Many* (1962) being written under Salter's supervision as part of Wiebe's master's program. The novel is the first work in Canada to be regarded as a Mennonite creation.

Set in 1944 in the fictional Mennonite community of Wapiti in northern Saskatchewan with the church as its centre, *Peace Shall Destroy Many* follows the maturing of eighteen-year-old Thom Wiens, who is pursuring his Christian commitment in a Mennonite landscape which does not permit violations of "the traditions of the fathers." The settlement's authoritarian founder and leader holds that Mennonites should withdraw completely from the secular world around them. Wiens slowly learns that people must come to know for themselves their own dependence upon Christ and the spiritual vision that permits the fulfilment of their identities. A debate between the liberal and conservative perspectives in Mennonite thinking, the novel sparked enormous criticism from many Mennonites, who reacted as savagely to their portrayal as did Jews to Richler's portrayal of them a decade earlier. Featuring a few romantic relationships between Mennonites and their mixed-race neighbours, it breaks out of the isolated, self-sufficient world of some Mennonite thinkers, positing a differently balanced vision of life. *Come Back* (2014), Wiebe's later novel, tells a semi-autobiographical tale of a father, Hal Wiens (an eight-year-old boy in Wiebe's first novel), a retired professor of literature whose twenty-four-year-old son, like Wiebe's own son, commits suicide in 1985.

---

[18] *A Voice in the Land: Essays By and About Rudy Wiebe*, ed. W.J. Keith (Edmonton: NeWest Press, 1981), pp. 127, 216, 244.
[19] Ibid., p. 126.

The other factor that plays into Wiebe's writing is his realization that the world of western Canada, his land of Saskatchewan and Alberta, is relatively untold in the pages of Canadian fiction: "There hadn't been much writing about the Canadian prairies, about my particular kind of world, so why not write about it? The Indians have always intrigued me, partly because they were a major part of the world I grew up with. I was born in Big Bear country, close to Turtle Lake."[20] Like Kroetsch, he found his world waiting to have its stories told, and he told the stories of people, including many Indigenous characters, with a firm commitment to the often harsh reality of his subject matter.

With *The Blue Mountains of China* (1970), Wiebe found his true voice as a novelist. In telling Mennonite history beginning in Russia in 1929, "the entire history of a people, scattered over 80 years of their life and scattered over four different continents,"[21] he chooses a new format, recounting the story from many points of view, with a semblance of order given by the recurrent perspective of an eighty-four-year-old woman, who was born in Manitoba, emigrated to Paraguay, and reappears as the narrative voice in the opening and three separate chapters; her reminiscences of her childhood and adolescence on the prairies reflect her secure faith. The novel fulfils his intention of penning Mennonite history, tracing family branches through diverse routes, and using a myriad of voices, all of them struggling with what it means for each of them to be a practicing Christian in the modern world.

From mapping Mennonite behavior in the past and the present, Wiebe turned to his other abiding interest, the Native peoples of the west, to create two historical biographies, *The Temptations of Big Bear* (1973) and *The Scorched-Wood People* (1977), the former of Big Bear, the latter Louis Riel, both men struggling heroically and fatally to stop the white man's exploitation of their minority followers. Big Bear, a wise chief of the Plains Cree, envisions a Northwest where Indians, Métis, and Whites live together in peace with one another and with the land; when young Native warriors kill nine white men in the Frog Lake Massacre of 1885, Big Bear is tried unjustly and convicted by a white court of "treason-felony," serving three years in prison, then, shortly after his release, dying as he is saying "the long prayer to The Only One that was his life." In *The Scorched-Wood People*, Riel, a political leader of the Métis, first of the Red River District and later of Saskatchewan, believes that he and his people "must preserve for our children that liberty, that possession of soil, without

---

[20] Ibid., p. 127.   [21] Ibid., p. 128.

which there is no happiness for anyone"; government forces defeat the Métis in the Battle of Batoche of 1885, and Riel is convicted of treason and executed. Both doomed leaders have the sympathy and compassionate understanding of their novelist.

The polyphonic structure of *The Blue Mountains of China* continues in Wiebe's historical fiction. Although narrated ostensibly by an omniscient voice, *The Temptations of Big Bear*, based on meticulous research, uses its cast of historical characters and their varied viewpoints to paint a portrait of Big Bear, the novel's central presence. Each group has a perspective, the white people generally maintaining an economic vision of the land, the Indians maintaining their religious understanding of the bond between the land and its people, and the slow but steady disappearance of Native-land rights increases the plight and the tragedy of the Indians. Big Bear is "a great and wise man who lives a tragic life. And no one knows much about him," Wiebe remarks. He is "a great hero of our past whom nobody has done much with. Even the Indians don't know much about him."[22] Wiebe brings to life the monstrous debates, the blunders and the hesitations, that make up the tragic history of Big Bear and his people.

Wiebe's first use of a specific overarching narrator comes in *The Scorched-Wood People* and its personal reminiscences of an elderly, scurrilous Métis poet, an epic singer of tales, who tells the story of the insurgent Riel and Gabriel Dumont, the Métis' military commander. Whether the story is factually accurate rests with the narrator's fluid memories. The emphasis falls not on the leaders' wisdom but on Riel's divinely inspired visions: he would have the Métis people bring "God's perfect kingdom" to fruition in this world. His dream of a new nation, not dissimilar to a Mennonite heaven on earth, contrasts bleakly with the eastern establishment's designs of economic exploitation of the land. And the two novels stand behind Vanderhaeghe's similar role as a historian of the past.

From his chronicling of his Mennonite heritage, Wiebe became a similar chronicler of the Canadian west. He resurrects, examines, and offers new understandings of two significant figures, Big Bear, comparatively unknown, and Louis Riel, often misrepresented. Both men conform to Wiebe's ideal of good people trying to bring their dreams to reality; both suffer ignoble defeat. Yet in their desire for peace, they articulate and live by standards and values totally in harmony with Wiebe's Mennonite vision, where pacifism is a virtue.

---

[22] Ibid.

Cast as an omniscient narrator's rendering of Sir John Franklin's first voyage to the Northwest Territories in search of the fabled Northwest Passage, *A Discovery of Strangers* (1994) recreates the first encounter of the Yellowknife Indians with the white men of Franklin's expedition, the Indians needed for the visitors as guides through the northland. At the novel's centre is the love story of twenty-two-year-old Midshipman Robert Hood and fifteen-year-old Yellowknife girl known to the British as Greenstockings; the pair create their own language to bridge their linguistic divide. Only twenty years after this abortive enterprise, the Yellowknifes will be reduced to almost nothing through a smallpox epidemic brought to them by their invaders. Once again Wiebe selects another minority, the Yellowknife Indians, and shows their earthly and spiritual goals, which are distinct from the intruders' ambitions. Using meticulous research into the Franklin archives, and imposing thoughtfully a love story which might well have happened onto the account of this expedition, he recreates a convincing story from the Canadian past.

Fundamentally Christian in his training and his beliefs, Wiebe acknowledges that his "major stories came from a certain kind of fairly narrow understanding of what the Bible was talking about, which is how I grew up. In some ways, I've simply never found a better way of thinking about the world."[23] From his fictional creation of Wapiti, the home of his Mennonite creations, he went on to fashion portraits of people, especially the Indians and the Métis, which deconstruct the traditional one-dimensional renditions of these racial minorities. He asks his readers to consider again the truthfulness and the beauty of these forgotten people. An archaeologist rather than a historian, he is rewriting or writing for the first time the history of the Canadian Northwest and the people who have inhabited and do inhabit it.

Known for more than thirty-five poetry volumes, George Bowering is also a prolific writer of fiction. Born in Penticton, British Columbia, with his youthful years spent in the Okanagan Valley, he took his BA in history and creative writing and his MA in English from the University of British Columbia. Initially interested in writing prose fiction, he read the writings of Americans, including Faulkner, Hemingway, and especially James T. Farrell. When he read the poetry of William Carlos Williams, he transferred his interest to poetry, consuming Canadian writers such as Irving Layton and Raymond Souster. Then, in 1963, he read *The Double Hook*: "I threw it across the room . . . . I hadn't understood a word of it."[24]

---

[23] Ibid., p. 242.   [24] *Always Someone to Kill the Doves*, p. 287.

Slowly, the power of the novel enfolded him: "The best novel to come out of the province . . .. More than any other Canadian novel, it is loved and referred to by the innovative poets and fiction writers who have arrived on the Canadian scene since 1959."[25]

Mirror on the Floor (1967), is a short, fast-paced account of the hero's unsuccessful efforts to form a relationship with a woman damaged by her parents' hatred of each other and her father's subsequent suicide. Experimenting with his technique while using the patterns of everyday speech, he creates a straightforward novel with only hints of his future fiction. *A Short Sad Book* (1977), a parody of famous Canadian people in fictitious incidents replete with the postmodern technique of frequent authorial intrusions, is an amusing history of deconstructed cultural myths. "My wife," confesses Bowering in the novel, "hates this novel she says I'm getting too far removed from my readers with all this obscure self-absorption."

In *Burning Water* (1980), the epitome of his experiments with the postmodern novel, the narrator alerts the reader at the beginning: "We are making a story, after all, as we always have been. Standing and speaking together to make up a history, a real historical fiction." Recreating the Pacific Northwest at the end of the eighteenth century, Bowering presents George Vancouver's voyages as well as his personal journey into madness and despair. Playing freely with the facts of his story, he places himself in the pages of his novel as the participating narrator. The story centres on finding not the Northwest Passages but the Peruvian Don Quadra, a Spanish leader fifteen years George Vancouver's senior. Vancouver and Quadra become lovers, leading their lives against the background of eighteenth-century imperial history. Quadra shows Vancouver that a deep commitment to duty is the avenue to a productive life. Bowering's ruminations on his own travels to Trieste and Florence and Costa Rica and San Francisco are interpolated to balance his descriptions of Vancouver's voyages, and such interruptions impede the flow of the narrative, as do his many literary allusions. His postmodern manipulation of history, while being playful, manages to undercut the seeming authenticity of his novel's factual basis.

His two novels set in the Okanagan Valley, his youthful home as well as the setting for *Deep Hollow Creek* and *The Double Hook*, are the best of his fiction writing. Set in the 1890s, *Caprice* (1987) is his rewriting of the typical western novel where he switches some genders and makes his lone

---

[25] *Bowering's B.C.: A Swashbuckling History* (Toronto: Viking, 2005), p. 314.

rider be a young French Canadian woman and a poet. Armed with a book of poetry and a deadly bullwhip, Caprice seeks vengeance on the American outlaw who murdered her brother, her quest taking her from the British Columbia interior to the southwestern United States and back again. Then a schoolteacher tries to have her abandon her quest: "This being a late-twentieth-century novel, he does get to enjoy sex with the heroine, and he does teach at the historical Kamloops Indian Residential School."[26] Caprice, however, will not desist; she succeeds in her quest, then rides away. No ordinary heroine of a western, where women are assigned the archetypal roles of loving wife, beleaguered prostitute, or prim school-marm, she is a driving and driven force, unique unto herself, who cannot be dissuaded from her mission.

Shoot! (1994) recounts the late 1870s deeds of the three Métis McLean brothers and their Métis friend Alex Hare in the Okanagan Valley. Bitter and antisocial, they are fated to become outlaws, murdering two men in cold blood. Trapped by a posse of more than one hundred men, the four are taken prisoner, tried, and then executed. Around this skeletal story Bowering studies the desperation of racism, at the same time inculcating himself into his narrative through his contemporary presence in the same region. A mixture of history, legend, and myth, the novel interweaves his autobiographical reflections with the facts of the McLeans, his novel being an account of racism and its dire consequences.

Although Bowering's fiction does not have the enduring power of Kroetsch's, his novels are important examples of British Columbia's engagement with its past. "I will be someone who did not write books," he admits, "to be placed in the mainstream of Canadian literature, but all the same someone whom they cannot write a history without mentioning. He was always pottering around in his garden, they will say, and once in a long while someone would come around and, well not really admire, but perhaps enquire about the odd-looking shrubs."[27]

Both Jack Hodgins (b. 1938), born in Comox, British Columbia, and Guy Vanderhaeghe, born in Esterhazy, Saskatchewan, acknowledge Kroetsch's determination to root their fiction in their own uncharted worlds. Both are skilled short-story writers as well as distinguished novelists, beginning their careers with acclaimed collections of short stories.

A graduate of the University of British Columbia and a high school teacher of English who became Professor of Creative Writing at the University of Victoria, Hodgins burst on to the literary scene with his first

[26] *How I Wrote Certain of My Books* (Toronto: Mansfield, 2011), pp. 103–104. [27] *Errata*, p. 16.

book, a collection of ten short stories titled *Spit Delaney's Island* (1976). The opening story, "Separating," begins: "People driving by don't notice Spit Delaney. His old gas station is nearly hidden now behind the firs he's let grow up along the road, and he doesn't bother to whitewash the scalloped row of half-tires someone planted once instead of fence." Then, in the closing story, "Spit Delaney's Island," the title character laments: "I feel like I walked out into the middle of somebody else's play, right in the middle of it, and nobody's told me what lines to say." The pair of stories serves as bookends of the collection, which captures the small exploits, imagined terrors, and many dilemmas of his characters.

This first book maps Hodgins's Vancouver Island. Frequently and mistakenly called "magic realism" – he does not write "anything unreal or unbelievable or even improbable"[28] – his writing depicts this rural world realistically, even though it may appear eccentric to urban sophisticates unable to understand the rugged beauty and the human complexity of his island. A staunch devotee of Faulkner and later Flannery O'Connor, and then a devoted reader of Munro, he makes his island a community of seemingly eccentric people, who are always trying to figure out their supposed marginalization as if their separateness were a source of anxiety. At the same time, his characters love their world with its ribald sense of humour and varied forms of entertainment; they seek to know how to love themselves and to love others, how to avoid the "separating" that cements people apart from others. Always fascinated with the space that separates people, he portrays the ultimately comic, indeed Chaucerian, nature of human experience. Like Chaucer, he groups together divergent people, happily contriving their main stories on the road to a mythical Canterbury, which may be near or far away.

Hodgins's world is equivalent to Faulkner's Yoknapatawpha County in Mississippi, and he returns again and again to these island people in their quests to know themselves and their worlds. Although he learned many fictional traits from Latin American novelists, for example, Colombia's Gabriel García Márquez and Peru's Maria Vargas Llosa, he asserts that "to a man those Latin Americans claimed to have learned it all from William Faulkner."[29] His island is Faulkner's world, his people their Faulknerian cousins.

---

[28] *Magic Realism: An Anthology Edited and with an Introduction by Geoff Hancock* (Toronto: Aya, 1980), p. 10.

[29] "Visions and Revisions: An Interview with Jack Hodgins (1981)," *On Coasts of Eternity: Jack Hodgins' Fictional Universe*, ed. J.R. (Tim) Struthers (Lantzville, British Columbia: Oolichan, 1996), p. 160.

The Barclay Family Theatre (1981), his second collection of connected stories, also has the opening and closing ones bookending the other six, a framing pattern for tales of the seven Barclay sisters. Each story is told by one daughter and one by the narrator himself. In the last story, "The Lepers' Squint," an older Barclay Philip Desmond, in Ireland with his wife and their three children, attempting to begin his novel, visits a cathedral where the lepers had been crowded into a room behind a wall, forced to see and hear through this single narrow slit. While Desmond is trying to fictionalize his Vancouver Island, he encounters a mysterious writer who engages his imagination. He realizes that he, too, has cut himself off like the lepers behind the squint, giving him the perspective necessary for writing his novel.

In his novels, Hodgins further explores his island, its history and its people. *The Invention of the World* (1977) brings together two stories: one, historical, centring on Donal Keneally, an egocentric materialist who led his faithful followers from rural Ireland to Vancouver Island in search of Eden, founding his Revelations Colony of Truth and making his followers his slaves; the other, contemporary, centring on Maggie Kyle, who runs on the original site of the colony a boisterous boarding house whose boarders include Keneally's elderly last wife. *The Resurrection of Joseph Bourne; or, A Word or Two on Those Port Annie Miracles* (1979) looks at Port Annie, a town sliding into the sea, when a beautiful woman is washed ashore by a tidal wave; comedy reigns supreme as Joseph Bourne, a disaffected poet, returns to his world through the ministrations of the woman. In the tradition of Kroetsch, Hodgins is telling seemingly tall tales, though he does not write "anything unreal or unbelievable or even improbable." His main focus is Vancouver Island in the present and in its past. Although he may remove himself now and then from Vancouver Island in his fiction, he always returns to his island home. In *The Master of Happy Endings* (2010), for example, he focuses on a retired high school teacher and widower of seventy-seven years, who seeks to break out of his now lonely and bereft paradise by offering his services as a tutor. He finds employment watching over an aspiring teenage actor who travels between his home in Victoria and the bright lights of Los Angeles. Back on his island, this man of principle realizes that his happiness was always with him in his constant pursuit of a life filled with good deeds.

In his trilogy, *The Macken Charm* (1995), *Broken Ground* (1998), and *Distance* (2003), set basically in Waterville, a thinly disguised rendition of his own birthplace of Merville, Hodgins crafts a comic vision of his island's rowdy life. The author's bildungsroman, *The Macken Charm* is one man's often hilarious first-person account of the summer before he leaves for university, filled with family dynamics and ribald happenings. The second volume, *Broken Ground*, is set both in 1922 with the returning soldiers who settled on the island and in the 1990s as one elderly survivor looks back on that early period. Narrated by ten characters, the opening section of *Broken Ground* explores the town's reaction to the historical fire of 1922. The multiple choral voices with their variety of narrations emphasize that the story itself rests in the voices, the visions, and the points of view of the people. One narrator, eleven-year-old Charlie MacIntosh, lives to see the 1990s film of the horrid fire, complete with misremembered details and sad exclusions. He finally reveals that the opening was based on interviews conducted by "a local fellow twenty years before ... [who] wrote it up the way he imagined we might have told it if we had told it all at once quite soon after the fire ..... There would always be another voice to hear from, or another version, or something new just remembered, or an older memory reconsidered." The novel is not total realism; conjecture about past events masquerades as factual reporting; stories that do not belong in the town's remembered history are marginalized. Perhaps the truth of the past can never be realized.

A modernist rather than a postmodern author, Hodgins writes human and humane comedies, even in *Broken Ground*, where he comes closest to writing a tragedy. Like Chaucer, he paints a wide canvas for the people of Vancouver Island, wanting his readers to know his Faulknerian world and experience the sense of community his world embraces. Like Kroetsch, he is telling tales of a landscape till now unrepresented in the pages of Canadian fiction.

For Vanderhaeghe, Kroetsch and his fiction were an early and permanent inspiration. A student at the University of Saskatchewan, he was firmly but secretly interested in a writing career, although every novel he had read was of foreign extraction: "Many of my professors, American and British exiles pining away for the bright lights of Iowa City and Newcastle, had encouraged in me a dismissive attitude toward anything Canadian." Then he stumbled on *The Studhorse Man*, which he purchased in a second-hand bookstore. "By the time that I had finished *The Studhorse Man* my assumptions had been shaken. After all, everything in the book took place right next door, in Alberta of all places. It was exposure to Kroetsch's novel that sent me looking for other Canadian writers in the hope that they could teach me how to write my own country."[30] He found the novel

---

[30] Guy Vanderhaeghe's Kroetsch Keynote Address, Sage Hill, Saskatchewan, Summer 2014.

revealing and liberating. "I remember, for instance, being very, very struck by Kroetsch's *The Studhorse Man*. And even though it was such a mythic book it had a tremendous amount of authenticity for me. And I think I said to myself, even before I had decided to write, this part of the world can be written about. Which sounds like an odd thing to say. But having read only British and American literature, it seemed to me that those were the places that one wrote about. I didn't consciously arge [stet] that but that reflex was likely part of my subconscious attitude. I couldn't imagine (until I had seen it on paper) the people around me actually figuring in on the process of making literature. And I remember that novel of Kroetsch's and it really struck me. So I sought out other books by him."[31]

A trained historian with a bachelor and master's degree in history from the University of Saskatchewan, he is a formidable short-story writer and a fine novelist. Regarding the disciplines of history and literature "as linked. I see history as literature and often I understand literature through historical perspectives."[32] "A novel is an aesthetic experience, but because I always had an intense interest in history, writing about the past or circling historical questions interests me and fascinates me," he comments. "I think the historical novel is always about contemporary issues in disguise .... The historical novel is always written by someone whose experience is contemporary, and so it's impossible to fully inhabit people of the past, or even to understand their issues the way they understood them."[33] His sources rest in the writers of the American South: "My own writing has been chiefly influenced by writers of the southern United States, and to a certain extent, by Alice Munro. These writers reflect an oral tradition of storytelling that developed in rural communities, although, of course, their work is much more refined and sophisticated."[34]

The seven stories of his first collection, *The Trouble with Heroes and Other Stories* (1983), range from the New Testament tale of Lazarus to the great Paris Exposition of 1889 to the contemporary prairie world. The narrators are a motley assortment, from first-person male narrators, the fifty-six-year-old who believes that "there is no more opportunity for heroism," the man who comes to claim the body of his foster brother in

---

[31] David Carpenter, "Inside Guy Vanderhaeghe," *NeWest Review* 8, 1 (September 1982): 9, 15.

[32] "Guy Vanderhaeghe," *Speaking for Myself: Canadian Writers in Interview*, ed. Andrew Garrod (St. John's, Newfoundland: Breakwater, 1986), p. 276.

[33] "Making History: Guy Vanderhaeghe," *Speaking in the Past Tense: Canadian Novelists on Writing Historical Fiction*, ed. Herb Wyile (Waterloo, Ontario: Wilfrid Laurier University Press, 2006), p. 26.

[34] "An Interview with Guy Vanderhaeghe," *Wascana Review* 19, 1 (Spring 1984): 22.

one of the biblical stories, and the thirty-five-year-old who arrives for a possible reconciliation with his dying father, to the omniscient third-person narrators. Obviously juvenilia, the stories typify Vanderhaeghe's concerns as a writer: the meaning of the heroic in a world where people seem merely to endure the problems of their social beings.

"No Man Could Bind Him" grew out of his sense of history and the idea of Western civilization as a balance of Greek and Hebrew thought. In his youth the first-person Greek narrator received a poor Jewish lad as his foster brother. "At the age of twenty, having been eight years with the family and after a season of hard drinking and dissipation, he raped my sister Persephone and disappeared." The narrator ultimately embraces an act of love in searching for his dying foster brother and coming to bury him. Showing "the humanity that lies behind all the trappings of aestheticism," the story reveals a "germ of love out of which both faith and doubt grow. I look on them as love stories."[35] Vanderhaeghe's fiction reveals the "germ of love" that resides, however deeply buried, in the recesses of the human heart.

"The oldest story is the story of flight, the search for greener pastures," says the narrator of "What I Learned from Caesar" from *Man Descending* (1982). "But the pastures we flee, no matter how brown and blighted – these travel with us; they can't be escaped." The twelve stories of *Man Descending*, published earlier than his juvenilia, are less tales of flight than tales of brown and blighted pastures that haunt, paralyze, and sometimes destroy their inhabitants. The range of his characters include young children watching the hypocrisy of pain of adulthood, teenagers observing the farcical dimensions of romance, young men descending prematurely into the pain of failed dreams, widowers confronting their fearful loneliness, and old men facing death. Vanderhaeghe's ability to create rich human beings is impressive; even more remarkable is his narrative ability, entering the mind of a young first-person narrator as easily as an elderly narrator.

A pair of closing stories, "Man Descending" and "Sam, Soren, and Ed," are a thirty-year-old's account of his failed attempts to reform his way of life. At the end of the second story, the narrator quotes Kierkegaard: "What ability there is in an individual may be measured by the yardstick of how far there is between his *understanding* and his *will*. What a person can *understand* he must also be able to force himself to *will*. Between understanding and willing is where excuses and evasions have their being."

---

[35] *Speaking for Myself*, p. 282.

Excuses and evasions are a way of life for many of the characters: the young children emulate their elders' quest for power; the widowers resort to physical violence to avoid their own pain; the aged flee to fantasy to avoid reality. In this bleak universe, there are only hollow rituals and biblical clichés; there is no real love, only the need for love, for that "germ of love" residing, so hidden, in the characters' foibles and failings. Rooted firmly in his western locale, Vanderhaeghe captures the moral void of the 1970s and 1980s, the desperate alienation of modern man, the hollow isolation of human beings, and those rare moments when people somehow transcend their aloneness and express their painful need.

From these short stories Vanderhaeghe moved into the novel. The final two stories of *Man Descending* led to *My Present Age* (1984), a novel focusing relentlessly on the about-to-be divorced Ed, "a fellow adrift in the sunset days of a long and blissfully cantankerous life." Searching for his estranged wife's hiding place in a wintry prairie city, he finds himself, as "Sam, Soren, and Ed" points out, "a malady of the modern age . . . entirely disassociated" from what he does. Vanderhaeghe creates a man who is almost an ugly alter ego of the author as his sad life cascades down to near madness. Yet the setting, so redolent of Saskatoon, is never named: "Something prevented me from putting a name to the city whose geography played as large a role in the psychology of my protagonist . . . . What seemed an insignificant matter then, does not, with hindsight, seem so insignificant now, but rather a retreat into evasion, a failure of artistic nerve, and a refusal to assert the validity of a place and a voice."[36] Paralleling this first novel is its companion piece, *Homesick* (1989), filled with prairie names and places, asserting "the validity of a place and a voice." Taking place in the fictional town of Connaught, Saskatchewan, in the late 1950s, it highlights the difficult relationships of one family: a widower, his proud widowed daughter, his grandson, and his omnipresent but unseen son, who, as later stated, died in 1946 in the Provincial Mental Hospital. The "germ of love" operates as people slowly accept the fact that they have needs which are achingly hidden and more achingly expressed.

As early as 1984, immediately after the publication of *My Present Age*, Vanderhaeghe was pondering an historical novel to capture the nineteenth-century worlds of western Canada, the United States, and perhaps England, too, bringing his historical sensibility to stories of his own landscape. His novel became the western trilogy: *The Englishman's Boy* (1996), *The Last Crossing* (2002), and *A Good Man* (2011).

---

[36] *The Urban Prairie*, p. 129.

The Englishman's Boy has two seemingly disparate narratives intersect to create a unified whole. Related in alternating chapters, the first story focuses on 1873 and the Englishman's boy, a young man who winds up in a posse in Montana chasing an Assiniboine raiding party who stole their horses; they pursue the thieves into Saskatchewan where vengeance is exacted in the Cypress Hills Massacre. The second narrative, set in 1920s Hollywood, focuses on Harry Vincent, a crippled journalist employed by a playboy moviemaker commissioned to retell the story of Cypress Hills, and his attempt in his own words to locate Shorty McAdoo, an aged actor of westerns who was involved in the massacre. Vincent must reconcile his own integrity with the crass ambitions of Hollywood.

The Last Crossing returns to nineteenth-century Montana. Charles Gaunt and his older brother Addington are dispatched by their father from his English estate to find Charles's twin brother Simon, a religious idealist, who travelled to America to convert the Indians to Christianity twenty-five years earlier. A frequent voice in the novel, Charles describes his anxiety about Simon, his troubled relationship to his tyrannical father and the perverse Addington, and his growing despair. Vanderhaeghe's method of alternating chapters from different viewpoints as well as his novel's frequent flashbacks study the worlds of the Wild West and of Victorian England.

In the conclusion to this triptych, *A Good Man* opens after George Custer's defeat at Little Bighorn in 1876. The Sioux feel emboldened, the United States is "having fits of hysterics," and Canada believes it could be the casualty of American efforts to solve its problems with the First Nations. Into this fractious time comes Wesley Case, haunted by a disgraceful military error in the Battle of Ridgeway in 1866 and eager to become "a good man" at a period when the practice of law and order is still "notional and shaky."

In this trilogy Vanderhaeghe shows a historian's meticulous attention to factual details, interweaving figures from history with his fictional creations. "When I'm writing fiction," he comments, "I don't attempt to teach or instruct, or any of those sorts of things. What's always first and foremost in my mind is that a novel is an aesthetic experience."[37] The aesthetic experience is his defining moment – he mingles facts and fiction to tell tales of the worlds of the nineteenth century that have not been recorded.

Kroetsch started a concerted effort to write the subjective history of western Canada, the complete history with its people of all nationalities

---

[37] *Speaking in the Past Tense*, p. 26.

including the major presence of Indigenous voices. Wiebe embarks on a similar journey, though without the comic dimensions of Kroetsch's fiction. While Bowering is postmodern in his intrusions into his narratives, Hodgins writes a human and humane history of his island. It remained for Vanderhaeghe, uniting his depictions of the aesthetic moment with his sensitivity to history, to write his dramatic accounts of his landscape and its history.

CHAPTER 7

Canada's Second Century

Atwood and Engel, Bowering and Kroetsch and Wiebe, Laurence and Munro and Thomas, these and many other writers published their first fiction volumes in the 1960s, a period of immense activity in writing and publishing as well as in public affairs. The Canada Council's support of writers and publishers was slowly bearing fruit, giving them financial assistance to write and publish their works. Canada was proclaiming a new sense of pride in its own nationhood.

In 1964, ninety-seven years after four provinces came together to form the Dominion of Canada, Lester B. Pearson, then prime minister, proposed the adoption of a national flag. Originally the flag was to be in two halves, English and French, united by the superimposed maple leaf. The flag received parliamentary approval in 1965 after it had been redesigned, as it is now, in a tripartite division: English, French, and other. But "other" raises questions. Where are the Native peoples? Where are the immigrants?

The year 1967 was Canada's centennial, the high point of the celebrations being the international exposition, Expo 67, in Montreal. Called "Man and His World," it had significance beyond the many countries bringing their exhibits to Canada. "The lasting impact of Expo 67 will be in the dramatic object lesson we see before our eyes today: that the genius of Man knows no national boundaries but is universal," Pearson stated at its opening on April 27, 1967. Expo boasted special importance for Canadians: "Anyone who says we aren't a spectacular people should see this. We are witnesses today to the fulfillment of one of the most daring acts of faith in Canadian enterprise and ability ever undertaken. That faith was not misplaced." Canada was no longer looking abroad; the world was now focused on Canada.

And Canada was changing. In 1963, Pearson had appointed a Royal Commission on Bilingualism and Biculturalism, which issued its report in 1969, promulgating the use of English and French as the official languages of Canada. In 1971, Pierre Elliott Trudeau, then prime minister, established a multiculturalism act, not a biculturalism act as was recommended. Canada would recognize and respect its multicultural heritage and ensure that measures were taken to protect it. In 1981, Canada passed its Charter of Rights and Freedoms, which recognized multiculturalism as part of the fabric of Canadian society. And in 1988, under Brian Mulroney, then prime minister, the Canadian Multiculturalism Act became law, preserving and enhancing multiculturalism. This multiculturalism, this plea for racial tolerance and an enhancement of the multicultural dimensions of Canadian society, testifies to the country's increasingly complex and multifaceted growth as a literary nation. And fiction writers were already charting their unique paths.

"At one time it was extremely difficult to be a Canadian writer. We still had for many, many years a kind of colonial mentality, a great many people felt that a book written by a Canadian couldn't possibly be good. It had to come from either New York or the other side of the Atlantic to be any good," reflected Margaret Laurence in 1972.

> The whole cultural climate has changed incredibly, and particularly in the last decade. My first book was published in 1960, and the change in those twelve years in the whole cultural situation has been enormous. Canadian writers are probably in a better position now than they have ever been before. Very few Canadian writers of any seriousness or worth do not find a considerable readership in their own country.[1]

Throughout the country new voices were writing, some fashioning reflections on the land and its peoples, others penning commentaries on their personal struggles with themselves, still others writing out of the freedom gained from such writers as Mordecai Richler and Sheila Watson. Going across the landscape provides a vision of the new writers who came to the forefront of Canadian fiction in the years leading up to the twenty-first century.

Quebec

In Montreal, Pearson's praise of Canadian enterprise had already been acknowledged by MacLennan, then Klein, then Richler. Now several others are joining the bandwagon.

Already an accomplished poet, Leonard Cohen (1934–2016) wrote his first novel, *The Favourite Game* (1963), a strongly autobiographical

---

[1] *Eleven Canadian Novelists*, p. 198.

bildungsroman about a young man coming of age in Montreal's middle-class Westmount world. Indebted to Richler's lower-class portrait of life in *The Apprenticeship of Duddy Kravitz*, and a "subtly balanced description of a sensibility," the novel was, Cohen remarked, "the best of its kind since James Joyce's *Portrait of the Artist as a Young Man.*"[2]

An episodic account of Lawrence Breavman slowly accepting his vocation as a poet, *The Favourite Game* both satirizes and sympathizes with his sensual aspirations. An ambitious child from a Jewish background who seeks to escape his ethnic enclave without fully relinquishing the heritage he both romanticizes and debases, the narcissistic Breavman drives through the Montreal streets at night in search of meetings with the ideal woman. Through his many sexual exploits, he does find freedom from his family, his friends, and even his lovers, though he also encounters a nagging spiritual lethargy; in the end, he cannot commit himself to anyone outside the self, and he bereaves others, in particular the women in his life. Mingling childhood and adolescence reminiscences with Cohen's own poetry, the novel is a paean of praise to the hero's obsession with sex: "Lust was training his eyes to exclude everything he could not kiss." He is essentially two distinct people: "the robot lover who made every night a celebration" and the romantic poet who watches, observing, but untouched, his sexual lifestyle and his place in it and apart from it; by focusing on himself, he captures an increasingly clear portrait of himself. By setting down the minute details of Montreal life, Cohen transforms his bildungsroman into a universal account of a sensitive though obsessed young man's movement into maturity. Without precedent in Canadian fiction, the novel is brutally self-analytical, never shying away from any taboos and never trying to exonerate Breavman's feelings or actions.

Beautiful Losers (1966), Cohen's other novel, is a dialectic between two narrators: the Anglophone "I," presumably Jewish, who narrates the first section, "The History of Them All," and the Francophone "F," a political revolutionary who, like Breavman, never foregoes an occasion of quoting himself, and writes the second section, "A Long Letter from F." These two bring their life stories to a collaborative biography of the Iroquois virgin saint, Catherine Tekakwitha, a seventeenth-century martyr, and then merge in the short third and concluding section, "Beautiful Losers: An Epilogue in the Third Person." The fourth character, the native-born

---

[2] Ian Rae, *From Cohen to Carson: The Poet's Novel in Canada* (Montreal: McGill-Queen's University Press, 2008), p. 60.

Edith, wife of "I," becomes sexually involved with F. as one of his disciples, then commits suicide.

In the first part, the historian "I" questions the standard categories of his profession, seeking to engage spiritually and sexually with the many versions of Catherine, the first being her fixed image on a colour postcard. To F., Catherine is a saint because she survives all the negative effects of contact with other peoples: the harsh effects of European colonization, the self-inflicted sufferings through Catholicism, and the constant pressures on her to beget children. This ability to change her personal sufferings into healing power is the prerogative of the saint and the artist.

Going back and forth in time and narration, aggressively experimental, *Beautiful Losers* eschews a linear progression in order to probe the inner workings of its characters inside and outside of time. In the end, they have telling conclusions: Catherine suffers an ignominious death; Edith is crushed in an elevator suicide; F. is incarcerated in a mental institution; and "I" is a dirty old man living in a treehouse. Although Catherine rejects bodily pleasures, the other three embrace them as the source of a new faith. Far from having a hero who is a close rendition of its own author, *Beautiful Losers* abandons any pretext of similarity between the author and his narrators in a comic yet serious exploration of sainthood in a contemporary context. It also tries to make sense of Canadian history and the coexistence of three nations, perhaps four including the Jewish, historically antagonistic but brought together to deal with their ideologies in contemporary reality.

For Ondaatje (b. 1943), Cohen "was a hero for our generation and for the next – stepping bravely into new forms, a great writer who then became a great songwriter."[3] Although he did not continue to write fiction, he retained a lasting place there. "As a songwriter, as a novelist, as a singer," observes Anne Michaels (b. 1958), "Leonard Cohen was at the heart of that incredible Canadian literary coming of age."[4]

In late 1970, in Montreal too, John Metcalf (b. 1938) organized a group of men, Hugh Hood (1928–2000), Clark Blaise (b. 1940), Ray Smith (1941–2019), and Raymond Fraser (1941–2018), to "work a shakedown on the poets, and divert the attention of their stupefied audiences to the more wholesome, godly, clearly more decent action of listening to stories

---

[3] "The Arts Community Remembers," eds. Josh O'Kane, Mark Medley, and Brad Wheeler, *The Globe and Mail*, 12 November 2016, p. A4.
[4] "Toronto's poet laureate pays tribute to a literary legend," Toronto *Star*, 13 November 2016, p. A3.

being read or told to them."[5] From early 1971 until the middle '70s, the "Montreal Story Teller Fiction Performance Group" gave readings from their short stories, "a group very much of our time and place and class-interests: no French, no women, no unseemly minorities."[6]

British-born and raised, Metcalf wrote Evelyn Waugh-like tales. While Fraser returned to New Brunswick to continue his career as a novelist, short story writer, and poet, Hood, a professor of English at the Université de Montréal, wrote a cumbersome twelve-volume *New Age* series of novels.

Two of the storytellers deserve attention. Born in Mabou, Cape Breton, Smith came to Montreal where he taught at Dawson College; after forty years in Montreal, he returned to his birthplace. His first collection of stories with the intriguing and ironic title, *Cape Breton Is the Thought-Control Centre of Canada* (1969), represents experimental fiction in the international tradition, the nine tales showing influences from Canada and beyond, and with Smith continuing in the postmodern tradition of Cohen's *Beautiful Losers*.

Lord Nelson Tavern (1974) brings together young people who have known one another since their school days, sharing their belief in the redemptive power of love. In his second collection *Century* (1986), the six stories, set mainly in Europe, question the chaotic absurdity of modern life. His second novel, *A Night at the Opera* (1990), continues Smith's habit of employing European settings, now the fictitious German city of Waltherrott, to examine satirically the crass folly of the deluded opera crowd. His finest novel, *The Man Who Loved Jane Austen* (1999), returns to 1990s Anglophone Montreal to depict the sad plight of a widower to maintain control of his teaching life and the lives of his two young sons against the cruel onslaught of his wealthy and cruel in-laws. Montreal is a sad place, riven by nationalistic fervor and human betrayals. At the end, he retreats to Nova Scotia, surrendering his sons to his manipulative in-laws. The book is a modern tragedy of familial deception.

Smith often salutes Richler in his writings. The protagonist of *The Man Who Loved Jane Austen* asks, "Mordecai Richler was staying – why shouldn't he?" And in *The Man Who Hated Emily Bronte* (2004), the hero looks out on "a glimpse of Lake Memphremagog where Mordecai Richler lived during his last years."

---

[5] Hugh Hood, "Trusting the Tale," *The Montreal Story Tellers: Memoirs, Photographs, Critical Essays* (Montreal: Vehicule, 1985), p. 8.
[6] Clark Blaise, "Portrait of the Artist as a Young Pup," *The Montreal Story Tellers*, p. 69.

Born in Fargo, North Dakota, to an Anglophone mother from Manitoba and a Francophone father from Quebec, Blaise emigrated to Montreal in 1966, teaching at Sir George Williams University (now Concordia University), then moving to Toronto in 1978 to teach at York University, before moving back to the United States in 1980. In his stories as well as his three novels, he wonders about questions of identity, his own and the haphazard world of people's confusions in contemporary North American life. His first novel, *Lunar Attractions* (1979), actually a series of short stories indebted to Munro's *Lives of Girls and Women*, traces the coming-of-age of David Greenwood, socially awkward and sexually inept, as he ventures forth from his home base of Florida to the town of Palestra farther up the Atlantic coast. Many of the stories concern David's confessions of his sexual fantasies as he explores his final high school years. The book is a semi-bildungsroman, the figure of David mirroring and yet not mirroring Blaise's own background.

Married to Bengali novelist and non-fiction writer Bharati Mukherjee (1940–2017), he often centres his work on immigrants trying to come to grips with their new and their old establishments. *The Meagre Tarmac* (2011), his tenth collection of short fiction, charts the lives of middle-class people of Indian origin, mostly from Calcutta, who come to North America with all the usual prejudices and all the customary hopes. The older generation usually wants finally to return to their homeland, the younger generation usually wants to stay in America. These stories capture the sorrowful voices of men and women trying to bridge the old ways of India and the dynamic and often soul-destroying chaos of life in America.

The Maritime Provinces: New Brunswick, Nova Scotia, and Prince Edward Island

Born in Stanley, Nova Scotia, Alden Nowlan (1933–83) was among the many Maritime writers who lauded Ernest Buckler: "*The Mountain and the Valley* is not only the best novel yet written by a Canadian, but one of the great novels of the English language."[7] Widely celebrated as a poet and published most often as a journalist, he produced four fiction titles. Although he penned the autobiographical novel *The Wanton Troopers* in 1960, it remained unpublished until 1988. His second novel, *Various Persons Named Kevin O'Brien* (1973), returns to his impoverished and isolated 1930s childhood, where encounters with his Maritime village filter

---

[7] "All the Layers of Meaning," *Ernest Buckler*, ed. Gregory M. Cook, p. 116.

through the now professional and journalistic eyes of the Native returning as educated city dweller. His two collections of short stories deal with the rural Maritime communities. "Morning Flight to Red Deer," for example, from *Will Ye Let the Mummers In?* (1984) interprets the author's experience of visiting western Canada on a reading tour; the visitor's enthusiasm for travel and conversation does not translate into a warm reception by locals. The pointed prose style he developed as a life-long journalist complements his boisterously metaphorical imagination. He often promoted his prose works in the guise of a parent standing up for his less successful child.[8]

Another of Nova Scotia's talents and a most gifted storyteller is from Cape Breton. Born in North Battleford, Saskatchewan, to Gaelic-speaking parents from Cape Breton, Alistair MacLeod (1936–2014) returned with his family to their roots in Inverness County, Cape Breton, when he was ten. Although he later obtained his doctorate at Notre Dame University in Indiana with a dissertation on Thomas Hardy and taught for more than thirty years at the University of Windsor, he never strayed far from his spiritual home of Cape Breton. In seventeen short stories and one novel, he captured the beauty and the horror of life in this constantly challenging environment with its many inhabitants and the ancestors who haunt their lives.

In his first story, "The Boat" (1968), MacLeod foreshadows many of the themes that dominate his later fiction: the stormy landscape, the fishermen who lead rugged lives, the wives who stay home and wait, and the son who flees this harsh realm. The narrator, who now teaches "at a great Midwestern university," recalls the time when he was fifteen and helped his father on his boat, remembering the harbour, the wharf, and the boat. Although his father longed to go to university, his duties as a husband and a father forced him to remain behind, a stern individual who made his living from the sea. Unlike his mother, whose horizons were "the very literal ones she scanned with her dark and fearless eyes," their son sought more distant and more challenging horizons. One November day, his father did not return from fishing. He "was found on November twenty-eighth, ten miles to the north and wedged between two boulders at the base of the rock-strewn cliffs where he had been hurled and slammed so many many times." The young man comes to know and appreciate his feelings for his parents and for the emotional price they paid for his

---

[8] For a relevant account of Nowlen, see David Adams Richards, "I Went Down to Meet Alden Nowlan," *Murder and Other Essays* (Toronto: Doubleday, 2019), pp. 215–24.

education. The Cape Breton men and women going about their daily lives against this harsh setting are the centre of MacLeod's realistic fiction. His world becomes equivalent to Hardy's Wessex, a remote area delineated with sensitive care and thorough understanding by a storyteller of that region. His characters are often stern individualists who earn their living from the sea, finding solace in their deep-rooted traditions.

"The Boat" and six other stories, including "The Golden Gift of Grey," his only story set not in Cape Breton but in Newfoundland, formed his first collection, *The Lost Salt Gift of Blood* (1976). All the stories focus on or are related by male narrators who are young people or are remembering a critical moment from their youth; their thoughts are riddled with difficulties as the men are forced to make decisions which set them on their future paths. With relentless attention to fraught individuals coming to assert, however tentatively, their choice, they are trapped in dueling desires to escape their present environment or to stay where they are. This is the crucial dilemma for each of the men: to move into a world beyond Cape Breton or to succumb to its demanding life.

His second collection of seven more stories, *As Birds Bring Forth the Sun and Other Stories* (1986), delves more deeply into the lives of his protagonists, often depicting their ancestors and the myths about them that grew into realities. With the title story's opening lines, "Once there was a family with a Highland name who lived beside the sea. And the man had a dog of which he was very fond," the tale captures not only childhood memories but family lore which dates back five generations. These tales from the past transcend time and prove the power and the timelessness of family traditions at the moment when the narrator is witnessing his aged father's final moments of mortality. "The Closing Down of Summer," looking to the future, features an elite team of coal miners suffering from Cape Breton's industrial decline and setting off for Africa to pursue their livelihood: "We have perhaps gone back to the Gaelic songs because they are so constant and unchanging and speak to us as the privately familiar." The Gaelic tradition haunts the men even as they are about to travel far from their Cape Breton families. In a still later story, "Clearances" (1999), a German couple are buying up the land for recreational purposes, the fears of cultural expropriation even more pronounced.

In the opening scene of MacLeod's novel *No Great Mischief* (1999), winner of the Dublin IMPAC Literary Award, Alexander MacDonald, a successful dentist in a southwestern Ontario city, is on his usual Saturday trip to Toronto to visit his eldest brother Calum in his sordid rooming house. Released from prison for his murder of a French Canadian miner,

Calum remembers his complete family history and the history of the clan MacDonald. Like the narrator of "The Boat," Alexander is an intellectual who abandoned Cape Breton for a successful career off-island; he shows the usual regret of the exile. After the sudden drowning of his parents, Calum becomes the leader of his immediate family, eventually becoming the head of the MacDonald clan and the leader of a hard-rock mining team. He is also the repository of his family's history, which has been passed on to him through his grandparents. Haunted by the past, he gives his detailed knowledge of his history to Alexander, who gathers together the many stories that form the novel. At the end Calum telephones Alexander to ask him to drive them both back to Cape Breton where Calum dies.

No Great Mischief celebrates the bonds of the clan and the permanent hold it has on its members, whether they are near or far. "The tightly knit, traditional family unit within a fully integrated communal society can provide a sense of identity, purpose, and security that is simply unavailable to the alienated individual in the fragmented, urbanized, industrial, modern world."[9] Although MacLeod is nostalgic for this civilized form of familial behavior, he is a sufficient realist to know that many people regard this pull of the homeland as a moment of transition which bodes ominously for the future. His novel becomes an elegy for a way of life which has passed and for the Gaelic language that is known now only by a very few people.

MacLeod expresses his undying faith in Cape Breton and its Gaelic traditions, though he recognizes that this heritage has mainly disappeared, living now most memorably on the pages of his fiction. He captures the conflicts of these sturdy families, and his fiction roots itself in carefully defined details only to transcend these settings in humane explorations of the personal struggles that often defeat men and women of all time. He delineates his characters and their dilemmas so thoroughly and so deeply that they become not only Cape Bretoners but easily recognized individuals from any region of the world.

Born in Newcastle, New Brunswick, David Adams Richards (b. 1950) had many literary influences. A mentee of Nowlan, devoted to MacLeod's fiction, in love with Buckler's fiction and non-fiction, schooled in the writings of Dickens, especially *Oliver Twist*, and Faulkner, Tolstoy, and Dostoevsky, and deeply indebted to the Bible, he creates his fictional

[9] David Creelman, *Setting in the East: Maritime Realist Fiction* (Montreal: McGill-Queen's University Press, 2003), p. 140.

universe out of his native Miramichi River Valley. Dependent upon shipping, mining, and small farming, the Miramichi area has been economically depressed, its population poorly educated and financially insolvent. Richards's characters, usually of the working class, struggle to preserve their moral courage and dignity in a world increasingly displaced by economic and social changes. Their sometimes violent lives hide, though not completely, the generosity and love in many of their relationships.

His first three novels focus on unaffected and engaging characters: the Dulse family in *The Coming of Winter* (1974); three generations of the MacDurmot family in *Blood Ties* (1976); and the history of the Terri family going back five generations in *Lives of Short Duration* (1981). Behind these lives of unremitting harshness and poverty stand fleeting moments of tenderness which partly redeem the violence. The novels form a trilogy which outlines the intersecting lives of working-class characters, frequently the disconnected, the disempowered, and the dispossessed, who live on the fringes of society. A second trilogy, *Nights below Station Street* (1988), *Evening Snow Will Bring Such Peace* (1990), and *For Those Who Hunt the Wounded Down* (1993), follows similar lives along the Miramichi. In *Principles to Live By* (2016), Richards leaves the Miramichi for the first time, resurrecting John Delano from *The Coming of Winter*, *Blood Ties*, and other novels. Now an elderly detective in Saint John, he must investigate a decades-old crime which pits him against corrupt leftists and disgraceful civil servants; meanwhile, in the photograph of his own lost son he sees only "hope and love," recalling the theme of *No Great Mischief*, "All of us are better when we're loved."

Far from being nostalgic for the worlds that once were, Richards looks at the contemporary scene, even when past history plagues his characters; he relishes the people's struggles, their heartaches, and their loneliness. Although they are often outcasts, he does not applaud the institutions – educational, governmental, or religious – that set out to control them, his disaffection with social system being unprecedented in Maritime fiction and recalling similar themes in Callaghan's fiction. The people who heed and follow the person within themselves, difficult as this route must always be, is the recipient of his highest praise. In making the Miramichi inhabitants the centre of his fictional universe, Richards does for his people what MacLeod did for Cape Bretoners. "He has produced a body of work exceptional in both quality and quantity and at the centre of his work is an understanding of the human heart possessed by relatively few of his contemporary writers," commented MacLeod. "He is careful and protective of this human heart that has been entrusted to his care yet he is also tough and brave enough to ensure its fierce safekeeping."[10]

Born in Port Hawkesbury, Cape Breton, Lynn Coady (b. 1970) received her BA from Carleton University and her MFA from the University of British Columbia. A short story writer and novelist, she is an insightful writer who often probes the hell her characters inhabit. Her subject matter is contemporary people often at odds with the world and with one another, struggling to find their own peculiar places. She offers the situations with ironic wit, willing to leave the final assessment of their often erroneous ways to her readers.

Her semi-autobiographical first book, *Strange Heaven* (1998), follows a nearly eighteen-year-old as she sits in a psychiatric ward of a Halifax hospital; she needs to recover from the ordeal of leaving her newborn child for adoption. Her connections with the other ward inhabitants are authentic, nightmarish, and amusing. When she returns to her Catholic Cape Breton home for Christmas, she finds her family members dysfunctional in their bizarre and often hilarious behaviour. Coady resets the common understanding of Maritimers, writing about them with ambivalence and humour. Both *Mean Boy* (2007) and *The Antagonist* (2011) feature first-person male narrators, the former satirizing aspiring young writers and respected poets in New Brunswick's Westcock University, the latter a nearly forty-year-old's reflections on being cast in life as a tough guy.

With sharp and refreshing wit, Coady's characters break free from their small and claustrophobic communities. They return to – or are still lodged in – their Maritime settings, gaining strength and some satisfaction through their searches into their pasts and their presents. For Coady, relationships have a unique way of hurting, of leaving a person alone, simple solutions being rarely effective or even possible.

For these Maritime authors, the pull of their home environment means that however far they are from the landscapes, they are still rooted there, capturing the hopes and promises, the follies and the failures of their people.

Newfoundland

In 1949 the tenth and final province, Newfoundland, joined Canada, no longer an independent political entity under British rule, but a province

---

[10] "On Staying the Course," *David Adams Richards: Essays on His Works*, ed. Tony Tremblay (Toronto: Guernica, 2005), p. 147.

within Canada. Its proud people had selected a destiny alongside but not a part of Canada; now, two referenda have made them a part of the larger country. "We were no longer an obscure, neglected, and bankrupt island-colony of Britain but a Province of Canada," the narrator says in the autobiographical novel *House of Hate* (1970) by St. John's Percy Janes (1922–99).

Although his writings date from the turn of the twentieth century, Norman Duncan was the first writer to make ordinary outport Newfoundlanders the centre of his fictional world. Later, in December 1940, Margaret Duley (1894–1968) lamented: "One of the things regarding a Newfoundland novel is that there are no writers from this country and I feel we must emerge sometime and nothing could be more auspicious than the enormous influx of Canadians into my country."[11] Born in St. John's and reading major British literary figures, she focused on women's lives in a time and place where women did not play significant roles, setting her novels in Newfoundland, "a country which the author loves and hates," as she wrote in a prefatory note to *Highway to Valour* (1941). Her first two novels, *The Eyes of the Gull* (1936) and *Cold Pastoral* (1939), romances reminiscent of Montgomery and de la Roche, focus on women fighting valiantly for their own existence in the outports and in St. John's. Her other two novels, *Highway to Valour* and *Novelty on Earth* (1942), expanding to include Labrador in their settings, are more realistic, focusing on women who fall hopelessly in love with married men; in the end, the two protagonists lead individual and fulfiling lives in their single state.

A strong feminist before feminism asserted itself, an ardent Newfoundlander who hated the narrow-minded insular mentality, she tried to do for her country what W.B. Yeats had done for Ireland, and what Norman Duncan had already done for Newfoundland, claiming it as a home where writers could set their tales in its harsh terrain. Although her novels are scarcely read today, she reflected on her fellow Newfoundlanders: "I have left them a heritage. In their library will be a little corner of Margaret Duley's works."[12]

In the 1950s Newfoundland was still being depicted artistically as a barren landscape. In 1952 Harold Horwood (1923–2006), also from St. John's, lamented that the new province was without literature, music,

[11] Alison Feder, *Margaret Duley: Newfoundland Novelist* (St. John's, Newfoundland: Cuff, 1983), p. 59.
[12] Ibid., p. 147.

or art. A pro-Canada politician in the 1949 debate about whether Newfoundland should become a province of Canada, he chose to devote himself to writing, first in his many newspaper columns, then in his articles and books on Newfoundland, and finally in his novels. His first and best, *Tomorrow Will Be Sunday* (1966), follows the plight of young Eli Pallisher as he comes of age in an outport known as Caplin Bight, "one of the backwaters of civilization." A hidden-away community which represents the most lethal form of strict evangelical Christianity, the benighted world tramples down anyone who upsets its tenets. Enter Christopher Simms, the son of a local retired magistrate, who went away to "the magic world of the cities" to attend university; his return promises a welcome alternative to Eli and a few others capable of responding to his vision; only those few with expansive imaginations can rise above the environment and its stranglehold. Horwood proves himself romantic rather than realistic, the tortured life of Caplin Bight melding finally into Eli's dive, literally, into a new order beyond the outport's toxic dead-end. *White Eskimo* (1972) moves to Labrador to rouse the Inuit to return to their fine, pre-Christian ways. With Horwood travelling extensively throughout this part of the province, the novel is another example of his continuing romanticism, preferring the life of the noble savage to the increasing sickness perpetrated by missionaries of the Protestant faith. In 1980 Horwood moved to Annapolis Royal, Nova Scotia, where he lived for the rest of his life, far from the Newfoundland he always depicted in his fiction and non-fiction. Romantic in his outlook, he left it to other writers to offer a realistic depiction of Newfoundland.

Born in suburban St. John's and the son of anti-Canada federates, Wayne Johnston (b. 1958) has written a host of historical novels and some contemporary, almost all of them set in Newfoundland. Two of his early novels, his first, *The Story of Bobby O'Malley* (1985), and his third, *The Divine Ryans* (1990), are first-person narratives of, respectively, sixteen-year-old Bobby O'Malley and nine-year-old Draper Doyle Ryan. Set in the Irish Catholic subculture, both novels are eye-witness accounts of the humorous lives of island people with the ultimate truths buried inside the comedy. At sixteen, after coming to terms with his father's unfortunate death, Bobby abandons his goal of becoming a priest and leaves the island. Equally upset by his father's death, Draper Doyle slowly discovers the tragic truth behind his family's cover-up.

Complemented later by *The Custodian of Paradise* (2006) and *First Snow, Last Light* (2017), *The Colony of Unrequited Dreams* (1998) is another first-person account, this time by real-life politician Joey

Smallwood, "a megalomaniac with an inferiority complex. In a way the quintessential Newfoundlander,"[13] who precipitated Newfoundland's federation with Canada and became the island's first premier. Narrated from his perspective, it voices his own deep passion to do something important for the greatness of his own land. Into his ruminations on his own life comes the fictional character of Sheilagh Fielding, "Smallwood's platonic lover, his greatest critic, best friend, and nemesis."[14] A hard-drinking newspaper columnist with a love–hate relationship with him, she writes cynical columns and personal journals along with her satirical *Condensed History of Newfoundland*, casting a haunting shadow on his tortured career. Their story recounts Smallwood's early years and the country's slow but steady path to Canadian federation.

When Joey is a young boy at Bishop Feild College, "a private school attended by the children of some of the city's better families," the students "were taught next to nothing about Newfoundland, the masters drilling into us instead the history and geography of England, the country for which they were so homesick that they acted as if they were still there, denying as much as possible the facts of their existence." In his fiction, most notably in *The Colony of Unrequited Dreams*, Johnston describes the colourful past, inspired by historical events and transfixed by his own imagination, in order to present a seemingly authentic portrait of his unique province.

While Johnston left the province in 1981 ultimately for Toronto, intermingling his residence there with frequent trips home to Newfoundland, others followed suit. Born in Jarrow, England, and moving at three with his family to Newfoundland, Michael Winter (b. 1965) graduated from Memorial University in economic geography. Starting with his first short story collection, *Creaking in Their Skins* (1994), he has fashioned his fiction from Newfoundland's people, their traditions and their loves, and while he departed the province for Toronto in 1999, he still spends his summers back home.

In his first novel, *This All Happened* (2000), he uses his fictional alter ego, Gabriel English, to record the latter's life and adventures in St. John's. Organized as a fictional diary of 365 entries from one year, the book chronicles his relationship with filmmaker Lydia Murphy as well as his progress on a novel he is writing about American artist Rockwell Kent.

[13] Wayne Johnston, *The Old Lost Land of Newfoundland: Family, Memoir, Fiction, and Myth* (Edmonton: NeWest, 2009), p. 23.
[14] Ibid., p. 24.

That novel becomes Winter's second novel, *The Big Why* (2004), a first-person account of Kent's departure from the bustling artistic world of New York City for Brigus, Newfoundland, before and at the start of World War I. This historical work, following Kent's desire to live honestly in keeping with the simplifying patterns of his art, is set against the Newfoundland landscape and its people.

Winter, one of the founding members of the St. John's writers' group, The Burning Rock Collective, worked on the collective with Lisa Moore, who was born in St. John's and graduated with a BA from the Nova Scotia College of Art and Design. Like Winter, she first published short fiction, her first collection, *Degrees of Nakedness* (1995), juxtaposing extreme emotions with common trivialities, her characters thinking about their love affairs or mistakes from their pasts as they contemplate everyday domestic life. In "Purgatory's Wild Kingdom," for example, a distraught father, now living in Toronto with an older woman, remembers his wife making him a sardine sandwich; when his daughter phones him, he cannot recall her name. Like Winter, too, she sets her fiction mainly in her native province where she resides.

Her novels testify to the diversity of her creativity. *Alligator* (2005), an interconnected series of stories by a host of narrators, offers a complete rendering of contemporary St. John's and its people. A seventeen-year-old wayward daughter, her mother grieving over the death of her husband, a Russian castaway, a young hotdog vendor, and several others tell their tales without making any connections to one another, despite their many opportunities to relate. Centring on a woman who was devastated decades earlier when her young husband drowned in the real-life sinking of the Ocean Ranger off Newfoundland's coast in 1982, *February* (2009) meditates on her personal emptiness as a practical woman left to raise alone her four children; the story rests, not in the boat's sinking, but in the aftermath and its impact on individual lives. *Caught* (2013), a fast-paced adventure novel or a thriller, focuses on a recently escaped convict attempting for the second time to smuggle marijuana from Colombia to Canada; it charts his abiding commitment to the drug trade and his sorry refusal to turn away from it. Each of the novels, so intriguing and so compellingly different, captures its own specific world.

A distinguished poet, Michael Crummey (b. 1965), who was born in Buchans, Newfoundland, and received his BA from Memorial University and MA from Queen's University, lived in Kingston, Ontario, for more than a decade before emigrating back to his home province. *Hard Light* (1998), his collection of poetry and stories told to him by his father, opens with "Rust": "It will be years still before the boy thinks to ask his father about that other life, the world his hands carry with them like a barely discernible tattoo. His body hasn't been touched yet by the sad, particular beauty of things passing, of things about to be lost for good. Time's dark, indelible scar." For Crummey, "Time's dark, indelible scar" haunts his fiction as he tries to recover or bid farewell to the world "about to be lost for good." *Flesh and Blood* (1998), his collection of thirteen short stories, focuses on the fictional mining town of Black Rock, Newfoundland, a scarcely disguised Buchans, as the residents of a disappearing rural lifestyle try to establish themselves in a rapidly changing era. People leave the town, people come back, all of them trapped, the stories an elegy to the town that once was and yet still is.

His five novels reveal his deep understanding of Newfoundland of the past and the present. Set on Newfoundland's beautiful but desolate northern shore two hundred years ago, *River Thieves* (2001) studies the problems of the growing European settlement and the simultaneously slow demise of the Beothuk, driven in part by the neigbouring Mi'kmaq tribes. In the story, a raiding party has been involved in the murder of two Beothuk men, while the European settlers attempt to connect to the land, only to learn that such a connection is ultimately impossible. Crummey presents the entire affair without moralizing or simplifying the story. Even the title shares his ability not to side with any one perspective. Are the river thieves the plundering Beothuk? Or the displacing settlers who move through a landscape which is not their own? The hostilities of the peoples collide, resulting in the decimation that occurs in the pages of history.

The Wreckage (2005) goes back to World War II and an expanded range of settings from Newfoundland's villages to St. John's, Chicago, Vancouver, and Japanese prison camps, following its heroine up to 1994. Aloysius (Wish) Furey, a Catholic drifter, catches sight of a sixteen-year-old girl on Little Fogo Island. Her Protestant family drives him from the island, though she tries to follow him. Furey, meanwhile, enlists in the British army and ends up a Japanese prisoner of war, encountering a sadistic guard, whose own background history included constant bullying when he grew up in Vancouver. Both men are products of bitter discrimination. Violence, Crummey suggests, is an essential part of people's cruelty, again emphasizing the desperate need for human connection.

Inspired by his reading of Márquez's *One Hundred Years of Solitude*, *Galore* (2009) begins with a whale beached on the shore of the impoverished outport of Paradise Deep, the townspeople planning to slaughter it. But inside is a man alive. This novel of magic realism chronicles the feuds between two warring dynasties and their descendants through many generations. A companion piece to *Hard Light*, it upholds the three-hundred-year folkloric tradition that stands behind every Newfoundlander: people are connected to a vanished way of life only by the stories they have learned from their parents and their grandparents.

Sweetland (2014) is an honest and unsentimental paean of praise and regret to an old world dying off in the onward march of humanity. There are two Sweetlands which draw attention to each other: one the island off the southernmost coast of Newfoundland, the other Moses Sweetland, the scion of the family who gave the island its name. The residents have voted overwhelmingly in favour of the government's lucrative voluntary reloca-tion if – and only if – every person agrees to leave; Moses is the sole holdout. As the novel moves back and forth in time, the reader is assured that the past is always present, that contemporary events are history repeating itself. *Sweetland* paints a desperate picture of a sad community in its final days, living precariously in its final moments, wondering what will be its future when the people become scattered to St. John's and beyond. In *The Innocents* (2019), Evered and Ada Best, "two helpless youngsters holding on to one another in the pitch" and orphaned siblings, live alone in a remote cove in Newfoundland's northern coastline in the eighteenth century; they learn to care for each other, never ceasing their love.

An astute, learned chronicler of Newfoundland, its history, peoples, and folkloric traditions, Crummey makes his province the home of people alive to old and new challenges to their way of living, alive as he is "with the desire to salvage, scavenge, to reconstruct, to preserve that wisdom, to go after, unearth and to imagine, then to hold fast," comments Lisa Moore.[15] By focusing closely on his people in their habitats, he offers seminal portraits of communities in Newfoundland or anywhere in the world.

Newfoundland has always been a land on the periphery, an island off the coast of Canada: "Geographically, we have always been an extremity: on the edge of a new, unknown world, the cusp of the Atlantic Ocean and the North American continent."[16] Today its many writers have made it a major avenue of fiction, so many of them intent on telling the past and the present of their own hitherto uncharted world.

[15] "Introduction," Michael Crummey, *Hard Light* (London, Ontario: Brick Books, 2015), p. 13.
[16] Michael Winter,"Introduction," *Extremities: Fiction from the Burning Rock*, ed. Michael Winter (Saint John's, Newfoundland: Killick, 1994), pp. xi–xii.

Ontario

Straddling the Quebec–Ontario border, Ottawa, the nation's capital, has not been a centre of literary activity. Although it was home, for example, to the nineteenth-century poet Archibald Lampman, he preferred the distant countryside to the noise of his city. Only in the post-centennial period has there been a new appreciation of Ottawa's artistic dimensions. Three writers, two coming from other areas of the province, the third a native of Ottawa, have made it their literary home.

Born in Owen Sound, Ontario, Elizabeth Hay (b. 1951) worked as an interviewer and a documentary maker, first in Yellowknife, then in Winnipeg and Toronto; after six years in New York City, she settled in Ottawa in 1992. "New York gives me Canada in a way that is more vivid, more sentimental, than Canada gives me itself. It gives me the emotional Canada that's so hard to find when you're there," she writes in *Captivity Tales: Canadians in New York* (1993). "My emotional tie to Canada is less the edgy one between husband and wife than the deeper, less describable one with a child: an all-enveloping and loaded combination of censure and acceptance." Juxtaposing personal reflections with objective commentary, her early collections of essays portray a woman in desperate need of finding herself by losing herself in her non-Canadian world.

Raised on the writings of Munro, the poetry of Margaret Avison and Elizabeth Bishop, and many other contemporary authors including Carol Shields, Hay penned *A Student of Weather* (2000), her study of two sisters and the young man who alters the projection of their lives. In January 1938 twenty-three-year-old Maurice Dove, sent by Ottawa to study the drought-ridden climate around Willow Bend, Saskatchewan, arrives on the doorstep of the Hardy farmhouse. Focusing on the two Hardy daughters, the beautiful Lucinda and the younger Norma Joyce, the novel follows thirty years in their lives, moving from Saskatchewan to New York and finally to Ottawa. Lucinda's housewifely endurance, Norma Joyce's persistent loneliness in New York, these are qualities which isolate and illuminate their dark lives. Other novels include *Garbo Laughs* (2003) about a woman addicted to movies; *Late Nights on Air* (2007) about a small radio station in Yellowknife; and *Alone in the Classroom* (2011) about a prairie teacher who believes "her role as a teacher was to lead children through an anxious passage into a mental clearing."

In *His Whole Life* (2015), Hay returns to New York City. Set in the looming Quebec referendum of the mid-1990s, the book has its characters haunted by the possibility that Quebec may secede; the stillness of the

Canadian woods rings true to its people while the sterility of New York has an increasingly negative effect on its inhabitants. In this work of fiction Hay returns to *Captivity Tales*, where she reflected: "All my thoughts are on Canada, the chief anchor in my life, which means I'm anchored to something falling apart." In drawing her stories from the immediate present, she writes detailed novels which reveal the humanity of her characters.

In contrast to Hay's preoccupation with the present, Francis Itani (b. 1942) tends to focus on the past. Born in Belleville, Ontario, and trained for the nursing profession, which she practiced for eight years, she became committed to writing after attending classes with W.O. Mitchell, who became her mentor. A children's writer, a short story author, and a poet, she wrote her first novel, *Deafening* (2003), after researching the problems associated with deafness, including taking lessons in sign language and doing volunteer work with the hearing-impaired. With meticulous attention to all the many details of her story, she writes a tribute to the problems and the heroism of deaf people. Focusing on the small pre-World War I town of Deseronto in eastern Ontario, where the O'Neil family owns a hotel, *Deafening* centres on Grania O'Neil, a girl who lost her hearing from scarlet fever when she was only five. Mamo, her grandmother, does not despair of Grania, but responds to her resolute nature, teaching her enough vocabulary so that she can have a normal life. Spending seven years in a segregated school introduces her to the hearing assistant to the school's doctor. She marries him before he leaves for the war, where he is a stretcher-bearer in Belgium and France. As an anti-war writer, Itani fills her authentic story with wartime atrocities.

Tell (2014), her sequel to *Deafening*, returns to Deseronto and focuses on other inhabitants of the same town. For example, Kenan, the husband of Grania's sister Tress, the recently returned soldier with one side of his face "sealed in rippled scars" and missing one arm, one eye, and one ear, is battling the many memories of his time in the trenches; slowly he, like other characters in the novel, must grapple with the burdens of the past. Itani's singular achievement is again her presentation of a sleepy town with its many secrets slightly below the surface. Prefacing certain chapters with the local items from the newspaper, the *Deseronto Post*, the novel depicts the time (November 1919 to January 1921) and the town, memorably preserved as a consequence of Itani's archival research. *That's My Baby* (2017), the third in her Deseronto trilogy, focuses on Honora Oak, septuagenarian writer and adopted daughter of Kenan and Tress, and her search into the befuddled worlds of her past.

Born in Ottawa, Alan Cumyn (b. 1960), a student of Alistair MacLeod, writes fiction about human rights and about World War I. *Man of Bone* (1998) and *Burridge Unbound* (2000) explore the dignity and the violation of human rights through first-person narration. In the former, Bill Burridge, on his first diplomatic positing away from Ottawa, finds himself on the South Pacific island of Santa Irene where third-world terrorism precludes his safe existence; he is kidnapped and tortured by rebel forces. In the latter he is home again in Ottawa trying to recover from the torture he endured and attempting to right the wrongful world. *The Sojourn* (2003) and *The Famished Lover* (2006) feature first-person narration as the narrator details his leave from the horrors of World War I on a ten-day leave in London where he meets his cousins and their family; in the second novel, freed from the tortures of a German prisoner of war camp, he returns to Montreal where he falls in love with a farm girl from the Eastern Townships, the horrors of the war years still haunting him. In these books Cumyn, like Itani, poses serious questions about the effectiveness of torture and war.

Two poets who ventured into fiction came to settle west of Ottawa in Kingston. Born in Toronto and educated at Queen's University in Kingston, Steven Heighton (b. 1961) travelled widely. He turned to prose with his collection, *Flight Paths of the Emperor* (1992), fourteen stories which capture the new Japan and the cultural differences between east and west from the perspective of the Canadian expatriate narrator. Still continuing as a poet and a short story writer, he wrote his first novel, *The Shadow Boxer* (2000), under the influence of, among others, Jack Kerouac and Thomas Wolfe, focusing on a young man from Sault Sainte Marie, Ontario, who is torn between his love of literature and his affinity for boxing, only to retreat to Rye Island in northern Lake Superior to confront his own loneliness. In his later novels, all of them adventure stories, he approaches groups isolated and trapped in worlds which become idyllic or survivalist. *Afterlands* (2005) reimagines nineteen people trapped on the ice floes after the Polaris expedition in the 1870s; *Every Lost Country* (2011) has a group of Tibetan refugees fleeing Chinese soldiers; *The Nightingale Won't Let You Sleep* (2017) examines contemporary Varosha, Cyprus, a derelict enclave of refugees and misfits slowly falling apart. First and foremost a poet, Heighton portrays the people he selects and their tragic worlds.

A second accomplished poet who turned to prose is Helen Humphreys (b. 1961), who was born in Kingston upon Thames, England, grew up in Toronto, and is now resident, too, of Kingston. Working within the tradition of British literature, particularly the feminist dimension, she creates in her nine novels, or more accurately novellas, detailed portraits of people often disconnected from the realities around them. Inspired by the photographs of Julia Margaret Cameron, *Afterimage* (2000), a Victorian novella, recounts the tribulations of a young woman who goes to work as a maid in a remote upper-class British estate, the indebtedness to *Jane Eyre* evident throughout. *The Lost Garden* (2002) begins on the day in 1941 when newspapers were reporting the drowning of Virginia Woolf, and Humphreys plays with Woolf's haunting presence. Using World War II as background in *Coventry* (2008) and *The Evening Chorus* (2015), she explores the intimate connection between human beings and the natural world around them. In *The Evening Chorus*, for example, a lyrical paean of praise to the constancy of nature amid war's horrors, a former grammar-school science teacher is shot down in the war's first full year. He then begins to study a pair of redstarts nesting on a wall just beyond the perimeter of his concentration camp. In his focus on the birds rests the importance of this novella. In the darkest days of war, nature can still assert her hold on humanity. Humphreys's natural world offers solace to people in their moments of despair, whether in a lost garden or elsewhere. People, she asserts, must not think of themselves as separated from nature.

In the second half of the century, Montreal was losing its title as the country's largest city. By 1976 its population was 2,802,500 in contrast to Toronto's 2,803,100, reflecting the rise of the Parti Québécois, the consequent flight of many Anglophones from the province, and the decline in immigrants; the centre of growth moved to Toronto. Montreal "was losing its character as the economic center of an English-speaking Canada and was simultaneously taking on its character as a regional, French-speaking metropolis," wrote Jane Jacobs.[17] Since the 1960s new publishers have been operating in Toronto, and writers – from across Canada – found their homes in these young organizations as well as in the older established firms. Toronto's metropolitan area, North America's third largest city (behind New York and Los Angeles), thus becomes a residence for many fiction authors, some of them even born in the city.

Born in Toronto, Timothy Findley began his career as an actor before Ruth Gordon and Thornton Wilder persuaded him to explore writing. Like Margaret Laurence, he believed the present day was the defining moment in Canadian literature, "the moment when it is going to happen,

---

[17] *The Question of Separatism: Quebec and the Struggle Over Sovereignty* (Toronto: Random House, 1980), p. 16.

when identity will blossom for individuals and people will suddenly realize, My god, we have writers."[18] Like Munro, he wrote out of the "Southern *Ontario* Gothic" tradition,[19] which looked back to Carson McCullers and Tennessee Williams. Like Wiseman, he found writing his mode of expressing anger and frustration at the human condition: "the writer goes down into the other world of hell for a few years and comes back up and tries to articulate the experience for everyone else."[20]

The Last of the Crazy People (1967) centres on the dysfunctional Wilsons and the blurred line between insanity and sanity, a constant theme in Findley's novels. "A short, swift plunge through the fog and terror of people who do *not* cry out when they should or move when they should,"[21] the book focuses on eleven-year-old Hooker Wilson. In the disintegrating world of his Ontario family – after giving birth to a stillborn, his mother keeps to her room; his father sits with his back to everything; his older brother commits suicide – he takes a gun to them, ending up in a mental hospital. Findley's delight in historical fiction is evident in *The Butterfly Plague* (1969), which chronicles the lives of the artistic and the crazy in 1920s and 1930s Hollywood, mirroring the ominous terrors of the impending World War II.

In *The Wars* (1977), Findley went back to World War I to follow the exploits of nineteen-year-old Robert Ross as he enters the war to escape the restrictive norms of his Victorian Toronto society. A sensitive and earnest young man, he enlists after his beloved older sister died from falling out of her wheelchair, while playing with her rabbits in the barn; his alcoholic mother had ordered Robert to murder the rabbits, his refusal prompting his father to hire someone to do the killing. As he goes off to war, he endures a series of unfortunate situations, including his killing of a horse, his experience of trench warfare, his brutal rape by four men, and his murder of his own captain. An archivist years later attempts to piece together his life from interviews with people Ross met, using first-, second-, and third-person narratives to shed light on Ross's tragic history. Findley creates his novel, Vanderhaeghe observes, "by piecing together a collage of arresting images and brief, telling scenes that not only cohere in a compelling narrative but whose form mimics the fractured lives of soldiers and civilians shattered by war."[22] Complementing *The Wars* is *Famous Last Words* (1981), set mainly during World War II. Hugh Selwyn Mauberley

---

[18] *Eleven Canadian Novelists*, p. 129.   [19] Ibid., p. 138.
[20] *Inside Memory: Pages from a Writer's Workbook* (Toronto: HarperCollins, 1990), p. 181.
[21] Ibid., p. 74.   [22] "Introduction," *The Wars* (Toronto: Penguin, 2005), p. xii.

(from the Ezra Pound poem of the same name) is forced to observe and ultimately to participate in the violence of his own world. No longer confined to one family, as in *The Wars*, the novel explores and exploits more than twenty fictional and more than fifty non-fictional people in a mixture of historical and fictional situations to underline the complicity of art and politics.

Subsequent novels develop related themes. *Not Wanted on the Voyage* (1984) is an imaginative rewriting of the story of Noah's Ark. *Headhunter* (1990) brings Conrad's Kurtz back to life in present-day Toronto with its omnipresence of violence and evil. *The Piano Man's Daughter* (1995) forces the central character to confront his mother's madness. *You Went Away* (1996), set in the first years of World War II, studies the devastating effects of the war on an Ontario family. And *Pilgrim* (1999) brings the title character – after his attempt at suicide – to Carl Jung's clinic in Zurich to regain his perspective on life.

Dealing relentlessly with the horrors of warfare, both public and personal, rewriting works of the past and challenging understandings of the present, Findley's fiction, in a statement mirroring Richler's perspective on fiction, witnesses the inhuman degrading of the contemporary world: "A writer is a witness. A witness of the present, a witness of the future, a witness of the past. Memory provides that witness with veracity. Yes; even our memory of the future."[23]

Born in London, Ontario, educated at the University of Western Ontario, then resident of Toronto, Graeme Gibson was a style innovator. His first novel, *Five Legs* (1969), and its sequel *Communion* (1971) document their characters' consciousness, as reflected in their unconnected perceptions, the radical and abrupt changes in their thinking, and the fragmentary sentence structure of their non-linear narratives. Following *The Double Hook*, Gibson expanded novel-writing to embrace experimental techniques, eager to make his reader an active participant in understanding the limitations of a linear reading. Like Marian Engel, whose early novels were written at the same time, he eschewed linearity to capture the radial discontinuity of his world.

Eight years in its writing and a telling disclosure of the southern Ontario puritan ethos, *Five Legs* falls into six parts: three from the perspective of Dr. Lucan Crackell, a repressed professor of English at the University of Western Ontario, and three from Felix Oswald, a confused graduate student. Both men are travelling to Stratford to attend the funeral of

---

[23] *Inside Memory*, p. 313.

Crackell's former student and Oswald's roommate. In his sections, Crackell, inhibited, finds his world closed to outside influences, strenuously committed to the acceptable norm, his dislike of his companion painfully evident; he is a pillar of southwestern Ontario's academic community. In his sections, Oswald ruminates about himself, his dislike of Crackell dominant. Although Oswald fears Crackell's inhibitions, his desire to opt out is matched only by his uncertainty about where he should run.

Communion, dealing with the convoluted fragmentation of the world outside of Oswald himself, locates him in Toronto, working as a veterinarian's assistant. Unrecognized by society as anything but a nobody, he loses connection to reality in his compulsive subjectivity. Escaping all human involvements, he perishes in flames in Detroit. Both novels display the legacy the individuals meet, their tendency to failure leading to spiritual malaise or death. Like Hawthorne's *The Scarlet Letter*, they emphasize the Calvinistic death visited upon closed people and the almost ritualistic death of young men in southwestern Ontario society.

In *Perpetual Motion* (1982), Gibson turned again to southern Ontario but in the late nineteenth century in a historical novel about Robert Fraser, who is driven by his fervent desire for power. "To authenticate the history of my region," he fashions "the attempt to dramatise a world I knew had to be there."[24] Fixated on inventing a perpetual motion machine which will harness natural energy, Fraser neglects and destroys both the nature around him and his own family as his rationality becomes tragic lunacy. *Gentleman Death* (1992), set in contemporary Toronto, studies one man, ambitiously searching for the meaning of life after the deaths of his father and his brother; his linear quest seeks reconciliation with his past.

Like Engel, Gibson returned to linearity in his later fiction. In his early novels, however, he, like Engel, charted a new path in post-1967 Canada.

Born in Baden-Baden, Germany, the daughter of a government auditor and his Lebanese-descended wife, and a graduate of the National Theatre School of Canada, Ann-Marie MacDonald (b. 1959), a playwright and a resident of Toronto, moved later into fiction. After writing for five years what she thought was another play, she published her first novel, *Fall on Your Knees* (1996). Telling the mysterious story of five generations of the broken Piper family and its many secrets, the book begins in 1898 in New Waterford, Cape Breton, "a small mining town near cutaway cliffs that

[24] Colin Nicholson, "Of Oracles and Orreries: Graeme Gibson and His Writing," *British Journal of Canadian Studies* 3, 2 (1988): 303.

curve over the narrow rock beaches below, where the silver sea rolls and rolls, flattering the moon." Eighteen-year-old James Piper, a self-taught piano tuner, meets and marries a woman who is but thirteen; they elope and have three children, the eldest sparking her father's amorous interest. As a consequence, he goes off to serve in World War I. When he returns, he is still dangerous to his family, his prurient desires reducing his children to helpless pawns of his tyrannical rule. *Fall on Your Knees* is a painful novel of human beings trapped in their arduous flight from their Cape Breton world. Given MacDonald's background in theatre, it is not surprising that her dialogue captures the many characters who populate her pages. Even more astonishing is her facility with narrative, the plot moving with ease through the generations.

The Way the Crow Flies (2003) turns to 1962 when the Cuban Missile Crisis occurred, when the race to the moon was taking place, when the Cold War was at its feverish height. The McCarthy family are returning from Germany to Canada where the father will direct an officers' training school. One of his daughter's teachers imposes after-school "punishments" on her and other young girls, which she will not divulge to her parents. At the same time, her father must resettle a German defector whose chequered past has been overlooked for political expediency. Her father is destroyed by this experience, his daughter, smarting from this wound, grows up to be a lesbian comedian in Toronto.

Adult Onset (2014) studies forty-eight-year-old Mary Rose MacKinnon, who has taken time off from her writing career to stay at home and tend her two young children in a trendy Toronto neighbourhood; her partner Hilary is out west directing *The Importance of Being Earnest*. While she is taking care of her two-year-old daughter, her mind drifts back to herself at the same age when she was parented by her own depressed mother, who was suffering from postnatal depression. She is continually harassed by painful memories of her past, including the time when she came out to her parents twenty years ago and they were in no way supportive. Compelled to examine her tense relationship with them, she seeks to understand her present anxiety.

Raised on the fiction of, among others, Dickens and the Brontës, MacDonald acknowledges her equal debt to Canadian writers, including Atwood and Findley.

Born in Midland, Ontario, resident in Toronto while working at Oxford University Press and Macmillan's, then residing for more than forty years in St Catharines where he taught English at Ridley College, Richard B. Wright (1937–2017) wrote fourteen novels which focus on men and women pursuing their tasks amid the hardships of contemporary life. His first novel for adults, *The Weekend Man* (1970), focuses on Wes Wakeham, a thirty-year-old publishing salesperson and the book's narrator. "A weekend man is a person who has abandoned the present in favour of the past or the future," he announces. "He is really more interested in what happened to him twenty years ago or in what is going to happen to him next week than he is in what is happening to him today." In the holiday season he must forge a new path for himself, all the while refusing to claw his way to the top of the corporate ladder. Amid the continuing turmoil of his failing marriage to Molly, the deceitful machinations of his secretary, and the drudgery of his publishing job, there is no illumination for him. Detached from the passing scene, he can be only an ironic commentator on his meaningless life.

Influenced by American writers such as Saul Bellow, Walker Percy, and Philip Roth, Wright continued in this sardonic vein. The hero of *In the Middle of a Life* (1973), "an unemployed greeting-card salesman," is an older version of Wes Wakeham. During one week, he relishes his debates with his ex-wife, he looks for a job, and he falls in love, all valiant attempts to confront the problems of daily living. Supremely aware of the difficulties and absurdities of human existence, Wright projects his characters' dilemmas against a post-Christian culture.

Farthing's Fortunes (1976) is a comic, Swiftian epic of Billy Farthing's life. Told from his present residence in an old-age home, Farthing, an Ontario farm boy, becomes a follower of the North American dream. Convincing in its depictions of the slums of Toronto, the Klondike gold rush, and World War I and the Great Depression, the novel traces its naïve hero as he succumbs to the mesmerizing power of an opportunistic and swindling American in his pursuit of economic success. Throughout his career, Wright evokes earlier times through a detailed placement of his characters in authentic settings.

In contemporary novels such as the shocking *Final Things* (1980), which watches a man deal with the rape and murder of his twelve-year-old son, the realistic *The Teacher's Daughter* (1982), which follows the love affair of a lonely woman and a petty criminal, and the comic *Tourists* (1984), where a Canadian couple meet boisterous Americans on their Mexican holiday, he explores the vicissitudes, both tragic and comic, of life.

In *The Age of Longing* (1995), originally titled *Presbyterian Blues*, the narrator, an editor in a publishing firm and just recovering from a heart attack, returns to his hometown of Huron Falls to sell his late mother's house, only to find himself journeying back to the time of his parents' failed marriage, his father a small-town hockey star, his mother a more principled and snobbish teacher. What the older narrator knows now helps him understand what his younger self witnessed. A fine depiction of small-town Ontario life in the 1930s and 1940s, *The Age of Longing* has Wright, like Munro, witness the world where important stories are often left to people's children to remember and to tell.

Clara Callan (2001), Wright's masterwork, returns to the period of *The Age of Longing*, the 1930s, to chronicle the lives of two sisters, Clara and Nora Callan, the former, a schoolteacher in her Ontario town of Whitfield, and the latter, her flighty younger sister, who flees to the excitement of New York City and radio soap-opera stardom. Told in Clara's prose and bringing together their many letters, the novel highlights many of the events of the 1930s as background to the Callan sisters' fortunes in a world sceptical of female independence. Wright's psychological studies of both the women and the worlds that surround them capture the female voices that are the novel's centre.

In keeping with the diversity of Wright's many works, *Mr. Shakespeare's Bastard* (2010) captures another historical period, the seventeenth century, with its taverns, beggars, and public hangings in a tale about a housekeeper who happens to be Shakespeare's illegitimate child, while his last novel, *October* (2016), returns to contemporary Toronto and a widower in his 1970s who learns that love can return to give form to his lonely life.

During his more than fifty years of writing, Wright was a masterful storyteller, be the stories set in Elizabethan England, present-day Toronto, or in-between. All good stories "remind us of the human adventure that we call life," he wrote in *A Life with Words: A Writer's Memoir* (2015), and his novels present men and women who embark on their adventures and who invite readers to identify with their usually quiet quests into the meaning of this transitory existence.

Also born in Midland, now resident in Toronto, is Susan Swan (b. 1945), a graduate of McGill University and influenced by Atwood and Engel. Her novels of the lives of women from the past complement her accounts of contemporary women trying to cope in their changing environments, most notably teenager Mary Beatrice "Mouse" Bradford, who grows up in Madoc's Landing, a thinly disguised Midland.

The Biggest Modern Woman of the World (1983) purports to be a first-person account of the Nova Scotian giantess Anna Swan (1846–88) and her involvement with P.T. Barnum. At the same time, the book undercuts the masculine traditions of autobiography to delineate her remarkable life from its prenatal beginning until her death. Swan, the writer, pushes the realistic autobiographical conventions to their limits, exploring her subject's life through literary texts, intertextual references, and parodies of the male-dominated field of historical writing. "I feel I am acting out America's relationship to Canada," Anna confesses to her mother. "We possess no fantasies of conquest and domination. Indeed, to be from the Canadas is to feel as women feel – cut off from the base of power." The book becomes an endearing and challenging account of one person's struggles to be a complete human being. *What Casanova Told Me* (2004) is a detailed portrait of two women separated by two centuries: Asked For Adams, whom Casanova convinces to set out on an adventure to Constantinople, and Luce Adams, Asked For's twenty-first-century descendant, who tries to unravel the true story of Casanova. What is revealed is the true nature of Casanova and his spell-binding hold on two women linked by blood and separated by centuries.

Then there is, in *The Wives of Bath* (1993), a contemporary account of Mouse's upbringing under the beleaguered eyes of her father, the town's principal physician and healer. Suffering from gross spinal curvature – polio having caused her back muscles to atrophy – she delights in observing the world around her, partaking in its robust and sometimes hurtful experiences.

In *The Dead Celebrities Club* (2019), Swan breaks this pattern, writing now of a sad and forlorn anti-hero, born in Toronto, whose male voice dominates the action. An amoral wizard at hedge-fund accounts, he finds himself in an upstate New York prison guilty of serious embezzlement and fraud, the novel being a dire warning about the evils of contemporary financial practices.

Born in Kingston, Ontario, educated at the University of Toronto and McMaster University, and settling in Toronto, Matt Cohen (1942–99) was a children's author, novelist, poet, and short story writer. His fictional writings include his initial four-novel series, *The Disinherited* (1974), *The Colours of War* (1977), *The Sweet Second Summer of Kitty Malone* (1979), and *Flowers of Darkness* (1981), chronicling life in the fictional town of Salem, Ontario, northeast of Kingston. The multi-generational story attempts to understand the Anglo-Protestant mentality that shaped so much of Ontario and Canadian social values and were cornerstones of much of the fiction of Davies and Findley, Munro and Wright.

After writing these books as an "outsider" to this mentality, Cohen turned to his Jewish inheritance and adapted the conventions of the historical novel to *The Spanish Doctor* (1984), an account of interfaith strife in medieval Spain; the novel was the first time he dealt directly with his heritage and a world bent on eliminating Jews. After *The Spanish Doctor*, he completed a second trilogy, the second, *Nadine* (1986), about a Parisian Jew who survives Hitler's maniacal manipulations and *Emotional Arithmetic* (1990) about a child who survives the Holocaust only to be immersed in a loveless marriage. "I feel I have to understand – although I know I won't – what happened to the Jewish-European dream," Cohen remarked. "Not simply because it ended in a tragedy greater than all other tragedies – perhaps it wasn't – but because it is in some way the life I was meant to inherit. Also, of course, if we cannot understand what in us has been destroyed then we can't understand how other peoples suffer in similar circumstances."[25]

Born in Belleville, the son of German immigrants and a graduate of the University of Western Ontario, now resident, too, of Toronto, Dennis Bock (b. 1964) wrote a semi-autobiographical collection of seven inter-connecting short stories, *Olympia* (1998), which follow a teenager's growth into full maturity in suburban Ontario. The central character and narrator, Peter, must navigate his difficult life, which includes his post-war German parents and their harsh memories of their past as well as his younger sister's death from leukemia. He struggles to make a coherent narrative from the fragments before him in an attempt to reconcile the memories of his relatives with his own insights. Set against the backdrop of the Nazis' glorification of the 1936 Berlin Olympics – two of Peter's grandparents were members of the German delegation – and the hostage-taking at the 1972 Munich Olympics, sections of history playing into Peter's reminiscences, the book is a haunting evocation of one man's search into his familial background to understand the pride and the shame of his extended family.

The Ash Garden (2001), his first novel, is a haunting tale of three people: Anton Böll, a German-born scientist who leaves Germany in 1940 because he disagrees with the decision to shift the focus of the atomic program from graphite to heavy water; Austrian Sophie Heinemann, a Jewish refugee, who finds herself interned in Canada and marries Böll; and a six-year-old Hiroshima-born Emiko Amai, who utters the novel's opening words, "*One morning toward the end of the summer they burned away my face*," and grows up to be a documentary filmmaker whose subject is the 1945 bombings of Japan and their aftermath. "We did what needed to be done. I am one of those people," Böll confesses. "It is not right or wrong to

---

[25] "Matt Cohen b. 1942," *Other Solitudes: Canadian Multicultural Fictions*, ed. Linda Hutcheon and Marion Richmond (Toronto: Oxford University Press, 1990), p. 177.

have used the bomb. But it was necessary." On the fiftieth anniversary of the bomb falling, the trio debate its effects on Japanese society and on themselves, all of them scarred by the bomb and by themselves. Once again historical personages interact with Bock's fictional creations.

Bock educated himself in the writings of Raymond Carver, John Cheever, and Richard Ford, not to mention such Canadians as Atwood, Gallant, and Munro. "I read Alice Munro five times straight," he notes. "So much of writing is accident, but you also have to have the craft, and she is obviously one of the greatest craftsmen going."[26] Whether Bock is recreating the past or embarking on new material, he brings to his writings a sophisticated imagination.

Born in Little Long Lac, Ontario, northwest of Thunder Bay, Jane Urquhart (b. 1949) settled in southern Ontario. Heavily indebted to Montgomery, the Brontë sisters, and other Victorian novelists and poets, she pens historical fiction. First known as a poet and later a short story writer, she writes prose that reflects her poetic training. *The Whirlpool* (1986) focuses on Niagara Falls, Ontario, in the summer of 1889 and various people caught up in the whirlpool's rhythmic swirl. *Changing Heaven* (1990), a complete immersion in the Victorian age, brings together a Brontë scholar's affair with an art historian and a balloonist's conversations with Emily Brontë's ghost, and *Away* (1993) examines an Irish woman and three generations of her descendants in Canada.

The Underpainter (1997) turns to art as it examines the life of a minimalist American painter who uses his art to isolate himself from human beings on the north shore of Lake Superior. Yet as an artist, he needs to understand the people around him. Therein lies the dilemma. In her later novel, *The Night Stages* (2015), Urquhart unites her two major interests, a passionate love of Ireland and its myths and a deep commitment to the expressive side of the painter. Set mainly in the Irish countryside, the book explores the haunting life of forlorn Tamara, an Irish woman in her thirties, who has just walked out on her lover and County Kerry where she has lived since before World War II. When her plane is grounded by fog at Gander Airport, she stares at the mural painted there by Kenneth Lochhead. Urquhart parallels Tamara's sad memories of her former life with the story of Lochhead's coming of age and his awakening to the creation of his mural.

Her major achievement is *The Stone Carvers* (2001), which focuses initially on Father Gstir, a Bavarian priest sent on a mission to the

---

[26] "Bock to the future," *The Globe and Mail*, 25 August 2001, p. D4.

German-settled area of Shoneval in southwestern Ontario in the years leading up to World War I. His many parishioners and their compatriots suddenly find themselves swept up in the war. The final resolution includes the Toronto sculptor Walter Allward whose ambitious plans include a memorial at Vimy, France, to honour the Canadian men who lost their lives in the war. Urquhart's fiction embraces a love of the past, Irish and Canadian, with a sentient feeling for the presence of all the figures from the past. Whether she is depicting the Victorian era, World War I, or later times, she brings to her fiction a poet's sensibility.

One of the few writers who was born, raised, and lives in Toronto is Anne Michaels. Her first two books were acclaimed volumes of poetry, and her later fiction partakes of a poet's sensibility. *Fugitive Pieces* (1996), which won the Orange Prize in 1997, is divided into two sections, the first narrated by Jakob Beer, a Holocaust survivor who emigrated to Canada and later published several volumes of poetry based on his own experiences, and the second by a young Jewish professor known as Ben whose study of the war sparks his fixation with Jakob and his writing. The world of memory is paramount, for "History is amoral: events occurred. But memory is moral; what we consciously remember is what our conscience remembers. History is the Totenbuch, The Book of the Dead, kept by the administrators of the camps. Memory is the Memorbucher, the names of those to be mourned, read aloud in the synagogue." In his narrative of catastrophe, Jakob gradually awakens to love as he discovers the redemptive power of memory, his pleasurable memories gradually transforming his wartime experiences and his Holocaust-haunted nightmares into a tentative movement towards human connectedness.

The Winter Vault (2009) is an absorbing study of loss and dislocation. Avery Escher, a young engineer whose mother's family died in the Holocaust, and his wife, Jean Shaw, a young botanist, met during the construction of the St. Lawrence Seaway, which obliterated towns Jean had loved. Then, in 1964 the couple are living on a Nile houseboat below the towering figures of Abu Simbel, where Avery is one of the engineers responsible for disassembling and moving Ramses II's famous temple from the rapidly rising waters of the Aswan Dam. Jean's pregnancy leads to a stillborn child, and Avery suggests that they separate when they return to Canada. This juxtaposition of communal and personal loss leads to the dislocation of the characters' lives. Jean has to learn that "To mourn is to honour. Not to surrender to this keening, to this absence – a dishonouring."

In her lyric fiction Michaels is an archivist employing poetic immediacy to make the past present. Like Heighton, Humphreys, and Urquhart, like Atwood too, she has a carefully constructed lens on life.

West of Toronto five writers have written challenging fiction, two of them moving their permanent residence to Toronto.

Living in Hamilton is Lawrence Hill (b. 1957), born in Newmarket, Ontario, "son of a black American Second World War veteran and a white American civil rights activist."[27] With a BA in economics from Laval University and an MA in writing from the Johns Hopkins University, he set out to be a Black Canadian writer investigating the question of identity in his society. "As a young man," he said, "I could have named Austin Clarke, but he was the only Black Canadian writer on my radar screen in the mid-late 1970s."[28]

His first novel, the semi-autobiographical *Some Great Thing* (1992), centres on a black investigative reporter for the *Winnipeg Herald,* who confronts the social issues of race and gender in his first job back home in Winnipeg. Armed with a BA in history and French from Laval and an MA in economics from the University of Toronto, he initially finds his social conscience when he is drawn into the battle over the constitutional rights of Manitoba's Francophones.

Set in 1995, *Any Known Blood* (1997) expands the focus of his earlier novel, telling the story of five generations of Langston Canes, a genealogy from Langston Cane the First, a Black American slave, through Langston Cane the Fifth, an African Canadian researching his family history to write his own account. Still somewhat autobiographical and including characters from *Some Great Thing,* the book is not history, though it has historical elements, but a novel. "My primary identity is as a novelist and a story-teller," Hill says. "I feel I can do something often which historians can't often do, which is to dramatize the past so that readers step naturally into it."[29] The son of a white mother and a black father, Langston Cane the Fifth, the narrator of his generational saga, seeks to uncover and know his past and his racial identity. Like Mahatma Grafton, he is trapped: "In Spain, people have wondered if I was French. In France, hotel managers asked if I was Moroccan. In Canada, I've been asked – always tentatively – if I was perhaps Peruvian, American, or Jamaican." As he tells his

---

[27] *Black Berry, Sweet Juice: On Being Black and White in Canada* (Toronto: HarperCollins, 2001), p. 6.
[28] Christian J. Krampe, *The Past is Present: The African-Canadian Experience in Lawrence Hill's Fiction* (Frankfurt: Peter Lang, 2012), p. 302.
[29] Ibid., p. 301.

discoveries, he blurs the line between fiction and history, summoning written documents from the past with a controlling power. From the classic slave narrative of Langston Cane the First through the family exclusions perpetrated by Langston Cane the Fourth, the novel maps out a genealogical history of racism, overt in the United States, more hidden in Canada, discovered by a man trying to know the truth about one-hundred-and-seventy years of the black experience in North America.

Continuing Hill's fascination with black history, *The Book of Negroes* (2007) is a first-person slave narrative, overtly fictionalized, of Animata Diallo and her enforced travels around the world. Self-assured, she points out that writing down her story has helped her cope with her traumatic experiences. Using four "Books" to give form to them, she recounts in the first her early years in Mali and her status as "property"; the second follows her slavery in North Carolina; the third charts her life as a fugitive slave in New York and then her passage to Canada; the fourth ends with her time in London, England, to support the abolitionist movement. Dramatizing "the past so that readers step naturally into it," Diallo's account is a firsthand collection of her own vivid memories.

In his three novels, Hill writes of black experiences in Canada and the world. Many black writers such as Hill explore black history which has remained hidden. A complete view of Canadian history is now available to writers and to readers, filling in the hitherto blank spaces of historical writing.

A plea for tolerance and kindness in a world where such qualities are notably absent, *The Illegal* (2015) is the plight of a young black runner who witnesses tragedies in his native Zantoroland. Setting the story in the near future, Hill studies the boy's perseverance in the face of dire obstacles. His mother is killed by marauders; his father, a famous journalist and intellectual, is arrested, beaten up, and left to die in his children's care. The boy flees his homeland, becoming "a stranger in a strange land whose only transgression was to exist in a place where his presence was illegal." The book is an indictment of the cruelties wreaked on people trapped in worlds which do not accommodate difference.

Hill plays a major role in Canadian fiction, reminding readers of the tragedies of those who continually evade their own background. The black experience must be embraced in order to have a complete vision of the country, his novels showing the deficiencies of a world where racism still haunts its people.

Southwest of Hamilton is Simcoe, the birthplace of Douglas Glover (b. 1948), who took his BA in philosophy from York University, his

M.Litt. in philosophy from the University of Edinburgh, and his MFA in creative writing from the University of Iowa. A novelist, short story writer, and literary critic, he claims among his mentors Milan Kundera, Vladimir Nabokov, the Canadian radical and writer Hubert Aquin, and psychiatrist R.D. Laing, who introduced him to a postmodern perspective on literature and culture; he also learned from the satires of Juvenal, Swift, Céline, and Nathanael West. In fact, he amassed readings of Canadian and world literatures as well as the writings of Eric Havelock, Walter Ong, and Marshall McLuhan. Now living in Vermont where he is a faculty member of Vermont College's MFA in writing, he has always been "a nomad, an expatriate, a wandering Canadian,"[30] dwelling in the United States while inhabiting a Canadian mindset, utilizing men and women first-person narrators, and presenting characters from every walk of life.

In "My Romance" from his fourth story collection, *16 Categories of Desire* (2000), Annie and her husband, the story's narrator, suffer the aftermath of their three-month-old son's death. Their sorrow has many manifestations: her uncontrolled crying, her heartsickness, his brief affair with the family physician. The grief opens them up to "a fleeting experience of something that might be called true love." The couple crack out of themselves and see each other fully for the first time. As Glover notes, "I am most interested in how we negotiate desire and love as we dance with another person and what redemptive possibilities inhere in that situation."[31]

Glover has written two pseudo-historical novels. In *The Life and Times of Captain N.* (1993), a somewhat true story of Captain Hendrick Nellis, a Tory guerrilla and redeemer of Whites abducted by the Indigenous, and his exploits on the Niagara frontier in the last days of the American Revolution. At the centre is his son Oskar, whom his father kidnaps into service as a reluctant hero for King George. Haunted by his dreams and by his books, Oskar is the teller and the shaper of the events that form his narrative. "I meant to portray all the cultures for what they were and not ascribe any excess of virtue or malevolence to either side. All cultures are ripe for satire. They constrain us in different ways, but if you can get any distance, they all look pretty weird," Glover observes.[32] Armed with

---

[30] "The Familiar Dead," *Notes Home from a Prodigal Son* (Ottawa: Oberon, 1999), p. 167.
[31] "Styles of Approach: Douglas Glover with Bruce Stone, March 2004," *The Art of Desire: The Fiction of Douglas Glover* (Ottawa: Oberon, 2004), p. 168.
[32] Ibid., p. 166.

abundant readings of the historical period and infusing satire into his recreation, he presents a subversion of conventional realism.

From the earliest days of the European colonization of North America comes his second pseudo-historical novel, *Elle* (2003), a first-person account by a young French woman marooned on the desolate Isle of Demons during Jacques Cartier's ill-fated third and final attempt to settle Canada. Based on the historical Marguerite de Roberval, the eponymous heroine is abandoned by her punitive uncle for acts of insubordination and sexual depravity and left to fend for herself in a world left to its own interpretation. Her uncle, meanwhile, imposes his French Protestant ways on the colonial outpost, producing only "a little France in the New World, a groaning, wretched copy of what he left behind." Glover admits that this book, too, is about love: "love is the moment when two selves meet and are as open to the risk of that encounter as they can be. I think there is some aesthetic satisfaction in exploring that subject."[33] As a fiction writer, he brings a thorough familiarity with major literatures, including his own, to deconstruct the conventions of realism in order to set up alternate versions of historical reality.

Further west is Leamington, the birthplace of Nino Ricci (b. 1959), now living in Toronto, who wrote a trilogy of novels out of his Italian-Canadian experiences, all of them narrated in the first person by Vittorio (later Victor) Innocente. In the first, *Lives of the Saints* (1990), set in Valle del Sole, a tiny mountain hamlet in the Italian Appenines, Vittorio, a seven-year-old boy, lives with his mother and his grandfather, his father having emigrated to Canada almost four years earlier. As he watches the town's superstitious behaviour at the sight of his mother's pregnancy, he loses his innocence. Covering a nine-month period from July 1960 to March 1961, the novel finishes on board a ship bound for Canada as his mother gives birth to a girl, then dies in the ordeal. The second, *In a Glass House* (1993), follows Vittorio to the small town of Mersea in southwest-ern Ontario where his father has a farm. The setting expands to include a metropolitan Toronto university and then a Nigerian boarding school where Vittorio teaches English in a poor, war-torn community. *Where She Has Gone* (1997), which closes the series, examines the relationship between Vittorio and his half-sister Rita in a psychological study of their incest. The three novels reveal the debilitating effects of superstitious Catholicism on its Italian adherents and followers. "I am certainly not Catholic in my life and really regard Catholicism less as a theme, per se,

---

[33] Ibid.

than as a particularly tempting corpse to dig my vulture claws into," remarks Ricci.[34]

Subsequent novels include *Testament* (2002), four different narrators and their unique accounts of Jesus Christ's life and his impact on them in a carefully researched study "based on what is known to us of the time and place in which Jesus lived," and *The Origin of Species* (2009), a frank account of a doctoral student in a seedy apartment in Mulroney-era Montreal contemplating the dysfunctional relationships in his own life.

Raised on the classics of literature, including Woolf and Munro, and venturing to embrace past and contemporary European literature, including Dostoevsky and Nabokov, Ricci also acknowledges Federico Fellini's films: "There is something in the pathos of Fellini's worldview, in the mix of irony and tragedy, in the willingness to include the whole range of human experience, that is very appealing."[35] Here is his sometimes sardonic view of the human condition.

Born in Windsor and living for many years in Toronto is Barbara Gowdy, who brings a razor-sharp delineation of the foibles and follies of her people with a wry insight which recalls Atwood's careful delineation of her characters. Her one collection, *We So Seldom Look on Love* (1992), focuses on the freakish, a necrophile, for example, or the forbidden, such as a transsexual whose transgender operation is not finished on his wedding night, arguing that these people are part of who and what human beings are. In the title story, a young woman in her thirties who works for an undertaker is a self-proclaimed necrophile: "my attraction to cadavers isn't driven by fear, it's driven by excitement, and that one of the most exciting things about a cadaver is how dedicated it is to dying." There is no replacement, she concludes, for the serenity of a cadaver. Frightening yet humorous the story is, but also human and heartbreaking.

Mister Sandman (1995) examines the Canary family: parents Gordon and Doris, closet homosexuals (unknown to each other), and their three "children," Sonja, the victim of a rape which produces Joan, raised by Gordon and Doris as their own, Marcy, a daughter, who seduces any available male. A pale speechless girl, Joan spends her life in a closet, and the other characters come to her for confession and consolation. Each one respects the others' privacy and secrets. Although the characters may seem strange, Gowdy makes them seem normal, trying to protect themselves in

---

[34] Marino Tuzi, "Interview with Nino Ricci," *Nino Ricci: Essays on His Works*, ed. Marino Tuzi (Toronto: Guernica, 2016), p. 255.
[35] Ibid., p. 256.

their various machinations. In *The White Bone* (1998), she humanizes a herd of elephants, another family in a realistic and terrifying portrait of their daily hunted lives, all the time acknowledging and delighting in their distance from human beings. Narrated from the perspective of the elephants, who communicate telepathically with one another, the book is populated almost solely by these animals. In *Little Sister* (2017), a chronic dieter, the operator of the Toronto repertory cinema the Regal, has a series of out-of-body experiences during a week of early summer thunderstorms. The book explores a tormented female psyche which, in contrast to her rational boyfriend, argues for an accepting understanding of the human condition. Gowdy seeks to humanize people (and animals, too) who are often ostracized by their seemingly freakish or outlandish lifestyles.

North and east of Windsor is Petrolia, the birthplace of Bonnie Burnard (1945–2017), who wrote two collections of short stories, *Women of Influence* (1988) and *Casino and Other Stories* (1994), and two novels, *A Good House* (1999) and *Suddenly* (2009). A patient observer of everyday lives, she moved to Regina in 1973, returning to the London area in 1995. Indebted to Engel, Munro, and Shields, she fashioned short stories, which, while describing the common trappings of daily life, convey universal truths. Often set in small Ontario or prairie towns, they depict heterosexual relationships and the trying circumstances underneath their apparent happiness. "Casino," for example, tells the brief stories of several marriages, entanglements, and even divorce as the people "remember the Casino and the Saturday-night dances." Examining the bonds that bind people together and sometimes break, *A Good House* begins in 1949 and continues until 1997, a family chronicle focusing on the Chambers family of small-town Stonebrook, Ontario, and the births, marriages, divorces, and deaths that represent every family's path through life; ultimately a celebration of the small town, the good house is the Chambers's modest storey-and-a half house. "Burnard is as familiar with the contemporary world and its violence as she is with the tenderness of human connection," exclaimed Shields. "She loves her characters too much to do them violence, and her affection for these people becomes, in short order, ours."[36]

Ontario fiction writers move farther afield in their fiction than their Maritime and Newfoundland counterparts usually do. They write of the past, for example, Ricci writes of the time of Christ, Wright of Elizabethan England, Gibson and Swan of nineteenth-century Canada, and Itani and Urquhart of early twentieth-century Canada. They delve into history,

---

[36] "The great Canadian novel at last?" Ottawa *Citizen*, 5 September 1999, p. C12.

sometimes their own, in order to pen their studies of people and places near and far.

The Prairies: Manitoba, Saskatchewan, Alberta

The prairies have always been a locale which attracts writers yet often refuses them a home; they are a locale where people from elsewhere in Canada settle down; for others, they are a place to flee. Ross had a career in banking there and in Montreal before leaving for the comparative safety of Greece; Wiseman and Laurence left for European and African worlds. In the post-centennial period, writers come to the prairies and also leave them behind.

Born in Morris, southwest of Winnipeg, to a Mennonite mother and a Métis father, and living first in Winnipeg and finally in Ottawa, Sandra Birdsell (b. 1942) finds the same mixture of races Grove first noted on the prairies. "Up near the hills in the west, the squares of land sustain whole communities of Ukrainians; closer to the lake, Icelanders; to the south, French-speaking communities," she writes in *The Missing Child* (1989), though there are now "colonies of black-clothed Hutterites and towns of German-speaking Mennonites." With a Bible in each house and discouraged from reading fiction and non-fiction, she has the Mennonite world stand behind her fiction with its emphasis on religious community and tradition and its themes of, for example, the appropriate amount of allegiance to the world outside the community and the relevance of church discipline.

Birdsell studied writing under Kroetsch's tutelage, expanding her knowledge of other writers, which included Joyce, Maxim Gorky, and Gabrielle Roy, and fostering her close kinship with Welty and O'Connor. "Flannery O'Connor is another writer who convinced me that it was important and legitimate to write out of my experience," she reflects.[37] In *Night Travellers* (1982), her first collection of stories, she studies working-class people, Métis and Mennonites, men and women, especially women, insisting on their ability to survive in a world which discourages dialogue. Like Laurence and Munro, she confronts the familiar and the unfamiliar in the fictional town of Agassiz south of Winnipeg. Maurice and Mika Lafreniere and their children are the centre of this study which consists of short stories that require the surrounding stories to complete

---

[37] "Falling into the Page: An Interview with Sandra Birdsell," Laurie Kruk, *The Voice is the Story: Conversations with Canadian Writers of Short Fiction* (Oakville, Ontario: Mosaic Press, 2003), p. 94.

the picture. Although the parents live lives of quiet desperation, their daughters, more honest with themselves and their partners, set aside the religious and sexual inhibitions that impeded their parents' growth. With its focus on one family, *Night Travellers* leads to *Ladies of the House* (1984), a less connected collection focused again on the people of Agassiz though no longer on one family. "I think knew I would be leaving Agassiz soon and so I was making an effort to record the place," one character says. "Like the soil of my valley, thick and black and sticky for days after a rain so that it spatters pant legs and has to be chipped or brushed free, I wanted the memory of that place to cling to me. I wanted to remember the heat of it, the discontent, the feeling of living in a shoebox." *The Missing Child*, her first novel, ends her delineation of Agassiz.

In her finest novel, *The Russlander* (2001), Birdsell refashions the close-knit group of Agassiz citizens in *The Missing Child* into the inhabitants of a wealthy Mennonite estate in Russia in 1910. In Katya Vogt's recollection of her family, she examines the prosperity of the ruling class and the poverty and growing disgruntlement of the estate workers. As tensions increase with World War I taking its toll, she must remember the Bolshevik Revolution and its terrible actions against her family. From tales of Mennonites in Russia, Birdsell orchestrates an epic of their departure from Russia and their arrival in Canada.

Although born in the fishing village of Port Edward, British Columbia and brought up in the predominantly Mennonite community of Niverville, south of Winnipeg, David Bergen (b. 1957) calls Winnipeg home in spite of his many travels. Educated in the literature of, among others, Carver, Hemingway, and Cormac McCarthy, he published his first collection, *Sitting Opposite My Brother* (1993), which examines contemporary characters grappling with familial dislocations and heartaches. His second, *Here the Dark* (2020), contains seven stories and the titular novella, all more powerful than the stories of the first collection, the final novella centring on a Manitoba Mennonite who attempts to break away from her religious background. His stories recall short fiction by Callaghan and Sinclair Ross.

Bergen's nine novels are far-ranging in their locales and their subjects. Occurring in the four seasons of one year, his first novel, *A Year of Lesser* (1996), watches the machinations of an apparently unspiritual man, an alcoholic and a philanderer, as he copes with the death of his wife and the pregnancy of his lover in the Manitoba town of Lesser. Weak but not unsympathetic, he is a tragic hero of his time and place. Brought up in the Mennonite faith, Bergen often studies wayward people who deal with personal loss and their individual routes to redemption; he delves into their inner lives, probing their psyches underneath their often ordinary existences. *See the Child* (1999) again explores small-town Manitoba, this time with a man learning to cope with the tragic death of his teenage son.

Moving out of Manitoba, he sets his novel, *The Time In Between* (2005), in Vietnam. After thirty years away, a former soldier returns to gain some understanding of a traumatic incident that happened to him. Superimposed upon his return is his children's search for their father who has gone missing. Drawing on his time in Vietnam, Bergen examines two searches and their devastating conclusion. In *Leaving Tomorrow* (2014), he writes – for the first time – in the first-person voice, the novel being the classic bildungsroman without the autobiographical connections that characterize many books of this genre. Raised in the fictional town of Tomorrow, Alberta, the protagonist, a sensitive individual who lives in the realm of words and writing, reveals his dreams as well as his failures. *Stranger* (2016) chronicles a young Guatemalan's affair with a married American physician and her subsequent pregnancy; the wealthy doctor's wife steals the woman's newborn girl and returns to the United States. Following the woman's relentless quest to locate her daughter, the novel sees her rise to heroic heights amid the startling divisions between the rich and the impoverished.

Whatever his settings, Bergen captures contemporary characters in trying situations where they reveal their strengths and their weaknesses. His fiction shows their motivations on the path to a reasonable existence and ultimately – if possible – to personal salvation.

Born to Mennonite parents in Steinbach, southeast of Winnipeg, Miriam Toews (b. 1964), with a BA in film studies from the University of Manitoba and a BJ in journalism from the University of King's College, moved to Montreal and London, England, before returning to Winnipeg and finally settling in Toronto. Unlike Wiebe, Birdsell, and Bergen, she invokes comedy in her depiction of her Mennonite background and her eventual hatred of its strict formulations.

In *Summer of My Amazing Luck* (1996) the narrator, a seventeen-year-old unmarried mother, offers her zany account of life in Have-a-Life welfare housing. She does not know the father of her infant son; her neighbour, a mother with four girls, pines for the fire-eating busker who fathered her twins. Little does the narrator realize that welfare regulations and her case worker will cause endless hassles. Toews found her natural voice, and her subsequent novels usually employ an articulate first-person female narrator to study and critique her Mennonite background. *A Boy of*

Good Breeding (1998), for example, has an omniscient voice tell the story of Algren, Manitoba, and the mayor who believes he is the illegitimate son of the Canadian prime minister.

Swing Low: A Life (2000) is Toews's biography-as-autobiography of her father's manic depression and eventual suicide. With "tracts, given to me by various visitors, and a Bible and a devotional book on Corinthians and a brochure advertizing a new housing development on the edge of town," her father finds elementary-school teaching an antidote to his depressive state. In this town "a good Mennonite wife is always more than capable of taking care of her husband. It's held to be her duty and her life, and [his wife], in spite of her independence and liberal views, couldn't move from under that yoke." When he retires, he ends his life. The "memoir," showing the hold the Mennonite tradition has on its followers, allows Toews to author her uniquely comic and tragic portrait of that tradition.

In *A Complicated Kindness* (2004), set in East Village, Manitoba, a small Mennonite community, one of its members, "the most embarrassing sub-sect of people to belong to if you're a teenager," is an insatiably curious and defiant sixteen-year-old whose constant questioning brings her into con-flict with her sanctimonious church pastor. *Irma Voth* (2011), set in Mexico's Chihuahuan desert, has the nineteen-year-old Mennonite title figure narrate her marriage to a non-Mennonite Mexican and her subse-quent estrangement from her religious father, ultimately fleeing with her mother's blessing to Mexico City with her two younger sisters. *All My Puny Sorrows* (2014) returns to East Village for an account of two loving sisters, the elder a world-famous pianist, happily married but wanting to die, and the younger, the narrator, divorced, destitute, and desperate to keep her sister alive. In all her novels, Toews reveals an exceptional talent for observing life in her own time, mixing hysterically funny moments amid the tragedies that engulf her people.

Women Talking (2018) captures the horrific world of contemporary Bolivia. Between 2005 and 2009, more than 130 women had been repeatedly poisoned at the ultraconservative Bolivian Mennonite Colony, then raped in their homes by men who were sometimes their relatives. Her novel has eight women gather after the men's arrests to decide on some action, and there is urgency to their conversations, for some men have gone to town to bail out their accused brothers, and the women have only limited time to talk freely without surveillance. "I've always been trying to challenge the patriarchy, specifically of my Mennonite community, but I'm concerned with the suppression of girls and women especially, and any place in the world that falls under fundamentalist, authoritarian thinking."[38]

Saskatoon is home for Yann Martel (b. 1963), who was born in Salamanca, Spain, the son of peripatetic Canadian diplomats. Educated at Trent University, he used the university as background to his remarkable title story of *The Facts behind the Helsinki Roccamatios and other stories* (1993). Trying to help his younger friend Paul who is dying of AIDS, the result of a blood transfusion he had in Jamaica, the nameless narrator conceives of a game for the remaining weeks until Paul's demise. The story becomes the narrator's tribute to Paul, "all I have kept – outside my head – is this record" of "one event of each year as a metaphorical guidelines. The twentieth century would be our mould." Every moment of his illness is graphically presented in the context of their relentless pursuit of their game, the story being authentic and deeply tragic.

Although his first novel, *Self* (1966), is a dizzying display of a seemingly fictional autobiography that transcends gender-specific boundaries, it was *Life of Pi* (2001) which won the Booker Prize. Falling into three loosely connected sections, the novel follows, first, the adventures of Piscine Molitor Patel, known as Pi Patel, and his espousal of three religions: Hinduism, Christianity, and Islam; his father, Director of the Pondicherry Zoo, instructs him in animal lore; finally leaving behind the dictatorial Mrs. Ghandi, the family flees India by ship. In the longer second section, after the tragic sinking of the cargo ship, Pi finds himself alone for 227 days on a lifeboat with a 450-pound Royal Bengal tiger named Richard Parker, a wounded zebra, a hyena, and an orangutan. The descriptions of their day-to-day existence make the fantastic journey plausible. The brief third section unites Pi with two sceptical men from the Maritime Department in the Japanese Ministry of Transport as he relives the events of the sinking. Although it questions the existence of God, this theme remains in the background.

The High Mountains of Portugal (2016) falls again into three seemingly disparate sections. In the first, "Homeless," set in 1904 Lisbon, a man, mourning the death of his wife and child, searches for a fabled crucifix. The second, "Homeward," takes place in a small Portuguese city on New Year's Eve of 1938 when a pathologist is visited by his wife for a long discussion of the curious connections between Agatha Christie's writings and the Christian gospels. In the third, "Home," Canadian Senator Peter

[38] "I needed to write about these women. I could have been one of them," *The Guardian*, 8 August 2018.

Tovy returns to the remote Portuguese village where he was born. Each person is searching for a good life, and Martel's novels question philosophical and ultimately theological matters.

Alberta is the home of Kroetsch and the adopted home of Wiebe, and both writers have been seminal influences on younger authors, their startling evocations of Alberta standing as the beginning of an Alberta-based fiction.

Born in Edmonton is Katherine Govier (b. 1948), who studied under Wiebe at the University of Alberta. Now resident in Toronto, she pens short stories and novels, studying characters trapped in their complicated existences. Traversing geographical locales, Toronto in *Fables of Brunswick Avenue* (1985) or Calgary in *Between Men* (1987) or Toronto again in *Hearts of Flame* (1991), she studies people in contemporary relationships, trying to find their own paths in a world riddled with doubt. In the first she focuses on modern people; in the second she explores the dissatisfaction of a Calgary marriage and the allure of political power; in the third she writes of similar dissatisfaction in Toronto. All three books are popular narrative romances of contemporary relationships.

Govier has also delved into the past, fashioning *Creation* (2002), a fictional biography of John James Audubon, who enlisted his son and a party of young gentlemen in 1833 to set sail for nesting grounds no ornithologist had ever seen; the treacherous passage between Newfoundland and Labrador becomes the setting for their fateful expedition. And *The Three Sisters Bar & Hotel* (2016) returns to historical fiction to write about the Bow Valley in the Rocky Mountains and its fictional town of Gateway during the past hundred years.

Born in Wetaskiwin, just south of Edmonton, Aritha van Herk (b. 1954) also studied at the University of Alberta under Wiebe's guidance. She received her BA and MA there and published her first novel, *Judith* (1976), her master's thesis, which captured immediate attention for its mixture of the biblical heroine Judith with Greek sorceress Circe, a monster who could turn men into pigs. Her second novel, *The Tent Peg* (1981), negotiates a new space for women when its heroine disguises herself as a boy to become a cook in an all-male mining camp. *No Fixed Address* (1986) watches its heroine confined by the constraints of traditional female roles. *Places Far from Ellesmere* (1990) frees the fictional Anna Karenina from her suicide. And *Restlessness* (1998) reworks the story of Scheherazade as a woman explains her life to the man she has engaged to kill her. Van Herk's five novels challenge both gender stereotypes and traditional myths, presenting their tales with humour amid their forceful lessons. *Places Far from Ellesmere* is subtitled "a geograficitione," pointing to further experimentation van Herk achieves in extending the limits of generic definitions and trying to illuminate further the relationship between cartography and plotting.

A professor at the University of Calgary since 1983 and a devoted scholar of Kroetsch's writings, she publishes books and essays which explore the themes of her fiction: the roles of women in contemporary society, the blurring of genre differences, the influence of place on human lives, and postmodernism itself, her own mode of fictional writing.

British Columbia

As the mountainous regions of Alberta yield to the Pacific coast, writers continue to use fiction to delineate their new landscapes. In the 1940s, Ethel Wilson wrote fiction of British Columbia. Then Sheila Watson and Audrey Thomas, George Bowering and Jack Hodgins had begun their delineations. Now younger novelists and short story writers join them.

Born in Vancouver, Joy Kogawa (b. 1935) found herself facing Japanese internment during World War II. The War Measures Act demanded that all Japanese living within one hundred miles of the Pacific Coast be removed from this "protected area" and sent to detention camps in interior British Columbia, their belongings and lands confiscated and sold. Kogawa and her family were sent away in 1942 to Slocan, British Columbia, then to Coaldale, Alberta, where she completed high school. *Obasan* (1981), her semi-autobiographical novel, is the first fictional treatment of the expulsion of Japanese Canadians during World War II.

Obasan introduces Naomi Nakane, a thirty-six-year-old, umarried grade-school teacher in Cecil, Alberta, in 1972, who has just received word that her elderly uncle passed away southwest of Cecil in Granton. Driving down to see his widow becomes a catalyst for reawakening her unresolved emotions from her childhood. As a five-year-old, she was uprooted along with her family, including her father, her older brother Stephen, and her uncle and his wife. Her mother had already made an ill-timed return to Japan with her own mother to visit relatives and is unable to come back. As a consequence of the War Measures Act, her family loses its property and its identity. Her mother never returns from Japan and dies in the atomic holocaust of Nagasaki, her father is dispatched to a road gang where he becomes fatally ill, and she and her brother, orphans at the end, are left in the care of their uncle and aunt, who maintain their dignity by choosing silence in the face of these excruciating circumstances.

Aunt Emily, Naomi's mother's sister, fled to Toronto during the period of internment. Now an activist member of the Co-operative Committee on Japanese Canadians, she helps Naomi come to terms with her story as she begins to piece together the fragments of her life, "a crowded collage of memories." She concludes: "Reconciliation can't begin without mutual recognition of facts."

Already a poet with her own poem at the beginning of her tale, Naomi offers a riveting history of the internment victims. Giving Naomi a package of papers about Japanese Canadian history, Aunt Emily is the political voice, Naomi's aunt and uncle the silent voices. Naomi must write her own ethnic history of the crisis that proved catastrophic for her people.

A deeply moving novel which reaches beyond Japanese Canadians to become a story about systemic racism in Canada, *Obasan* became a guide for subsequent political action. It educated the public to the injustices Japanese Canadians suffered during and after the war, becoming the authoritative voice in the campaign for an official apology and monetary compensation.

A sequel to *Obasan*, *Itsuka* (1992) continues Naomi's first-person account of her life until 1988. After Obasan's death, Aunt Emily insists that her niece come to live in Toronto. Naomi now works for a multicultural magazine, she has a romantic involvement with her employer, and she becomes part of the movement for Japanese Canadian redress, which ends with Brian Mulroney's apology in 1988 and financial settlements for all the victims. Although the main characters from *Obasan* reappear, *Itsuka* lacks the lyrical cry that made her first book such a impassioned statement about internment and the racism behind it. *The Rain Ascends* (1995), her third and final novel, is autobiography-as-fiction. When the father, a respected Anglican priest, is discovered to be a paedophile, Kogawa tries to balance the glaring truth with forgiveness.

Shining a steady and uncompromising light on the injustices suffered by Japanese Canadians, *Obasan* stands as their plaintive cry. Kogawa thus accomplishes what Indigenous voices were doing for their peoples.

Born in Port Alberni on Vancouver Island, SKY Lee (b. 1952), a graduate of the University of British Columbia in Fine Arts, wrote a four-generation saga of a Chinese Canadian family, *Disappearing Moon Café* (1990). Opening in 1892 when Wong Gwei Chang is entrusted by the Chinese community to travel to western Canada to gather up the bones of Chinese labourers who died building Canada's transcontinental railway, and closing in 1986 when his great-granddaughter Kae Ying Woo narrates the story digging up family secrets, the book focuses on the Wong family, a potential dynasty, as individual members try to perpetuate their family name. Chang's wife oversees a Chinese restaurant, the Disappearing Moon Café, as if she were a tyrant speaking condescendingly to all her people. Her daughter-in-law Fong Wei is subject to her constant humiliations for not producing offspring, even though, as the narrator later informs the reader, her husband was impotent.

What is the cultural cost of survival for these Chinese Canadians, particularly for generations of Chinese women, "a lineage of women with passions and fierceness in their veins"? Some maintain connections with China; many others, Canadian-born children, forsake the conflicts of the old world with its clear traditions for the less clear-cut values of Canada. With powerful reminiscences of past events, letters embedded in the narrative, and multiple perspectives on the story, Lee creates a wrenching portrait of her people. Often relegated to a minor place in fiction, Vancouver's Chinese community has rarely been so clearly and so well defined, and it is to the credit of Lee, a feminist author, that she creates this canvas.

Vancouver-born Wayson Choy (1939–2019) took a year's sabbatical in 1976–77 from his teaching position at Humber College in Toronto to study creative writing at the University of British Columbia, where he had graduated years earlier as the first Chinese Canadian student admitted to their creative writing program. In 1976 his teacher in fiction was Shields. "Her mastery as my teacher," he wrote, "had inspired me to awaken all the similar goodness I saw for the first time in my Chinatown past."[39] His two novels, *The Jade Peony* (1995) and *All That Matters* (2004), reveal Vancouver's Chinatown in the 1930s and 1940s.

The first popular novel by a Chinese Canadian, *The Jade Peony*, an intimate portrait of an immigrant Chinese family living in the inner city of Vancouver before and during World War II and struggling with racism, has three sections with a different child of the Chen family narrating his or her experience of growing up in Chinatown: Jook-Lang, the only sister; Jung-Sum, the second brother; and Sek-Lung, the third brother. The first child born in Canada, Jook-Lang forms an unlikely friendship with an older man; the second brother, adopted into the Chen family when his parents died, needs encouragement in his new family; often ill, the third brother is obsessed with the impending World War II. Their grandmother and family matriarch, a major influence on them, acknowledges the

---

[39] "My *Seen-Sang*, Carol Shields: A Memoir of a Master Teacher," *The Worlds of Carol Shields*, ed. David Staines (University of Ottawa Press, 2014), p. 303.

traditional ways of China that they must balance while hoping for a modern life in the New World. All three narrators are first-generation Canadians. In *All That Matters*, the sequel to *The Jade Peony*, Kiam-Kin, the first son, narrates his arrival in Vancouver in 1926 with his father and grandmother and his subsequent battle with racism, dishonesty, and poor living conditions, all the time struggling with Chinese traditions while adjusting to the New World and realizing the benefits of his own community.

While SKY Lee paints a wide canvas to reveal the nearly century-long machinations of the Wong family, Choy narrows his perspective to paint one family's hardships. Along with Kogawa, these three West Coast novelists enlarge the base of Canadian fiction, bringing forward from the sidelines Japanese and Chinese people to share the main stage.

Though born in Edmonton, Caroline Adderson (b. 1963) went to the University of British Columbia, settling in Vancouver. Indebted to Gallant and Munro and reading Canadian literature as well as writers from American and other literatures, she began her career with a collection of ten short stories, *Bad Imaginings* (1993), which have diverse times and settings (most of them in the West). An effete gold prospector in 1861, a chambermaid in Victoria in World War I, a Ukrainian immigrant who brings rain to southern Alberta's Palliser Triangle in the drought-ridden Depression, and two friends trying to understand feminism in 1980s Vancouver, all these and others balance their own idiosyncrasies with the outside world's definition of normalcy.

Her first novel, *A History of Forgetting* (1999), chronicles two lovers, Malcolm and Denis, who have come from Paris to Vancouver, Denis suffering from advanced Alzheimer's. When one of Malcolm's associates is killed by homophobic thugs, Malcolm and his co-worker Alison leave for Auschwitz in order to understand their past in a modern-day pilgrimage to the darkness at the centre of the twentieth century. Meanwhile, Denis, placed in a care facility, succumbs to his encroaching disease. *Ellen in Pieces* (2012) chronicles the life of Ellen McGinty, passionate, lovable, and exasperating, who, abandoned by her husband, sells her North Vancouver home and becomes a potter in Kitsilano. The book assumes the shape of Ellen's own life, taking on a man-boy lover, reintegrating with her estranged father who then commits suicide, and being diagnosed with stage-four breast cancer. Slowly and tragically, many of the characters come to learn the true meaning of selfless love, which can unite people.

A master at showing the complexity of the human situation, watching the mingled state of this comedy-tragedy called life, Adderson presents complex portraits of women and men piecing together the many parts of their too brief existences.

Many writers performed their craft while teaching in university settings, Bowering, for example, at Simon Fraser University and Hodgins at the University of Victoria. And many of their students have gone on to be writers themselves.

Born in Kamloops, British Columbia, Gail Anderson-Dargatz (b. 1963) earned her creative writing degree from the University of Victoria, where she studied with Hodgins, her mentor. In her first book, *The Miss Hereford Stories* (1994), the setting is Likely, Alberta, "a half-horse town; we had no newspaper, the coffee shop was 'the Café,' the hotel was 'the Hotel' and the tavern was 'the Tavern.' If you wanted fancy you went to Camrose." The narrator of this earthy coming-of-age collection is Martin Winkle, ten years old in the first story and continuing on through his teenage years, who watches closely the follies and shenanigans of the local population.

Another first-person coming-of-age story is her first novel, *The Cure for Death by Lightning* (1996), which charts fifteen-year-old Beth Weeks and her adolescence on a British Columbia farm during World War II. Mentally unstable, her father becomes a sexual predator in his own home by molesting Beth, while her mother, unwilling to acknowledge her husband's actions, retreats into conversations with her dead mother, clutching her scrapbook to avoid the trauma of her marriage. The struggle to find love in this forlorn landscape is pivotal for Beth's upbringing. Overarching this plot is the presence of the hermit, Coyote Jack, who may or may not be a murderer, or else the culprit is the spirit of a coyote, for the Native peoples play a solid role. More than forty recipes and remedies lend the novel further coherence.

A Recipe for Bees (1998), saturated with bee lore, is a third-person account of the forty-eight-year marriage of a psychic beekeeper and her mild-mannered husband. Now living in a tiny senior citizen's apartment up island from Victoria, she awaits news of her beloved son-in-law's brain surgery, and the endless waiting allows her to remember her often dismal life on her parents' farm and later on her father-in-law's sheep farm in rural British Columbia.

In *The Spawning Grounds* (2016), Anderson-Dargatz brings together her knowledge of white people and their aboriginal counterparts who live on the opposite side of the river in a tale suffused with First Nations mythology. Eighteen-year-old Hannah Robertson lives with her brother and their grandfather on the family ranch by the fictional Lightning River in British Columbia; across the river is a Shuswap community which includes Alex, Hannah's best friend. Once one of the mightiest salmon runs in the world, the river's waters are nearly depleted; because of decisions taken by farmers and land developers, the river is scarcely a trickle, choked as it is by silt. The First Nations are protesting the hideous development of the area, urging local settlers to desist from fishing. Hannah's grandfather represents the opposing view, "When are you Indians going to get over the fact that this land belongs to us now." The novel is a scathing indictment of the painful confrontation with nature and the revenge nature demands from such unsuspecting people.

Domestic-centred, Anderson-Dargatz's fiction explores people dwelling primarily in British Columbia. Indebted to the writings of Sheila Watson and espousing her own connection with writers on the Pacific Coast, including Márquez, she focuses on the interactions of people dwelling there, both Native and White, and the salient problems in their relationships.

From all regions of the country, these many writers – more than forty in this chapter – testify to the startling increase in fiction in Canada. No longer reliant solely on American or British sources, they now partake of their own culture, many of them expressing indebtedness to Atwood or Engel, Kroetsch or Laurence, Munro or Richler, Watson or Wiebe, or many others. Canada now has a distinct literary tradition for many fiction writers.

Robertson Davies began this new tradition, using Leacock's writings as the background to his early fiction. The writers of the later century now express indebtedness to Canadian authors as well as to American and European authors as the sources of their creativity. Robert Kroetsch, for example, expresses his obligation to his first mentor, Hugh MacLennan, and Engel lauds Margaret Laurence's heroines for the depiction of troubled women. This pattern continues throughout the country. Mordecai Richler stands behind the fiction of Leonard Cohen and Richard B. Wright, Alden Nowlan pays homage to Ernest Buckler, and Buckler, Nowlan, and Alistair MacLeod stand behind David Adams Richards's writings. Alice Munro inspires the fiction, for example, of Elizabeth Hay and Jane Urquhart, and of Clark Blaise and Guy Vanderhaeghe. Lawrence Hill is indebted to Austin Clarke, and Rudy Wiebe, George Bowering, and Gail Anderson-Dargatz regard Sheila Watson as a force in their creativity. The maturity of Canadian fiction is evident when writers turn to Canadian sources while never denying influences, too, from outside the country.

In its second century the country is experiencing many fine fiction writers who focus on their own worlds be they near at hand or, in some cases, far away. Now these native-born writers need to be complemented by the increasing number of Indigenous voices as well as by the non-native-born writers who have come to Canada and contribute significantly to its fiction.

CHAPTER 8

Indigenous Voices

"For First Nations, Métis Nations and Inuit peoples in Canada, these early colonial relationships were not about strength through diversity, or a celebration of differences," Prime Minister Justin Trudeau announced at the 72nd Session of the General Assembly of the United Nations on 21 September 2017. "For Indigenous peoples in Canada, the experience was mostly one of humiliation, neglect and abuse." His words acknowledge the many centuries of systemic maltreatment of Indigenous men, women, and children that hindered the development of Indigenous voices in Canadian fiction.

Long before the four provinces of Nova Scotia, New Brunswick, Quebec, and Ontario created the nation of Canada in 1867, long before English and French colonizers started to arrive in the late fourteenth century, the Indigenous peoples constituted the population of North America for thousands of years. Once the settler immigrants came to Canada, they profited initially from the guidance of the Native population and their knowledge and experience of the land and its resources. The French and then the English settlement of Canada began in the early seventeenth century where different Indigenous populations acted as partisans and allies on both sides. The settlers' relationship with the Indigenous came to be shaped by economic pressures, by shifting alliances, and, last but not least, by governmental policies of subordination and assimilation to the supposedly superior cultures of England and France. There were and are, however, distinct voices from the First Nations and Inuit peoples of the country, and though historians have joked about mixed-blood people having their origins nine months after the first Europeans settled in Canada, the mixed-race people, too, have been present since the dawn of colonization in the country.

For Indigenous peoples, the dominant mode of communication and memory was oral. From earliest times, they used the oral form to express themselves, their history, their stories, and their dreams. For example, the

Haida people on islands off northwest British Columbia [formerly the Queen Charlotte Islands, now the Haida Gwaii], who have lived there for at least 7,500 years, used both visual arts and oral cultural traditions to express their ideas. When Europeans arrived there in the eighteenth century, the Haida's intellectual and literary world soon ceased to be the region's dominant culture. Traders, Christian missionaries, naval officers, all these newcomers saw only lands to be colonized, not people whose knowledge and traditions differed radically from their own.

The process of colonization subjugates the existing population to the needs, beliefs, and whims of the colonizers. Human nature often uses racism to justify the superiority of the colonizing culture. For example, colonizers did not consider mixed-race people a group with valid legal rights. When Manitoba joined Canada in 1870 and the Manitoba Act guaranteed these people titles to their lands, the Indian Act of 1876 entrenched rules for keeping the Indians on their reserve land and away from the colonial settlers, stripping women, for example, and their descendants of their status rights as Indian if they married European men. Such acts encouraged assimilation, making Indigenous peoples slowly merge into Euro-Canadian society. This same Indian Act made all Indians wards of the state with no rights to vote in federal or provincial elections.

By the early nineteenth century, Canada had become a staging ground for European settlers to uphold their superior status to the Indigenous peoples. Residential schools, the centre of the settlers' policy, began in earnest in the 1820s.[1] Native children were taken to segregated, government-sponsored boarding schools, which rarely offered nourishing or even passable food; they were forbidden to speak languages other than English or French, though many children only understood their Native languages; they were subjected to mental and physical abuse from their instructors; they were forced to Christianize themselves, while Indigenous spiritual traditions were denigrated. Later years found thousands of graves of malnourished and mistreated youths. In Indigenous homes parents risked imprisonment for performing traditional Indigenous ceremonies.

Created with the acknowledged support of the Anglican, Catholic, and Methodist churches, residential schools integrated and assimilated Indigenous students into Euro-Canadian society, eradicating all things Indigenous in the children. "We were made to speak English, to forget

---

[1] For residential schools and their problems, read, as a beginning, Celia Haig-Brown, *Resistance and Renewal: Surviving the Indian Residential School* (Vancouver: Tillacum Library, 1988).

the sacred ways of our people, and to learn to kneel before a cross we were told would save us," *Ragged Company* (2008) by Richard Wagamese (1955–2017) makes clear.

In 1883, Prime Minister John A. Macdonald described his intention to Members of Parliament:

> When the school is on the reserve the child lives with its parents, who are savages; he is surrounded by savages, and though he may learn to read and write, his habits and training and mode of thought are Indian. He is simply a savage who can read and write. It has been strongly pressed on myself, as the head of the Department, that Indian children should be withdrawn as much as possible from the parental influence, and the only way to do that would be to put them in central training industrial schools where they will acquire the habits and modes of thought of white men.[2]

It would take generations for Indigenous communities to assert their distinctive voices.

In 1847 George Copway (1818–69), an Ojibway, published *The Life, History, and Travels of Kah-ge-ga-gah-Bowh*, his autobiography and the first book in English written by an Indigenous person. A convert to Christianity and subsequently an ordained minister, he was strongly anti-pagan and remarkably supportive of his new faith. "The Christian will no doubt feel for my poor people, when he hears the story of one brought from that unfortunate race called the Indians," he exclaimed. "The mind for letters was in me, *but was asleep*, till the dawn of Christianity arose, and awoke the slumbers of the soul into energy and action." No doubt for Copway, Christianity was the best avenue out of "that unfortunate race called the Indians."

While her two older brothers and older sister attended residential schools, E. Pauline Johnson (1861–1913), a mixed-race, was too sick to leave her home in Brantford, Ontario, on the Six Nations Reserve. Her father was a distinguished Mohawk chief, her mother a transplanted English woman, and their respectable, Anglican, middle-class family represented the hopes of a mixed-race community. As a young woman, she was reading books from her parents' library, including Scott and Longfellow, Keats, Tennyson, and Browning; she later recommended *Wacousta* as a Canadian novel which depicted Indigenous people in a positive manner. As her literary reputation grew, she tried to make European Canada accept the centrality of the Native experience in understanding the country and

---

[2] Tanya Talaga, *Seven Fallen Feathers: Racism, Death, and Hard Truths in a Northern City* (Toronto: House of Anansi, 2017), p. 60.

its history, advocating a continuing role for the equal partnership between the Native and the European. And she became part of the late-nineteenth-century/early-twentieth-century feminist movement which struggled against the boundaries of acceptable femininity.

As a poet, Johnson was often a first-person narrator, extolling the fine virtues of the natural world and the human, frequently the Native presence in it, claiming in 1890 to stand by her blood and her race. Focusing primarily on Indigenous peoples, their history and their natural haunts, she recited her poetry in public in both Indigenous attire and fashionable British dress, the oral tradition embedded in her poetry granting her the ennobling position of a true bard of her people.

In the 1890s Johnson moved into prose, fashioning often sentimental but effective short stories about the need for Native-White co-existence and harmony. In "The Shagganappi" (1913), for example, young Fire-Flint Larocque, now a freshman at an eastern college, meets the governor general, who corrects the principal; the young man is not a half-blood, but a half-breed: "As you come of Red Indian blood, dashed with that of the first great soldiers, settlers and pioneers in this vast Dominion, that you have one of the proudest places and heritages in the world; you are a Canadian in the greatest sense of that great word." He becomes a good friend to the most popular boy in the college, the son of Sir George Bennington, and ends up rescuing him from drowning. Then, to the extreme consternation of other students, the young Bennington announces that his own mother is a half-breed. All ends happily in a testimonial to the efficacy of sound relationships between Natives and Whites, more wish-fulfilment on Johnson's part than a mirror of her contemporary reality.

In other stories Johnson studies the corrosive effects of poor relationships between Natives and Whites. In "A Red Girl's Reasoning" (1893), a woman reveals to a society hostess that her parents were married in a traditional Native rather than a Christian ceremony. When her husband accuses her of publicly humiliating him, she leaves him: "Why should I recognize the rites of your nation when you do not acknowledge the rites of mine?" In "As It Was in the Beginning" (1899), Esther of mixed blood is taken away from her home by Father Paul, who denies her upbringing: her outfits, her language, and her religion. Although she falls in love with a white man, the priest instructs her beloved to marry a white woman, an example of the clergy's prejudice against Indians. Esther departs at night: "They account for it by the fact that I am a Redskin, but I am something else, too – I am a woman." In a few other stories, "The Derelict" (1896), for example, a white man gains strength from his Indian wife to oppose the hypocrisy of the

Anglican Church. "She was a woman. Her arms were about him, her lips on his; and he who had, until now, been a portless derelict, who had vainly sought a haven in art, an anchorage in the service of God, had drifted at last into the world's most sheltered harbor – a woman's love."

Brought up a strict Anglican, Johnson moved away from her faith as her career progressed. The early adherent slowly became unorthodox, condemning religion's hypocrisy and showing no commitment to it. In her non-fiction "A Pagan in St. Paul's Cathedral" (1906), an Indian is drawn into the midst of worshippers in London's great cathedral and finds there is no difference between his form of worship and theirs. "The spiritual grandmother to *all* Native writers"[3] and the first major writer of Indigenous ancestry, Johnson believed in worshipping a higher power, living in harmony with nature, and, above all else, respecting all people regardless of their race or religious beliefs.

Johnson's optimistic outlook on Native peoples and their interchanges with Euro-Canadians fell on deaf ears, and after her death in 1913, sixty years would go by before an Indigenous writer would again be published in Canada.

As residential schools continued to flourish, they effectively severed whatever influence Johnson may have had on younger generations; she remained a single voice, the voices of her society stilled by governmental decree. In 1913, too, Duncan Campbell Scott, an advocate for the assimilation of Canada's Indigenous populations, became Deputy Superintendent and Head of Indian Affairs, a position he held for nineteen years. In the Indian Act of 1920, he introduced compulsory attendance at residential schools, declaring attendance as mandated for every Indigenous child between the age of seven and fifteen and leading to the complete assimilation of all Indians into Euro-Canadian society: "Our object is to continue until there is not a single Indian in Canada that has not been absorbed into the body politic and there is no Indian question, and no Indian Department, that is the whole object of this Bill."[4] The last residential school did not close its doors until 1996.

Since Confederation, Indigenous peoples have the right to vote if they abandon their Indian status. In 1924 Indigenous veterans of World War

---

[3] Armand Garnet Ruffo, "Introduction," *An Anthology of Canadian Native Literature in English*, 4th edition, eds. Daniel David Moses, Terry Goldie, and Armand Garnet Ruffo (Don Mills, Ontario: Oxford University Press, 2013), p. xxx.

[4] From a speech to a Special Committee of the House of Commons, cited in John Leslie and Ron Maguire, eds., *The Historical Development of the Indian Act* (Ottawa: Treaties and Historical Research Centre, 1978), second edition, p. 114.

I received the right to vote. But only in 1960 were all First Nations and Inuit peoples finally enfranchised. Mixed-race people, on the other hand, had the right to vote since they did not live on reserves.

The collective movement of writing by Indigenous peoples gained momentum in the 1970s when writers sought to tell their stories in autobiographies and then autobiographical fiction. In *Halfbreed* (1973), Maria Campbell (b. 1940), the first mixed-race voice to reach Indigenous and non-Indigenous Canadians, chronicles her life as "a Halfbreed woman in our country. I want to tell you about the joys and sorrows, the oppressing poverty, the frustrations and the dreams." Forcing her Euro-Canadian readers to re-examine their attitudes to Halfbreeds, she sees her status not as deficient but as enlightening, giving access to different cultures and perspectives. Open to people of diverse ethnicities, she boasts in her autobiography of having a Euro-Canadian friend. The object of her first love is a Swede, she makes friends with Chinese people, and she encounters Indians who allow her entry into their private circles.

Recalling first the atrocities against mixed-race people, culminating in the Northwest Rebellion of 1885, Campbell recreates her childhood years in a close-knit community in northern Saskatchewan where malicious taunts and other forms of abuse meet her every day: "The townspeople would stand on the sidewalks and hurl insults at us. Some would say, 'Halfbreeds are in town, hide your valuables.' If we walked into stores the white women and their children would leave and the storekeepers' wives, sons and daughters would watch that we didn't steal anything." Instead of reading or doing homework, she recalls cleaning the dorms and hallways as well as the punishment she received for speaking Cree in her residential school. Racism is part of the fabric of her daily life. "Racism is for us, not an ideology in the abstract, but a very real and practical part of our lives," observes Stó:lō Lee Maracle (b. 1950) in *I Am Woman* (1988). "The pain, the effect, the shame are all real."

Noting that personal as well as historical trauma continue to impede Campbell's personal growth, *Halfbreed* reflects the injustices enacted not only on her own family but on her people. Christianity, a forceful agent of colonization, tries to control its followers whereas the land itself is her hope and life-spring. Her struggle to survive her life of poverty within a loving family leads to a new understanding of her former years.

Breaking down the silence about Métis history and life, Campbell addresses Indigenous and non-Indigenous readers to proclaim what it is to be Métis. Surprisingly, she ends her book on an optimistic note. "I've stopped being the idealistically shiny-eyed young woman I once was," she concludes. "I believe that one day, very soon, people will set aside their differences and come together as one. Maybe not because we love one another, but because we will need each other to survive." Yet this reconciliation will come only in the future when need creates tolerance.

A storyteller and a community teacher, Campbell was a good friend of Margaret Laurence, a spiritual writer who wrote respectfully of the different cultures she was describing. Out of the many pieces of her own variegated life, she created a harrowing autobiography. Before the publication of *Halfbreed*, the titular term was pejorative; now it highlights a person living within two cultures with open access to these differing but equal worlds. The 2019 edition of *Halfbreed* reinstates the pages of her youthful rape by a Royal Canadian Mounted Policeman, excised by her publisher at the time because the only other corroboration came from her then deceased Cree great-grandmother.

Two years after *Halfbreed* appeared, Lee Maracle published her autobiography, *Bobbie Lee: Indian Rebel*, with its subtitle, *Struggles of a Native Canadian Woman* (1975). Written to document her upbringing, it sees Native struggles as examples of national liberation among colonized peoples. In her writing career, where Maracle has balanced fiction and nonfiction, she sees individual struggles as an essential part of the formation of a fully formed and independent human being.

In *I Am Woman*, where she inscribes stories from "the people of my passion," Maracle writes for the Native population. "It is inevitable, Europeans, that you should find yourself reading my work. If you do not find yourself spoken too, it is not because I intend rudeness – you just don't concern me now," she asserts. Her book "addresses the Native people in desperate circumstances, who need to recover the broken threads of their lives." With the clarion call, "Racism is an essential by-product of colonialism," she sees life as a journey, difficult yet necessary, towards a new dawn, when "the imprisonment of a Native mind in the ideology of the oppressor" leads to an acceptance. "Will Europeans ever look at me and see an equal, not an aborted cripple but a human being with all my frailties, my separate history and our common future?"

Maracle's fiction never abandons the outlooks and biases of her nonfiction. In her novel *Ravensong* (1993), set in 1954 British Columbia, a bridge connects the marginalized Native population in one town from the largely white Euro-Canadian population across the river. Desiring at first to be part of "white town," the Salish protagonist slowly transforms herself into a new person, decolonizing her mind and expressing an appreciation for her own roots. Her mother, on the other hand, represents the old world: she "had left for residential school just like the others. They were all scrubbed clean and deloused; even Momma, who had no lice, was deloused. It was such an indignity." Colonialism also plays a pivotal role in *Celia's Song* (2014), a hopeful multigenerational tale about the indignities suffered by First Nations people. The intricate plot, which involves a storm damaging a funerary structure on British Columbia's northern coast, unearths residential school abuse and the pernicious and lasting effects of racism. Maracle is a tireless critic of the abuses of the Indigenous population, particularly women, at the hands of Euro-Canadians.

Influenced also by Campbell's *Halfbreed*, Métis Beatrice Culleton Mosionier (b. 1949) writes autobiographical fiction of honest emotion. Using her background in her first novel, *In Search of April Raintree* (1983), a scathing indictment of racism in Canadian society, she observes two mixed-race sisters who suffer from their family's collapse and the injustices of social services. Their father, Henry Raintree, must move to Winnipeg from his northern Manitoba town because of his tuberculosis, and he and his wife soon descend into despair, becoming the victims of their self-destructive obsessions. The two daughters, placed in separate foster homes, become distanced from their parents and from each other. Their daughter April, the novel's narrator, rejects her parents and her sister because she cannot abide being treated as Indigenous: "I just felt embarrassed to be seen with natives." She accepts the negative stereotypes of Indigenous people, while her younger sister Cheryl relishes her Indigenous identity.

Although April marries a non-Indigenous businessman in Toronto, his prejudiced mother ends their relationship, and April returns to Winnipeg with a generous divorce settlement. Meanwhile, Cheryl sees the injustices carried out against her people, thus idealizing the Indigenous tradition and a return to a purely Indigenous culture. She sinks into a depression of violence, drinking, and drugs, even becoming a prostitute. Stigmatizing racism makes both daughters its victims. Learning slowly to accept her Indigenous heritage and her own past, April comes to cherish her identity. As Mosionier concludes in *Come Walk with Me: A Memoir* (2009), "In surviving as a Métis woman, April will embrace her Indian spirituality. This is the source of Native strength that the churches and governments had tried to suppress, the power that survives imposed religion, the power that sustains the Indian spirit against all odds." *In Search of April Raintree* reveals the destructive processes of stereotypical racist perspectives. Indigenous peoples need to tell their truths openly, sharing their life stories and thereby dismantling the collective myths, created by European settlers, of their own identities. Once again, Margaret Laurence and her many books were a defining presence in Mosionier's cultural upbringing.

In 1990 Jeannette Armstrong (b. 1948), an Okanagan, observed: "Our children, for generations, were seized from our communities and homes and placed in indoctrination camps until our language, our religion, our customs, and our societal structures almost disappeared. This was the residential school experience."[5] That experience stands behind the opening pages of her first novel *Slash* (1985), where a male narrator, Thomas Kelasket, later renamed Slash, records the events and the people who influenced him in his account of the Indigenous struggle for human rights and self-determination in Canada and the United States. Residential schools "made people mean inside from being lonely, hungry, and cold," Slash remembers. "Kids were even beat up for talking Indian."

Slash records his life journey as he encounters the racism of the assimilationist school system and of North American society as well as the economic marginalization of his people. His hatred of white oppression leads him again to alcohol. Going through a series of personal transformations and rejecting the choices that white acculturation has forced on Indigenous peoples, he finally becomes proud of his Okanagan heritage, of the "pride and power in being Indian." Talking with a non-Indian friend near the end of the novel, he hears him observe: "We came from across the ocean looking for a new world because ours was so polluted and overcrowded. We wanted freedom. We wanted to be able to be free as humans and live comfortable, instead of just a few aristocrats owning everything and the commoners always poor. In our search we reached here. I am beginning to see the things you people are up against. Your people could show us a lot if only we had the sense to listen. I hope we start to listen before it's too late." Slash learns to take the best of what he has witnessed and create a unique and multiple vision for his life, armed with the ability to comprehend and to reinvent the traditional practices of his community.

Indebted to Pauline Johnson and to *Halfbreed* and *Bobbie Lee: Indian Rebel*, Armstrong records the Indigenous worlds of the 1960s and 1970s and their confrontations with colonialism and racism. At the end, Slash addresses his son: "You are our hope. You are an Indian of a special generation. Your world will be hard but you will grow up proud to be Indian." As in *In Search of April Raintree*, the novel's final focus is on a

---

[5] "The Disempowerment of First North American Native Peoples and Empowerment Through Their Writing," *An Anthology of Canadian Native Literature in English*, p. 256.

child who represents a new generation which will exist without dominant ideologies or defined parameters.

A political activist, Armstrong has penned books for children, poetry collections, and a second novel, *Whispering in Shadows* (2000), a semi-autobiographical account of a young Okanagan artist becoming involved in contemporary political movements; she also co-edited with Douglas Cardinal *The Native Creative Process* (1991). Her greatest achievement, however, may be as founder and director of the En'owkin Centre of International Writing, the first centre in the world where Indigenous men and women learn and teach how to write and publish their literatures; along with its own publishing house, Theytus Books, the centre plays a major role in the history and development of Indigenous writing in Canada.

Tomson Highway (b. 1951), a Cree from northwestern Manitoba, had a distinguished career as a playwright – he finds drama the natural extension of the oral storytelling tradition – before he turned to fiction, writing his one novel, the autobiographical *Kiss of the Fur Queen* (1998), rooted in his own landscape and representing his confrontation with the residential schools, which he and his brother René experienced at a young age.

"Among my favourites are the novels of William Faulkner and Fyodor Dostoyevsky. Those are the two novelists in particular that I have a tremendous admiration for," Highway confesses. "And a lot of the Southern writers in the United States: people like Katherine Ann Porter, Eudora Welty, Carson McCullers, Flannery O'Connor, and those people, because they wrote about working-class people – well, grassroots people, very ordinary people – and turned their stories with the art of storytelling and great technique into major visionary works."[6] In this way he, too, aligns himself with Alice Munro and the Southern writers who inspired her.

In the novel two brothers, Champion and Ooneemeetoo Okimasis of northern Manitoba, are taken from their family and sent to a Catholic residential school. They cannot speak their native Cree language, which is demonized by the priests; they are forced to cut their hair; their names are changed to Jeremiah and Gabriel. Moreover, the priests physically and sexually abuse them, and this treatment leads to Jeremiah's celibacy and Gabriel's inability to form successful relationships. Watching over the

[6] Hartmut Lutz, "Tomson Highway," *Contemporary Challenges: Conversations with Canadian Native Authors* (Saskatoon, Saskatchewan: Fifth House, 1991), pp. 89–90.

young pair is the playful Fur Queen, a shape-shifting trickster, who pro-
tects them throughout their lives. Jeremiah moves to Winnipeg to pursue
his musical interests, and Gabriel joins his brother there to pursue his
passion for dance. He then embraces his homosexuality, taking alcohol and
drugs and turning to prostitution as he relives in his mind the abuse he
endured from his teachers' hands.

The destructive forces of residential schools lead to serious repercussions
on the young boys whose lives are traumatized by its horrors. In reliving
the past, Highway charts a new route to assert one's own life after the
many repressive incidents of the past. Nowhere in Canadian literature has
there been such a realistic and evocative portrait of the school system and
its deleterious effects on young people. In addition, *Kiss of the Fur Queen*
becomes a celebration of the Cree way of life and a dramatic assertion of
the need to preserve it.

"A pioneering work, as it dealt with two subjects that up to that time
were not widely spoken about: the abuses, both physical and sexual, that
took place at the residential schools set up for First Nations children, and
gay lifestyles and identities among First Nations people," claims Atwood.
"This novel was among the first books to tackle such long-repressed and
inflammatory subjects, particularly the residential schools abuses. That
story has been unfolding in the eyes of the public for over a decade now,
but it may fairly be said that Tomson Highway wrote the first chapter."[7]

In 1980 Thomas King (b. 1943), born in California to a Greek mother
and a Cherokee father, came to Canada to teach in the Department of
Native Studies at the University of Lethbridge, finally settling at the
University of Guelph. Finishing his doctorate at the University of Utah
and armed with a fundamental knowledge of Native and non-Native
literatures, he brings a fine understanding of Native traditions, a vibrant
sense of humour, and a familiarity with contemporary critical modes of
writing. Not part of the residential school system that influenced
Indigenous writing in Canada, he has other and new perspectives on the
fiction of his adopted country. As he says in his introduction to *All My
Relations: An Anthology of Contemporary Canadian Native Fiction* (1990),
"the limitations placed on us by non-Native expectations are simply
cultural biases that will change only when they are ignored." In the thirty
years since, his fiction and non-fiction have gone far to reducing and
perhaps even ignoring such long-standing biases.

---

[7] "The 25 Most Influential Canadian Books of the past 25 years," *Literary Review of Canada*,
anniversary edition, 2016, p. 3.

As a critic, King transformed understandings of Native writings. Arguing that "post-colonial" privileges European thinking, making Native literature only a response to colonialism, he sees Native-centred writing as existing outside any European framework. "Post-colonial" writing, he asserts, severs Native traditions "that were in place before colonialism ever became a question, traditions which have come down to us through our cultures in spite of colonization." Although a critical form which tries to break the old colonial relationships, it reinforces them. With the post-colonial approach to Native writing totally inappropriate, he prefers the term "associational literature," confirming the continuing values of Native cultures: "in addition to the usable past that the concurrence of oral literature and traditional history provide us with, we also have an active present marked by cultural tenacity and a viable future which may well organize itself around major revivals of language, philosophy, and spiritualism."[8] The critical vocabulary must not recreate terms which invoke colonialism. In his novels he practices what he preaches.

In *Medicine River* (1990), which King regards as a cycle of stories, Will, the first-person narrator and the son of Rose Horse Capture, returns home to Medicine River, Alberta, "an unpretentious community of buildings banked low against the weather that slid off the eastern face of the Rockies." A photographer by trade, he studies the day-to-day lives of contemporary First Nations people in eighteen humorous chapters. His friend, Harlan Bigbear, "who had a great respect for the truth, though on occasion he had difficulty finding all the parts, tended to be more temperate in his insistence on the whole truth all at once," is a social convener who always tries to darn up the threads of his people, sometimes beneficially, sometimes poorly. A Coyote figure, he invests his presence in his community. He is insistent that Will open a shop as the town's only Native photographer. While Will enters the town as a foreigner, he slowly becomes a part of this gentle community.

"I wasn't concerned about the white community in *Medicine River*. My focus really was on the Native community," reflects King. "Whatever kinds of mistakes the people make in *Medicine River* I wanted to make sure that they were Native mistakes that they made."[9] This is precisely what he depicts: a group of people, totally realistic and determinedly themselves, engaged in their everyday lives.

---

[8] "Godzilla vs. Post-Colonial," *World Literature Written in English*, 30, 2 (1990): 12, 14.
[9] "Thomas King," *Contemporary Challenges*, p. 111.

Green Grass, Running Water (1993) abandoned the safe confines of Medicine River and its inhabitants, now breaking all boundaries of time and place. Using a postmodern structure where such divisions seem irrelevant, King interweaves history and contemporary Indigenous culture and theology. Set in a contemporary First Nations Blackfoot community in Alberta, the novel tells a fantastical tale of four men, Lone Ranger, Ishmael, Robinson Crusoe, and Hawkeye, who escape from a mental asylum, all figures from imperial master narratives; they become four women respectively, First Woman, Changing Woman, Thought Woman, and Old Woman, thus echoing Coyote's unique ability to change genders. Coyote, a greedy lecher, constantly interferes with the ways of the world in his singing and dancing. At the same time, the trickster figure represents the steady endurance of Indigenous communities although their belief systems have been marginalized or obliterated by Eurocentric establishments.

Opening with an unknown narrator explaining "the beginning," *Green Grass, Running Water* explores and explodes the Judeo-Christian creation myth, placing it alongside Native creation myths. The novel's characters are real or literary figures from Judeo-Christian stories, Indigenous figures from recent times, and historical people only thinly disguised. The novel also examines the historical basis of treaties about Native peoples in the story of Eli Stands Alone, who returns from his University of Toronto professorship to live in his mother's home by a local dam. At the annual traditional Blackfoot Sun Dance ceremony, the dam breaks, caused by Coyote's machinations, Eli himself and his home are destroyed, and the waterway returns to its natural course. The territorial integrity of the Blackfoot reservation is restored, and their lands are restored to their proper usefulness.

Deriving its title from the Canadian government, which promised Indigenous peoples rights to their land "as long as the grass is green and the water runs," *Green Grass, Running Water* subverts the dominating power of Eurocentric traditions. Revising racial, religious, and sexual hierarchies, it removes the authority of Judeo-Christian patriarchal beliefs and systems, setting up an alternative *and* Indigenous vision of life. "The most ambitious, complex novel yet by an Aboriginal writer coming out of Canada (if not exactly from Canada)," writes Ojibway author Drew Hayden Taylor (b. 1962), "it represented a shift in form and structure and broadened the scope of Aboriginal fiction in Canada."[10]

[10] "The Most 'Influential and Essential' List," *Futile Observations of a Blue-Eyed Ojibway: Funny You Don't Look Like Now*, #4 (Penticton, British Columbia: Theytus, 2004), p. 104.

Similar in tone to *Medicine River*, *Truth and Bright Water* (1999) returns to the more traditional narrative structure of the earlier novel. Truth, a tiny rural Montana town, and Bright Water, a Canadian reserve, are separated by the Shield River; a half-completed bridge supposedly connects the two towns. Tecumseh, the fifteen-year-old first-person narrator, recounts his adventures with Soldier, his proud boxer dog, and his older cousin and best friend Lum. His coming-of-age story involves his estranged parents, whom he would like to see reconciled, and Monroe Swimmer, "Famous Indian Artist," a trickster, who has returned from Toronto to the reserve to buy an abandoned Methodist mission church and paint it – a magical trompe l'oeil – "out of" the landscape. He eventually learns that Monroe painted the village and the Indians back into the painting of *Sunrise on Little Turtle Lake* in order to save the world.

Despite its tragic ending, *Truth and Bright Water* continues King's recasting of the Indigenous people who populate this book with a significant place within society. With wry humour, he lambasts both the buckskin German tourists at the Bright Water Indian Days powwow and the Indigenous artisans who declare anything to be traditional if the price is acceptable. Yet at the novel's centre is a loving portrait of small-town life on both sides of the border and an unfinished bridge, a symbol of the still-to-be-completed understanding and acceptance of the Indigenous place within society.

The Back of the Turtle (2014) continues King's ability to weave Native culture into frightening tales of contemporary Native and non-Native realities. Set in the fictional community of Samaritan Bay near the Pacific Ocean, the novel follows the plight of Gabriel Quinn, a successful scientist of First Nations descent, who works for the multinational chemical firm Domidion. He has returned to Samaritan Bay and Smoke River, the Native reserve in British Columbia, with the intention of committing suicide for his involvement in the creation of GreenSweep, which destroyed the local environment and its community. Meanwhile, Domidion's CEO is implicated in another environmental disaster in the Athabaska Oil Sands. Less demanding on its readers than *Green Grass, Running Water*, the novel is a politically charged account of highly relevant subject matter.

The Back of the Turtle, begun in the early 2000s, was interrupted by eight years King devoted to *The Inconvenient Indian: A Curious Account of Native People in North America* (2012). "The fact of Native existence," he avers, "is that we live modern lives informed by traditional values and contemporary realities and that we wish to live those lives on our terms."

Frequently comic in his novels with their depiction of Indigenous peoples and their ways of life, King presents a tragic vision of these men and women trying to live their lives according to their own terms; he notes the indignities suffered by them, setting up a paradigm of equality which embraces all human beings. In so doing, he repositioned Indigenous fiction as an essential part of contemporary writing.

Heralding Richard Wagamese, an Ojibway originally from Northwestern Ontario, as "the real deal,"[11] a writer "you could put yourself into his characters, you could feel what they were feeling, see what they were seeing. He was an incisive writer in that way,"[12] King saluted an author who had suffered the loss of his parents at the age of three – he would not see his mother or his extended family for twenty-one years – the aloneness of his many foster homes, his adopted Presbyterian family, alcoholism and drug abuse, and extreme poverty and jail to become a major fiction and non-fiction writer. "I found a peace in being a male Ojibway human being that I never knew was possible," writes Wagamese in his autobiography *For Joshua: An Ojibway Father Teaches His Son* (2002). "I just needed an earnest desire to learn and it had been granted me."

Wagamese's first novel, *Keeper 'n Me* (1994), recounts the first-person autobiography of Ojibway Garnet Raven, whose early life bears much resemblance to its author's own story. Taken from his home on a north-western Ontario Indian reserve at the age of three by the Ontario Children's Aid Society, he finds himself placed in a series of foster homes. In his mid-teens he escapes to the streets of Toronto. In time burdened with alcohol and substance abuse, he is found guilty of possession with intent to traffic and sentenced to five years on a work farm. There he receives a surprise letter from his long-forgotten Indigenous family. The sudden communication from his past incites him to return to the reserve following his release. Back in his home territory, he discovers a sense of self, buoyed in this enterprise by Keeper, a friend of his grandfather and an experienced guide into his people's ways. As a consequence, Garnet learns about the ways of the Ojibway people. "Be a storyteller," he is told. "Talk about the real Indyuns. About what you learned, where you traveled, where you've been all this time. Tell them. Tell them stories on accounta them they all need guides too." The child of residential school survivors, Wagamese has a sympathetic understanding of Indigenous peoples, and

---

[11] "Ojibway author found salvation in stories," *The Globe and Mail*, 25 March 2017, p. S12.
[12] "Love and tributes for Ojibway storyteller Richard Wagamese," CBC Radio, 20 March 2017.

the endings of his novels offer resolutions which highlight Ojibway excellence while not diminishing the achievements of non-Ojibway peoples.

Dream Wheels (2006) and *Ragged Company* expand and deepen his study of human beings trapped in trying circumstances. In the former, he continues threading Native Canadian spirituality into his first third-person story: Joe Willie Wolfchild, a young Ojibway-Sioux and eight seconds away from becoming the #1 "All-Round Cowboy," is crippled by a legendary bull and retreats to the family ranch. Meanwhile, in a bleak suburb, a fifteen-year-old boy drifts into drugs and robbery, spurred on by the trauma of seeing his black mother beaten by her white boyfriend. Thanks to an enterprising young detective, the mother and son move to the ranch where Joe Willie's Sioux mother restores their relationship through the healing powers of the Sioux. While the ranch proves a fruitful home to all these characters, *Ragged Company* has four characters who are homeless in an unnamed Canadian city. Attending a movie matinee, they stumble upon a winning lottery ticket, though they do not have proper identification to claim their prize. One man comes to their aid, and their five perspectives form the substance of the novel. Though only two of them are Indigenous, they come to realize that home is an area they must knowingly accept, trust being the bond that can unite them. Each story is a spiritual biography of the characters' sense of loss and their belated acceptance of the possibility of redemption.

In *Indian Horse* (2012), Saul Indian Horse, an Ojibway from northwestern Ontario, journeys back in this first-person memoir for an understanding of who he was in the 1960s and '70s and who he is now. Taken forcibly from his dead grandmother and incarcerated in a residential school at the age of eight where he is constantly victimized by a priest, he reveals the potential of becoming a great hockey player. His career, however, is accompanied by racist taunts and brawls, leading him to cultural alienation. Only when he returns to his roots, only when he confronts the demons of his past, does he realize the wisdom of Ojibway teachings about human beings in this landscape. "I have been lifted up and out of this physical world into a place where time and space have a different rhythm," he confesses. "I always remained within the borders of this world, yet I had the eyes of one born to a different plane. Our medicine people would call me a seer." In *Medicine Walk* (2015), an Ojibway teenager, Franklin Starlight, is summoned to visit his estranged and sadly decimated father Eldon, who wants to be buried in the way of his ancestors, sitting up, facing east, "in the warrior way." Realizing his filial duty, he agrees to conduct him into the British Columbia interior as Eldon narrates tales of his difficult life. For the son, this final journey leads to acceptance, if not forgiveness, of his father. The landscape becomes a healing presence to both the loquacious father and his uncertain son. In Wagamese's posthumously published and incomplete novel, *Starlight* (2018), Starlight, now an older man and tied to his solitary life, offers an abused white woman and her young daughter a place to live and to work for him.

Wagamese wrote with deep compassion of the trials and the sufferings of the Ojibway people, reaching out to the love that ultimately connects them and highlighting the healing power of family, of tradition, and of the landscape that engulfs them. The land, he stated in *One Native Life* (2008), "is our salvation. The time we spend in communion with the earth is the time, my people say, that we are truly spiritual. It enhances, empowers and frees us." His books capture the Ojibway mind in scenes that speak to Ojibways and all peoples who find themselves reflected on his pages. His role "was to be just that: a teller of stories, a communicator, a keeper of the great oral tradition of my people."

Robert Arthur Alexie (1957–2014), a First Nations novelist and land claim negotiator, was born in Fort McPherson in the Northwest Territories, making his literary home in the same northern area, where he set his account of the residential school system. In *Porcupines and China Dolls* (2002), set initially in 1962, two six-year-old boys are dragged from their parents to attend a mission school, living now without their families in a world where there is no hope. "The girls had been scrubbed and powdered to look like china dolls and the boys had been scrubbed and sheared to look like porcupines," comments Thomas King in *The Truth About Stories: A Native Narrative* (2003). The novel then moves to 1999 when the two have grown up, though chronic mental anguish still plagues their lives. "When will it end? How long do we carry the hate, the anger, the rage 'n the sorrow?" Alexie writes about the schools with stark clarity and horror, showing how to write fictionally about the school experience and especially its aftermath. The novel is "primarily for a Native audience," continues King, "making a conscious decision not so much to ignore non-Native readers as to write for the very people they write about." In *The Pale Indian* (2005), his other novel, an eleven-year-old Indian from Aberdeen in the Northwest Territories and his six-year-old sister come to Calgary in 1972 to live with their adoptive and kind white family, having been removed from their parents and their home. Although the boy promised never to return, a job with a drilling company brings him back in 1984 to the home of his people. Now he must confront the truth of his parents' lives as well as of his own life. Less broad than its predecessor, focused more on an individual and his own livelihood, *The Pale Indian* suggests a future direction for this gifted novelist, who, unfortunately, took his own life.

Displaying deep respect for Thomas King by using an epigraph from his writings for her third novel, *Son of a Trickster* (2017), Eden Robinson (b. 1968), a Haisla/Heiltsuk and a creative-writing graduate of the University of Victoria and the University of British Columbia, was born on the Kitamaat Reserve of the Haisla Nations traditional lands in northern British Columbia, where she often sets her fiction. "When I write," she confesses, "I'm interpreting a Haisla world through English words,"[13] and her books introduce Haisla mythology into her accounts of contemporary life.

Trap Lines (1996), three short stories, all with first-person narrators, and a novella, contains two white stories enclosed by more Native stories, the lurid sadism of the two central stories held in place by the endemic familial dysfunction of the opening and closing stories. The four tales, focusing on adolescents restricted by their age and their class, are grim fairy tales about these young people and their relationships with psychopaths and socio-paths. Among her mentors are Edgar Allan Poe and Stephen King.

Her first novel, *Monkey Beach* (2000), takes place in her home community of Kitimaat. Lisamarie Michelle Hill, its teenage Haisla narrator, learns that her brother, an Olympic hopeful swimmer, has disappeared at sea. Her world is haunted by premonitions and ghosts; her life is burdened by the deaths of loved ones; her use of drugs cripples her. Wracked and wrecked, she enters her own memory when she and her brother first saw the sasquatch. She has a special gift which enables her to see and hear spirits and ask for their help. The novel becomes a mystery and a spiritual journey, with its contemporary realism and its Haisla mysticism and spirituality.

"You're buying into a religion that thought the best way to make us white was to fucking torture children," her Uncle Mick states. Her Aunt Trudy tells Lisa: "There were tons of priests in the residential schools, tons of fucking matrons and helpers that 'helped' themselves to little kids just like you. You look at me and tell me how many of them got away scot-free." Her Uncle Mick and her Aunt Trudy "had both suffered through residential school together." Although Lisa did not attend these schools, the older generation knew them. Although Robinson, like Lisa, is part of

---

[13] *Luminous Ink: Writers on Writing in Canada*, eds. Tessa McWatt, Rabindranath Maharaj and Dionne Brand (Toronto: Cormorant, 2018), p. 6.

the first generation after the residential schools, they still hold sway over the Indigenous inhabitants of remote Katimaat.

Robinson returns to Kitimaat in *Son of a Trickster* (2017), the first of a Trickster trilogy, a first-person account of sixteen-year-old Jared Martin's coming of age in a dysfunctional and violent family. A "random town Native," the sensitive but substance-abusing teenager bakes and sells homemade pot cookies to his fellow high school students, thereby financially supporting his divorced father; he also helps out his elderly neighbours who lodged him when his mother went into a rehabilitation institute. The gritty realism is counterbalanced by frequent supernatural intrusions: Jared meets a talkative raven who asserts that he is his real father, and he also sees animal spirits. His mother finally confesses that his father was a trickster named Wee'git. In *Trickster Drift* (2018), the second in the series, the first-person narration gives way to the omniscient third person as Jared, now seventeen, moves to East Vancouver to enrol in a diagnostic medical sonography program. Although he lives with his mother's estranged sister, an activist poet, he cannot shake off his magical nature. A ghost lives in her apartment, there is a creature living in his room's wall, and creatures appear constantly; the spirits and the supernatural activity plague Jared, who remains a selfless individual ministering to people in distress.

All Robinson's tales are invested with humour, the realism counterbalanced by her sharp wit and humane compassion for her characters. She focuses mainly on families that function poorly though they never completely fall apart, and her focus is the young people who lead frequently depressing lives. Haisla mythology neither plays into her fiction nor is it superimposed upon it; it is an essential component of her fiction and her vision of life, and Robinson is one of the major chroniclers of contemporary Indigenous life.

The Trickster or Nanabush is the centre of Drew Hayden Taylor's *Motorcycles & Sweetgrass* (2010). A fine dramatist and short story writer, he paints a sleepy Otter Lake Reserve in Ontario, which is pleasantly disturbed by the arrival of a handsome, blond white man on a 1953 Indian Chief motorcycle. The intruder, offering the reserve many names for his identity, "brings truth, love, and chaos in his wake, but in so doing, lays bare festering wounds, unacknowledged losses, and unhealthy secrets that must be dealt with if the community has any hope of a healthy future."[14]

---

[14] Daniel Heath Justice, *Why Indigenous Literatures Matter* (Waterloo, Ontario: Wilfrid Laurier University Press, 2018), p. 92.

Maggie Second, the reserve's chief, falls in love with him while her son is wary. "Besides the fact that Nanabush is make-believe, John is White," he says. "I assume Nanabush would at least look a little Indian." His mother openly asserts that "Nanabush was a charming and inventive character from Ojibway mythology. A symbol. A teaching tool. That was all." John proves to have the Trickster's true and multiform lineage. Otter Lake has many raccoons with long memories who have called the place their home. They recognize John for what he is despite his fear of them, reflecting an earlier time when his hunger drove him to kill and eat a raccoon. When they defile his beloved motorcycle, he accepts responsibility for his cruelty. The raccoons can even dominate a human trickster, leaving human beings to confront the learning that comes from the other-than-human world.

Determined to educate Indigenous and non-Indigenous people on issues which reflect and celebrate Indigenous life, Taylor offers an honest portrayal of their lifestyles, often highlighting their attempts to reconcile their heritage with the society in which they live. He underlines, too, what is lacking in Indigenous writing. Frustrated by repeated attempts to put together an anthology of Indigenous science fiction, he confesses in his foreword to his comic collection, *Take Me to Your Chief* (2016): "I wanted to take traditional (a buzzword in the Native Community) science-fiction characteristics and filter them through an Aboriginal consciousness." Thus he finds himself taking the first step towards such an anthology. "As we're well into the twenty-first century, the time has come to explore the concept of Native Science Fiction, a phrase that I submit should no longer be considered a literary oxymoron." Immersing itself in the traditions of science fiction filtered through a distinctly Indigenous sensibility, the collection – each story takes place on the reserve – fills a literary void.

His second novel, *Chasing Painted Horses* (2019), also takes place on the Otter Lake Reserve and straddles the line between young adult and adult fiction. Recounting the meeting of three children with a gifted and equally young artist, the novel shows imagination's power to absorb young people's attention and control. Echoing the short stories of Sinclair Ross, it captures the frightening yet awesome power of a child's encounter with the world outside of herself.

At the same time that Maracle, Armstrong, and Highway, King and Wagamese, Robinson and Taylor were writing their fictions, Joseph Boyden (b. 1966) was learning about Indigenous peoples. Spending winters in Toronto and summers on Georgian Bay, he travelled extensively before graduating from York University and a subsequent master's program in creative writing at the University of New Orleans where he is now a professor. He also spent two years as a professor of Aboriginal programs for Northern College in Cree communities on the west coast of James Bay. Although not Indigenous, he researched Indigenous life extensively, imbuing his three novels with appropriate details and facts.

Three Day Road (2005), his first novel, chronicles the plights of best friends Xavier Bird and Elijah "Whiskeyjack" Weesageechak, united by their separate times in residential schools and then their service abroad in World War I. In their many combats they face racist taunts as they prove themselves adept at shooting and killing the enemy. Although Xavier becomes the best shot in his company, he comes to hate the murderous war. Elijah, on the other hand, loves the war's bloodthirstiness. His leg amputated in the war, Xavier returns home to the local train station where he is unable to continue unassisted; his aunt Niska, an Oji–Cree medicine woman, paddles her only relative on his three-day journey to his home in the white settlement of Moose Factory, all the time offering him healing stories of her past and the past of their people, the Cree of northern Ontario. Told by two narrators, Xavier and Niska, the novel is a powerful indictment of the savagery and ultimate pity of war. *Through Black Spruce* (2008) brings the Bird family into the present, again choosing two narrators, Will Bird, now mostly comatose in Moose Factory, and his niece Annie Bird, now sitting beside his hospital bed. As the two reveal their secrets, they share their own natural resilience. *The Orenda* (2013) tells the four-hundred-year-old story of the first contact between foreigners and the Indigenous peoples from an Indigenous perspective. A trusted warrior and statesman of the Huron nation kidnaps a young Iroquois girl, who reminds him of his own lost daughter. Meanwhile, a charismatic Jesuit missionary lives among the Hurons, trying to understand their customs and language and guiding them to Christian salvation. These three narrators engage in a long and detailed series of duplicitous and tragic meetings. Buoyed by his own meticulous research, Boyden creates harrowing images of Indigenous life in the distant past, the near past, and the present. Whether or not one accepts "appropriation of voice" arguments, his novels engage with issues confronting Indigenous peoples.

The Inuit population, approximately four percent of the Indigenous population of Canada, lives in the northernmost regions of the country: northern Quebec, northern Labrador, and the western Arctic, which includes the Northwest Territories and the Yukon. There have been roughly 4,000 years of human history in the Arctic area, and parallels operate to some degree to the other Indigenous peoples in Canada. In the eighteenth and nineteenth centuries, for example, the arrival of explorers, whalers, missionaries, and scientists saw the Inuit acting as guides and traders, yet all the while Inuit culture persisted, the Inuit language, Inuktitut, and its six dialectical variants reinforcing the distinct Inuit identity. The eighteenth and nineteenth centuries, too, witnessed the marshalling of young people into residential schools, which sought to assimilate children into a Eurocentric vision of Canada. European education disrupted traditional Inuit methods of learning and often resulted in cultural dislocation. The pattern of family, extended family, and community elders instructing the youth was no longer endorsed: children were taken from their families, sent to faraway church-run schools, and denied their own language. Similar to the residential schools, these schools were often the site of interracial feuding, a chronic lack of food, and physical and sexual abuse from white employers and teachers.

As early as the 1790s, some Inuit children, for example, were educated in mission schools in Labrador, removing them from the traditional influences of family and culture and ultimately assimilating them to the Eurocentric perspective in a system regarded as ideal. Not until about by 1970, almost two centuries later, did the decrease in church-run schools lead to federally funded school constructions in many villages.

Although the Inuit have been expressing their oral culture in songs and stories for more than a thousand years, and their pictorial culture, in bone and stone sculptures and in prints and drawings, is now applauded, Inuktitut, the Inuit common language, has prevented the culture from flourishing in Canada's southern areas. From earliest times the Inuit had no written language, the world of writing introduced only by the arrival of Christian missionaries. Literacy then began to spread, though the spread was slow. The Hudson's Bay Company's endeavours focused on trade, not on improving literacy, and while the missionaries and Hudson's Bay dominated the landscape, there were few attempts to educate the Inuit in written languages.

Not until after World War II did the Canadian government focus seriously on the north, establishing centralized communities and creating a formal educational system. From the 1960s on, the quality of education increased with a significant number of young people writing now in English; the federal and territorial governments established Inuktitut language programs, though some believed the programs would facilitate transition to English or French. In the 1970s bilingual and bicultural education was beginning, and in the 1980s almost all printed material was published bilingually (Inuktitut and English) or trilingually (Inuktitut, English, and French). With this increase came a strong desire to express in poetry and prose the unique features of Inuit culture and history, and written Inuit literature is inexorably connected to the oral tradition that stands behind it.

From an oral to a written culture is a long journey. "As long as Inuit were isolated and nomadic hunters they had little use for a written language, but as soon as they began to absorb philosophies and information from outside the culture, as soon as they expanded their social units beyond the boundaries of the extended family, as soon as they had a desire to record factual reality as well as mythic reality, they quickly began to fix words on paper," writes Robin McGrath. "There has never been any resistance to the written word or the printed word among Inuit; rather they have accepted it as a useful tool for maintaining family relationships, developing political autonomy and encouraging cultural survival."[15] In a newly literate society, autobiographies are the dominant form of early writing: diaries and journals, followed by accounts of one's life, were detailed and plentiful.

In the winter of 1950 Thomas Kusugaq (c. 1915–73)[16] enunciated eight Nassilingmiut (Central Arctic Inuit) oral legends or traditional stories he had learned as a child to Alex Spalding (1924–2002), who transcribed them in 1979 as *Eight Inuit Myths/Inuit Unipkaaqtuat Pingasuniarvinilit.* "A powerful testament to the history, culture, and future of his people,"[17] Kusugaq's rendition evokes Inuit mythology, reflecting the immense history of its culture. In the beast fables, for example, humans encounter and even marry animals, often showing that respect for the animal world is tantamount to respect for all living objects.

Originally published in Ikutitut in 1967, *Harpoon of the Hunter* (trans. 1970), the novel by Patsauq Markoosie (1941–2020) and the first by an Inuk, follows the life of sixteen-year-old Kamik. His father encounters a marauding white bear and sets off with his son and other men to find and kill it. "A bear with rabies could be the most dangerous animal to walk this land. If it fought with other bears, then they would get rabies too." The father is killed by another bear, and seven men, except for Kamik, die in their hunt. When Kamik returns, he falls in love with the daughter of one of his rescuers, and, when she and his mother drown while crossing an open channel at sea, he impales himself on his harpoon. Indebted to his

---

[15] *Canadian Inuit Literature: The Development of a Tradition* (Ottawa: National Museums of Canada, 1984), p. 24.
[16] The birthdate is impossible to verify.
[17] Keavy Martin, *Stories in a New Skin: Approaches to Inuit Literature* (Winnipeg, University of Manitoba Press, 2012), p. 47.

grandmother's tales as well as Farley Mowat's *People of the Deer* (1952), the story, translated into English and many other languages, unites an old Inuit legend with a European-style love affair. Here, at last, was, according to James McNeill's forward to the 1970 edition, "a story of life in the old days, not as it appeared to southern eyes, but as it has survived in the memory of the Eskimos themselves." While Markoosie was penning his novel in the Northwest Territories, Mitiarjuk Nappaaluk (1931–2007) from northern Quebec was completing in the 1950s and 1960s her novel, *Sanaaq* (trans. 2014), though it was not published until 1984. Sanaaq, a feisty, independent, and strong-willed widow, lives with her young daughter among the semi-nomadic Inuit families just before the first Europeans arrived. She marries a young Inuit man, and the novel follows the joys and sorrows of their lives together, including a hunter losing his eye to scalding water, the arrival of the first Catholic missionaries and the establishment of a Catholic Church, the landing of the region's first airplane, the first visit from a Northern Affairs agent, and conjugal violence and Sanaaq's subsequent removal by air to a southern hospital. The novel, covering the early 1930s to the aftermath of World War II, is a compelling document of the hopes and the tragedies of an earlier Inuit life.

Although the novels anticipate a new stature in Inuit fiction, this stature consists almost exclusively of short stories, not the long, involved tales of Gallant or Munro, but brief ones which sometimes hearken back to the mythological tales, sometimes reflect the curious dichotomy between the old ways of the Inuit and the new, and sometimes focus on the dilemmas of contemporary Inuit life.

Essayist and poet, cartoonist and editor, Alootook Ipellie (1951–2007) spent the early part of his multi-faceted career working for *Inuit Monthly* (later named *Inuit Today*) where he was illustrator and frequent contributor. His poetry, drawings, and short stories are featured in Robin Gedalof's *Paper Stays Put: A Collection of Inuit Writing* (1980) and his self-illustrated collection of twenty tales, *Arctic Dreams and Nightmares* (1993), the first collection of short stories by an Inuit author. His stories were originally published in English and in Inuktitut. "The challenge for all Inuit today is in trying to retain what they can about all aspects of their once rich, traditional culture and heritage. They've ridden a bumpy road travelling from virtually a stone-age era to the twentieth century within a very short span of time," he wrote in his introduction. "It is the will and the perpetual pride of our elders that has helped us to retain the old myths, stories and legends so that our present generation can absorb them and pass them on to future generations."

In "Nipikti the Old Man Carver," one of Ipellie's early stories, Nipikti is bringing his latest work of art to the co-op to be sold. As he travels, he witnesses the inevitable destruction of everything he knows and loves, displaying a healthy regret for the past as well as a strong belief in the future, a vision rooted in traditional Inuit values. The intended new road for the community may be redirected so that the useful and familiar rocks where he rests may be saved, as Inuit society may also be saved. In other stories, Ipellie lambasts the colonial attitudes towards the Inuit, often choosing satire. In "Miami Beach, Here We Come!" Nanook and his family, with a heat wave sweeping the north, plan to leave Grise Fiord for a month in snow-covered Miami, for example, or "N.W.T. Separates from Canada" explores a proposed referendum on separation from Canada.

Although he concluded his foreword to the English translation of *The Diary of Abraham Ulrikab* (2005), "Whether displayed in a zoo or an art gallery, Inuit people are still treated as exotic specimens," he devoted his entire life to a delineation of the old Inuit dying culture and the new Inuit lifestyle. A mixture of the two cultures, he saw himself as uniquely positioned to summon up remembrances of the old and reflect upon the new and changing. His stories bridge both worlds, looking back with nostalgia and looking directly at the present with hesitant acceptance. His last book, *The Inuit Thought of It: Amazing Arctic Innovation* (2007), is testimony to his Arctic home and way of life, addressed as it is to an essentially non-Inuit audience. Subsequent fiction writers would follow in Ipellie's footsteps, believing that they are now becoming a part of their own tradition.

While Inuit fiction in English and in Inuktitut was emerging slowly, there was still much to be done to bring it into an acknowledged place within Canadian fiction. In 1971 a group of Inuit people formed Inuit Tapiriit Kanatami [United with Canada] to advocate for all the Inuit peoples. They studied carefully the development of the North, and they supported the preservation and the promotion of the Inuit language and heritage.

Literacy levels among the Inuit are still far below the national level, and close to sixty percent have less than a high school education. The residential school system had undermined traditional educational practices, yet its final disappearance left the survivors and their families traumatized. There remains a tremendous urgency to teach and train the youth – fifty percent of the Inuit population are under the age of twenty-five – and secure for them access to post-secondary education. There remains a tremendous urgency to unite the Inuit with their fellow Canadians to the south in a fulfiling and lasting relationship, based on coexistence.

In 2008 the Truth and Reconciliation Commission was created as a consequence of the Indian Residential Schools Settlement Agreement of 2007, which had allocated a multi-billion dollar settlement, the largest in Canada's history, to residential school survivors. The commission's final report, *Honour the Truth, Reconciling for the Future*, submitted in 2015, demands that Canada move from apology to action. Yet Justin Trudeau's words, which opened this chapter, still hold true for the Canadian nation. Some fiction works, however, do presage a new hope for writings by First Nations, Métis, and Inuit authors. The future is theirs, united with Canada as the Inuit say, not through assimilation but through an acknowledgement of their own place within Canada and its fiction writing.

CHAPTER 9

Naturalized Canadian Writers

Although naturalized Canadians, Canadians born outside of Canada, were a relatively uncommon feature in the country's landscape before World War II – Frederick Philip Grove being an exception – the war years and the years immediately following altered the fabric of Canadian society. The devastation of many countries around the world had their economic, political, and social upheavals laid bare, resulting in a desire for large-scale emigration. Canada's immigration policy, which largely reflected the country's colonial beginnings, now underwent reluctant but significant changes. The country's wide open spaces and sparse population made it a beacon for immigrants looking for a land of freedom and stability. Three naturalized writers led the way for the growing number of emigrant men and women coming into the country.

Born in Vienna of Jewish parents, and then fleeing the newly imposed Anschluss in 1938, Henry Kreisel spent eighteen months (May 1940–November 1941) as an enemy alien in internment camps in New Brunswick and Quebec before arriving in Toronto, where he attended the University of Toronto, obtaining his doctorate. He became a Canadian citizen and settled in Edmonton where he became Professor of English and Comparative Literature and Vice-President of the University of Alberta.

Raised on the classics of Austrian and German literature, Kreisel chose to write in English, not his family's German or Yiddish languages. Finding the literary art of Canada woefully unacknowledged, he struggled to overcome this national ignorance. Adopting as his master Joseph Conrad, a Pole who used only English in his writings, he turned in 1942 to the poetry of A.M. Klein to learn to find in his memory his deepest roots; without their sustenance, he could not function as a creative artist. He became a writer with a double understanding: seeing European experiences through his Canadian perspective and seeing Canadian experiences through his European perspective. His two novels and many short stories brought the life of the European immigrant into Canadian fiction.

The Rich Man (1948) follows the decision of Jacob Grossman to leave his home in Toronto and return to Vienna, the city of his earlier life. The year is 1935. The Nazis have assassinated Engelbert Dollfuss, the chancellor of Austria, and anti-Semitism is publicly encouraged. Grossman's journey is a voyage home, a futile attempt to renew his familial relationships. Contrasting Canada and Europe, the new world and the old, the novel portrays him confronting the now outdated world of his upbringing. *The Betrayal* (1964) reverses the pattern of *The Rich Man*, bringing a Viennese man to Edmonton and depicting the European war experience through Canadian eyes. In his intimate first-person account, a young history professor, confronting three people who have emigrated from Vienna, must witness the guilt fostered during the Jewish persecutions in Austria. The past is not merely history but something that evokes powerful responses in the present. Studying the relationship between Canada and Austria, Kreisel crafted a unique contribution to fiction. No longer portraying the new settlers who come to the prairies, as Grove did, he presents the harsh urban experience of new immigrants, inviting readers to assess the damages of the European upheavals to their own lives in Canada.

Born an illegitimate child and raised in Barbados, Austin Clarke (1934–2016) was schooled in the major classics of British literature. "Barbados," he wrote in *Growing Up Stupid Under the Union Jack* (1980), "was known as Little England." He taught high school and later became a factory worker to earn funds for his 1955 escape from Barbados and his arrival in Toronto. He studied at the University of Toronto; he wrote some poems and short stories before turning to the novel, publishing eleven novels, six short story collections, five autobiographical works, and one volume of poetry. And he, too, became a Canadian citizen.

His first two novels, *The Survivors of the Crossing* (1964) and *Amongst Thistles and Thorns* (1965), are set in Barbados. The semi-autobiographical *Amongst Thistles and Thorns*, the first written of the pair, focuses on a nine-year-old Barbadian boy, the illegitimate child of a washerwoman, and his search for his father. Mirroring the idioms and rhythms of many levels of Barbadian society, the novel studies the gulf between the rich and the poor, between white and black, in contemporary society, yet despite the humiliation of the downtrodden blacks visible everywhere, there is an exuberance to the people, especially the boy's mother, a formidable figure of determination and love. In *The Survivors of the Crossing*, a man who emigrated from Barbados to Canada writes home to alert his friends to the great opportunities for employment in his new country. His letter inspires a labourer on the sugar plantation to organize a strike to tell management, the upper and middle classes, of the indignities endured by his fellow labourers. Practically every page reveals Clarke's anger at management's insensitivity and his pity for the workers' sufferings.

The 1960s made Clarke aware of his unique calling. "No Canadian writer, in 1963 – and even today, there are very few – had dealt, in a realistic way, its limitations not withstanding, with the 'presence' of black people on the Toronto landscape of whiteness." Writers such as Ralph Ellison, Richard Wright, and James Baldwin, "my spiritual brother," were his "nearest models, so far as geography and a veneer of cultural-racial context were concerned," he stated in his autobiography *'Membering* (2015), and they became forces in his writings and in the developing world of Canadian fiction. He found that the racial problems in the United States existed, though in a more subtle manner, in Canada too, and his Toronto trilogy, *The Meeting Point* (1967), *Storm of Fortune* (1973), and *The Bigger Light* (1975), explores the blackness of white Toronto, the exploitation of lower-class Barbadian women, and the persistent discrimination of black people.

The Meeting Point, for example, studies Barbadian women who immigrate to Toronto to work as domestic helps, including its protagonist Bernice Leach. "It was a community of immigrants: immigrants who were not Anglo-saxon. Like her, these immigrants had suddenly realized they were lost in a foreign land." They labour in a white world with the cultural and social differences between employers and employees always evident. The women must suppress their natural personalities in order to be accepted in their working environment. The household where she works is a Jewish family, themselves once immigrants to Canada and now representative of the degree the outsider travels in order to be joined in this new world. The truth, however, is that the Barbadian helps can never assimilate to this world; they will always stand outside, looking inside but unable to join.

His tenth and finest novel, *The Polished Hoe* (2002), returns to Barbados in 1952 to present Mary Mathilda's confession to Sergeant Percy of murdering her employer, Mr. Belfeels, the powerful owner of a sugar plantation and a wealthy man known for his mistreatment of his workers. She is a seductive woman of about sixty who lives midway between the plantation and the village as the "outside" woman of the owner. The twenty-four-hour confession becomes a meandering history of her dependence upon the owner ever since he raped her at the age of eight, her mother standing by silently. She has been his mistress and the mother of his only son. She eventually discovers her mother's secret that she herself is Belfeels's daughter, which prompts her to murder him.

The Polished Hoe encapsulates the major themes of Clarke's fiction: the rigid hierarchy among peoples that is terrifyingly enforced; the desperate search for retribution that is rarely achieved; and the portrait of an island with slavery embedded in its past and its present. He incites Barbadians to look into a mirror and see themselves and their identity. In looking back at Barbados, he is also looking at contemporary Toronto, trying to disabuse it of its belief in its racial innocence.

The father of Black Canadian literature and the first naturalized Canadian from a Commonwealth country, he steadfastly adhered to his depiction of contemporary reality with its positive and its negative traits intact. His influence on other Canadian writers is immense. "I first read Austin Clarke's work when I came to this country in the early seventies," Dionne Brand (b. 1953) reflects. "As a young writer at the time its presence within Canadian writing assured me of the possibilities for Black writers in Canada."[1]

The year after Clarke arrived in Canada, Jane Rule left the United States, fleeing the McCarthy witch-hunts that permeated American news. Originally from New Jersey with a bachelor's degree in English from Mills College in California, she taught at Concord Academy in Massachusetts before settling on the West Coast of Canada and becoming a Canadian citizen.

Her first novel, *Desert of the Heart* (1964), published the same year as Clarke's first novel, reintroduced lesbian relationships to Canadian fiction. Evelyn Hall, a professor of English and married for sixteen years, has come to Reno to arrange for a divorce. In her boarding house she meets Ann Childs, a young cartoonist who works in a casino and is fifteen years her junior. Their growing interest and concern for each other lead to a happy union. Herself an open lesbian, Rule offers the couple a safe haven where such attitudes as the necessity of marriage and child-bearing are now irrelevant; she allows them a happy ending.

This Is Not for You (1970) is an unmailed letter from Kate George to her friend Esther Woolf, who has entered a convent and taken a vow of silence. Vowing at all times to be conventionally proper, Kate refuses to transmit what she senses to be the chaos of her lesbianism to her relationship with Esther. Behind her wrong-headed integrity is Rule's liberating anger at people's refusal to risk the challenges that confront them in their sexual behaviours. Later novels continue her exploration of

---

[1] Stella Algoo-Baksh, *Austin C. Clarke: A Biography* (Toronto: ECW Press, 1994), p. 216. See also David CharIandy, "As Man," *Luminous Ink*, pp. 43–9.

homosexual as well as heterosexual relationships. Using the boarding-house pattern already employed in *Desert of the Heart*, *The Young in One Another's Arms* (1977) studies a variety of responses to vulnerability in matters of love.

While fiction, both novels and short stories, are Rule's focus, she also published a series of essays as well as *Lesbian Images* (1975), her scholarly study of the ways in which lesbian experiences have been reflected in several writers. A socially committed writer, she offers a sensitive analysis of the intricacies and dilemmas of the human heart. She wants her characters to grow into fine communities where tolerance is the key to their success. "Everything she wrote was aimed at a more inclusive world, a more accepting world," remarks Atwood; "she valued those qualities because she had experienced their opposites."[2]

From these early naturalized Canadians come eight writers who adapted to their new homes and relished its space to write fiction of their new lands as well as their homelands.

Playwright and poet, novelist and short story writer, Carol Shields, born in Oak Park, Illinois, arrived in Canada with her Canadian husband in 1957. They lived in Vancouver and Toronto before they settled in Ottawa where her husband accepted an engineering position at the University of Ottawa in 1968; they moved to Vancouver in 1978, then settled in Winnipeg in 1980 where she taught at the University of Manitoba and became Chancellor of the University of Winnipeg. In 2000 they retired to Victoria.

Her first non-fiction book, *Susanna Moodie: Voice and Vision* (1976), based on her University of Ottawa master's thesis, looks at Susanna Moodie in the context of her own time. Based on material left over from her thesis, Shields wrote her first novel, *Small Ceremonies* (1976), about the narrator Judith Gill, the biographer of Moodie, and her travails in academia. Here is Shields's own voice: observant, wry, and ironic, looking in detail at the world in front of her. Influenced strongly by Atwood in her style and by Munro in her vision, indebted as well to Montgomery, and paying homage to great female writers such as Austen and Woolf, she examines contemporary middle-class men and women, especially women, in their daily lives, making ordinary details and facts absolutely riveting. In the parodic *Swann: A Mystery* (1987), her favourite book among her many, she returns to the Canadian past as various contemporary people, much as

Shields did with Moodie, argue about the reputation of the late poet Mary Swann. Poetic scraps, scattered biographical facts, and sentimental conclusions, however, highlight this willful distortion of academic sleuthing, for Swann was primarily a fabrication created by scholars concerned only with their own reputations.

The Stone Diaries (1993), which won the Pulitzer Prize and was a finalist for the Booker Prize, looks back to Wilson's *The Innocent Traveller*, Laurence's *The Stone Angel*, and Pat Lowther's posthumous poetry collection *A Stone Diary* (1977) for its story of one woman and her journey through her ordinary life. Born in Manitoba in 1905 and dying in Florida in the 1990s, Daisy Goodwill Flett maps her own intimate story. Her early years lead to her marriage and children; she loves her work as a gardener and a journalist; she suffers when she loses both her husband and her job and later has a heart attack. When she moves to the Canary Palms Convalescent Home, she takes joy from the small pleasures of her residence. She accepts all the changes life brings her, moving from one event to another, never believing in her own – or anyone else's – ability to offer any ultimate meaning to her life. Daisy is, commented Shields, "like so many women of this century who became, in fact, nothing. Their lives did not hold many choices. They were this huge army of women, they were mainly voiceless, they were defined by the people around them."[3]

After her examination of one woman's life in *The Stone Diaries*, Shields turns to the problems of a late-twentieth-century male, thirty-six-year-old Larry Weller, in *Larry's Party* (1997), winner of the Orange Prize. A maze and labyrinth designer, he represents the struggle of a man to find and understand his own identity. Studying the private, domestic male provides Shields with an avenue into men at a time of new thinking about gender when definitions of masculinity were being seriously challenged. In her last novel, *Unless* (2002), another finalist for the Booker Prize and her most overtly feminist work, a nineteen-year-old woman leaves home to beg at a street corner with a sign hanging from her neck, "Goodness." Her family searches desperately for the reasons why she has abandoned them, her boyfriend, and her university studies. For Shields, the sense of a person's nothingness is the first step on the road to true humility, which in turn leads to goodness.

"She gave her material the full benefit of her large intelligence, her powers of observation, her humane wit, and her wide reading," reflects

---

[3] Eleanor Wachtel, *Random Illuminations: Conversations with Carol Shields* (Fredericton, New Brunswick: Goose Lane, 2007), p. 51.

Atwood. "Her books are delightful, in the original sense of the word: they are full of delights."[4] Younger writers such as Hay and Urquhart learned from Shields's authentic fiction.

A naturalized Canadian, Michael Ondaatje, born in Colombo, Ceylon (now Sri Lanka), spent a peripatetic childhood, attending Saint Thomas College in Colombo, then moving to England at the age of nine to attend Dulwich College, then immigrating to Canada in 1962, where he obtained his BA at the University of Toronto and his MA at Queen's University. An acclaimed poet, he authored, for example, *The Collected Works of Billy the Kid* (1970), focusing primarily on Billy's final outlaw year and mixing freely the few historical facts of his life of crime with an imaginative reconstruction of his legend. Researching his mythic American hero and fashioning a poem which combines biography, historical romance, lyrical reflections, and oral anecdotes, he follows Sheila Watson and Robert Kroetsch in adding another dimension to Canadian literature, embracing a new vision for literary creativity: "The air currents of literary influences that result in the merging of art forms, subject matter, alternate perspectives, and above all, translations, alter our world subliminally and more profoundly than we know. We move, drift, climb into, and tunnel from one country to another. It is the central story of our time."[5] The "merging of art forms" and tunnelling "from one country to another" become a constant refrain in his mingling of fact and fiction.

In his first novel, *Coming Through Slaughter* (1976), which is influenced by *The Double Hook* with its taut style, Ondaatje mixes poetry, prose, and fictional documentary for a biography of Buddy Bolden (1877–1931), a cornet player whose band is often credited with what came to be known as jazz. Intrigued by a brief newspaper clipping, "Buddy Bolden who became a legend when he went berserk in a parade" in 1907, the narrator travelled to Louisiana to learn what little there was about Bolden's life; he used tapes of jazzmen's memories of him, books about Bolden's Storyville district in New Orleans, and records of the East Louisiana State Hospital, where he finally lived, mad, until his passing in 1931.

Unchronological as the novel is, *Coming Through Slaughter* divides itself into three sections: the first is essentially narrative, the second occurs in Bolden's mind, and the third mingles his thoughts in various mental hospitals with historical documentation, narrative, and the reflections of the author. His playing appears to be formless because "he tore apart the

---

[4] "To the Light House," *The Worlds of Carol Shields*, p. 6.
[5] "A Port Accent," *Luminous Ink*, p. 213.

plot" trying to describe the music. He is unthinking until he meets E.J. Bellocq, a photographer of Storyville's prostitutes, who introduces him to calculated art, privacy, and silence. After Bellocq's suicide, he meditates on his own music. He contrasts himself with John Robichaux, who "dominated his audiences"; he wants audiences "to come in where they pleased and leave when they pleased and somehow hear the germs of the start and all the possible endings at whatever point in the music that I had reached *then*. Like your radio without the beginnings or endings." In the parade where he goes "mad," he realizes his goal, becoming one with his music.

In 1977 Ondaatje collaborated with Kroetsch on a film adaptation of *Badlands*. Although the cinematic version never entered production, it indicated Ondaatje's constant attempts to merge art forms.

Ondaatje's first formal novel, *In the Skin of a Lion* (1987) has a tripartite division in its depiction of Toronto in the early years of the twentieth century. Book one, for example, introduces the protagonist, Patrick Lewis, a young boy from eastern Ontario. It also recounts the lives of immigrants building Toronto's Bloor Street Viaduct, including Nicholas Temelcoff, a worker from the Balkans who rescues a nun falling from the bridge. The novel then returns to Lewis, who has become a searcher for the notorious millionaire, Ambrose Small, who disappeared in 1919. Subsequent books include Lewis's meeting with Small, his love affair with Small's friend Clara Dickens, his later affair with Alice Gull, the nun who fell from the bridge, his adoption of her daughter Hana, and a section on a Toronto thief named David Caravaggio. Like his first novel, this book mingles fictional characters with real-life people, though Ondaatje states at the beginning, "This is a work of fiction and certain liberties have at times been taken with some dates and locales."

In the Skin of a Lion studies Toronto's history through the eyes of an outsider, Lewis, Canadian-born but from Toronto's surrounding area. He finds himself adrift in the metropolis, crammed as it is with thousands of immigrant workers who often fail to speak their new home's language. Rowland Harris, Commissioner of Public Works, sees immigrant labourers as being indispensable as well as invisible to society. Ondaatje sees the city as a possibly new community not based solely on industrial capital. Evident is the gulf between rich and poor, between Small or Harris and the immigrant labourers.

Winner of the 1992 Booker Prize and winner, too, of the Golden Man Booker Prize in 2018, *The English Patient* is the sequel to *In the Skin of a Lion* with the setting no longer Toronto in the 1920s and 1930s but the deserted Villa San Girolamo, north of Florence, Italy, towards the end of

World War II. In this sequestered place lies an English patient, who has been burned beyond recognition, attended by Hana, a twenty-year-old nurse and Patrick Lewis's adopted daughter; then two others arrive, David Caravaggio, Hana's father's friend from Toronto, who has become a spy in the war, and Kirpal Singh, known as Kip, a Punjabi Sikh from a British sapper unit, who wants to clear the Villa of explosives. As the English patient remembers his activities before and during the war, the other three, exhausted by war, testify to the complexity of the present situation and attempt to make sense of their lives.

The title suggests a new understanding of what it means to be English, a form of cultural authority which can define the self-image of other nations. The patient is, in fact, Hungarian Count Ladislaus de Almásy, a desert explorer whose true identity Caravaggio first proposes. Kip and the patient are "both international bastards – born in one place and choosing to live elsewhere," the patient observes. "Fighting to get back to or get away from our homelands all our lives." Alarmed by "One bomb. Then another. Hiroshima. Nagasaki," and seeing himself as one of "the brown races of the world," Kip flees the Villa, ending up back in India as a doctor fourteen years later. Meanwhile, Hana has returned to Canada, "Ideal and idealistic in that shiny black hair!" Ondaatje explores national differences through the developing relationships among the four main characters.

Once again Ondaatje mingles history and fiction, as he states in the acknowledgements: "While some of the characters who appear in this book are based on historical figures, and while many of the areas described – such as the Gilf Kebir and its surrounding desert – exist, and were explored in the 1930s, it is important to stress that this story is a fiction and that the portraits of the characters who appear in it are fictional, as are some of the events and journeys." His extensive list of research studies again reflects the thorough background he sets out, as he did in *Coming Through Slaughter* and *In the Skin of a Lion*.

Anil's Ghost (2000) depicts contemporary Sri Lanka, steeped in cultural traditions but now immersed in civil war. Whereas his semi-fictional autobiography, *Running in the Family* (1982), gazed playfully and affectionately on Sri Lanka as a postcolonial nation, *Anil's Ghost* casts a bleak gaze on the country's unending sectarian conflicts and tragedies. Thirty-three-year-old Anil Tissera returns home to Sri Lanka after completing her studies in England and the United States. A forensic pathologist, she works for the Centre for Human Rights in Geneva and seeks to understand various murders connected to the civil war. Her imposed Sri Lankan partner, archaeologist Surath Disasena, often seen as a friend or a foe to

Anil's investigation, becomes a martyr to her cause, proving that his fidelity to justice is vindicated. In his acknowledgments, Ondaatje again cites numerous books and articles which "were invaluable in the writing of this book," a continuation of his closing pattern at the end of his first three novels.

Divisadero (2007), his fifth novel, studies a nuclear family, though its members are not blood-related, on a farm in Northern California in the 1970s as Ondaatje goes back and forth in his narration of their lives. A father has three children, Anna, his natural daughter, Claire, his daughter who was adopted as an infant at the time of Anna's birth, and Cooper, his son who was orphaned and adopted at the age of four. The children's escapades, including an incident of violence when Anna begins a sexual relationship with Cooper, lead to their separate journeys through this fragmentary existence.

A haunting reflection on the coming of age of a young boy from Sri Lanka, *The Cat's Table* (2011) is told by the boy as an adult, moving slowly again back and forth in time. In August and September of 1954, the large ship *Oronsay* is transporting its passengers on a twenty-one-day trip from Ceylon through the Indian Ocean, up the Suez Canal into the Mediterranean, and on to England. Among the people onboard is an eleven-year-old boy named Michael who is going to England to meet his mother. Alone on the ship, he is seated at insignificant Table 76, known as the Cat's Table, as far from the Captain's Table as can be, along with two other young boys and an assortment of strange fellow passengers. As the story progresses from the ship's holds to the narrator's adult years, it unravels a spellbinding tale about the often forbidden discoveries of childhood and the burden of merited understanding, about a lifelong journey which began – unexpectedly – with this voyage. In his confrontation with the past, with this voyage and the time both before and after, Michael invites readers to examine the self-portrait he is sketching. The autobiographical form makes the book a moving account of one man's search for himself amidst the lives around him and during one remarkable sea voyage.

"In 1945 our parents went away and left us in the care of two men who may have been criminals," *Warlight* (2018) opens. "We were living on a street in London called Ruvigny Gardens, and one morning either our mother or our father suggested that after breakfast the family have a talk, and they told us that they would be leaving us and going to Singapore for a year." Thus begins fourteen-year-old Nathaniel Williams's account of his and his sister's curious life. Their father leaves immediately, their mother stays until school starts, "as if our mother had arranged things so there would be no tearful goodbyes." Abandoned by their parents, the pair grow up "protected by the arms of strangers." In the second part of the novel, Nathaniel, twenty-eight and working for the British Foreign Office, is reviewing files covering the war years. He seeks to solve the riddle that was his late mother and her fleeting appearances in his life. Propelled into another life of intelligence work, she became someone driven and remarkable, a woman with a double life as a spy. Like Anil Tissera and young Michael, Nathaniel must travel the depths of his memory to piece together his own life and the murder of his mother, revealing to himself "that confused and vivid dream of my youth."

Whether the settings of Ondaatje's fiction be Louisiana or downtown Toronto, Italy or Sri Lanka, California and France, on a ship or in war-torn London, they testify to the learned diversity of his imagination. As he explores them, he provides his intimate and intense knowledge of each. He moves back and forth in time, judging the settings and the people in them from his own natural perspective. Sometimes, as in *Coming Through Slaughter* and *In the Skin of a Lion*, he steps back in order to provide a voice for those individuals marginalized or displaced by cultural modernity. Sometimes adopting a first-person narrator, as in *Anil's Ghost*, *The Cat's Table*, and *Warlight*, allows him to assess the events and his protagonist's place in their unfolding.

Born, too, in Colombo though a generation younger than Ondaatje, Shyam Selvadurai (b. 1965), the son of a Sinhalese mother and a Tamil father, emigrated with his family to Toronto at the age of nineteen because of the ethnic riots of 1983, obtaining his BFA from York University and his MFA from the University of British Columbia. His fiction has focused on Sri Lanka, a country he cannot abandon.

Funny Boy: A Novel in Six Stories (1994) charts young Arjie's coming of age during the seven years before the 1983 riots when the majority Sinhalese violently attacked the minority Tamils. A first-person bildungsroman of the young Sri Lankan's sexual and political awakening within his wealthy family, the novel finds its hero doubly endangered as a homosexual and as a Tamil, for both these identities prove intolerable in Sri Lanka. As the riots encroach on his family, he no longer feels at home in his own country.

Cinnamon Gardens (1998) studies Sri Lanka in the 1920s when the characters may acknowledge their true inclinations and desires. One woman seeks to navigate herself between an arranged marriage and independence, which may ostracize her; one man tries to maintain his status as a married man while struggling with his homosexuality. Such threatening personal choices confront the figures in this painful analysis. His young adult novel, *Swimming in the Monsoon Sea* (2005), studies Sri Lanka in 1980 when a happy fourteen-year-old receives a visit from his Canadian cousin; his ordered life now involves his homosexual love for his visitor. Selvadurai's first setting of part of his work in Canada, *The Hungry Ghosts* (2013) explores the chequered past and present of Sri Lanka: the Liberation Tamil Tigers and the government continue to exhaust each other's forces, leaving thousands missing or dead. An immigrant novel, it centres on Shivam Rassiah in the present time; like Selvadurai, the son of a Sinhalese mother and a Tamil father, he narrates the story of his family, including his wealthy and overpowering grandmother, his sexual coming out, and his eventual emigration to Canada, all these tales within the defined framework of Sri Lanka's civil war. Dickens stands behind the novel as Selvadurai weaves Shivam's story forwards and backwards in time and place. Shivam, now residing in his thirties in Vancouver, prepares to return to Sri Lanka to bring his grandmother to Canada to die. He confronts himself at last; he cannot escape from his past, which ultimately becomes an embrace of all that has been and is, and in that embrace comes hope for his future.

From the Caribbean come three writers who further adjust the face of Canadian fiction: Dionne Brand, Neil Bissoondath (b. 1955), and André Alexis (b. 1957).

Born in Guayguayare, Trinidad, and emigrating to Toronto in 1970, Brand obtained her BA and MA from the University of Toronto and became Professor of English and Canada Research Chair at the University of Guelph. A distinguished poet, she continues and augments Clarke's racial worlds both of the Caribbean and of Toronto.

In Another Place, Not Here (1996) chronicles two colliding worlds, the realm of the first narrator, Elizete, a sugarcane cutter speaking in Trinidadian dialect, who enters Toronto illegally, and that of the second narrator, Verlia, a cosmopolitan Marxist who returns to the island from Toronto to proselytize for her Black Power Movement. As the two women become lovers, they know the island's poverty and abuse and the inherent racism that disillusions immigrants to Canada. A novel of a woman turning to love in a lesbian relationship, the book centres on the defeat of socialism, the troublesome assimilation of blacks into dominant white cultures, and the failure to achieve equality for women and racialized people.

Expanding her scope to span continents and centuries, *At the Full Change of the Moon* (1999) focuses on Marie Ursule, queen of a secret society of militant slaves called the Sans Peur regiment, who leads a mass suicide on a Trinidad estate in 1824, then is hung. Her daughter Bola is smuggled away, surviving to conceive a large brood who will stay at home or travel abroad, going to North America and Europe, and embodying slavery's legacy of pain and shame. Bola's children, grandchildren, and great-grandchildren will be haunted by Marie Ursule's commitments and dreams as the twentieth century reaches its close.

Toronto is the centre of Brand's next two novels. "This city hovers above the forty-third parallel; that's illusory of course," opens *What We All Long For* (2005), the city maintaining a vital presence in the overlapping stories of second-generation people in their early twenties. There is the lesbian avant-garde artist, the daughter of Vietnamese immigrants, in love with her best friend, a biracial bicycle courier, who must deal with her brother's frequent acts of delinquency. There is the jazz-loving poet, who dropped out of university without his Jamaican-born parents' knowledge; he is in love with a black woman who dates only white men. Friends since high school, this quartet creates their own lives in Toronto, supporting one another in their battles with their migratory parents and their complex families. The first Canadian novel to portray a multicultural and multiracial urban world, it offers a vision of people longing for the diasporic concept of home, struggling with belonging to their families and communities, and encountering discrimination everywhere. Overlapping, too, are the many stories of *Love Enough* (2014). Brand again eschews a linear plot to focus on the lives of only slightly connected people living in Toronto. Love is in short supply, and almost all the characters struggle to know the nature of human love. A little peace, a little comfort, a little rest, how much more is possible in Brand's fictional universe! *Theory* (2018), set again in Toronto, is a first-person academic travelogue in the voice of an unnamed and genderless narrator. In their late thirties, they are trying to complete an ambitious dissertation on the past, present, and future of art, race, class, gender, and politics.

A strong, impassioned writer of fiction of the past and of the contemporary world, Brand delights in the seething postmodernism of Toronto that witnesses racial cultures coexisting in always tense proximity.

From the West Indies, too, comes Neil Bissoondath, who was born in Arima, Trinidad. He left the island at eighteen, moving to Toronto where he obtained his BA from York University. He resides in Quebec City where he is Professor of Creative Writing at Laval University.

In his first collection of stories, *Digging Up the Mountains* (1985), he maps the path of much of his fiction, immigrants longing for a new home in Canada yet unable to leave behind their old home; their culturally alienated lives become a series of exiles, buoyed by domestic upheaval and often death. He captures their varied reactions, his all-too-vivid characters experiencing the loneliness of dislocation and the longing for home in the far-from-idyllic world of Toronto. People leave one world only to discover prejudice and terror in the new landscape. Whether his figures leave Trinidad or Japan, whether they live in Canada, Europe, or Latin America, they share the naïve belief that a refugee finds a home. When they leave one location – the Caribbean settings, for example, are stifling, constricting, and destructive to Natives and non-Natives alike – they bring the old world with them, the real settings becoming ultimately internal: the fears and frustrations of immigrants, trapped in the rootlessness of modern life. Bissooondath's stories enter marginalized areas of society without moving outside the conventions of literary realism.

In his first novel, *A Casual Brutality* (1988), the first-person hero, a thirty-five-year-old physician from fictional Casaquemada, a thinly disguised Trinidad, takes his medical training in Toronto and returns to his island to practice. The island itself is on the verge of political and military chaos, and so, too, is he as his life disintegrates. In flashbacks, he draws a detailed and sensitive portrait of his life, building to a nightmarish conclusion which sadly reflects the world around him and inside him. Moving easily between the Caribbean and Canada, the novel follows the physician as he is caught between his homeland's violent corruption and his adopted country, both places rife with racism. On the one hand, *The Innocence of Age* (1993) focuses on an increasingly racist Toronto; on the other, *The Worlds Within Her* (1998) returns its middle-aged heroine from Toronto to her Caribbean birthplace, a place of political instability. *The Unyielding Clamour of the Night* (2005) uses a fictional South Asian nation, modeled on Sri Lanka, to probe again this world's complexities. An idealistic young schoolteacher moves to a southern village beset by political demonstrations. Here his fundamental belief in the goodness of humanity is severely tested as the encompassing war becomes, for some, a solid source of business.

Like many naturalized Canadians, Bissoondath writes globally themed fiction, his writings being set in Canada and the Caribbean, Europe, Japan, and Southeast Asia. Indebted to such major writers as Conrad and Milan Kundera, Solzehenitsyn and Tolstoy, and V.S. Naipaul, his uncle, he studies contemporary people, at first mainly immigrants, who cannot find peace in themselves or in the chaos surrounding them. By exploring universal human themes and experiences, he attempts to build and even to strengthen the mutual understanding that should be acknowledged in this world.

Born in Port of Spain, Trinidad, emigrating to Canada at the age of four and settling shortly thereafter in Ottawa, André Alexis has portrayed Ottawa directly and forcefully, eschewing the themes of Brand and Bissoondath with the plight of immigrants. His first book, the collection, *Despair and Other Stories of Ottawa* (1994), mixes veiled autobiography ("his parents lived in Blossom Park ... although he *was* of Trinidadian origin he was Canadian as could be"), authentic descriptions, and surrealistic overplays to create a philosophical investigation of the human psyche, drawing the sombre, dream-laden world of his characters' lives.

In his first novel *Childhood* (1998), middle-aged Thomas MacMillan, with a birthdate identical to Alexis's birth, looks back on his life, including his early years with his unconventional Trinidadian grandmother in Petrolia, Ontario. In a novel of elegiac recollection, he finds displacement and absence confronting him. An outsider in his grandmother's house as well as in his hometown, he meets racism because of his brown skin. After his grandmother's death, his mother moves him to Ottawa where he lives in the home of a Trinidadian amateur scientist. As he carefully recounts his past, "it has form, the past, but it is distance that makes it something other than wisp." Although Alexis moved to Toronto in the nineties, his fictional home remained Ottawa for *Asylum* (2008), a first-person account of the political machinations during Brian Mulroney's prime ministership. While the novel opens in Italy in 2003, the narrator looks back longingly to Ottawa, his mid-twenties, and his social life centring on the Fortnightly Club, a motley group of civil servants, academics, and business people who ponder philosophy and ideas. In a large book which reflects its author's reading of Tolstoy, Joyce, and Henry James, the various club members show their higher callings and their betrayals in their Ottawa lives.

From the two Ottawa novels comes Alexis's next project, a quincunx, a cycle of five interrelated novels using forgotten or abandoned literary forms and investigating the meaning of, among much else, faith. In the first, *Pastoral* (2014), Father Christopher Penny, originally from Ottawa, is assigned to the town of Barrow in southwestern Ontario. Though the setting is bucolic, the inhabitants of his new parish are far from the simple shepherds of the traditional pastoral, and his trial of faith involves his sense that organized religion may be extraneous in confronting nature itself. The book is a miraculous contemporary version of an older form of pastoral that is being celebrated while being undercut. The second, *Fifteen Dogs* (2015), is a contemporary parable about fifteen dogs in a Toronto veterinary clinic who are granted human consciousness. Subtitled "An Apologue," an allegorical story intended to convey an appropriate lesson, it raises major existential questions through the dogs' newly conferred powers of reason and speech. More detailed and deeper than George Orwell's *Animal Farm*, the book maps out the human issues of personal fulfilment and love. The fourth, *The Hidden Keys* (2016), tells a quest narrative or adventure story of stealing objects left in a will to five siblings in the low-class as well as the tony areas of central Toronto. The fifth, *Days by Moonlight* (2019), uses the travelogue to recount the journey through southwestern Ontario in search of fabled memories of fictitious poet John Skennen.

Well-versed in world literatures as well as Canadian literature, Alexis probes the innermost thoughts of his central characters, be they human or animal.

Rohinton Mistry (b. 1952), a Parsi native of Bombay who received his BSc from the University of Bombay, emigrated to Canada after his graduation, finding employment in a bank's accounting department. Banking, however, did not satisfy him, and he enrolled on a part-time basis at the University of Toronto in pursuit of his second bachelor's degree, this time in English and philosophy. Raised as a child on Enid Blyton and other writers, he began reading authors such as Joyce and Bernard Malamud, Chekhov and Turgenev, and Davies and Richler. "One Sunday," his first story and destined to become one of eleven stories in *Tales from Firozsha Baag* (1987), won the University of Toronto's Hart House Literary Competition in 1983.

A collection of linked stories, *Tales from Firozsha Baag* combines the immediacy of daily life in a Bombay apartment complex with the perspective Kersi Boyce achieves by emigrating to a new home in Toronto. An objective study of Kersi and his childhood friends, the stories follow him as he takes up his position as an immigrant, powerless in his new Canadian world and powerless, too, in his Indian world. From each of his friends, he learns something, and yet at the end he has not reached a solution. The trauma he experiences is the trauma of the immigrant, for he has learned in the earliest stories that he is destined to emigrate to Canada, and each story reveals why he wants to leave his homeland and why he never leaves his homeland. Like the immigrants in Bissoondath's stories, he is sick of his home and sick for his home.

A modern Tiresias whose emigration leaves him throbbing between his Bombay life and his new Toronto home, not yet realizing that his existence is neither one nor the other but a cultural hybrid who can take possible delight in both, Kersi surfaces in Don Mills, a suburb of Toronto, in the final story, "Swimming Lessons," which functions as an epilogue to the first ten stories. A duet between his Toronto world and the world back home as mirrored in his parents, the story bundles up the previous ten stories as a gift to them. They now know that their son would be a writer; he has a vocation, something that lifts him up to be on the level with his older brother, a social worker outside of Bombay; Kersi has a calling. The first ten stories depict his childhood, his upbringing, his world of Firozsha Baag. By becoming a beginning writer, by seeking to transform the people of Bombay into the figures of his fiction, he is signalizing that the words and the worlds of fiction do not make the horrors of his life disappear; they do, however, offer him through his writing a mode of rendering his former world a permanent fixture of his past while the past continues to haunt and destabilize him. Kersi does not seek to make everything worthwhile; he seeks only to record for himself and his readers what have become his memories of Bombay.

Tales from Firozsha Baag, a detailed recreation of the world of the artist's childhood, is a loving recreation which is also a partial glimpse at that earlier world, a world which is no longer, at least to the participant who is also the writer. This unique pattern found its early iteration in *Sunshine Sketches of a Little Town*, which Mistry knew from his readings, and from Richler's collection of stories, *The Street* (1969), another recreation he also knew. In this way, he inherits a longstanding Canadian literary tradition, adapting it to his Indian background.

In his three novels, *Such a Long Journey* (1991), *A Fine Balance* (1995), and *Family Matters* (2002), all Booker Prize finalists, he looks at contemporary India, using his position in Canada at a removed perspective on his other home. Like Ondaatje and Bissoondath, he adopts his new country and writes from afar about his former place of residence.

Set in Bombay with India's turbulent national politics complemented by worse tensions on the international level – the political backdrop is the Indo-Pakistani war in Bangladesh in 1971 – *Such a Long Journey* teems with the life of the city and the people who travel its streets. The protagonist, a dedicated and somewhat innocent Parsi bank clerk, finds his familial and professional lives unraveling as his son eschews filial piety, his best friend involves him in political intrigue, and his own rationality and morality confront a world in severe change.

In *A Fine Balance*, the abuses of political power threaten to destroy the dignity of the individual. Set against the emergency measures imposed by Indira Gandhi in the mid-seventies, the novel's monumental account of the struggle "to maintain a fine balance between hope and despair" is a powerful and painful examination of a humanity beset by social and political regression. Into Parsi Dina Dalal's widowed life and tiny flat arrive three migrants to Bombay to share her meagre abode: a young Parsi student from a hill station near the Himalayas seeking a better education, and two Hindu tailors, lower-caste people driven from their village for their challenge to the caste system and seeking shelter from the senseless and brutal belittlements they have endured. The quartet come together soon after the government declares a "State of Internal Emergency," lasting twenty months and providing the novel's background. Initially aloof from the tailors, Dina comes to recognize their goodness and their humanity; she has come to know the pair and their sufferings. When the rent collector confronts her with the crime of operating a factory with three men, she replies that they are her husband Ishvar and their two sons. The lines of demarcation have been erased; caste members are human beings. Although many people populate the pages, the one person, almost a fifth main character, who appears only once, is Mrs. Gandhi herself, an omnipresence who denies any rights under the law to her people in the "Emergency." The political realm stands behind the entire book, yet the political realm is also the personal realm; the two are one and the same, and there is no event where the political realm does not infringe upon and even determine it.

In the novel's epilogue, set in 1984 after the assassination of Mrs. Gandhi, the two tailors come daily through the backdoor to Dina's new home, though they cannot come on weekends when other members of her family would be there. As for the Parsi student, he commits suicide in Dubai, far less prepared than the two tailors to face the horror of life.

The poor and the powerless, the dispossessed and the forlorn, the most vulnerable members of society, these are the people, and theirs is the unending struggle, always through suffering, to affirm human dignity. *A Fine Balance* is a cogent warning about the human terrors that await a society without compassion; it is, at the same time, a testimony to the enduring greatness of the human spirit.

In *Family Matters*, set in Bombay in the mid-1990s, Nariman Vakeel, a seventy-nine-year-old Parsi widower suffering from Parkinson's disease, lives in a once-elegant apartment with his two middle-aged stepchildren. When a broken ankle complicates his precarious situation, one stepchild plots to hand over his round-the-clock care to his daughter Roxana, and she moves him into her own residence. Like Dina Dalal, she decides to nurse her father in an act of mercy and solidarity, for bonds of blood demand such acts of solidarity.

Unlike *A Fine Balance, Family Matters* takes place within the four walls of two flats: the first from which Nariman is cruelly cast out and then Roxana's apartment where her husband Yezad regards Nariman as an unwanted invader. Although Yezad must gain some degree of flexibility and kindness in order to accommodate his father-in-law, he sacrifices his liberal tolerance to become a religious fundamentalist. The ideal family is a matter not of birth but of caring, compassion, and humanity. For Mistry, this humanism is the only way "to maintain a fine balance between hope and despair."

With a deeply compassionate understanding of the human condition, Mistry creates equally compassionate accounts of Parsi Bombay in his novels and of Bombay and Toronto in his short stories. While Kersi Boyce has to plan his new life as an immigrant in Toronto, the novels chart the chaos that ensues when kindness absents itself from the human scene. Dina and Roxana come to realize that their acts of compassion celebrate the triumph of the human spirit in a world often stifled by the exigencies of manipulation and greed. True identity is found not in the large frame of national discourse but in the inspired dignity of the human and humane individual.

Born in Nairobi, Kenya, of Indian descent and raised in Dar es Salaam, Tanzania, M.G. Vassanji (b. 1950) received his BS from the Massachusetts Institute of Technology and PhD from the University of Pennsylvania before coming to Canada that same year as a postdoctoral fellow at Atomic Energy of Canada and then research associate at the University of Toronto. A novelist, short story writer, and non-fiction author of books on India and East Africa, he often writes about the lives of East African Indians, their migratory patterns and their subsequent migrations to Europe, Canada, or the United States. His accounts include discussions of the Indian community in East Africa, the native Africans, and the consequences of colonial administration from the Germans and from the English.

In his first novel, *The Gunny Sack* (1989), Salim Juma inherits his great aunt's old gunny sack, a vinyl legacy hiding the forgotten relics of her past. Far away from the Dar es Salaam of his childhood, he uncovers the history of his immigrant family in Tanzania and Kenya: "I stopped to examine the collective memory – this spongy, disconnected, often incoherent accretion of stories over generations." His search for origins and inheritances interweaves the intimate details of ordinary families to harsh political events, including the disenfranchisement of Asians, thus shaping a century of history under the gaze of Arab, German, and British colonialism. In this way, Vassanji gives order through his fiction to a series of collective memories of a largely unexplored and unrecorded past of East Africa. *No New Land* (1991) follows the pattern established by Mistry in setting his story in Don Mills, where Indians from Tanzania congregate in their apartments. This "community of exiles – so tight, so self-contained, so alienated from the mainstream – is that of an almost classic ghetto," comments Bissoondath. "It is not an extreme of multiculturalism but its ideal: a way of life transported whole, a little outpost of exoticism preserved and protected."[6] In a tragicomic mode, including its ironic title, Vassanji explores his protagonist's struggle to adapt to the bitter realities of Toronto. "We are but creatures of our origins, and however stalwartly we march forward, paving new roads, seeking new worlds, the ghosts from our pasts stand not far behind and are not easily shaken off." The ghosts accompany these immigrants as they discover Toronto is no new land. As Vassanji will do in his subsequent fiction, he divides his writings in almost alternation between East Africa and the new world of Canada.

In *The Book of Secrets* (1994), Pius Fernandes, a former schoolteacher who has worked for several decades at a community school in the former German colony and British protectorate of Tanzania, accidentally gets hold of an English-language diary in Dar es Salaam in the late 1980s. Written between 1913 and 1914, it is a fragmentary treatise by Alfred Corbin, a British colonial officer. Fernandes embarks on writing a scholarly history of Tanzania from German colonial rule to the end of the 1980s. In reading the diary, he becomes intrigued by the characters of Pipa, a shopkeeper and a minor character from *The Gunny Sack* and *Uhuru Street* (1992), and his wife Mariamu, who becomes an obsession for him. When she marries Pipa, she is no longer a virgin, raising the question of who is the father of her child. That question is never answered. In the novel, filled as it is with the diary, commentaries, and notes, Fernandes becomes excessively involved in the history he is going to write.

An ostensibly historical novel, *The Book of Secrets* employs the diary to reconstruct Fernandes's Africa and the Indians who lived there. His narrative frame, revealing the imperfect process of uncovering the mysteries of the past, also sheds light on the meaning of historical knowledge and the meaning of home for the diasporic migrant who can settle in England or any country but is always summoned back to the place of origin.

From the safe haven of Ontario, Vikram Lall, the first-person narrator of *The In-Between World of Vikram Lall* (2003), travels back to his formative

---

[6] *Selling Illusions: The Cult of Multiculturalism in Canada* (Toronto: Penguin, 1994), p. 110.

roots in Kenya in the 1950s. He comes from the ultimate in-between social group, an Indian in East Africa. His grandfather was "recruited from an assortment of towns in northwest India"; his father is a member of the Asian Home Guards employed by the British to suppress the Africans; he himself is Kenyan, and his status is suspect, neither a native of the land nor the child of British colonials. The Mau Mau uprisings are increasing, sometimes killing entire families in attempts to rid the country of British rule. Later, a liberated Kenya in the 1970s enlists Lall in politics, though corrupt politicians cast aside his innocence; he is essentially a man caught up in the times: "I therefore prefer my place in the middle, watch events run their course. This is easy, being an Asian, it is my natural place." The African elite now behave like their British predecessors, and the colonial police are security advisers for the new rulers. The novel is an indictment of the futility of revolutions and the pains they cause.

Nostalgia (2016) travels to a not-too-distant future Toronto where a physician meets a patient suffering from leaked memory syndrome or, as it is commonly known, Nostalgia. In this world rejuvenated bodies need rejuvenated identities; all traces of a person's past can now be erased, and a new, complete, and idyllic fiction can be implanted in the mind. But on occasion, cracks appear in these rejuvenated identities, and reminders of discarded lives appear and begin to take control. Laced with satire, this novel is a frightening account of a future where forgetting the past is a mainstay of the present. And, in a continuing alternation between Toronto and foreign shores, *A Delhi Obsession* (2019) has a recent widower and agnostic writer, born in Kenya and living in Toronto, visiting for the first time Delhi, the city of his ancestors, where he begins a passionate and tragic love affair with a married Hindu woman.

For Vassanji, his record of Indian life in East Africa is an ordering through fiction of a world never before charted, bringing an unknown or alternate history to the attention of his readers. Through the perspective gained through distance in Canada, he presents the history of his worlds, its past, its present, and its possible future as well as its migratory patterns for Indians, their coming to Africa, their present status, and, for some, their eventual displacement leading to a second migration.

For these naturalized Canadian writers, all of them Canadian citizens, the country is a secure home from which they write about their new home and about their homelands. From the distance it affords them, from the freedom they enjoy, they feel under no compulsion to adapt to their new country; they can write about their own landscapes as well as their new country. Some, like Shields and Alexis, author studies of Canadian society; others, like Ondaatje or Mistry or Vassanji, write about their worlds here and far away.

As the country's population continues to diversify, the country is welcoming this new fiction. As Vassanji reflects,

> The "new Canadian" writer is for the most part accepted as a Canadian writer, extending the bounds of literary appreciation; rewriting notions of the country's past, or history of its people; questioning its traditional symbols and representations. Of course, this thrust does not come without resistance. There are always those who bring out their calipers to measure how Canadian you are, or your work is. But new Canadians arrive every year. The movement can only be forward.[7]

[7] "So As Not to Die," *M.G. Vassanji: Essays on His Works*, ed. Asma Sayed (Toronto: Guernica, 2014), p. 326.

CHAPTER 10

Canadian Fiction in the Twenty-First Century

There is no simple distinction in Canadian fiction between the late twentieth and the early twenty-first century. Many authors, for example, Margaret Atwood and Dionne Brand, Elizabeth Hay and Wayne Johnston, Thomas King and Rohinton Mistry, Lisa Moore and Alice Munro, Michael Ondaatje and M.G. Vassanji, are publishing important fiction as they did in the twentieth century. What distinguishes the periods is the still increasing diversity of writers who find a natural home in their adopted land, "extending the bounds of literary appreciation," as Vassanji states. The naturalized writers work alongside but frequently not in tandem with more traditional Indigenous and native-born writers, all of them contributing to the multicultural and multiracial worlds of contemporary Canadian fiction. In the development of Canadian fiction, writers are writing of the past, the present, and the future; they are writing of lands far away as well as nearby; they are writing what they need to write in terms that appeal to them. A pattern established in the seventh chapter now leads to a similar way of regarding nineteen writers who have emerged in the twenty-first century as commanding and distinctive fiction authors.

Montreal, like Toronto and the West Coast, welcomed foreigners to its growing number of fiction writers. Quebec law seeks newcomers who speak or at least would learn the French language, and Rawi Hage (b. 1964), born in Beirut, fled Lebanon in 1984, emigrating to New York City and finally settling in Montreal in 1991, Arabic and French being his native languages. He studied at the New York Institute of Photography before continuing his studies at Concordia University.

In his first novel, *De Niro's Game* (2006), winner of the Dublin IMPAC Literary Award, he paints a devastating portrait of war-torn Beirut in the early 1980s, a city of bloodshed, where violence and revenge are the way of life. Bassam, young and aimless, who refuses to join the militia, spends his days planning his escape from Beirut while awaiting the next bomb attack;

he dwells outside the corrupt regime, an antagonist to the state's scientific thinking. His childhood friend George, known as De Niro, is drawn into the treacheries and blackmails of the civil war, finally entering the domain of drugs and vice. He can escape his self-defined torture chamber only through death; he accepts, lives, and dies by the rules of the militia's agenda. The denouement owes much, as the novel's title implies, to the culminating scene of Michael Cimino's film, *The Deer Hunter. De Niro's Game* captures the malaise, despondency, and despair that are modern Beirut in a book which invites comparison with such existential influences as Camus, Kafka, and Sartre.

In the comically dark and carnivalesque *Cockroach* (2008), Hage, like Ondaatje, Mistry, Vassanji, and others, turns to his new home, contemporary Montreal, to focus on a nameless immigrant-narrator from the Middle East and his impoverished life on the edges of society. Sitting in a psychiatrist's office, where he has been sentenced by the state to undergo therapy sessions, the man raises existential questions about his life, his attempted suicide, and his mental condition, including his imagined belief that his desires transform him into a cockroach. *Carnival* (2012) has two kinds of taxi drivers – the spiders and the flies, the spiders who patiently sit in their cars and await their calls and the flies who wander in search of their customers. Fly is the novel's first-person narrator in a nameless city, a thinly disguised Montreal. Raised in the circus, he drifts along in his taxi, observing everything in its beauty and its ugliness, witnessing its clowns, drug dealers, magicians, and ordinary people, and finding his library of books the only possible comforter and shelter.

Beirut Hellfire Society (2018) returns to Lebanon, chronicling the life of Pavlov, the son of the local undertaker, during the civil war that ravaged Beirut in 1978. Told in the third person, the first time Hage has employed this form of narration, it focuses on the war-weary townspeople. When Pavlov's father falls victim to the war's random violence, one of the founders of the Hellfire Society, a secretive sect that reveres fire and cremates their dead, invites Pavlov to assume his father's position and take care of the city's atheistic and homosexual people: "Our members want to be buried outside the religious apparatus, which as you know is almost impossible in our conservative society." Pavlov accepts his role of Charon to this marginalized society as he picks up the remains of bodies; he becomes the unwitting survivor-chronicler of his fading community, witnessing its inevitable decline. The book is, as Hage states in his acknowledgements, "a book of mourning for the many who witnessed senseless wars, and for those who perished in those wars."

Hage is a major voice in contemporary Canadian fiction, bringing his knowledge of and familiarity with literary and critical works outside the Canadian tradition. As a global citizen, he is not restrained by national boundaries, becoming, instead, an international writer based in Montreal.

Heather O'Neill (b. 1973), on the other hand, chooses a unique area of Montreal for her complex fiction. Born and raised on the rough edges of Notre-Dame-de-Grâce, except for more than two years at the age of five when her parents divorced and she lived with her mother in the United States, she grew up with her father and her two sisters there before attending McGill University. When she turns to fiction, she chronicles the harsh realities of her lower-class world, painting the lives of women in tawdry and seemingly hopeless conditions.

Her first novel, *Lullabies for Little Criminals* (2006), follows two years in the life of twelve-year-old Baby, an irrepressible girl learning to navigate Montreal's harsh Saint-Laurent Boulevard in the 1980s. Though she is the daughter of a heroin-addicted father – her mother died soon after her child was born – she still sees the miraculous in the tawdry, her eyes full of the wonder and curiosity of young people coming into their own. She wanders the streets, eventually being placed in a foster home while her father recovers in hospital from tuberculosis. Told in first-person narration by Baby herself in a voice that recalls Salinger's Holden Caulfield, the novel is an illuminating account of Montreal's underbelly, the frantic and often chaotic life that underpins the more respectable lives of the city's citizens. Far from MacLennan's more urban world, Gallant's middle-class observers, or Richler's Jewish regions, O'Neill's Montreal is a distinctly lower-class part of the city.

The Girl Who Was Saturday (2014) returns to the same area of Montreal in 1995, the time of Quebec's second referendum. Nineteen-year-old Nouschka Tremblay and her twin brother Nicolas are the children of a once famous singer, now a faded Québécois celebrity associated with the sovereignty movement. Told in first-person narration by Nouschka, the novel highlights the attempts to make a documentary about the Tremblays in scenes of familial togetherness which did not take place, for the twins never knew a father's presence. With astonishing exactness O'Neill charts her story of this francophone family from the heart of the family enclave and from the gritty neighbourhood of a Montreal whose spine is Saint-Laurent Boulevard with its trash heaps, petty crime, and wasted decadence.

The Lonely Hearts Hotel (2017) goes back to 1914 and an orphanage on Montreal's northern boundary. Rose and Pierrot, abandoned after birth by teenage mothers, end up there, Rose creative, theatrical, and introspective,

Pierrot brilliant and musical, both swearing at a young age to love each other for the rest of their lives. Written in the third person, the novel studies their cruel upbringing among repressed evil nuns, followed by Rose's employment as governess in a wealthy Westmount home and Pierrot's adoption in light of his musical gifts by a wealthy elderly Westmount man during the period of the Great Depression. Although their new homes long separate them, they descend slowly and separately into the underworld, a home to crime, drugs, and sex peopled by addicts, drug dealers, and gangsters. When the pair are finally reunited, their happiness gives way to Pierrot's ultimate death while Rose triumphs in her own ruthless world.

O'Neill's fiction successfully transforms Montreal into a universe where the poor and downtrodden exist side by side with the upper classes, the line between these two poles of society being slim indeed. Although she focuses on young people trapped in their godless universe, her focus is finally the young women, Baby, Nouschka, and Rose, who try to rise out of their worlds. Rose learns to assert herself in traditionally masculine terms, running a huge heroin-smuggling operation. O'Neill creates engaged women learning their own ways of succeeding. Based on her knowledge of Dickens and his contemporaries as well as her familiarity with the grand European and Russian novelists, she has her Montreal engage with the problems of her time.

From the Maritimes comes the fiction of Nova Scotia–born Darren Greer (b. 1968), a gay activist and the son of a father who discovered late in life his Indigenous family. Educated at the University of King's College and Carleton University, he wrote his first novel, *Tyler's Cape* (2001), to show the sad impact of religion on a rural Nova Scotian family of three young sons; the first-person account is penned by the youngest, who is homosexual. A bildungsroman of the children's growth into personal maturity, it showcases an interesting writer's observations on his own community, referencing his indebtedness to Alistair MacLeod with his coastal traumas and David Adams Richards with his fictional worlds on New Brunswick's Miramichi River.

In his fourth novel, *Advocate* (2016), another first-person narrative, Jacob McNeil, a thirty-two-year-old reclusive health counsellor for gay men in Toronto, returns home to Advocate, Nova Scotia, in 2008, summoned by his mother's telephone call about his grandmother's imminent death. Burdened by his long-standing hatred of his grandmother, he has to understand the petty animosities and personal hatreds of this backwater town. His grandmother epitomizes the small-minded sterility that engulfs Advocate. Behind Jacob's return is his memory of his Uncle David, who returned to the town in 1984 in search of a home where he could die peacefully from AIDS. As David's illness became known, he deteriorated physically, and Advocate distanced itself, not granting him care, sympathy, or mercy. The only people who stood by him were the poor, the men and women from the local reservation, and the town's only black resident. Jacob's grandmother did not attend his funeral.

Greer effectively captures a time when AIDS was still the unnamed disease, David's final months offering a portrait of a town which seeks to remove itself from the painful realities of the present. Jacob's current employment in Toronto gives credence to the possibility of a life of service after Advocate. Between his childhood and his present counselling position, between Advocate's punitive reaction to David and Jacob's present employment, lies the harsh world of homophobia in any small town in Nova Scotia, Canada, or the world.

Ottawa is represented by Colin McAdam (b. 1971), born in Hong Kong, his father working in Canada's Foreign Service. He attended Ashbury College there, one of many Canadian cities where he spent his childhood and adolescence. After completing his BA in English literature at McGill University, his MA at the University of Toronto, and his PhD at Cambridge University, he embarked on a fiction writing career. Set in Ottawa, *Some Great Thing* (2004), his first novel, reveals the power, greed, and corruption visited upon people whose lives are controlled by single-minded ambitions. Set again in Ottawa, *Fall* (2009) follows the comic and tragic escapades of students at Saint Ebury's, an elite private boarding school and a thinly disguised Ashbury College.

His major work, *A Beautiful Truth* (2014), is a fine portrait of the thin line separating animal nature and human nature. Animals and humans have far more in common than people admit, and such a conclusion goes back to Seton and Roberts and their animal portraits. A childless couple living in Vermont adopt a chimpanzee, Looee, born in Sierre Leone, and raise him as their son. After a violent event, he is suddenly dispatched to the Girdish Institute in Florida where many chimpanzees are studied. Abandoning his human characters in favour of Looee and his colony of friends, McAdam invites the reader to undergo the harrowing experiences of the chimpanzees, Looee becoming a research subject for a pharmaceutical organization, a "perverse abattoir where the animals were efficiently denied their deaths." The humans turn their back on Looee, and the apes suffer unendurable hardship and death.

Resident of Ottawa, Montreal, and now Toronto as well as a host of international cities, McAdam brings his varied backgrounds and unique educations to his explorations of Ottawa and the Vermont-Florida axis of a forlorn African animal. The loneliness of his characters, be they human or animal, underscores the tragedy of our blindness to their condition.

From Toronto come four writers who reveal further trends in contemporary fiction. Born in metropolitan Toronto, the son of Caribbean immigrants, David Chariandy (b. 1969) received his BA and MA from Carleton University and his PhD from York University and now teaches at Simon Fraser University. As one of the first doctoral students to write a dissertation on Black Canadian literature, he often examines racialized experiences. "The future I yearn for is not one in which we will all be clothed in sameness," he writes in his literary non-fiction *I've Been Meaning to Tell You* (2018), "but one in which we will finally learn to both read and respectfully discuss our differences."

Inspired in part by his own experiences with a black mother and a South Asian father who immigrated to Canada from Trinidad, *Soucouyant* (2007) takes place in Scarborough in the east end of Toronto, one of the global capitals of African-Caribbean culture. The time is 1989, and an immigrant family from Trinidad finds its younger of two sons coming home to care for their mother, who is suffering from dementia. (Chariandy's mother did not have dementia, though his great-aunt did.) As he regards his past, he remembers the taunts he and his brother received from their racist schoolmates, his mother being denied a seat at a pie shop because of her colour, and his parents' home being robbed and vandalized out of sheer hatred. The novel examines the effects of racism on the community while presenting a stunning portrait of the final and fatal effects of dementia on the mother and those close to her. Scarborough is again the home for his other novel, *Brother* (2017), set in the early 1990s. The story focuses on two brothers, the younger one being the narrator, and their mother, who juggles many jobs to maintain their meagre life, all this happening under the shadow of local violence and police brutality. The narration begins ten years after his brother's violent death at the hands of the police, the community still mourning the loss; over-policed and crime-inflicted, it is structured according to the theory that reproduces poverty from one generation to the next with limited chance for change. As the narrator reflects on his and his brother's past, he confronts the racism that has permeated and still permeates his tight-knit community.

Chariandy follows in the growing tradition of Black Canadian writers, including Austin Clarke, whom he has called the first Black Canadian writer, Dionne Brand, and Lawrence Hill.

Born in Riga, Latvia of Jewish parentage, David Bezmozgis (b. 1973) came to Toronto with his family when he was six. Educated with a BA in English at McGill University and an MFA from the University of Southern California's School of Cinema-Television, a director and film-maker as well as a writer, he found immediate success with his first volume, *Natasha and Other Stories* (2004), a cycle of seven stories about Roman and Bella Berman and their son Mark, Russian Jews who fled Riga for their desired abode in Toronto, modelled to some degree after the writings of Saul Bellow, Richler, and Philip Roth. Narrated by Mark at various stages of his growth into adulthood, the stories capture the immigrant experience with humour and sensitivity. In the title story, for example, Mark experiences his sexual awakening in the person of his fourteen-year-old cousin, who has immigrated from Russia. The seven stories offer a sympathetic account of a Jewish family and their life in a new homeland. *Immigrant City* (2019), a second collection of seven independent stories, focuses again on immigrants navigating their way through the sometimes bizarre complexities of their Canadian lives.

In his two novels, Bezmozgis further delineates the plight of refugees from the Soviet Union. Set in Italy in 1978, *The Free World* (2011) chronicles the experiences of Jewish refugees originally from Russia, who have journeyed from Latvia to Ukraine to Czechoslovakia to Austria to Rome. There, Samuil Krasnansky, who was unwilling to leave Latvia, despises his elder son Karl for eagerly embracing any opportunity emigration offers, and his son Alec for his carefree philandering, for Alec's life has always been a game. Knowing his characters too well to have any illusions about their self-interested natures, Bezmozgis overturns the regrettable clichés of immigrant idealism, offering instead a large family's six months of nostalgia and dislocation as they adapt to the perilous hope of a new life. And *The Betrayers* (2015) focuses on the political and moral acts of supposedly enlightened individuals. Betrayed in Russia forty years ago by a fellow Jew and suffering a thirteen-year incarceration in the gulag, Baruch Kotler subsequently moved to Israel where he betrays his wife by taking his much younger lover on a sentimental journey to Yalta, the now-dilapidated Crimean resort of his youth. In the twenty-four hours that is the time frame of the novel, Kotler must acknowledge those who have betrayed him as well as those family members in Israel he betrayed.

Told in economical prose, Bezmozgis's fiction looks knowingly at the problems of immigrants, be they in Toronto, Rome, or Yalta, studying them closely as they confront their new experiences. Their fate is to endure situations which are often far from easy. Fundamental questions are raised about human morality, especially in the complexities of Rome and its personal ramifications in Yalta.

Born in Toronto to a Hungarian Jewish family and educated at the University of Toronto, Sheila Heti (b. 1976) began her writing career in short fiction, penning thirty brief, fable-like stories, *The Middle Stories* (2001), which look out on a bleak world where friendships are rare, abiding love even rarer. In "The Man with the Hat," for example, the almost thirty-nine-year old title figure must make a plan for his career: "If I should write an honest diary, what should I say? Alas, that life has halfness, shallowness." The story then concludes: "Every plan fails. That's what the man had refused to tell him. Every single body's. But that, my friend, is precisely life's sorrow."

Her first novel, *Ticknor* (2005), a work of historical fiction set in nineteenth-century Boston and narrated by an aging bachelor named George Ticknor about his friend, the eminent historian William Hickling Prescott, is an incisive depiction of the narrator's ruination as he confides his bitter feelings about the man who has made something of his life. Obsessive about Prescott's power and equally obsessive about his own inferiority, mingling a viewpoint filled with resentment and self-pity, Ticknor reveals his own jealousy which has destroyed his being.

In her next two novels, *How Should a Person Be?* (2010) and *Motherhood* (2018), Heti defines her position as a fiction writer, transforming her own personal anxieties into a fictional mantle to create what could be called non-fiction fiction. The former is a bildungsroman of two women, Sheila and Margaux (the real-life artist Margaux Williamson, to whom the book is dedicated), one a novelist and the other a painter, striving to become accomplished artists. Their growths are charted in their travels, exploratory exposition, and recorded conversations. Suffering as she continually tries to finish a play commissioned years earlier by a small feminist theatre company, Sheila constantly expresses her uncertainty about herself and her tendency to heed other people's reflections on herself. The consequence is a freewheeling memoir, passing itself off as a novel.

In *Motherhood*, the first-person narrator, Sheila again, is thirty-six years old, living in Toronto with her lawyer-boyfriend Miles, who has a daughter from a previous relationship. Over three years, she seeks an answer to the question of motherhood: "If I want a child, we can have one, he said, *but you have to be sure*." Despite his profession of neutrality, it becomes clear that he does not seek more children. Preoccupied by her meandering reflections on this topic – the book's structure is cyclical rather than linear – Sheila writes a work which may overcome her need for a child, the novel itself being a feminist narrative of her thoughts on the place of children and childbearing in our society. In writing her non-fiction fiction, Heti believes that her own anxieties, however personal they may be, can be re-created in a new art form which partakes of the novel while being rooted firmly in her questioning self.

Born in a Lao refugee camp in Thailand, Souvankham Thammavongsa came to Toronto when she was a year old, sponsored by a Canadian family. She graduated with a BA from the University of Toronto. An accomplished poet, she brings to her first prose volume, *How to Pronounce Knife* (2020), a poet's sensibility, including the ability to capture her characters' feelings and thoughts with scalpel-like precision and disarming humour. She is indebted, among others, to Carson McCullers and Alice Munro. Her fourteen stories reveal the trials, the burdens of inequality, and the need to belong with its ceaseless yearning for some sense of home. The refugee-immigrant Laotians who populate the stories have lost their sense of rootedness in their nameless North American cities.

In "You Are So Embarrassing," for example, a woman's "small blue car was parked in an alley. She was hoping to catch a glimpse of her daughter, who left work every day at around four in the afternoon." She then recalls a day almost twenty years ago when she went to meet her daughter at her high school locker, for the daughter had not yet come outside. "And can you *not* talk to my friends, please?" the daughter scolds her. "You are so embarrassing." Now, the mother, the recovered victim of a stroke, cannot even approach her daughter. In so many of these stories, the plights of the Laotians, with the desires and the disappointments in their lives, are heartbreaking.

Chariandy, born in Toronto to West Indian immigrants; Bezmozgis, born in Latvia and raised in Toronto; Heti, born in Toronto to Hungarian Jewish parents; and Thammavongsa, born in Thailand and living in Toronto, represent the new voices in fiction who have found residences in Canadian cities.

London, Ontario, became home in 1998 for Emma Donoghue (b. 1969), the Dublin-born dramatist, novelist, and short story writer, children's author, literary historian, and screenwriter, who became a Canadian citizen in 2004. She received her BA from University College Dublin and her PhD from Cambridge University. As a literary historian, she has penned many books on lesbian love, beginning with *Passions between Women: British Lesbian Culture 1668–1801* (1993).

Exposed from an early age to literatures from around the world, she admires, among Canadian writers, Atwood, Munro, and Shields. An author of historical and contemporary fiction, she chronicles true incidents from the fourteenth to the nineteenth centuries in her short story sequence, *The Woman Who Gave Birth to Rabbits* (2002), a love triangle in 1790s London in her novel *Life Mask* (2004), and an 1860s divorce in her domestic thriller *The Sealed Letter* (2008).

Room (2010), a Booker Prize finalist, is narrated by five-year-old Jack, who lives in a secured eleven-foot by eleven-foot room, the soundproofed, lead-lined backyard shed, with his beloved Ma; since he has never been outside, he believes that the room and the things it contains (including Ma and himself) are real. His Ma, who does not want her son disappointed, allows him to believe that the rest of the world exists only on television. To her – and Jack does not know this – room is a prison where she has been the contained since she was nineteen. The only other person Jack has ever seen is "Old Nick," who comes by with necessities at night, Jack being totally unaware that "Old Nick" kidnapped his mother, regularly rapes her, and has imprisoned her for seven years. Jack himself is the result of one rape. Jack and his mother eventually escape room, but the seeming horrors of this lifestyle are at the same time the idyllic time he spent there. Although the outside world is a frenzy of new activities, Jack wants to keep his mother to himself, as they had been. The novel is a beautifully rendered portrait of a caring mother and her young son.

The Wonder (2016) turns to the past, 1859 to be exact, to follow the trials of Elizabeth Wright, a nurse trained under Florence Nightingale, as she comes from England to a remote area of Ireland to assess the condition of an eleven-year-old girl who has been starving for four months supposedly without food. The girl is healthy and vital, a true wonder child at a time for its many such wonders. The novel becomes a battle between Elizabeth's proper thinking and the benighted Irish community that surrounds the girl. The people believe in the repressive dogma of the Catholic Church, and when Elizabeth confronts them with her version of the truth, they are too blind to accept it, the child becoming the willing victim of their torturous techniques. *Akin* (2019) has an almost eighty-year-old New York widower assume the temporary guardianship of his eleven-year-old grandnephew during a one-week vacation in Nice, France. Their unlikely pairing cannot dull their quest to find information about the widower's mother and her involvement with the Nazis during World War II. And *The Pull of the Stars* (2020), "a fiction pinned together with facts," makes the fever/maternity ward of a 1918 Dublin hospital the traumatic setting for a harrowing account of the influenza pandemic. Interposing her fiction with the real-life figure of Dr. Kathleen Lynn, a physician considered a criminal by the police, Donoghue offers a staggering portrait of three days of anxiety and death.

Gripping as a historical writer in her attention to the background and details of her plots and equally gripping as a writer of the present with its troubles and tribulations, Donoghue is a welcome addition to the myriad voices that are modern Canadian fiction.

Manitoba boasts an important new Canadian fiction author. A Métis born and raised in Winnipeg and, like Thammavongsa, a fine poet, Katherena Vermette (b. 1977), who received her MFA from the University of British Columbia, wrote her first novel, *The Break* (2016), about the Break, "a piece of land just west of McPhillips Street. A narrow field about four lots wide that interrupts all the closely knit houses on either side and cuts through every avenue from Selkirk to Leila, that whole edge of the North End." One evening, a young Métis mother, babe in her arms, looks out her window and sees a young Métis girl being raped in this abandoned landscape. The novel then becomes an intergenerational saga about life in the North End, ten people offering their perspectives on the incident, some in the first person, some in the third, some alive, some dead, some girls, some women, and one male voice, the Métis police officer investigating the case; some of them drift into the past, others focus relentlessly on the present. As the novel pushes inexorably towards its unforeseen conclusion, the various voices try to make some sense of the tragic event and of their own lives. No one person, they slowly realize, is completely alone, completely separate from one another. Women need to respect one another in order to bring to an end the patterns of abuse that cripple many of their lives.

Published exactly sixty years after Wiseman's account of the Jewish world of Winnipeg's North End in *The Sacrifice*, *The Break* heralds a new voice in fiction, a Métis voice who does not apologize for her story but tells it directly, complete with all its harrowing details, which make it applicable to all Métis women, indeed to all women and men. The distance from the early writers of Indigenous fiction to *The Break* is immense, though only a few decades in duration. In her acknowledgements, Vermette observes: "Thank you to those who blazed the trail, Lee Maracle, Beatrice Culleton Mosionier, Eden Robinson," and closes, "And, of course, big thanks to the Indigenous Writers Collective – I don't know where I would be without you." She is writing now within an established and thriving tradition of authors who are telling their stories to Indigenous and non-Indigenous readers, mapping out their own territories. While Inuit storytellers are beginning to create their writing tradition, the Métis have a tradition which sees their written works as part of a continuum with earlier works in their fiction.

Further west, many writers have emigrated to Vancouver and Victoria to complement the many authors who already live there.

Born in Venezuela, Timothy Taylor (b. 1963) grew up in West Vancouver before attaining his BA at the University of Alberta and his MBA from Queen's University. After working in banking in Toronto, he returned to Vancouver to pursue a writing career. His first novel, *Stanley Park* (2001), a paean to the sights and sounds of contemporary Vancouver, is a modern morality play. An aspiring food connoisseur runs his fledgling restaurant while his anthropologist father camps out in Stanley Park to study the homeless and solve the mystery of two dead children found there. Financial ruin threatening his ambitions, the son falls into the hands of an evil coffee magnate who seeks to bail him out. Taylor brings his readers into the inner workings of the city's culinary world and kitchen politics. *Story House* (2006), another paean to Vancouver, ventures into the still rarer world of architectural design. Although two half-brothers, the sons of the late, famous architect Packer Gordon, are barely on speaking terms, they come together, one an architect himself, the other a professional counterfeiter, to restore a boarded-up building which had been an early design of their father's. Structured on classical Greek tragedy, the novel plots their growing interdependence as they question the value of authenticity in design. Both novels are detailed accounts of two different worlds, the culinary and the architectural.

Set in the near future, *The Blue Light Project* (2011) abandons Vancouver for an unspecified contemporary city as bland as any advertiser can possibly delineate it. Into this mixture of violence and depravity comes a disgraced former journalist, summoned to interview a violent hostage taker, and his interview is his entrance into this frenetic world. Focusing on the four days of the crisis, the novel does not accept easy solutions in a world of creeping fascism. The answer to the human predicament is the ability to imagine, but how difficult is this in Taylor's restricted universe. In *The Rule of Stephens* (2018), set again in Vancouver, the survivor of a serious commercial airplane crash, who had always believed in a rational world, begins to raise fundamental questions about life itself as she believes that her luck has turned against her. Her once cherished worldview slips away in its explanatory power so that the universe becomes inexplicable.

Save for one novel, Taylor's fiction maps the Vancouver terrain with care and intelligence. Although his worlds are many and diverse from the culinary to the chaotically internal, he studies them with awe and with savage disgust, always frightened of the measures that restrict the human capacity to wonder.

More compelling are four novels by Vancouver-born Steven Galloway (b. 1975), a BA graduate from the University of British Columbia and an MFA graduate of its creative writing program. His first, *Finnie Walsh* (2000), recounts the life and death of the title character in a first-person narrative by his best friend, Paul Woodward. Meeting in the third grade in 1980, the pair are from opposite sides of the track in small-town Portsmouth, Finnie the son of the owner of the local mill where Paul's father works the nightshift. Both boys emulate their hockey heroes, and their fourteen-year tale follows their escapades on and off the ice. The novel introduces a wealth of major and subsidiary characters who bring to life the problems and the tragedies of the Walsh and Woodward families.

Salvo Ursari, the hero of *Ascension* (2003), a sixty-six-year-old tightrope walker, meets his death as he walks between the twin towers of Manhattan's World Trade Center in 1976. He had grown up in Transylvania and moved to Budapest where he becomes involved with a high-wire act; his brother and sister join him, and the Ursari family leaves for America to become part of the legendary Fisher-Fielding circus. Galloway paints effectively Ursari's Transylvanian roots, his life in Budapest, and his singular focus and sheer exhilaration high above the ground.

Set in the 1990s Bosnian War, *The Cellist of Sarajevo* (2008) opens with a cellist sitting by a window playing Albinoni's *Adagio* while a group of people outside wait to buy bread in the marketplace. Moments later, a mortar-shell explodes and all the people are killed. Suggested by real-life Vedran Smailovic, the principal cellist of the Sarajevo Symphony Orchestra transports his instrument to the street and plays the *Adagio* daily for twenty-two days, a day for each person killed. Three characters are the novel's centre: a sniper who shoots only soldiers, a man who goes out to collect drinking water for his family and his downstairs neighbour, and a baker who lives in the past. Galloway makes the people, both real and imagined, his own creations, revealing their hope that the seemingly unending war has not destroyed everything of value.

The mixture of real and imagined characters continues in *The Confabulist* (2014), which uses the facts of Harry Houdini's life to create a new story that interlaces history with imagination, truth with invented scenes and situations. The novel reimagines the illusionist's life and death along with the story of Martin Strauss, the narrator, the possessor of a rare degenerative brain disorder, which causes him to lose his memories, and the novelist's invention as the fabled puncher who ended Houdini's life. Strauss seeks to tell his story while he can still recall it.

Galloway moves from the small town of Portsmouth to the American and European landscapes of his last three novels. Endowing his people with often heartbreaking reflections on their anxieties and their worlds, he fashions intricate plots in which they reveal themselves with frightening clarity.

Two other writers who have made Vancouver home are Anosh Irani and Madeleine Thien. Both of them born in 1974, Irani comes from Bombay, Thien from Vancouver itself. Irani moved to Vancouver in 1988. They came to study creative writing at the University of British Columbia.

Following in the footsteps of his literary idol Rohinton Mistry, Irani sets his four novels in India. In his fourth and best, *The Parcel* (2016), he recounts the terrifying life of the underbelly of Kamathipura, Bombay's red-light district. Madhu, a retired transgender sex worker, has been part of this close-knit group of workers, identifying herself as a hijra, a person belonging to the third sex, neither man nor woman. Most hijras are born as female souls trapped in male bodies and eventually have themselves castrated; they are migratory beings, constantly trying to find home not just within their own bodies but within society too. Madhu is given the task of training a "parcel," code for a young girl who has been trafficked from the provinces into the red-light district. Training means preparing for the harsh reality that is to come. In regarding her parcel, Madhu watches her own emotions spiral out of control as her own past returns to haunt her. Her carefully constructed identity threatens to disappear as she tries to save the young woman from personal debasement.

In his acknowledgments, Irani writes: "I grew up opposite Kamathipura. From the time I was born until I was seven years old, I lived in a compound called 'The Retreat,' a stone's throw away from the red light district. Even when my family moved, the area was only ten minutes away, and the red light district continued to haunt and inspire me; it does so to their very day. Normally, when an author writes a book, there are specific people he can thank; however, in this case, I am unable to individually list the transgendered people, sex workers, and residents of Kamathipura who opened up their hearts and minds to me over the years." *The Parcel* is an inspired account of the third gender and their trials and tribulations as they go about their daily lives, written with passionate force by a man who had observed them closely.

While Irani used Vancouver to study carefully his home world of India, Thien used the setting only for her first book, *Simple Recipes* (2001), a novella and six short stories which frequently capture the domestic pain of Vancouverites. Underneath the stories' plots is a longing for something more, for a permanence against the losses encountered in looking back at the past. As the protagonist of "The Map of the City" reflects, "Last Sunday, I drove out to Hastings Street and the neighbourhood where I grew up. I looked for the old store, but the glass storefronts had changed too much."

In her novels, *Certainty* (2006), *Dogs at the Perimeter* (2011), and *Do Not Say We Have Nothing* (2016), she roots her protagonists in contemporary Canada in order to wonder about the familial, social, and increasingly political problems that have occurred in Borneo, Cambodia, and China respectively.

From the perspective of contemporary Vancouver, *Certainty* studies a family whose past goes back to World War II and the Japanese occupation of British North Borneo. A thirty-year-old radio documentary producer in Vancouver, the protagonist is haunted by her family's history in war-torn Borneo. She travels back in time to discover that, as a child, her father lived in Sandakan, which the Japanese controlled. What she learns are the lives people lived before emigration; then people remade themselves with painful effects on them and their families. More overtly political than *Certainty*, *Dogs at the Perimeter* studies another family whose past goes back to Cambodia when it was under the Khmer Rouge. When a Japanese Canadian neurologist walked out of Montreal's Brain Research Centre and disappeared, his colleague sets out to find him, travelling back to her Cambodian home. She relives her childhood thirty years earlier as she witnesses the steady darkness that engulfed her country.

A finalist for the Booker Prize, *Do Not Say We Have Nothing* depicts the long periods of Chinese unrest from Mao Zedong's revolutionary army's first battles to the Tiananmen Square massacre to life in contemporary China. A three-generation story that bridges Canada and China, the novel opens in contemporary Vancouver where Marie, also known as Jiang Li-Ling or Girl, the Chinese Canadian narrator, reviews and recreates her life which has led to her position as professor at Simon Fraser University. Back in 1990 she and her mother were trying to understand a letter written in state-sanctioned simplified Chinese, which was imposed by Chairman Mao Zedong. Marie's father, she recalls, has committed suicide the preceding year by jumping from a ninth-floor window when she was only ten years old; his death coincided with the Tiananmen Square massacre. The letter asks her mother to take care of a young girl who fled post-Tiananmen suppression and wants the comparative freedom of Canada.

The girl's father, a famous composer named Sparrow, mentored Marie's father in the 1960s when both of them were studying at Shanghai Conservatory of Music. Slowly but carefully Marie pieces together her father's story and that of his country.

Mixing real-life events and such noted personages as Mao Zedong and He Luting, the president of the Shanghai Conservatory, with her fictional characters, Thien captures the recent decades of Chinese history and their terrifying effects. Towards the novel's end, Marie reflects: "I believe these pages and the Book of Records return to the persistence of this desire: to know the times in which we are alive. To keep the record that must be kept and also, finally, to let it go. That's what I would tell my father. To have faith that, one day, someone else will keep the record." Thien's book shows "the times in which we are alive. To keep the record that must be kept."

In 2017 Thien published a short story of a young girl named Sothea, a refugee from Cambodia, who comes to Goderich, Ontario, with her family. "Alice Munro," Sothea writes, "described the town's river, referred to in her stories as the Maitland, the Meneseteung, and sometimes the Wawanash. 'I am still partly convinced that this river – not even the whole river but this stretch of it – will provide whatever myths you want, whatever adventures.'" Titled "Alice Munro Country," the story acknowledges Thien's indebtedness to Munro and her fiction.

From Vancouver, then, come three artists with different fictional worlds. Timothy Taylor depicts Vancouver; Steven Galloway tells stories of Canada, the United States, and Europe; Anosh Irani presents scenes of his native India, and Madeleine Thien captures the immigrant's life in Vancouver before she turns to Asian landscapes.

Complementing them is Kathy Page (b. 1958), who arrived from England in 2001 to settle on Salt Spring Island in the Strait of Georgia between mainland British Columbia and Vancouver Island. With a BA from England's York University and an MA from the University of East Anglia and armed with a thorough familiarity with English literature, she had already published four novels by the time she came to Canada.

Munro's influence is evident in her two collections of short fiction, *Paradise & Elsewhere* (2014) and *The Two of Us* (2016). The former is a series of deeply upsetting stories in barely recognizable settings from times remotely distant as well as the present. Even more enthralling is the latter, some stories set in England, some in Canada, and one in Santa Fe, New Mexico. All her stories are realistic, highlighting, for example in *The Two of Us*, the trying relationship between couples, whether they be teacher and pupil, swimming coach and young athlete, or husband and wife – and many have open endings. Her characters tend to develop into situations where they have an intense moment or moments which leave them trying for more, hoping for more, desperately watching for the next stage of their development. Page reminds her readers that there are many times when people cannot enter into a meaningful relationship with others until they can resolve their own complexities. Although there is the human need for connection, there are also attendant difficulties involved in trying to honour that connection.

Munro's influence is evident, too, in Page's eighth novel, *Dear Evelyn* (2018), a masterful portrait of two people whose seventy-year marriage witnesses a gradual deterioration in their compatibility. Harry Miles, born between the two World Wars, is the son of working-class parents in south London with an exceptional love of poetry, fostered by his teacher. He meets Evelyn Hill, from a similar background to his own, on the steps of the Battersea library, and his infatuation is immediate and lasting. In the war years they are married, Harry going off to battle while Evelyn has the first of three daughters. From then on, their infatuation, indeed their love, diminishes in their ability to grow together. Their seemingly compatible but divergent personalities remain committed, but not devoted, to each other. Evelyn becomes increasingly domineering, Harry increasingly resentful, her strong-mindedness becoming intolerance. He can only accept that "what she desired now was his absence from her daily life." Their marital plight is a heartbreaking depiction of love's erosion.

Page writes of the bonds that tie together, often to exhaustion, people's hearts and minds. Like Munro, she flashes a careful light on ordinary people whose lives are anything but ordinary, making the ordinary something extraordinary in her art.

Born in Sidney, Vancouver Island, Patrick DeWitt (b. 1975) travelled extensively before settling down in Portland, Oregon. *Ablutions* (2009), his first novel, presents the gritty, tragic, and also hilarious account of a barman, using only the second person in his narrative voice, as he encounters a weird group of down-and-out people in his Hollywood drinking hole. Indebted to Charles Bukowski with its morbid tone and its cast of strange people, the book chronicles the protagonist's descent into alcoholism, losing his wife and much else along the way to oblivion.

The Sisters Brothers (2011), a Booker finalist, cements DeWitt's reputation for mixing the comic with the tragic. A work of historical fiction, it follows two hired assassins, Charlie and Eli Sisters, intent on their next assignment in 1851 Oregon and California; they seek out their next victim, assigned as their latest prey by the enigmatic and powerful figure known as the Commodore; they follow their leader's orders without question. DeWitt maps out the traditional Western in a picaresque reformulation, impregnating it with heavy irony and creating a darkly comic tour-de-force. The assassins themselves go through their own series of picaresque adventures, from the obligatory scene with a failed local dentist to meeting with deranged prospectors and luring prostitutes and scenes of gruesome murders. At the conclusion of their journey, they are no closer to the point of knowing about themselves, and they return home, filled with no more self-knowledge than when they set out. *The Sisters Brothers* is a deeply comic reworking of the Western novel.

Undermajordomo Minor (2015) is the droll story of seventeen-year-old Lucien (Lucy) Minor. Friendless, purposeless, and a compulsive liar, he leaves an uncomfortable home environment in the village of Bury to accept a position as undermajordomo at a remote Alpine castle. Heading out into the world for the first time, he encounters mysterious men and women, thieves and villains, and, of course, love. People never give up in their search for this elusive dimension of human existence, the novel a Gothic fairytale. In *French Exit* (2018), an Upper East Side domineering widow sets sail for Paris with her adult son, fleeing penury, Paris serving as backdrop not for romance but for economical ruin. Again uniting the comic with the tragic, DeWitt makes a classic tragedy of manners which parodies high society while displaying a mother–son relationship which goes awry.

In these novels, each of them with different geographical settings, he captures the increasingly hilarious worlds of his people, always recounting a tragic story with comic intentions.

Resident now of Victoria, British Columbia, Esi Edugyan (b. 1978), the daughter of Ghanaian immigrants, was born and raised in Calgary. She travelled west to the University of Victoria to take a degree in creative writing with Jack Hodgins, following this with an MA from the John Hopkins University.

Discovering the real-life black settlement of Amber Valley north of Edmonton, which was originally founded by African Americans from Oklahoma, Edugyan sets there her first novel, *The Second Life of Samuel Tyne* (2004). Examining Tyne's difficult and ultimately lonely life, a Ghanaian immigrant in 1975 and now, fifteen years later, a solid citizen in Calgary, it watches a bureaucratic civil servant who hates his pedestrian job. Tyne's uncle bequeaths to him his old mansion in Aster, Alberta, on the Athabasca River, a fictional rendering of Amber Valley; he forsakes the

drudgery of the city to move with his wife and their two daughters to the
seeming simplicity of the small town and his uncle's home. The idealized
Aster of Tyne's imagination turns out to be a false dream, his family's
veneer of acceptance of their new life remains only a veneer, and the town's
small-mindedness and racism eventually turn on the Tynes themselves.
When mysterious fires start to consume local edifices, Tyne's new beginning proves a sham.

  Half-Blood Blues (2011), a Booker finalist, focuses on Hieronymus Falk,
a brilliant twenty-year-old Afro-German jazz musician, who is arrested by
the Nazis and never heard from again. The son of a white German mother
and a black African soldier, Hiero is a mixed-race German, one of the
people who came to be known as "Rhineland bastards," a stateless population refused their citizenship and horribly victimized by the controlling
Nazis. A member of the interracial jazz ensemble, he has a life which is in
double jeopardy: the Nazis labeled jazz the degenerate music of both blacks
and Jews. Out of Hiero's wartime story comes the novel, set in 1992,
which tries to recover his story and, ultimately, himself. *Half-Blood Blues*
belongs in the expanding traditions of Black Canadian fiction, in which
the biracial experience represents the challenge of uniting or reuniting
black and national identities.

  The popularity of American jazz suffuses the European world. Even
Louis Armstrong makes telling appearances. The novel's narrator, Sid, the
only witness of Hiero's arrest, ventures back to Poland to find out what has
happened to him. Thus begins his slow journey to redemption through a
fascinating and little-known world of Nazi persecutions and into the heart
of his own guilty conscience. From Sid's journey, too, comes his unique
portrayal of Hiero's genius.

  Confining her space to this musical world under the Nazis, Edugyan
probes a racist world which has hitherto been little explored, and she
populates it with some real-life personages, bringing the further suggestion
of complete factuality to her fiction. The novel is a revealing account of
racism within a story about friendship and music. There is racism everywhere, Sid realizing that a chance meeting on the street or at a train station
can mark the end of one's life, and the fate of Germany's black population
under the Nazis is a hidden world now examined and awaiting further
exploration. The novel about a mixed-race man without a place in his
society reveals Edugyan's incisive handling of racism in the distant world of
Nazi Germany.

  Her third novel, *Washington Black* (2018), another Booker finalist,
travels back in time to the first half of the 1830s. In this first-person

narrative, an eleven-year-old slave boy lives on a Barbadian sugar plantation, where Big Kit, a mother figure to him, becomes his protector. He
becomes the manservant and assistant of Christopher Wilde, the brother of
the cruel plantation owner. An eccentric abolitionist as well as a scientist,
Wilde creates a hot-air balloon he has named "Cloud-cutter." But young
Washington witnesses the death of Wilde's cousin, and this sight places a
bounty on his head. Wilde then flees with the boy in "Cloud-cutter," the
pair embarking on adventures which takes them initially to Virginia, then
places more remote.

Edugyan treats slavery as she treats freedom: she wants to understand
and illuminate their bitter and hostile relationship. Washington has a
friendship with Wilde, though they are never equals; the power imbalance
is too severe. In understanding freedom, Washington is seeking an answer.
"What does it feel like, Kit? Free?" he wonders. She responds that it is the
ability to "go wherever it is you wanting." He is freed from his field slavery
by Wilde; he is later freed when he becomes assistant to a natural scientist.
But he is haunted by the scars of his gradually increasing freedom, feeling
at times afraid of what it means, its capacity to unsettle his identity and
"the terrible bottomless nature of the open world, where one belongs
nowhere, and to no one. There are many acts of violence in the novel
which continually threaten to undercut and even to destroy the slow
progress towards some degree of freedom; these acts become a barometer
of the frequently appalling attitudes of society to slavery and to freedom.

Edugyan studies internalized enslavement, first in Alberta, where one
man commits himself to his solitary destiny, then in 1920s Paris, where
one lone genius is executed, and finally in 1830s Barbados, where a young
boy learns hope in embracing some freedom.

Born in Victoria and educated with a BFA from the University of
Victoria, where he, too, studied with Jack Hodgins, and an MFA from
the University of Virginia, Steven Price (b. 1976), a fine poet, writes novels
remarkable for their depictions, first of contemporary Victoria, then of
different historical periods.

Set in Victoria, *Into That Darkness* (2011) begins when two massive
earthquakes devastate the West Coast. Amid the city's total destruction,
survivors push the bonds of civility to their limit, with frequent robberies
and murders encroaching on the now forlorn landscape; only the tilting
Empress Hotel stands as the last vestige of civility. After every catastrophe,
there is one seminal question, which is frequently debated in the novel: if
there is a divine being, why does he or she allow such unimaginable pain
and suffering? The response is perhaps non-existent. Only the

protagonist's belief in the eternal efficacy of nature itself stands as an antidote to the doom that has levelled the city.

A captivating historical novel and a tribute to the sensational novels of late Victorian England, *By Gaslight* (2016) depicts 1885 London, its fog-encrusted cityscapes, and its deftly handled journey through sewers and séance halls. William Pinkerton, the son of Allan Pinkerton, the founder of the Pinkerton National Detective Agency, has arrived to search for Edward Shade, who had obsessed his father for much of his life. A series of flashbacks include the tales of the American Civil War, with the closing chapter in 1913 Oregon. Meticulously told by a master, the novel recalls Wilkie Collins ("a reader of sensation novels," a Chief Inspector says. "That Wilkie Collins and the like. Desk is full of them. I never could stomach a detective who was a reader.") and Dickens (The attendant at the Public Record Office recounts, "That Mr. Dickens come here regular, once. I remember him well, I do. We used to talk about songbirds. We both liked them birds of a season. Fascinating man, that Mr. Dickens. Don't much care for his writing though."); these two writers penned similarly long and intricate stories, though the author's note cautions that the novel's "characters, both real and imagined, are creations of the author. The gaslit London of its pages never existed." Still, there is no finer introduction to late Victorian England.

Lampedusa (2019) is a fictional recreation of the life, especially the final days, of Giuseppe Tomasi di Lampedusa, the author of *The Leopard*, his only novel. The 1950s world of Palermo, the novel's setting, epitomizes the change that time wreaks, meaning loss and despair, the two qualities that perfectly describe Tomasi: "Though he knew he would die in this city of his birth what he felt for it was not love but a fierce desolation that took the place of love." He has lost everything, including his mother, his childhood palazzo in the bombing of Palermo, and his father's wealth. Now, in his last days and suffering fatally from emphysema, this once noble man wanders the streets trying to have the courage to finish his novel. Without ever knowing it would be published, he dies at sixty, a year before its publication. Situated between the past and its vanished old world and the depressing present, the novel recalls the similar pattern of *The Leopard*, Tomasi representing the final cry of a failing Sicily. "We are from a world that no longer exists. If I do not write that world, write it down, then what will become of it?" *Lampedusa* is a fine portrait of Tomasi's malaise and despair. When Price is writing of the past, be it London or Palermo, he brings to life these earlier worlds through his research and through his narrative skill.

These eight writers, some of them born in Canada, others born outside of Canada, represent the wide range of contemporary Canadian fiction. While Taylor paints contemporary Vancouver, Galloway writes of Canada and abroad, Irani studies India from away, and Page often writes of England from away, DeWitt and Edugyan, Price and Thien rework and broaden the historical novel: DeWitt writes of the past and the present in America and in Europe, Edugyan recounts the past in Canada, Europe, and Barbados, Price writes of contemporary Victoria as well as earlier times in England and Italy, and Thien, starting in present-day Vancouver, ventures into the recent history of Borneo, Cambodia, and China, each time her protagonists beginning their search into the past from Canada. Boasting an abundance of real or imagined characters with distinctive traits and distinctive voices, these eight function as a microcosm of the diverse and diversified fiction penned now throughout the country.

These nineteen writers represent the newest addition to the growing number of fiction authors populating the landscape. They represent fiction's steadily developing worlds, heralding a cosmopolitan understanding of their unique universe. Twenty-first-century writers continue and expand what the preceding generation of writers had already started, be they from Canada or Europe or Asia. They write of Canada and the United States; they write of Europe and Asia; their borders are unlimited.

Afterword

As recent fiction has been pointing out, Canada is a multicultural, multi-national, and multiracial country which resists any simple or simplified definition. From its early stages, when the country was a colony paying service to far-off mother countries, it grew slowly into its own land, a growth mirrored in Canada's maturing fiction. When early writers charted their ways into the landscape, they often looked abroad for their sources. Then they looked to their own country's writers for further sources. From the mid-twentieth-century's flinging off that colonial mentality, writers came to realize they were building on their own traditions and espousing their own understandings of the country and its inhabitants. With the emergence of Indigenous voices, then of naturalized Canadian authors, writers became an essential segment in a distinctive society. Canada now boasts of a multicultural group of writers unafraid of the country or of one another; they are not frightened of choosing their own settings, their own landscapes. They write as they want – on subjects they have the freedom to choose.

The story of Canadian fiction is the movement from colony to nation to global village – a global village being a nation beyond nationalism – where the nation's fiction writers are so multifaceted that the distinction between national and international no longer holds. And this situation is almost unique to Canada where the country's writers, native-born as well as naturalized voices, coexist, operating independently with some degree of cross-over, a case of life lived at the crossroads. What the imagination can conceive is what the writers now do.

Following MacLennan's national novels of the 1940s, for example, came almost immediately Richler's Jewish Montreal, Watson's interior British Columbia, Laurence's prairie worlds, and Kroetsch's Alberta, all these new writers concentrating on the people who occupy the already defined landscapes. Today these writers are joined, for example, by Ondaatje writing about Toronto and many other parts of the world, Thien writing about Vancouver and Asian settings, and Edugyan writing about Alberta and Europe and Barbados.

Fiction writers represent the world that is now Canada. They look at life here and abroad. They wonder about lives lived inside and outside of Canada. They are all rooted in Canada, even if their fiction does not exclusively depict Canadian scenes. They stand for multiculturalism, with the number of native-born Canadian writers increasingly augmented by naturalized Canadian voices, who are not frightened to tackle their new Canadian worlds as well as their chosen landscapes from their countries of origin. This is the new Canada, home to a diversity of ethnicities, birth countries, languages, and religious faiths unprecedented in the nation's history and unprecedented in the nation's fiction. This diversity is a societal experiment not replicated elsewhere in the world. A crossroads of people from every nationality of the world, Canada remains a work in progress, a work both achieved and always to be achieved. And the multifaceted fiction mirrors this continuing dramatic evolution.

This present condition in Canada may ultimately reflect the newness of its literature. Still quite young, the fiction does not seem to suffer from the chauvinism of the United States or other and older lands, which have so much at stake in their country's history. The country is young enough that there is little pressure to uphold what is already there.

Canadian fiction has come a long way in the past two centuries. It has moved from being on the circumference to embracing in the mid-twentieth century a self-sufficiency in place, a *here* defined without reference to *there*. Now the *here* of Canadian fiction is not defined but indefinable. For the twenty-first-century Canadian writer, *here* encompasses Canada and the world, an area with no centre and therefore no periphery, with neither the possibility nor even the need of definition.

Just like the life of the country, fiction no longer shows a balance between the best of the British and the best of the American. It is rather a balancing of voices in a country whose citizens and their works are at once native-born and naturalized. This has happened in the fiction, and it is happening, too, in the tapestry of Canada where terms like national and international have dissolved.

Select Bibliography

CANADIAN LITERATURE

Atwood, Margaret. *Survival: A Thematic Guide to Canadian Literature*. Toronto: House of Anansi Press, 1972.

Benson, Eugene and William Toye, eds. *The Oxford Companion to Canadian Literature*. Don Mills, Ontario: Oxford University Press, 1997.

Blodgett, E.D. *Configuration: Essays in the Canadian Literatures*. Toronto: ECW Press, 1982.

Five-Part Invention: A History of Literary History in Canada. University of Toronto Press, 2003.

Buss, Helen M. *Mapping Our Selves: Canadian Women's Autobiography in English*. Montreal: McGill-Queen's University Press, 1993.

Clarke, George Elliott. *Odysseys Home: Mapping African-Canadian Literature*. University of Toronto Press, 2003.

Demers, Patricia. *Women's Writing in Canada*. University of Toronto Press, 2019.

Fiamengo, Janice, ed. *Home Ground and Foreign Territory: Essays on Early Canadian Literature*. University of Ottawa Press, 2014.

Frye, Northrop. *The Bush Garden: Essays on the Canadian Imagination*. Toronto: House of Anansi Press, 1971.

Divisions on a Ground: Essays on Canadian Culture. Toronto: House of Anansi Press, 1982.

Gerson, Carole. *Canadian Women in Print 1750–1918*. Waterloo, Ontario: Wilfrid Laurier University Press, 2010.

Groening, Laura Smyth. *Listening to Old Woman Speak: Natives and alterNatives in Canadian Literature*. Montreal: McGill-Queen's University Press, 2004.

Hamill, Faye. *Canadian Literature*. Edinburgh University Press, 2007.

Howells, Coral Ann and Eva-Marie Kroller, eds. *The Cambridge History of Canadian Literature*. Cambridge University Press, 2009.

Keith, W.J. *Canadian Literature in English*. Erin, Ontario: Porcupine's Quill, 2006.

Kertzer, Jonathan. *Worrying the Nation: Imagining a National Literature in English Canada*. University of Toronto Press, 1998.

King, Thomas, Cheryl Calver, and Helen Hoy, eds. *The Native in Literature*. Toronto: ECW Press, 1987.

Klinck, Carl F., ed. *Literary History of Canada: Canadian Literature in English.* University of Toronto Press, 1965.

Kröller, Eva-Marie, ed. *The Cambridge Companion to Canadian Literature.* Cambridge University Press, 2017.

Martin, Keavy. *Stories in a New Skin: Approaches to Inuit Literature.* Winnipeg: University of Manitoba Press, 2012.

McGrath, Robin. *Canadian Inuit Literature: The Development of a Tradition.* Ottawa: National Museums of Canada, 1984.

McGregor, Gaile. *The Wacousta Syndrome: Explorations in the Canadian Langscape.* University of Toronto Press, 1985.

McMullen, Lorraine, ed. *Re(Dis)covering Our Foremothers: Nineteenth-Century Canadian Women Writers.* University of Ottawa Press, 1990.

McWatt, Tessa, Rabindranath Maharaj, and Dionne Brand, eds. *Luminous Ink: Writers on Writing in Canada.* Toronto: Cormorant, 2018.

Moses, Daniel David, Terry Goldie, and Armand Garnet Ruffo, eds. *An Anthology of Canadian Native Literature in English* (fourth edition). Don Mills, Ontario: Oxford University Press, 2013.

Moss, Laura, ed. *Is Canada Postcolonial? Unsettling Canadian Literature.* Waterloo, Ontario: Wilfrid Laurier University Press, 2003.

New, W.H. *Borderlands: How We Talk about Canada.* Vancouver: University of British Columbia Press, 1998.

A History of Canadian Literature. Montreal: McGill-Queen's University Press, 2003.

Land Sliding: Imagining Space, Presence, and Power in Canadian Writing. University of Toronto Press, 1997.

New, W.H., ed. *Encyclopedia of Literature in Canada.* University of Toronto Press, 2002.

Literary History of Canada: Canadian Literature in English (second edition), vol. 4. University of Toronto Press, 1990.

Nischik, Reingard, ed. *History of Literature in Canada: English-Canadian and French-Canadian.* Rochester, NY: Camden House, 2008.

Redekop, Magdalene. *Making Believe: Questions about Mennonites and Art.* Winnipeg: University of Manitoba Press, 2020.

Siemerling, Winfried. *The Black Atlantic Reconsidered: Black Canadian Writing, Cultural History, and the Presence of the Past.* Montreal: McGill-Queen's University Press, 2015.

Staines, David. *Beyond the Provinces: Literary Canada at Century's End.* University of Toronto Press, 1995.

Staines, David, ed. *The Canadian Imagination: Dimensions of a Literary Culture.* Cambridge, MA: Harvard University Press, 1977.

Stouck, David. *Major Canadian Authors: A Critical Introduction.* Lincoln: University of Nebraska Press, 1984.

Tremblay, Tony. *The Fiddlehead Moment: Pioneering an Alternative Canadian Modernism in New Brunswick.* Montreal: McGill-Queen's University Press, 2019.

Twigg, Alan. *For Openers: Conversations with 24 Canadian Writers.* Madeira Park, British Columbia: Harbour, 1981.
  Strong Voices: Conversations with Fifty Canadian Authors. Madeira Park, British Columbia: Harbour, 1988.
Walcott, Rinaldo. *Black Like Who?: Writing Black Canada.* Toronto: Insomniac Press, 2003.
Waterston, Elizabeth. *Survey: A Short History of Canadian Literature.* Toronto: Methuen, 1973.
Woodcock, George. *The World of Canadian Writing: Critiques & Recollections.* Vancouver: Douglas & McIntyre, 1980.

CANADIAN FICTION

Cameron, Donald. *Conversations with Canadian Novelists.* Toronto: Macmillan, 1973. Two volumes.
Coleman, Daniel. *White Civility: The Literary Project of English Canada.* University of Toronto Press, 2006.
Craig, Terrence. *Racial Attitudes in English-Canadian Fiction, 1905–1980.* Waterloo, Ontario: Wilfrid Laurier University Press, 1987.
Creelman, David. *Setting in the East: Maritime Realist Fiction.* Montreal: McGill-Queen's University Press, 2003.
Davies, Gwendolyn. *Studies in Maritime Literary Activity, 1760–1930.* Fredericton, New Brunswick: Acadiensis, 1991.
Dean, Misao. *Practising Femininity: Domestic Realism and the Performance of Gender in Early Canadian Fiction.* University of Toronto Press, 1998.
Dooley, D.J. *Moral Vision in the Canadian Novel.* Toronto: Clarke, Irwin, 1979.
Dragland, Stan. *Strangers & Others: Newfoundland Essays.* St. John's, Newfoundland: Pedlar Press, 2015.
Fiamengo, Janice. *The Woman's Page: Journalism and Rhetoric in Early Canada.* University of Toronto Press, 2008.
Gadpaille, Michelle. *The Canadian Short Story.* Don Mills, Ontario: Oxford University Press, 1988.
Garrod, Andrew, ed. *Speaking for Myself: Canadian Writers in Interview.* St. John's, Newfoundland: Breakwater, 1986.
Gerson, Carole. *A Purer Taste: The Writing and Reading of Fiction in English in Nineteenth-Century Canada.* University of Toronto Press, 1989.
  Three Writers of Victorian Canada and Their Works. Toronto: ECW Press, 1983.
Gibson, Graeme, ed. *Eleven Canadian Novelists.* Toronto: House of Anansi Press, 1973.
Goldman, Marlene. *DisPossession: Haunting in Canadian Fiction.* Montreal: McGill-Queen's University Press, 2012.
  Paths of Desire: Images of Exploration and Mapping in Canadian Women's Writing. University of Toronto Press, 1997.
Greenstein, Michael. *Third Solitudes: Tradition and Discontinuity in Jewish-Canadian Fiction.* Montreal: McGill-Queen's University Press, 1989.

Heidenreich, Rosmarin. *The Postwar Novel in Canada: Narrative Patterns and Reader Responses*. Waterloo, Ontario: Wilfrid Laurier University Press, 1989.

Hill, Colin. *Modern Realism in English-Canadian Fiction*. University of Toronto Press, 2012.

Howells, Coral Ann. *Private and Fictional Worlds: Canadian Women Novelists of the 1970s and 1980s*. London: Methuen, 1987.

Hoy, Helen. *How Should I Read These? Native Women Writers in Canada*. University of Toronto Press, 2001.

Hutcheon, Linda. *The Canadian Postmodern: A Study of Contemporary English-Canadian Fiction*. Toronto: Oxford University Press, 1988.

Jones, Joseph and Johanna. *Canadian Fiction*. Boston: Twayne, 1981.

Keefer, Janice Kulyk. *Under Eastern Eyes: A Critical Reading of Maritime Fiction*. University of Toronto Press, 1987.

Kruk, Laurie. *Double-Voicing the Canadian Short Story: Birdsell, Findley, Hodgins, King, MacLeod, Shields, Vanderhaeghe*. University of Ottawa Press, 2016.

Kruk, Laurie, ed. *The Voice is the Story: Conversations with Canadian Writers of Short Fiction*. Oakville, Ontario: Mosaic Press, 2003.

Löschnigg, Maria. *The Contemporary Canadian Short Story in English: Continuity & Change*. Trier, Germany: Wissenschaftlicher Verlag Trier, 2014.

Lynch, Gerald. *The One and the Many: English-Canadian Short Story Cycles*. University of Toronto Press, 2001.

Lynch, Gerald and Angela Arnold Robbeson, eds. *Dominant Impressions: Essays on the Canadian Short Story*. University of Ottawa Press, 1999.

Moss, John. *A Reader's Guide to the Canadian Novel* (second edition). Toronto: McClelland & Stewart, 1987.

Nischik, Reingard, ed. *The Canadian Short Story*. Rochester, New York: Camden House, 2007.

Northey, Margot. *The Haunted Wilderness: The Gothic and Grotesque in Canadian Fiction*. University of Toronto Press, 1976.

O'Flaherty, Patrick. *The Rock Observed: Studies in the Literature of Newfoundland*. University of Toronto Press, 1979.

Petrone, Penny. *Native Literature in Canada: From the Oral Tradition to the Present*. Don Mills, Ontario: Oxford University Press, 1990.

Porter, Ryan. *You Can't Get There from Here: The Past as Present in Small-Town Ontario Fiction*. University of Toronto Press, 2019.

Ricou, Laurence. *Vertical Man/Horizontal World*. Vancouver: University of British Columbia Press, 1973.

Rae, Ian. *From Cohen to Carson: The Poet's Novel in Canada*. Montreal: McGill-Queen's University Press, 2008.

Sugars, Cynthia. *Canadian Gothic: Literature, History and the Spectre of Self-Invention*. Cardiff: University of Wales Press, 2014.

Sugars, Cynthia and Eleanor Ty, eds. *Canadian Literature and Cultural Memory*. Don Mills, Ontario: Oxford University Press, 2014.

Thomas, Clara. *Canadian Novelists 1920-1945*. Toronto: Longmans, 1946.

Woodcock, George. *George Woodcock's Introduction to Canadian Fiction*. Toronto: ECW Press, 1993.

Wyile, Herb. *Anne of Tim Hortons: Globalization and the Reshaping of Atlantic-Canadian Literature*. Waterloo, Ontario: Wilfrid Laurier University Press, 2011.

Speaking in the Past Tense: Canadian Novelists on Writing Historical Fiction. Waterloo, Ontario: Wilfrid Laurier University Press, 2006.

Speculative Fictions: Contemporary Canadian Novelists and the Writing of History. Montreal: McGill-Queen's University Press, 2002.

Index